A Bibliography of

Danish Literature

in English Translation

CAROL L. SCHROEDER

A Bibliography of
Danish Literature
in English Translation
1950-1980

With a Selection of

Books about Denmark

DET DANSKE SELSKAB

Published with a grant of
The Danish Bicentennial Foundation of 1976

by Det danske Selskab
The Danish Institute for Information about Denmark
and Cultural Cooperation with other Nations
Kultorvet 2, DK-1175 Copenhagen K
Tel. 01 - 13 54 48   Cables: PIONER COPENHAGEN

Edited by Grethe Jacobsen, Ph.D.
Graphic design by Finn Christensen
Printed in Denmark by Mammens Bogtrykkeri A/S, Odense

ISBN 87-7429-044-4

Acknowledgements

A poet could perhaps work alone on a hilltop, but not so the bibliographer, whose very work is made up of the works of others. Many sources must be referred to, all the works of different hands, and many individuals consulted. I am grateful to have found such helpfulness and generosity in those I approached during the compilation of this work, and wish to express my thanks to all of them.

My main source of information was the University of Wisconsin Memorial Library, whose impressive collection in Danish literature I wish continued growth in the future. In Denmark, both the Copenhagen Public Library and the Royal Library were most useful, including of course the numerous well-respected bibliographies which the Royal Library publishes.

Individual authors, translators, publishers, scholars and fellow bibliographers were most generous in answering my queries and providing valuable data, and I shall miss corresponding with them. Special thanks to Danish children's literature bibliographer Karen Nelson Hoyle, to bibliographers Aage Jørgensen and Larry Syndergaard, and to translators Anne Born, Joan Tate, Heðin Brønner and especially Alexander Taylor and Nadia Christensen, who have done so much to promote contemporary Danish literature in translation in this country.

When I began this project in 1972, it was Elias Bredsdorff's bibliography from 1950 which provided my inspiration, and it has been a great pleasure to me to have had his advice and support over these past eight years. During and after my studies in the Scandinavian Studies department at the University of Wisconsin I received the generous help of Professor Harald Naess in questions of Scandinavian bibliography, and of Professor Niels Ingwersen in researching many elusive details about works of Danish literature. I am also most grateful to Folmer Wisti and Det danske Selskab for their willingness to undertake and encourage this long-term research project.

Although it may be a cliché to thank one's spouse for supporting the writing of a book, I would like to give my husband Dean special credit for his endless patience with my, at times incomprehensible, enthusiasm for compiling this bibliography, sometimes at the expense of other activities, over so many years of our shared business and married life.

And lastly, there are two individuals who worked on this project with such dedication that they were an inspiration to me: Deirdre Roden, who did typing, filing and who xeroxed over 5,000 individual file cards, and Grethe Jacobsen, who helped research many questions and problems in Danish libraries and who carefully proof-read hundreds of pages of detailed copy. Without them this work would never have been as complete as it stands today.

Carol L. Schroeder, M.A.

Madison, Wisconsin
March 1981

Table of Contents

Preface

By *Elias Bredsdorff*,
formerly Reader in Scandinavian Studies
in the University of Cambridge

During my years as Queen Alexandra Lecturer in Danish in University College London, 1946-9, I compiled a Bibliography of Danish Literature in English Translation, which was first published in Copenhagen in 1950 and reprinted in Westport, Connecticut, in 1973. My aim was, as I stated in the preface »to give a complete list of all translations of Danish literature into the English language, since the first Danish book was translated in 1533 (Christiern Pedersen's »The richt vay to the Kingdome of heuine«) up to the middle of the twentieth century«. I was fully aware at the time of the inevitability of something having been overlooked and today I realise the shortcomings of my bibliography.

Fortunately there have been many translations from Danish into English after 1950, and during the last thirty years many articles and books have been written in English on subjects related to Denmark and Danish culture, and so the need for a continuation of my early bibliography has become more and more obvious. When, some years ago, the Head of the Danish Institute in Copenhagen asked me whether I would be prepared to follow up my own bibliography with a volume covering the period after 1950 I reluctantly had to decline the invitation, and at that time I knew of no one else who would be prepared to undertake that very demanding task.

I was extremely happy, however, when shortly afterwards I was informed that Carol L. Schroeder, then a young American research student of Danish literature in the University of Wisconsin, Madison, had agreed to undertake this important task. I now realise that the choice could not have been better. I have had the great privilege of following closely Carol Schroeder's work, and I can say how deeply impressed I am with her enthusiasm for the subject, with the conscientiousness with which she has worked, and with her competence as a bibliographer. Carol Schroeder's bibliography is indeed one of very high quality, and I am sure that over the years to come thousands of readers, both in Denmark and in the entire English speaking world, will feel greatly indebted to her for the important new tool she has given everybody interested in the cultural exchange between Denmark and the English speaking world.

Elias Bredsdorff

Copenhagen
May 1981

Introduction

The purpose of this bibliography is to help make Danish literature and information about Denmark more readily accessible to those who do not speak a Scandinavian language. It covers Danish literature in English translation and a selection of books in English about Denmark.

It was my original intention to update Elias Bredsdorff's *Danish Literature in English Translation,* so the beginning date for inclusion in this bibliography is 1950. The closing date is December, 1980. As in Bredsdorff's work, all examples of Danish literature published in English anywhere in the world are included, from individual poems to book-length works. The criteria for inclusion is that the piece of literature be written in Danish originally, or written by a Danish-born writer.

Poems, essays, novels, plays and short stories by an author are arranged alphabetically according to the English title. Each entry contains the English title, the location of the translation and whenever possible the name of the translator. In addition, the original Danish title, genre and year of publication are, in most cases, provided. Many works appear in anthologies, collections or periodicals featuring mumerous translations, and for these the location of the translation may be given in abbreviated form. A guide to these abbreviations will be found on page 13.

Each listing of translations is followed by a list of »Previous Translations« which are taken from Elias Bredsdorff's *Danish Literature in English Translation,* by permission of the author. Translations which have been included as current translations are not duplicated in the »Previous Translations« lists.

In order to aid further study of Danish authors or genres, a bibliography of articles and books published in English about the writer or the genre then follows.

There are three Danish authors about whom a great volume of material exists in English: Hans Christian Andersen, Isak Dinesen (Karen Blixen) and Søren Kierkegaard. For these writers only book-length works are listed, and those wishing to do more in-depth research are referred to specialized bibliographies listed among the works about these authors.

Hans Christian Andersen is also more widely translated than any other Danish author, and in Bredsdorff's bibliography translations of his works make up a special supplement. In this book Hans Christian Andersen is included in the alphabetical listing of authors, but the translations are divided by genre. Within each genre, titles are arranged alphabetically and then chronologically. Although it is impossible to track down all of the hundreds of children's editions of Andersen's stories, many of them retellings rather than translations, an attempt was made to be as complete as possible, especially in regard to legitimate translations.

The section »Books about Denmark« covers the same time period (1950-80). It is a selection of books in English dealing with a Danish topic and primarily intended for the general reader. Works are included if they have more than 16 pages of English text. Publications of 15 pages or less or of a strictly technical or very specialized nature are, on the other hand, excluded, as are books that are pan-Scandinavian in scope.

The section is arranged according to topic. A guide to the subject headings is to be found on page 152. Within each topic the listings are arranged alphabetically, either by author, editor, public or corporate body or by the title, according to the publication data provided.

Abbreviations

Note: Complete information for collections
and anthologies is found in the »Literature in Translation« section
under the individual author or under anthologies

AD
Dinesen, Isak. **Anecdotes of Destiny.** 1958.

ADL
Anthology of Danish Literature. Ed. P. M. Mitchell and F. J. Billeskov-Jansen, 1972.

AScL
An Anthology of Scandinavian Literature. From the Viking Period to the Twentieth Century. Ed. H. Hallmundsson. 1965.

ASR
American-Scandinavian Review. Periodical. (New York). Published by the American-Scandinavian Foundation. [Replaced in 1975 by *Scandinavian Review*.]

AtW
Hansen, Martin A. **Against the Wind. Stories.** 1979.

BoDB
A Book of Danish Ballads. Selected and intro. by Axel Olrik. 1939; rpt. 1968.

BoDV
Book of Danish Verse. Selected and annotated by Oluf Friis. 1922; rpt. 1976.

Books
Books (London) no. 17 (Winter 1974/75). »In Denmark« issue. Ed. Clifford Simmons. London: The National Book League, 1975.

CARNIVAL
Dinesen, Isak. **Carnival: Entertainments and Posthumous Tales.** 1977.

CDPl
Contemporary Danish Plays. An Anthology. Ed. Elias Bredsdorff. 1955; rpt. 1970.

CDPo
Contemporary Danish Poetry. An Anthology. Ed. Line Jensen [et al.]. 1977.

CDPr
Contemporary Danish Prose. An Anthology. Ed. Elias Bredsdorff. 1958; rpt. 1974.

CrS
Malinovski, Ivan. **Critique of Silence. Selected Poems.** 1977.

Daguerreotypes
Dinesen, Isak. **Daguerreotypes and Other Essays.** 1979.

DB&FS
Danish Ballads and Folk Songs. Ed. Erik Dal. 1967.

DFOJ
Danish Foreign Office Journal. Periodical. (Copenhagen). Published by the Danish Ministry of Foreign Affairs. [Replaced in 1968 by *Danish Journal.*]

DI
The Devil's Instrument and Other Danish Stories. Ed. Sven Holm. 1971.

Diss. Abstr.
Dissertation Abstracts. (Ann Arbor, Michigan).

DJ
Danish Journal. Periodical. (Copenhagen). Published by the Danish Ministry of Foreign Affairs. [Supersedes *Danish Foreign Office Journal.*]

Dk-JVJ
Jensen, Johs. V. **Denmark's Johannes V. Jensen.** 1955.

FaF
Four and Forty. A Selection of Danish Ballads Presented in Scots. Tr. Alexander Gray. 1954.

FMoScPl
Five Modern Scandinavian Plays. 1971.

FPl-H
Holberg, Ludvig. **Four Plays.** 1946; rpt. 1971.

FPl-KM
Munk, Kaj. **Five Plays.** 1953, 1964.

FSS
Faroese Short Stories. Ed. Heðin Brønner. 1972.

FtDP
Blicher, Steen Steensen. **From the Danish Peninsula: Poems and a Tale.** 1957.

GScT
The Genius of the Scandinavian Theater. Ed. Evert Sprinchorn. 1964.

HBD
Historical Ballads of Denmark. Tr. Alexander Gray. 1958.

HinS
A Heritage in Song. Ed. Johannes Knudsen. 1978.

HoS
A Harvest of Song. Ed. S. D. Rodholm. 1953.

IDIWB
In Denmark I Was Born ... A Little Book of Danish Verse. Selected by R. P. Keigwin. 1950.

LD
Sarvig, Ole. **Late Day.** 1976.

LitR-Dk
The Literary Review - Denmark Number. (Teaneck, N.J.: Fairleigh & Dickinson) vol. 8, no. 1 (Autumn 1964).

A Little Treasury
A Little Treasury of World Poetry. Ed. and intro. Hubert Creekmore. New York: Charles Scribner's Sons, 1952.

LR
Lines Review. (Midlothian, Scotland) no. 46 (September 1973): Five Danish Poets.

LT
Dinesen, Isak. **Last Tales.** 1957.

MoDA
Modern Danish Authors. Eds. Evelyn Heepe and Niels Heltberg. 1946; rpt. 1974.

MoDP
Modern Danish Poems. Ed. Knud K. Mogensen. 1951.

MoNPl
Modern Nordic Plays: Denmark. Intro. Per Olsen. 1974.

MoScPl
Modern Scandinavian Plays. By August Strindberg and others. 1954.

Nobel Prize Reader
Nobel Prize Reader. Ed. Leo Hamalian and Edmund L. Volpe. Intro. Robert J. Clements. New York: Eagle Books (Popular Library), 1965. Also as **Great Stories by Nobel Prize Winners.** New York, Noonday Press, 1959.

Nor
The Norseman. Periodical. (London). Ceased publication in 1958.

Orbis
Orbis. Periodical published by the International Poetry Society, Bakewell, Derbyshire. »Modern Danish Lyric Poetry« Number, vols. 27/28 (June, 1977).

Orbis Litt.
Orbis Litterarum. Periodical. (Copenhagen).

POEMS
Andersen, Hans Christian. **Poems.** Tr. Murray Brown. 1972.

Portland
The International Portland Review 1980. Portland, Oregon: Portland State Univ., 1980. p 504. [Danish-English text.]

PW
Gress, Elsa. **Philoctetes Wounded and Other Plays.** 1969.

RG
The Royal Guest and Other Classical Danish Narrative. Tr. P. M. Mitchell. 1977.

Scan
Scandinavica. Periodical. (Norwich, England).

ScPlTC
Scandinavian Plays of the Twentieth Century. Intro. A. Gustafson. 1944; rpt. 1972.

ScSoB
Scandinavian Songs and Ballads. Modern Swedish, Danish and Norwegian Songs. Ed. Martin S. Allwood. 1953.

SeBDV
A Second Book of Danish Verse. Tr. Charles Wharton Stork. 1947; rpt. 1968.

SeGT
Dinesen, Isak. **Seven Gothic Tales.** 1963, 1969, 1972. [Original 1934 ed. used for page numbers.]

SeOPl
Holberg, Ludvig. **Seven One-Act Plays.** Tr. Henry Alexander. 1950; rpt. 1972.

Seven Poems
Andersen, Hans Christian. **Seven Poems. Syv Digte.** Tr. R. P. Keigwin. 1955, 1970.

Snow Queen
Andersen, Hans Christian. **The Snow Queen and Other Poems.** 1977.

SotN
Swans of the North and Short Stories by Modern Danish Authors. Tr. Evelyn Heepe. 1953.

SP-BA
Andersen, Benny. **Selected Poems.** 1975.

SP-HN
Nordbrandt, Henrik. **Selected Poems.** 1978.

SP-KR
Rifbjerg, Klaus. **Selected Poems.** 1976.

SR
Scandinavian Review. Periodical. (New York). Published by the American-Scandinavian Foundation. [Supersedes the *American-Scandinavian Review.*]

SS
Scandinavian Studies. Periodical. (U.S.A.). Published by the Society for the Advancement of Scandinavian Studies.

SW-Gr
Grundtvig, N. F. S. **Selected Writings.** 1976.

TaT
Brandt, Jørgen Gustava. **Tête à Tête.** 1978.

TC
Holberg, Ludvig. **Three Comedies.** 1957.

TCScP
Twentieth Century Scandinavian Poetry: The Development of Poetry in Iceland, Denmark, Norway, Sweden and Finland, 1900-1950. Ed. Martin S. Allwood. 1950.

THB
Ballad. **The Heart Book: The Tradition of the Danish Ballad.** 1965.

Tiger
Sørensen, Villy. **Tiger in the Kitchen and Other Strange Stories.** 1956, 1957, 1969.

TMoS
Branner, H. C. **Two Minutes of Silence.** 1966.

TS
Blicher, Steen Steensen. **Twelve Stories.** 1945; rpt. 1972.

Versuch
Versuch: Literarische Beiträge von College-Studenten. Lawrence, Kansas: Dept. of Germanic Languages and Literatures. Univ. of Kansas.

WR
Jensen, Johs. V. **The Waving Rye.** 1958, 1959.

WT
Dinesen, Isak. **Winter's Tales.** 1961. [Original 1942 ed. used for page numbers.]

Bibliographical Abbreviations

b.	born	*pb.*	paperback
comp.	compiled by	*pl.*	plates
c	copyright	*pub., publ.*	published by, publisher
diss.	dissertation	*pr.*	press
ea.	each	*pseud.*	pseudonym
ed.	edited by, edition, editor	*ref.*	referring to, reference
enl.	enlarged	*rpt.*	reprinted, reprint
exp.	expanded	*resp.*	responsible
hb.	hardback	*rev.*	revised
ill.	illustrated by, illustration	*tr., trans.*	translated by, translation,
intro.	introduced by, introduction		translator
n.d.	not dated	*univ.*	university
no., nr.	number	*unp., unpag.*	unpaginated
p, pp	page, pages	*v., vol., vols.*	volume, volumes

Note on Alphabetization

The letters *å* (identical with *aa*), *æ* and *ø* are special Danish vowel signs. Entries containing these letters are alphabetized as follows:

> *å* and *aa* = *aa* (before *ab*)
> *æ*   = *ae*
> *ø*   = *o*

Den, det and *de* are Danish articles equivalent to *the* and therefore ignored in alphabetization *(Det danske Selskab*, e.g., is arranged under *danske)*.

DANISH LITERATURE
IN ENGLISH TRANSLATION
1950-1980

A. Individual Authors

JEPPE AAKJÆR (1866-1930)

The Farmer. Tr. S. D. Rodholm. *HoS* pp 165-166. [*Bondevise*, poem from the collection *Samlede Værker*, I, 1918.]

Georg Brandes. Tr. R. P. Keigwin. *TCScP* p 40. [*Til Georg Brandes*, poem written in 1927, published in *Samlede Digte*, II, 1947.]

Golden Sun. Tr. S. D. Rodholm. *HoS* p 147. [*Gylden Sol*, poem published in *Politiken*, 15. april 1917, and in *Samlede Værker*, II, 1918.]

Heart, Be Still. Tr. S. D. Rodholm. *HoS* p 46. Also *HinS* hymn 99. [*Aften* from *Ræbild-Kantate*, published in *Politiken*, 4. august 1912, and in *Samlede Værker*, II, 1918.]

Here I Stand with Tinkling Bells Galore. Tr. S. D. Rodholm. *HinS* song 97.

History. Tr. S. D. Rodholm. *HoS* pp 131-132. [*Historiens Sang*, poem published in *Skive Folkeblad*, 6. juni 1917, and in *Samlede Værker*, II, 1918.]

If I Should Give My Heart Away. Tr. S. D. Rodholm. *HinS* song 98. [*Gylden Sol*, poem published in *Politiken*, 15. april 1917, and in *Samlede Værker*, II, 1918.]

Jutland. Tr. Robert Silliman Hillyer. *BoDV* pp 156-160. [*Jylland*, poem from the collection *Fri Felt*, 1905.]

The Oats. Tr. Charles Wharton Stork. *SeBDV* pp 102-103. [*Havren*, poem published in *Politiken*, 3. september 1916, and in *Samlede Værker*, II, 1918.]

The Oats. Tr. S. D. Rodholm. *HoS* pp 163-164. [*Havren*, poem.]

Oats. (stanzas) Tr. R. P. Keigwin. *IDIWB* p 95. [*Havren*, poem.]

Off for the Day. Tr. W. Glyn Jones. *CDPr* pp 29-40. [*Da Hyrdedrengen skulde i Skoven*, short story from the collection *Hvor Bønder bor*, 1908.]

Pæ' Sivensak. Tr. Robert Silliman Hillyer. *BoDV* pp 155-156. [*Pæ' Sivensak*, poem published in *Tilskueren*, oktober 1908, and in *Samlede Værker*, I, 1918.]

Prelude. Tr. Robert Silliman Hillyer. *BoDV* p 154. [*Forspil*, poem from the collection *Rugens Sange*, 1906.]

The Rye Field. Tr. Charles Wharton Stork. *SeBDV* pp 100-101. [*Ved Rugskjellet*, poem from the collection *Rugens Sange*, 1906.]

The Shepherd. Tr. S. D. Rodholm. *HoS* pp 157-158. [*Ole sad pua en Knold*, poem from the collection *Samlede Værker*, I, 1918.]

Songs of the Heath. (Cerddi'r grug.). Tr. John Glyn Davies. Talsarn, Llanfairfechan, N. Wales: H. Glyn Davies, 1962. p 42. Includes 3 translations into Welsh. [Mimeographed.]

The Sower. Tr. R. P. Keigwin. *IDIWB* pp 91-93. [*Sædemand*, poem published in *Land-mands-Almanakken*, 1914, and in *Samlede Værker*, II, 1918.]

The Stonebreaker. Tr. Charles Wharton Stork. *SeBDV* pp 104-105. [*Jens Vejmand*, poem published in *Politiken*, 22. september 1905, and in *Samlede Værker*, I, 1918.]

The Stonebreaker. Tr. R. P. Keigwin. *IDIWB* pp 87-89, and *TCScP* pp 39-40. [*Jens Vejmand*, poem.]

To Bundgaard. Sculptor. Tr. R. P. Keigwin. *TCScP* p 40. [*Til Billedhugger Bundgaard*, poem from the collection *Glimmersand*, *Smaa Vers*, 1919.]

Previous Translations:

The Tramp's Christmas Eve.
A Song of the Rye.
The Morning of Battle.
The Shining Brook.
She Held Me Out Her Mouth to Kiss.
The Oat.

EMIL AARESTRUP (1800-1856)

A Dinner. Tr. R. P. Keigwin. *IDIWB* p 61. [*En Middag*, poem from the collection *Digte*, 1838.]

Early Parting. Tr. S. Foster Damon. *BoDV* pp 101-105. [*Tidlige Skilsmisse*, poem written 1825-1837.]

Evening Sigh. Tr. Charles Wharton Stork. *SeBDV* pp 38-39. [*Et Aftensuk*, poem from the collection *Digte*, 1838.]

Fear. Tr. S. Foster Damon. *BoDV* p 101. [*Angst*, poem from the collection *Digte*, 1838.]

Morning Walk. Tr. S. Foster Damon. *BoDV* pp 100-101. [*En Morgenvandring*, poem from the collection *Digte*, 1828.]

Punishment. Tr. Charles Wharton Stork. *SeBDV* pp 37-38. [*Straf*, poem from the collection *Digte*, 1838.]

Ritournelles. Tr. S. Foster Damon. *BoDV* pp 105-108. [*Ritorneller*, poems published in various collections including *Digte*, 1838.]

The Sleeper. Tr. S. Foster Damon. *BoDV* p 99. [*Den Sovende*, poem published in *Gæa*, *æsthetisk Aarbog*, published by P. L. Møller in 1846.]

22 **To a Friend.** Tr. Charles Wharton Stork. *SeBDV* p 37. [*Til en Veninde*, poem from the collection *Digte*, 1838.]

Previous Translations:

Holy Chimes.

KJELD ABELL (1901-1961)

Anna Sophie Hedvig. Tr. Evelyn Heepe. *MoDA* pp 61-82. [Extract from Act II of *Anna Sophie Hedvig*, play, 1939.]

Anna Sophie Hedvig. Tr. Hanna Astrup Larsen. *ScPITC*, 2nd series: pp 223-298. Also in Corrigan, Robert W. ed.: *Masterpieces of the Modern Theater: Scandinavian Theater.* New York: Collier Books, 1967. [*Anna Sophie Hedvig*, play, 1939.]

Ants and Contrariness. Tr. Eileen MacLeod. *CDPr* pp 257-262. [*Myrer og Modsigelseslyst*, short story, 1940. Original title when read aloud, *Myrerne*.]

Days on a Cloud. Tr. A. I. Roughton and Elias Bredsdorff. With an Introduction by Elias Bredsdorff. *GScT* pp 466-535. [*Dage på en Sky*, play, 1947.]

The Queen on Tour Tr. J. F. S. Pearce. *CDPl* pp 105-172. [*Dronning gaar igen*, play, 1943.]

The Soul of the Theatre. Tr. Harry G. Carlson. *GScT* pp 402-407. [*Teatrets Sjæl*, essay, *Perspektiv*, vol. 6, no. 2, February, 1955.]

Three from Minikoi. Tr. A. I. Roughton. London: Secker & Warburg, 1960. p 319. [*De tre fra Minikoi*, novel, 1957.]

Previous Translations:

The Melody That Got Lost.
The Ants.
A Postcard from Spain.
Eve [a Short Extract]: Apotheosis.

Works about Kjeld Abell

Madsen, Børge Gedsø. **Leading Motifs in the Dramas of Kjeld Abell.** *SS* vol. 33, no. 3 (1961) pp 127-136.

Marker, Frederick J. **Kjeld Abell.** New York: Twayne Publishers, 1976. p 172. [World Authors Series.]

OVE ABILDGAARD (b. 1916)

Excursions. Tr. Helge Westermann and Martin S. Allwood. *MoDP* p 36. Tr. also with Sonia Cannata Westermann. *TCScP* pp 92-93. [*Togter*, poem from the collection *Uglegylp*, 1946.]

Glimpses of a Childhood. Tr. Foster W. Blaisdell, Jr. *LitR-Dk* pp 43-46. [*Glimt af en Barndom*, short story from the collection *Det langsomme Foraar*, 1957.]

Jørgen. Tr. Alexander Taylor. *CDPo* p 167. [*Jørgen*, poem from the collection *Og Lises Hånd i min*, 1972.]

Navel. Tr. Helge Westermann and Martin S. Allwood. *TCScP* p 92. [*Navle*, poem from the collection *Uglegylp*, 1946.]

Terndive. Tr. Alexander Taylor. *CDPo* pp 164-166. [*Ternedyk*, poem from the collection *Og Lises Hånd i min*, 1972.]

12 Eggs. Tr. Alexander Taylor. *CDPo* p 167. [*12 æg*, poem from the collection *Og Lises Hånd i min*, 1972.]

Winter Dream. Tr. Alexander Taylor. *CDPo* p 166. [*Vinterdrøm*, poem from the collection *Og Lises Hånd i min*, 1972.]

HANS AGERBEK (1798-1869)

Watch and Wait Unafraid! Tr. S. D. Rodholm. *HoS* pp 84-85. [*Uforsagt, vær paa Vagt*, hymn written 1850, published in complete version in *Bibelske Sangbog*, 1864.]

JOHANNES ALLEN (b. 1916)

Data for Death. Tr. Marianne Helweg. London: Hogarth Press, 1971. p 191. [*Data for din Død*, novel, 1970.]

It's a Swinging Life. Tr. Keith Bradfield. London: Hogarth Press, 1966. p 160. Ill. [*I disse skønne Tider*, novel, 1961.]

Operation Charlie. (Resume with quotations of reviews in English and French). *World Theatre* (Paris) vol. 15, no. 2 (1966) p 180 (Technical Data: Denmark). [*Operation Charlie*, play, 1965.]

Relations. New York: World Publishing Co., 1970. p 159. [*Nu*, novel, 1967.]

Tumult. A Novel. Tr. Frederick Marker. London: The Hogarth Press, 1969. p 168. London: Pan Books, 1969. p 122. pb. [*Nu*, novel, 1967.] See also *Relations* (American version).

Young Love. Tr. Naomi Walford. London: Hogarth Press, 1958. p 167. New York: Alfred A. Knopf, 1959. p 215. Greenwich, Conn.: Fawcett Pubs., 1960. p 141. pb. London: Pan Books, 1960. p 153. [*Ung Leg*, novel and moviescript, 1956.]

MURAT ALPAR

Murat Alpar, born in Turkey, has lived in Denmark since 1967 and writes in Danish.

The Foreign Workers. Tr. from Danish by Alexander Taylor. *SR* vol. 66, no. 1 (March 1978) p 16. [*Gæstearbejderen*, poem from the collection *Gæstearbejderen Memet*, 1978.]

Foreign Workers Live Two Lives. Tr. from Danish by Alexander Taylor. *SR* vol. 66, no. 1 (March 1978) p 14. [*Gæstearbejderen besidder to Liv*, poem from the collection *Gæstearbejderen Memet*, 1978.]

Memet. Tr. Alexander Taylor. Copenhagen: Augustinus Forlag; Willimantic, CT: Curbstone Press, 1980. p 25. [*Gæstearbejderen Memet*, poetry collection, 1978.]

Memet's Apartment. Tr. Alexander Taylor. *SR* vol. 66, no. 1 (March 1978) pp 74-75. [*Memet's Lejlighed*, poem from the collection *Gæstearbejderen Memet*, 1978.]

Memet's Children Go to School. Tr. Alexander Taylor. *SR* vol. 66, no. 1 (March 1978) pp 76-77. [*Memet's Børn går i Skole*, poem from the collection *Gæstearbejderen Memet*, 1978.]

Viktoria Street. Tr. from Danish by Alexander Taylor. *SR* vol. 66, no. 1 (March 1978) pp 36-37. [*Viktoriagade*, poem from the collection *Gæstearbejderen Memet*, 1978.]

BENNY ANDERSEN (b. 1929)

Alcoholism. Tr. Alexander Taylor. *SP-BA* p 101. [*Alkoholisme*, poem from the collection *Det sidste øh*, 1969.]

All This. Tr. Alexander Taylor. *SP-BA* p 119. [*Alt dette*, poem from the collection *Her i Reservatet*, 1971.]

The Amiable Skeleton. Tr. Anne Born. *Orbis* p 34. [*Det elskværdige Skelet*, poem from the collection *Personlige Papirer*, 1974.]

Analysis. Tr. Alexander Taylor. *SP-BA* p 7. [*Analyse*, poem from the collection *Den musikalske Ål*, 1960.]

At Home. Tr. Anne Born. *Orbis* p 34. [*Hjemme*, poem from the collection *Personlige Papirer*, 1974.]

Atmosphere. Tr. Alexander Taylor. *Moons and Lion Tailes* (Minneapolis) vol. 2, no. 4 (1978) p 81. [Poem.]

Autonomous. Tr. Alexander Taylor. *SP-BA* p 71. Also *Contemporary Literature in Translation* (Vancouver, B.C.) no. 7 (Spring 1970) p 27. [*Uafhængig*, poem from the collection *Kamera med Køkkenadgang*, 1965.]

Between Us. Tr. Alexander Taylor. *LR* p 54. Also *SP-BA* p 109. [*Mellem os*, poem from the collection *Det sidste øh*, 1969.]

Certain Days. Tr. Alexander Taylor. *Contemporary Literature in Translation* (Vancouver, B. C.) no. 15 (Spring 1973) pp 31-32. Also *SP-BA* pp 79, 81. [*Visse Dage*, poem from the collection *Portrætgalleri*, 1966.]

Charity Concert. Tr. Alexander Taylor. *LR* p 55. Also *SP-BA* p 61 and *Contemporary Literature in Translation* (Vancouver, B.C.) no. 9 (Winter 1970) p 23. [*Velgørenhedskoncert*, poem from the collection *Kamera med Køkkenadgang*, 1965.]

The Critical Frog. Tr. Alexander Taylor. *SP-BA* p 35. [*Den kritiske Frø*, poem from the collection *Den musikalske Ål*, 1960.]

The Critical Seed. Tr. Anne Born. *Orbis* p 33. [*Den kritiske Frø*, poem from the collection *Den musikalske Ål*, 1960.]

Dear Enemies. Tr. Alexander Taylor. *SP-BA* p 97. [*Kære Fjender*, poem from the collection *Det sidste øh*, 1969.]

Dear Friends. Tr. Alexander Taylor. *SP-BA* p 99. [*Kære Venner*, poem from the collection *Det sidste øh*, 1969.]

Earthworm. Tr. Michael Sanner. *Versuch* vol. 11 (1972) p 8. [*Regnorm*, poem from the collection *Det sidste øh*, 1969.]

Earthworm. Tr. Alexander Taylor. *SP-BA* p 105. Also *CDPo* p 247. [*Regnorm*, poem from the collection *Det sidste øh*, 1969.]

Experiences. Tr. Alexander Taylor. *Contemporary Literature in Translation* (Vancouver, B. C.) no. 15 (Spring 1973) pp 31-32. Also *SP-BA* pp 91, 93. [*Erfaringer*, poem from the collection *Det sidste øh*, 1969.]

Family Idyll. Tr. David Allen. *Versuch* vol. 11 (1972) p 30. [*Familieidyl*, poem from the collection *Det sidste øh*, 1969.]

Family Idyll. Tr. Alexander Taylor. *SR* vol. 67, no. 2 (June 1979) p 16. [*Familieidyl*, poem from the collection *Det sidste øh*, 1969.]

The Forgotten Son. Tr. Alexander Taylor. *SP-BA* pp 9, 11. Also *Prism International*

24

(Vancouver, B.C.) vol. 11, no. 3 (1972) pp 78-79. [*Den glemte Søn*, poem from the collection *Den musikalske Ål*, 1960.]

Friendship. Tr. Alexander Taylor. *SP-BA* pp 41, 43. [*Venskab*, poem from the collection *Den indre Bowlerhat*, 1964.]

Generation Gap. Tr. Alexander Taylor. *SP-BA* p 103. [*Generationsforskel*, poem from the collection *Det sidste øh*, 1969.]

Goodness. Tr. Alexander Taylor. *SP-BA* pp 37, 39. Also *CDPo* p 243, *Trans-Pacific* (Yellow Springs, Ohio) p 36 and *World Literature Today* (Oklahoma) vol. 52, no. 4 (Autumn 1978) p 550. [*Godhed*, poem from the collection *Den indre Bowlerhat*, 1964.]

The Hanged Informer. Tr. Alexander Taylor. *SP-BA* p 87. [*Den hængte Stikker*, poem from the collection *Portrætgalleri*, 1966.]

Happiness. Tr. Alexander Taylor. *SP-BA* p 49. [*Lykken*, poem from the collection *Den indre Bowlerhat*, 1964.]

Headliner. Tr. Alexander Taylor. *SP-BA* p 25. [*Hovedsagen*, poem from the collection *Den musikalske Ål*, 1960.]

Hiccups. Tr. Leonie Marx. *Mundus Artium* (Athens, Ohio) vol. 8, no. 2 (1975) pp 30-32. [*Hikke*, short story from a collection of short fiction called *Puderne*, 1965.]

High and Dry. Tr. Alexander Taylor. *LR* p 56. Also *SP-BA* p 67, *CDPo* p 248 and *Prism International* (Vancouver, B.C.) vol. 11, no. 3 (1972) p 76. [*Paa det tørre*, poem from the collection *Kamera med Køkkenadgang*, 1965.]

High and Dry. Tr. Phillip Marshall. *LitR-Dk* p 77. [*Paa det tørre*, poem from *Kamera med Køkkenadgang*, 1965.]

High Time. Tr. Anne Born. *Orbis* p 32. [*Paa høje Tid*, poem from the collection *Den indre Bowlerhat*, 1964.]

A Hole in the Earth. Tr. Alexander Taylor. *SP-BA* p 141. Also *CDPo* p 249. [*Et Hul i Jorden*, poem from the collection *Personlige Papirer*, 1974.]

In the Bar. Tr. Alexander Taylor. *SP-BA* p 69. [*I Baren*, poem from the collection *Kamera med Køkkenadgang*, 1965.]

The Intellectual. Tr. Hanna Gliese-Lee. *Prism International* (Vancouver, B.C.) vol. 12, no. 1 (1972-1973) p 96. [*Den intellektuelle*, poem from the collection *Kamera med Køkkenadgang*, 1962.]

It's High Time. Tr. Alexander Taylor. *West Coast Review*, June 1973. Also *SP-BA* pp 51, 53. [*På høje Tid*, poem from the collection *Den indre Bowlerhat*, 1964.]

Jelly Fish. Tr. Alexander Taylor. *LR* p 55. Also *SP-BA* p 65. [*Goplerne*, poem from the collection *Kamera med Køkkenadgang*, 1965.]

Just to Be Sure. Tr. Alexander Taylor. *LR* p 53. Also *SP-BA* p 95, and *Poetry Now* (Eureka, Ca.) vol. 4, no. 6 (1979) p 30. [*For en Sikkerheds Skyld*, poem from the collection *Det sidste øh*, 1969.]

The Last Er. Tr. Alexander Taylor. *LR* p 51. Also *Maine Edition* (September 1973) and *SP-BA* p 117. [*Det sidste øh*, poem from the collection of the same title, 1969.]

The Last Poem in the World. Tr. Alexander Taylor. *Moons and Lion Tailes* (Minneapolis) vol. 2, no. 4 (1978) pp 79-80. [*Det sidste Digt i Verden*, poem from the collection *Det sidste øh*, 1969.]

Life Is Narrow and High. Tr. Alexander Taylor. *SP-BA* p 133. Also *CDPo* p 246. [*Livet er smalt og højt*, poem from the collection *Personlige Papirer*, 1974.]

Light Night. Tr. Anne Born. *Orbis* p 35. [*Lys Nat*, poem from the collection *Personlige Papirer*, 1974.]

Love Declaration (Man to Woman). Tr. Alexander Taylor. *SP-BA* p 123. [*Kærlighedserklæring (fra Mand til Kvinde)*, poem from the collection *Her i Reservatet*, 1971.]

Love Declaration (Woman to Man). Tr. Alexander Taylor. *SP-BA* p 121. [*Kærlighedserklæring (fra Kvinde til Mand)*, poem from the collection *Her i Reservatet*, 1971.]

M. Tr. Alexander Taylor. *SP-BA* p 83. Also *CDPo* p 244. [*M.*, poem from the collection *Portrætgalleri*, 1966.]

Melancholy. Tr. Alexander Taylor. *SP-BA* p 139. Also *CDPo* p 248. [*Melankoli*, poem from the collection *Personlige Papirer*, 1974.]

Memories. Tr. Alexander Taylor. *SP-BA* p 59. [*Minderne*, poem from the collection *Den indre Bowlerhat*, 1964.]

Morning Prayer. Tr. Alexander Taylor. *SP-BA* p 13. [*Morgenbøn*, poem from the collection *Den musikalske Ål*, 1960.]

The Musical Eel. Tr. Alexander Taylor. *SP-BA* p 33. [*Den musikalske Ål*, poem from the collection by that name, 1960.]

Now It's Said (Man, about 30). Tr. Alexander Taylor. *SP-BA* pp 125, 127. [*Så er det sagt (Mand, ca. 30 År)*, poem from the collection *Her i Reservatet*, 1971.]

Obituary. Tr. Alexander Taylor. *SP-BA* p 23. Also *Contemporary Literature in Translation* (Vancouver, B.C.) no. 13 (Summer 1972) p 6. [*Nekrolog*, poem from the collection *Den musikalske Ål*, 1960.]

On Dry Land. Tr. Anne Born. *Orbis* p 35. [*Paa det tørre*, poem from the collection *Kamera med Køkkenadgang*, 1962.]

Optimist. Tr. Alexander Taylor. *LR* pp 51-52. Also *SP-BA* p 73 and *Prism International* (Vancouver, B.C.) vol. 11, no. 3 (1972) p 75. [*Optimist*, poem from the collection *Kamera med Køkkenadgang*, 1965.]

The Pampered Mermaid. Tr. Alexander Taylor. *SP-BA* p 85. Also *Poetry Now* (Eureka, Ca.) vol. 4, no. 6 (1979) p 30. [*Den forvænte Havfrue*, poem from the collection *Portrætgalleri*, 1966.]

The Pants. Tr. Hanne Gliese-Lee. *Mundus Artium* (Athens, Ohio) vol. 5, nos. 1-2 (1972) pp 44-51. [*Bukserne*, short story from the collection *Puderne*, 1965.]

The Passage. Tr. Paula Hostrup-Jessen. *DI* pp 247-260. [*Passagen*, short story from the collection *Puderne*, 1965.]

The Persistent Worshipper. Tr. Alexander Taylor. *SP-BA* p 89. [*Den ihærdige Tilbeder*, poem from the collection *Portrætgalleri*, 1966.]

Photographs. Tr. Alexander Taylor. *LR* pp 49-50. Also *Maine Edition* (September 1973), *SP-BA* p 29, *CDPo* pp 244-245 and *Poetry Now* (Eureka, Ca.) vol. 4, no. 6 (1979) p 30. [*Fotografierne*, poem from the collection *Den musikalske Ål*, 1960.]

Relaxation. Tr. Alexander Taylor. *SP-BA* p 61. [*Løsning*, poem from the collection *Kamera med Køkkenadgang*, 1965.]

Rural Station. Tr. Alexander Taylor. *SP-BA* pp 3, 5. [*Landstation*, poem from the collection *Den musikalske Ål*, 1960.]

Sabina. Tr. Alexander Taylor. *SP-BA* pp 135, 137. [*Sabine*, poem from the collection *Personlige Papirer*, 1974.]

Selected Poems. Tr. Alexander Taylor. Princeton: Princeton University Press, 1975. Hardback Danish-English version; paperback ed. with English only. p 142. Individual poems listed separately under *SP-BA*.

Shut Up. Tr. Anne Born. *Orbis* p 34. [*Hold op*, poem from the collection *Kamera med Køkkenadgang*, 1962.]

Skeptical Prayer. Tr. Alexander Taylor. *SP-BA* p 19. Also *Contemporary Literature in Translation* (Vancouver, B.C.) no. 13 (Summer 1972) p 6. [*Skeptisk Bøn*, poem from the collection *Den musikalske Ål*, 1960.]

Sleepless Hours in the Summer House. Tr. Alexander Taylor. *LR* p 54. Also *SP-BA* p 31. [*Søvnløse Timer i Sommerhuset*, poem from the collection *Den musikalske Ål*, 1960.]

Slug-a-bed. Tr. Alexander Taylor. *SP-BA* pp 45, 47. [*Syvsover*, poem from the collection *Den indre Bowlerhat*, 1964.]

Smile. Tr. Alexander Taylor. *SP-BA* pp 55, 57. Also *World Literature Today* (Oklahoma) vol. 52, no. 4 (Autumn 1978) p 553. [*Smil*, poem from the collection *Den indre Bowlerhat*, 1964.]

Soul. Tr. Anne Born. *Orbis* p 33. [*Sjælen*, poem from the collection *Den indre Bowlerhat*, 1964.]

Table Prayer. Tr. Alexander Taylor. *SP-BA* p 17. [*Bordbøn*, poem from the collection *Den musikalske Ål*, 1960.]

Tenderness. Tr. Alexander Taylor. *LR* p 51. Also *SP-BA* p 21. [*Ømhed*, poem from the collection *Den musikalske Ål*, 1960.]

This Is. Tr. Alexander Taylor. *LR* pp 52-53. Also *SP-BA* pp 75, 77 and *Prism International* (Vancouver, B.C.) vol. 11, no. 3 (1972) pp 79-80. [*Her er*, poem from the collection *Portrætgalleri*, 1966.]

This Uncertainty. Tr. Alexander Taylor. *SP-BA* p 107. Also *CDPo* p 242. [*Denne Uvished*, poem from the collection *Det sidste øh*, 1969.]

Time. Tr. Alexander Taylor. *SP-BA* pp 129, 131. Also *CDPo* pp 245-246 and *World Literature Today* (Oklahoma) vol. 52, no. 4 (Autumn 1978) p 552. [*Tiden*, poem from the collection *Her i Reservatet*, 1971.]

To a Strong Woman. Tr. Nadia Christensen. *SR* vol. 67, no. 2 (June 1979) pp 17-18. [Excerpt from *Til en stærk Kvinde*, poem from the collection *Under begge Øjne*, 1978.]

The Uncertainty. Tr. Alexander Taylor. *LR* p 54. Also *Maine Edition* (September 1973). [*Denne Uvished*, poem from the collection *Det sidste øh*, 1969.]

Widescreen. Tr. Alexander Taylor. *SP-BA* p 27. Also *World Literature Today* (Oklahoma) vol. 52, no. 4 (Autumn 1978) p 551. [*Widescreen*, poem from the collection *Den musikalske Ål*, 1960.]

Winter Prayer. Tr. Alexander Taylor. *SP- BA* p 15. [*Vinterbøn*, poem from the collection *Den musikalske Ål*, 1960.]

Women. Tr. Alexander Taylor. *Moons and Lion Tailes* (Minneapolis) vol. 2, no. 4 (1978) pp 76-78. [*Damer*, poem from the collection *Den indre Bowlerhat*, 1964.]

Your Dress Without You. Tr. Alexander Taylor. *SP-BA* pp 111, 113, 115. [*Din Kjole uden dig*, poem from the collection *Det sidste øh*, 1969.]

Works about Benny Andersen

Marx, Leonie. **Exercises in Living: Benny Andersen's Literary Perspectives.** *World*

26 *Literature Today* (Oklahoma) vol. 52, no. 4 (Autumn 1978) pp 550-554.

Taylor, Alexander. **In Defence of Humor.** *Moons and Lion Tailes* (Minneapolis) vol. 2, no. 4 (1978) p 75.

HANS CHRISTIAN ANDERSEN (1805 - 1875)

Arranged as follows:
1) Autobiography, Travel Description, Letters
2) Collections of Poetry
3) Individual Poems
4) Collections of Tales
5) Individual Tales
6) Books about Hans Christian Andersen

Note: Dramatizations follow the listings of translations of collections and individual tales.

1) Autobiography, Travel Description, Letters

The Andersen-Scudder Letters: Hans Christian Andersen's correspondence with Horace Elisha Scudder. Ed., with trans. and explanatory notes by Waldemar Westergaard. Intro. Jean Hersholt. Interpretive essay Helge Topsøe-Jensen. London: Cambridge, 1950. p 181.

The Fairy Tale of My Life. Tr. W. Glyn Jones. Ed. H. Topsøe-Jensen. Ill. Niels Larsen Stevns. Copenhagen: Nyt nordisk Forlag, 1954. London: Maxsons & Co., 1955. New York: British Book Centre, 1954, 1955. p 350. [Based on the 1951 Danish edition edited & annotated by H. Topsøe-Jensen.] [*Mit Livs Eventyr*, 1855-67.] [Printed in Denmark.]

The Fairy Tale of My Life. An Autobiography. 1871; rpt. New York and London: Paddington Press, 1975. p 569. Ill. [*Mit Livs Eventyr*, 1855 and 1868.]

Hans Andersen's Diary of His Visit to Dickens in 1847. Ed. by Elias Bredsdorff. In Bredsdorff, Elias: *Hans Andersen and Charles Dickens.* Cambridge: W. Heffer & Sons, 1956. [Printed in Copenhagen.] [An edition of *Hans Andersen and Charles Dickens. A Friendship and Its Dissolution.* Copenhagen: Rosenkilde & Bagger, 1956. p 140.]

The Mermaid Man. The Autobiography of Hans Christian Andersen. Tr. and abridged by Maurice Michael. London: Arthur Barker; New York: Library Publishers, 1955. p 240. [*Mit Livs Eventyr.*]

A Prospect from My Window in Naples. Tr. Charles Beckwith. *ADL* pp 217-221. [*Udsigt fra mit Vindue*, travelogue from *En Digters Bazar*, 1842.]

A Visit to Portugal, 1866. Tr. and with notes and intro. Grace Thornton. London: Peter Owen, 1972. Indianapolis, Ind.: Bobbs-Merrill, 1973. p 105. Ill. [*Et Besøg i Portugal*, 1866.]

A Visit to Spain and North Africa, 1862. Tr. and ed., with an intro. by Grace Thornton. London: Peter Owen, 1975. p 198. [UNESCO collection of representative works: Danish series.] [*I Spanien*, travel description, 1863.]

2) Collections of Poetry

Poems. Tr., selected and ed. Murray Brown. Berkeley, Ca.: Elsinore Press, 1972. p 114. Individual poems listed separately under *POEMS*.

Seven Poems. Syv Digte. Tr. R. P. Keigwin. Odense: H. C. Andersen's House, 1955, 1970. p 21. [Danish and English texts included.] Individual poems listed separately under *Seven Poems.*

The Snow Queen and Other Poems. Tr. and intro. Anne Born. Richmond: The Keepsake Press, 1977. p 16. [Contains parallel Danish and English text of five poems.] [Limited edition of 185 copies.] Individual poems listed separately under *Snow Queen.*

3) Individual Poems

Alhambra. Tr. Murray Brown. *POEMS* p 53. [*Alhambra*, poem, 1863.]

All Things Rush On like Wind. Tr. Murray Brown. *POEMS* p 92. [*Kommer aldrig igjen!* poem, 1868.]

Alphabet Bouquet. Tr. Murray Brown. *POEMS* pp 18-20. [*Alphabet-Bouquet*, poem, 1846.]

August. Tr. Murray Brown. *POEMS* pp 82-85. [*August*, poem, 1832.]

The Beech Tree. Tr. Murray Brown. *POEMS* p 81. [*Bøgetræet*, poem, 1830.]

The Bogeyman Has Done It! Tr. Murray Brown. *POEMS* pp 54-61. [*Det har Zombien gjort*, poem, 1838.]

The Briefest Night. Tr. Murray Brown. *POEMS* p 97. [*Den korteste Nat*, poem, 1875.]

Bury Me There. Tr. Murray Brown. *POEMS* p 100. [*Mol-Toner*, poem, 1831.]

The Carrot Wedding. Tr. Murray Brown. *POEMS* pp 71-72. [*Spørg Amagermo'er*, poem, 1871.]

The Chicken and the Lark. Tr. Murray Brown. *POEMS* p 80. [*I Foraaret i Kjøge*, poem, 1875.]

The Children of the Year. Tr. Murray Brown. *POEMS* p 7. [*Aarets Børn*, poem, 1840.]

From **A Child's Notebook.** Tr. Murray Brown. *POEMS* p 12. [Af: *Et Barns Skriftemaal*, poem, 1875.]

Copenhagen. Tr. Murray Brown. *POEMS* pp 27-28. [*Kjøbenhavn*, poem, 1875.]

The Cottage. Tr. Murray Brown. *POEMS* p 25. [*Hytten*, poem, 1831.]

Cradle Song. Tr. Murray Brown. *POEMS* p 2. [*Agnetes Vuggevise*, poem, 1867.]

Critique. Tr. R. P. Keigwin. *Seven Poems* p 15. [*Recension*, poem, 1830.] [Danish text included.]

Dance, My Little Puppets, Dance! Tr. Murray Brown. *POEMS* p 5. [*Dandse, dandse, Dukke min*, poem, 1871.]

The Dying Child. Tr. Murray Brown. *POEMS* p 86. [*Det døende Barn*, poem, 1827.]

The Dying Child. Tr. S. Foster Damon. *BoDV* p 109. [*Det døende Barn*, poem, 1827.]

The Dying Child. Tr. R. P. Keigwin. *Seven Poems* p 19. [*Det døende Barn*, poem, 1827.] [Danish text included.]

Evening Landscape. Tr. Murray Brown. *POEMS* p 17. [*Aftenlandskab*, poem, 1829.]

A Foreground with a Little Green. Tr. Murray Brown. *POEMS* p 16. [*En Forgrund med en Smule Grønt*, poem, 1833.]

Forest Peace. Tr. Norman C. Bansen. In *Christmas Chimes.* An annual Christmas publication. Vol. 38. Ed. Edward C. Eskildsen. Blair, Nebraska: Lutheran Publishing House, 1958. p 64. [Poem.]

Good-by, Italy. Tr. Murray Brown. *POEMS* p 67. [*Farvel til Italien*, poem, 1834.]

Holger Danske. Tr. Murray Brown. *POEMS* pp 40-42. [*Holger Danske*, poem, 1830.]

I Dreamt I Was a Little Bird. Tr. Murray Brown. *POEMS* pp 14-15. [*Jeg drømte jeg var en lille Fugl*, poem, 1833.]

I Have a Dread That Stops My Breath. Tr. Murray Brown. *POEMS* p 94. [*Jeg har en Angst som aldrig før*, poem, 1864.]

I Love the Ocean. Tr. S. D. Rodholm. *HoS* p 168. [*Hvad jeg elsker*, poem published in *Phantasier og Skizzer*, 1831.]

If You Walk on Thin Ice. Tr. Murray Brown. *POEMS* p 33. [*Gaaer du paa Glatiis*, poem, 1871.]

In Cartagena II. Tr. Murrray Brown. *POEMS* p 47. [*De dandse med Castagnetter*, poem, 1862.]

In Denmark I Was Born. Tr. R. P. Keigwin. *Seven Poems:* p 9. Also *IDIWB* pp 63-65. [*Danmark, mit Fædreland*, poem published in *Fædrelandet*, 1850.] [Danish text included in *Seven Poems.*]

In Denmark I Was Born. Tr. Murray Brown. *POEMS* p 1. [*Danmark, mit Fædreland*, poem, 1850.]

The Infant Jesus in the Manger Lay. Tr. Murray Brown. Ill. Axel Andersen. *ASR* vol. 56, no. 4 (December 1968) frontispiece. Also *POEMS* p 96. [*Barn Jesus i en Krybbe laae*, poem, 1832.]

Jutland. Tr. R. P. Keigwin. *Seven Poems* p 10. [*Jylland*, poem, 1860.] [Danish text included.]

Jutland. Tr. Murray Brown. *POEMS* p 69. [*Jylland*, poem, 1860.]

Life's the Traveller's Gale. Tr. Murray Brown. *POEMS* p 45. [*Det er Liv at rejse*, poem, 1842.]

Little Verse. Tr. Murray Brown. *POEMS* p 91. [*Smaavers*, poem.]

Little Viggo. Tr. Murray Brown. *POEMS* p 73. [*Lille Viggo*, poem, 1832.]

Live Well, Jenny Lind. Tr. Murray Brown. *POEMS* p 43. [*Levvel til Jenny Lind*, poem, 1843.]

The Man from Paradise. Tr. Murray Brown. *POEMS* pp 48-53. [*Manden fra Paradis*, poem, 1830.]

Melodies of the Heart. Tr. Murray Brown. *POEMS* pp 30-32. [*Hjertets Melodier*, poem, 1830.]

The Merry Night of Halloween. Tr. Murray Brown. *POEMS* p 6. [*St. Hans's lystige Nat*, song from *Bruden fra Lammermoor*, 1832.]

Mother and Child. Tr. Murray Brown. *POEMS* p 3. [*Moderen med Barnet*, poem, 1829.]

Mottoes with Presents. Tr. Murray Brown. *POEMS* p 79. [*Deviser med Presenter*, poem, 1831.]

My Childhood's Home. Tr. Murray Brown. *POEMS* p 4. [*Mit Barndoms Hjem*, poem, 1875.]

My Mother's Little Cottage. Tr. Murray Brown. *POEMS* p 24. [*I Hytten hos min Moder*, poem, 1831.]

My Song. Tr. Murray Brown. *POEMS* pp 98-99. [*Min Vise*, poem, 1832.]

Oktober. Tr. Murray Brown. *POEMS* pp 88-91. [*Oktober*, poem, 1832.]

Odense. Tr. Murray Brown. *POEMS* pp 77-78. [*Odense*, poem, 1875.]

On Being Informed of Michael Wiehe's Death. Tr. Murray Brown. *POEMS* p 38. [*Ved Efterretning om Michael Wiehe's Død*, poem, 1864.]

The Pearl. Tr. Charles Wharton Stork. *SeBDV*

28

p 40. Also *A Little Treasury* p 510. [*Man har et Sagn - et Eventyr* (first line), a poem published in *Kjøbenhavns Flyvende Post*, 1830.]

From **Phantasus.** Tr. Murray Brown. *POEMS* p 10. [Af: *Phantasus*, poem, 1829.]

A Poem about Wives. Tr. Murray Brown. *POEMS* pp 34-35. [*Et Digt om Konerne*, poem, 1839.]

A Poet's Last Song. Tr. Murray Brown. *POEMS* p 104. [*En Digters sidste Sang*, poem 1844.]

A Poet's Last Song. Tr. R. P. Keigwin. *Seven Poems* p 21. [*En Digters sidste Sang*, poem, 1844.] [Danish text included.]

Poetry. Tr. Murray Brown. *POEMS* pp 106-107. [*Poesien*, poem, 1831.]

Push Out, O Golden Woodruff. Tr. Murray Brown. *POEMS* p 8. [*Skyd Frem, Skovmærke*, song from *Sneemanden*, 1861.]

Rabbi Meyer. Tr. Murray Brown. *POEMS* pp 62-65. [*Rabbi Mejer*, poem, 1839.]

The River King's Bride. Tr. Anne Born. *Snow Queen* pp 12-13. [*Elbkongens Brud*, poem 1831.]

The Rose. Tr. Anne Born. *Snow Queen* pp 14-15. [*Rosen*, poem, 1832.]

The Rose on the Coffin. Tr. Murray Brown. *POEMS* p 74. [*Rosen paa Kisten*, poem, 1849.]

The Rosebud. Tr. Charles Wharton Stork. *SeBDV* pp 40-41. [*Rosenknoppen*, poem, 1836.]

The Rosebud. Tr. Murray Brown. *POEMS* p 22. [*Rosenknoppen*, poem, 1836.]

The Rosebud. Tr. Anne Born. *Snow Queen* pp 10-11. [*Rosenknoppen*, poem, 1836.]

The Rose-Elf. Tr. Murray Brown. *POEMS* p 74. [*Rosen*, poem first published in *Iversens Fyens Stifts Avis*, 1832, and in *Samlede Værker*, vol. XII, p 140.]

She Is So Pure, Love of My Heart. Tr. Murray Brown. *POEMS* p 44. [*Hun er saa hvid, min Hjertenskjær*, poem, 1832.]

The Snow Queen. Tr. Murray Brown. *POEMS* p 23. [*Snee-Dronningen*, poem, 1829.]

The Snow Queen. Tr. Anne Born. *Snow Queen* pp 6-7.

The Soldier. Tr. Murray Brown. *POEMS* p 37. [*Soldaten*, poem, 1830.]

From **The Son of the Desert.** Tr. Murray Brown. *POEMS* p 26. [Af: *Ørkenens Søn*, poem, 1831.]

Spring Song. Tr. Murray Brown. *POEMS* p 75. [*Foraarssang*, poem, 1870.]

Study from Nature. Tr. Murray Brown. *POEMS* p 9. [*Studie efter Naturen*, poem, 1830.]

The Tear. Tr. Murray Brown. *POEMS* p 93. [*Taaren*, poem, 1830.]

From **Thorvaldsen.** Tr. Murray Brown. *POEMS* p 39. [Af: *Til Thorvaldsen*, poem, 1838.]

From **A Traveller.** Tr. Murray Brown. *POEMS* p 68. [Af: *En Reisende*, poem, 1839.]

Twaddle, Twaddle. Tr. Murray Brown. *POEMS* p 36. [*Pjat, Pjat*, poem, 1830.]

Twilight. Tr. Murray Brown. *POEMS* p 101. [*Aftendæmring*, poem, 1830.]

The Two Birds. Tr. Anne Born. *Snow Queen* pp 8-9. [*De to Fugle*, poem, 1833.]

Two Brown Eyes. Tr. R. P. Keigwin. *Seven Poems* p 17. [*Hjertets Melodier*, Stanzas I-VIII, 1831.] [Danish text included.]

From **The Venerable Man.** Tr. Murray Brown. *POEMS* p 102. [Af: *Oldingen*, poem, 1874.]

From **Vignettes Dedicated to Danish Poets.** Tr. Murray Brown. *POEMS* p 87. [Af: *Vignetter til danske Digtere*, poem, 1831.]

Wandering in the Wood. Tr. Murray Brown. *POEMS* p 70. [*Vandring i Skoven*, poem, 1852.]

What I Love. Tr. Murray Brown. *POEMS* p 103. [*Hvad jeg elsker*, poem, 1831.]

The Woman with the Eggs. Adapted by Jan Wahl. Ill. Ray Cruz. New York: Crown Publishers, 1974. p 31 ill. [An adaptation of a poem by H. C. Andersen published in *Den danske Bondeven*, 1836.]

The Woman with the Eggs. Tr. R. P. Keigwin. *Seven Poems* p 13. [*Konen med Æggene*, poem, 1836.] [Danish text included.]

The Woman with the Eggs. Tr. Murray Brown. *POEMS* pp 11-12. [*Konen med Æggene*, poem, 1836.]

4) Collections of Tales

Andersen Stories for Pleasure Reading. Ed. Edward William Dolch. Champaign, Ill.: Garrard Pub. Co., 1956.

Andersen's Fairy Tales. Intro. William T. Atwood. Ill. Frederick Richardson. Philadelphia: Winston, 1957. p 278. Ill. [The Children's Classics.]

Andersen's Fairy Tales. Ill. Leonard Weisgard. Garden City, N. Y.: Doubleday, 1958. p 217. Ill. [Junior deluxe classics eds.]

Andersen's Fairy Tales. Retold by Rose Dobbs. Ill. Gustav Hjortlund. Prepared under the supervision of Josette Frank. New York: Random House, 1958. p 63. Ill.

Andersen's Fairy Tales. Adapted by Charlotte Dixon from Caroline Peachey's translation. Ill. Janusz Grabianski. New York: Duell,

Sloan & Pearce, London: Jonathan Cape, 1963. p 320. Ill. [A Splendor Book.] [British edition titled *Hans Andersen's Fairy Tales.*] [Printed in Austria.]

Andersen's Fairy Tales. Ed. versions of translations by Mrs. E. V. Lucas, Mrs. H. B. Paull and Signe Toksvig. Ill. Lawrence Beall Smith. Afterword by Clifton Fadiman. New York: The Macmillan Co., London: Collier-Macmillan Ltd., 1963. p 542. Ill. [The Macmillan Classics Series no. 10.]

Andersen's Fairy Tales. Tr. E. V. Lucas and Mrs. H. B. Paull. Ill. Leonard Vosburgh. New York: Grosset & Dunlap, 1963. p 311. Ill. [Companion Library.]

Andersen's Fairy Tales. Ed. Freya Littledale. Ill. John Fernie. N.Y.: Scholastic Book Services, 1966. p 128. Ill.

Andersen's Fairy Tales. Ill. Birgitte Bryan. Chicago: Children's Press, 1970. p 192. Ill. [Fourteen tales with vocabulary notes, brief biography of Andersen and a description of Denmark.]

Andersen's Fairy Tales. Ed. E. Haldeman-Julius. Girard, Kansas: Haldeman-Julius Co., 19--, (not dated.) p 64. Ill. [The Little Blue Book no. 156.]

Ardizzone's Hans Andersen: Fourteen Classic Tales. Selected and ill. Edward Ardizzone. Tr. Stephen Corrin. London: A. Deutsch, 1978. p 191. Ill.

The Bell, and Other Tales. Franklin, New Hampshire: Hillside Press, 1967. p 51. Ill. [Limited edition of 210 numbered copies, each 60 mm high.] [Contains The Bell, The Real Princess, The Leaping Match and a bibliography of microscopic and miniature editions.]

The Best of Hans Christian Andersen. Adelaide: Rigby, 1974. p 164.

The Best Stories of Hans Andersen. Tr. from the Italian ed. Ill. Nardini. London: Daily Mirror Newspapers, 1959. p 44. Ill. [Printed in Italy.] [Translated from the Italian ed., *Fiabe di Andersen,* 1959.]

The Bronze Boar, and Other Stories. Retold from Hans Andersen. London: Collins, 1955. p 96. Ill. [Silver Torch Series, no. 80.]

A Christmas Greeting to My English Friends. Tr. Reginald Spink. Intro. Erik Dal. Illustrations from different countries. Copenhagen: Høst og Søn, 1965. p 68. Ill. [First published in London in 1847; now newly translated.]

The Complete Andersen. All of the 168 Stories by Hans Christian Andersen (some never before translated into English and a few never before published) now freshly translated by Jean Hersholt, with an appendix containing the unpublished tales, a chronologic listing,

and the editor's notes. Ill. Fritz Kredel. New York: Heritage Press, 1952. 3 vol. p 298 & 446 & 430. Ill. [Originally published 1949.] See also *Complete Stories.*

The Complete Fairy Tales and Stories. Tr. Erik Christian Haugaard. Intro. Virginia Haviland. Garden City, New York: Doubleday, 1974. Foreword Naomi Lewis. London: Victor Gollancz, 1974. p 1101. [156 stories and fairy tales with the author's notes.]

Complete Stories. Tr. Jean Hersholt. Ill. Fritz Kredel. New York: The Heritage Press, 1950. 3 vol. [Textually identical with the six vol. *Complete Andersen,* Ltd. Editions Club, 1949.]

Dean's Gift Book of Hans Christian Andersen Fairy Tales. Ill. Janet and Anne Grahame-Johnstone. London: Dean, 1975. p 60. [Dean's gift books.]

Dulac's The Snow Queen and Other Stories from Hans Andersen. Ill. Edmund Dulac. London: Hodder and Stoughton, 1975. Garden City, N. Y.: Doubleday, 1976. p 143. Ill. [Contains The Snow Queen, The Emperor's New Clothes, The Wind's Tale, The Nightingale and The Little Mermaid.] [This collection originally published with illustrations by Edmund Dulac in 1911.]

Fairy Tale Book, Ten Favorite Stories. Tr. Anne Scott. Ill. Benvenuti. New York: Golden Press, 1962, c1959. p 154. Ill.

Fairy Tales. World Edition. In 4 volumes, containing 84 tales. Ed. Svend Larsen. Tr. R. P. Keigwin. Intro. Elias Bredsdorff. Illustrated with drawings reproduced from the originals in the Andersen Museum in Odense. Vol. I. Ill. Vilhelm Pedersen. p 395. Vol. II. Ill. Vilhelm Pedersen. p 368. Vol. III. Ill. Vilhelm Pedersen and Lorenz Frølich. p 368. Vol. IV. Ill. Vilhelm Pedersen and Lorenz Frølich. p 399. Odense: Flensted, 1950-1960. Reprinted periodically. New York: Scribner, 1950-. London: Edmund Ward, 1951-. [Printed in Denmark.]

Fairy Tales. Intro. Margaret and W. J. Jeffrey. Ill. Vernon Soper. London: Collins, 1954. p 318. Ill. [Collins New Classics series.]

Fairy Tales. London: Preview Publications, 1954. p 80. [Hamlyn classic series.]

Fairy Tales. Vol. 1-4. Tr. R. P. Keigwin. Ill. Gustav Hjortlund. Ed. Svend Larsen. Odense: Flensted, London: Wm. Heinemann, 1955-. Each vol. p 56. Ill. [Printed in Odense.] [British ed., Heinemann's Illustrated Hans Andersen series.]

Fairy Tales. Tr. Mrs. E. V. Lucas and Mrs. H. B. Paull. Ill. Arthur Szyk. 1945, New York: Grosset and Dunlap, 1955, 1972. p 343. Ill. [Illustrated Junior Library.]

30   **Fairy Tales.** Tr. Alice Lucas. Ill. by the brothers Robinson. London: Dent, 1956. p 407. Ill. [Everyman's Library, 4. For young people.]

Fairy Tales. Tr. Eve Wendt. Ill. Axel Mathiesen. Copenhagen: Jespersen & Pio, 1956, 1961. New York: Heinemann, 1962. p 126. Ill. [Contains 16 tales.] [Also listed under title *The Little Mermaid, and Other Fairy-tales* (1961 ed.).]

Fairy Tales. Ill. Leonard Weisgard. Garden City, N. Y.: Junior Deluxe Editions, 1956. p 217. Ill.

Fairy Tales. Adapted by Anne Terry White. Ill. Lowell Hess. New York: Simon and Schuster, 1958. p 72. Ill. [A Giant little golden book.]

Fairy Tales. With 25 illustrations in full color by children of eighteen nations. New York: Crown (Orion Press), 1958. London: Deutsch, 1959. p 355. Ill.

Fairy Tales. Vol. 1-3. Tr. Marie-Louise Peulevé. Ill. Svend P. Jørgensen. Odense: Skandinavisk Bogforlag, 1964. p 94 ea. Published in the United States by Dufour Editions, Inc.: Chester Springs, Pa., 1964. [27 tales in each vol.]

Fairy Tales. Retold by E. Jean Robertson from the original English version by Caroline Peachey. Ill. Shirley Hughes. London: Blackie, 1961, 1978. p 264. Ill. London: Peal Press, 1965. p 264 ill. or p 190 not ill. London: Blackie, 1970, available in one vol. or two, as *Fairy Tales by Hans Andersen* and *More Fairy Tales.* London: Pan Books, 1974. p 174. Ill. [A Piccolo Book.]

Fairy Tales. Tr. L. W. Kingsland. Ill. Ernest H. Shepard. London: Oxford University Press, 1961. p 327. Ill. [Oxford illustrated classics.]

Fairy Tales. Abridged ed. London: Dean & Son, 1962, 1974. p 247.

Fairy Tales. London: Children's Press, 1963. p 188. [Boys' and girls' library.]

Fairy Tales. London: Blackie, 1964. p 286. [Famous books, no. 12.]

Fairy Tales. Ill. V. Pedersen and M. L. Stone. New York: Parents' Magazine Press, 1964. p 352. Ill.

Fairy Tales. Adapted by Kathleen N. Daly. Ill. Gian Berto Vanni. New York: Golden Press, 1964. Unp. Ill. [A Big Golden Book.]

Fairy Tales. Ann Arbor, Michigan: University Microfilms, 1967. p 351. Ill. [A Legacy library facsimile.] [Rpt. of the 1884 ed.]

Fairy Tales. Ill. Ridolphi. London: Golden Pleasure Books, 1967. p 244. Ill. [Gold star library.]

Fairy Tales. London: Rylee, 1967-1968, 1970. p 263. Ill. [Clear Print Classics, no. 15.]

Fairy Tales. Tr. Valdemar Paulsen. Ill. Milo Winter. New York: Rand McNally, 1972. p 286. Ill.

Fairy Tales. Intro. and ed. May Lamberton Becker. Ill. Jean O'Neill. Cleveland: Collins World, 1975. p 318. Ill. [A Rainbow Classic.]

Fairy Tales. Tr. Erik Christian Haugaard. Ill. Robert Lo Grippo. Ltd. ed. Franklin Center, Pa.: Franklin Library, 1977. p 543. Ill. [The collected stories of the world's greatest writers series.]

Fairy Tales and Legends. Ill. Rex Whistler. London: Bodley Head, 1959, 1978. [On label inside front cover - published in the United States by Dufour Editions, Chester Springs, Pa.] New York: Macmillan, 1960. p 470. Ill. [47 tales illustrated with black and white etchings.] [Previous ed. 1935.]

Fairy Tales and Stories. Ed. Signe Toksvig. Intro. Francis Hackett. Ill. George and Doris Hauman. New York: Macmillan, 1953. p 270. Ill. [New children's classics.] [Originally published in 1921.]

Fairy Tales and Stories. Tr. and intro. Reginald Spink. Ill. with papercuts by Hans Christian Andersen. London: J. M. Dent & Sons, Ltd., New York: E. P. Dutton & Co., 1960. p 416. Ill. [Everyman's Library.] [Includes all selections previously pub. in *Hans Andersen's Fairy Tales*, 1958.]

Fairy Tales by Hans Christian Andersen. Ill. Harrison Weir, V. Pedersen, M. L. Stone, A. W. Bayes and others. New York: Avenel Books. Div. of Crown Publishers, 1975. p 351. Ill. [Facsimile of 1884 ed.]

Fairy Tales from Andersen and Grimm. Retold in words chiefly of one syllable by A. Pitt-Kethley. Ill. John Harris. London: Shoe Lane Publishing Co., 1953. p 93. Ill. [One syllable series.]

Fairy Tales from Hans Andersen. London: Hudson House, 1953. p 188. [Hudson House classic series.]

The Fairy Tales of Hans Christian Andersen and Charles Perrault. Ill. Harry Clarke. New York: Illustrated Editions Co., n.d. New York: Three Sirens Press, 19-. p 251. Ill. [Cover title: *Andersen's Fairy Tales*.]

Fairy Tales Retold for Little Children. Ill. James Caraway. New York: Wonder Books, 1952. [Wonder books, 599.] Manchester: World Distributors, 1964. p 20. Ill. [Big wonder books.]

Fairy Tales Retold for Young Children. Ill. James Caraway. New York: Grosset & Dunlap, 1952. Manchester: World Distributors, 1956. p 28. Ill. [Big Treasure Books.]

Famous Fairy Tales from Andersen and Grimm. Retold for younger readers. London: Golden Pleasure Books, 1963. p 192. Ill. [Printed in Czechoslovakia.]

Favourite Fairy Tales. London: Collins, 1966, 1976. p 45. Ill. [Contents: The Snow Queen, The Flying Trunk, The Ugly Duckling.]

Favourite Fairy Tales from Andersen. Retold by Marie Holz. Ill. Sharon Stearns. London: Foulsham, 1954. p 24. Ill. [Bonnie Books series.]

Favourite Fairy Tales from Andersen. Ill. Paul Durand. London: Hamlyn, New York: Golden Press, 1973. p 140. Ill. [American edition *Favorite Fairy Tales.*]

Favorite Stories from Hans Andersen. Ill. René Cloke. New York: British Book Centre, 1950. p 100. Ill. [See also *Hans Andersen's Fairy Tales.*]

Favourite Tales of Hans Andersen. Tr. M. R. James. Ill. Robin Jacques. London: Faber & Faber, 1978. p 165. Ill. [Faber fanfares.]

Favourites from Hans Andersen. Freely adapted by M. Deleau. Ill. H. LeMonnier. London: Bancroft & Co., 1959. p 60. Ill. [Printed in Holland.] [New Heritage Library.]

First Three Tales. The Tinder Box, Little Claus and Big Claus, The Princess and the Pea. Tr. David Hohnen. Intro. Erik Dal. Illustrations from different countries. Copenhagen: Høst & Søn, 1960. p 64. Ill. 2nd ed. 1965. 3rd ed. 1968. [*Fyrtøiet, Lille Claus og store Claus, Prindsessen paa Ærten*, stories, 1835.]

The Flying Trunk . . . [*Twenty-four Stories.*] Tr. Lyda Jensen. Ill. Renate Goetz. Chicago: Scott, Foresman, 1951. p 317. Ill.

Forty-two Stories. By Hans Andersen. Tr. M. R. James. Ill. Robin Jacques. London, New York: Faber & Faber, 1953 and 1968. p 346. Ill. New York: A. S. Barnes & Co., 1959. p 346. Ill. [Previous ed. 1930, as *Forty Stories.*] [A Wonderful World Book.]

Fourteen Classic Tales. See *Ardizzone's Hans Andersen: Fourteen Classic Tales.*

Hans Andersen Bedtime Book. London and Glasgow: Children's Press, 1958. p 92. Ill.

Hans Andersen, His Classic Fairy Tales. Tr. Erik Haugaard. Ill. Michael Foreman. London: Gollancz, 1976. p 188. Ill. [These translations originally published in *The Complete Fairy Tales and Stories*, 1975.]

Hans Andersen Stories. Ill. René Cloke. London: Spring House, 1975, 1977. p 18. Ill. [Fairyland favorites.] [Contents: Thumbelina, The Princess and the Swineherd, The Shepherdess and the Chimney-sweep.]

Hans Andersen's Fairy Stories. Retold by Jane Carruth. London: Octopus Books, 1978. p 208. Ill.

Hans Andersen's Fairy Tales. Ill. Maxwell Armfield. New York: Dutton, 1953. p 278. Ill. [The Children's Illustrated Classics.]

Hans Andersen's Fairy Tales. A new translation by Reginald Spink. Ill. Hans Baumhauer. New York: E. P. Dutton, London: J. M. Dent & Sons, Ltd., 1958. London: J. M. Dent & Sons, 1973, 1976. p 245. Ill. [The Children's Illustrated Classics.]

Hans Andersen's Fairy Tales. A Selection. Tr. L. W. Kingsland. With the original illustrations by Vilhelm Pedersen and Lorenz Frølich. Intro. Naomi Lewis. London: Oxford University Press, 1959. p 349. Ill. [The World's Classics no. 571.]

Hans Andersen's Fairy Tales. Tr. L. W. Kingsland. Ill. Ernest H. Shepard. London: Oxford University Press, 1961. New York: Henry Z. Walck, 1962. p 327. Ill.

Hans Andersen's Fairy Tales. Ill. Jeanne Lagarde. London: Ward Lock & Co., 1961. p 91. [Rainbow Storybook.]

Hans Andersen's Fairy Tales. Tr. Mrs. E. Lucas. Ill. Charles Mozley. London: Caxton Publishing Co., 1965. p 257. [Printed in Hungary.] [Caxton Junior Classics.]

Hans Andersen's Fairy Tales. Ill. René Cloke. London: Ward Lock, 1966, 1979. p 95. Ill.

Hans Andersen's Fairy Tales. Ill. W. Heath Robinson. London: Pan Books, 1976. 2 vol. p 144 & p 160. [Piccolo gift books.] [These translations and illustrations originally published in one volume in 1913.]

Hans Andersen's Fairy Tales: a Selection. Maidenhead: Purnell, 1977. p 138. Ill. [A Purnell classic.] [Originally published London: Bancroft, 1966.]

Hans Christian Andersen. Abridged by P. Bolsover. Ill. Carlo Tora, etc. Brighton: Litor Publishers, 1967. [Printed in Helsingborg.] [Children's Classics series.]

Hans Christian Andersen's Fairy Tales. Ill. Jiří Trnka. London: Golden Pleasure Books, Spring Books, 1959. Also London: Hamlyn, 1960, 1964. p 253. Ill. [Printed in Czechoslovakia.]

Hans Christian Andersen's Fairy Tales. Ill. Jenny Thorne. Maidenhead: Purnell, 1977. p 187. Ill. [A Purnell deluxe classic.]

Hans Christian Andersen's Fairy Tales to Read Aloud. Compiled by Oscar Weigle. Ill. Jill Elgin. London: Spring Books, 1960. p 143. Ill. [Printed in Czechoslovakia.] [Read-aloud Books.]

The Little Elf, and Other Stories. Retold by Jane Carruth. Ill. Benvenuti. London: Odhams Books, 1964. p. 72. Ill. [Printed in Milan] [Odhams Royal Fairy Tale Series.]

The Little Mermaid and Other Fairy Tales. Tr. R. P. Keigwin. Ill. Gustav Hjortlund. Biography of H. C. Andersen by Svend Larsen.

32

Odense: Flensted, 1960. New York: Platt & Munk, 1963. p 122. Ill. [Heirloom edition, 1963.]

The Little Mermaid and Other Stories. Retold by Ann MacLeod. London: Collins, 1967. p 44. Ill.

More Hans Andersen's Fairy Tales. Retold by E. Jean Roberton from the original English version by Caroline Peachey. Ill. Shirley Hughes. London: Pan Books, 1976. p 157. Ill.

More Tales from Andersen. Retold by Shirley Goulden. Ill. Benvenuti. London: W. H. Allen, 1958. p 56. Ill. [Printed in Milan.] [Splendour Books, no. 9.]

My Bumper Fairy-Tale Book. Selections from the Tales of Grimm and Hans Andersen. Ill. Doreen Baxter. London and Glasgow: Collins, 1960. p 124.

My Favourite Book of Fairy Stories. (By Grimm and Andersen). Ill. René Cloke. London: Ward Lock, 1969. p 157. Ill. [Andersen stories originally published in 1966.]

My First Book of Hans Andersen Stories. Ill. Esmé Eve. London: Nelson, 1967. p 45. Ill.

My First Picture Book of Hans Christian Andersen. Ill. René Cloke. New York: Derrydale Books, Div. of Crown Publishers, by arrangement with Award Publications, 1975. Unp. Ill. [Printed in Hungary.]

My Treasury of Hans Christian Andersen. Retold by Jane Knight. Ill. Nans van Leeuwen. London: Purnell, 1969. p 124. Ill.

My World of Fairy Tales. Stories from Grimm, Perrault, and Andersen. Ed. Jane Carruth. Chicago: Rand McNally, 1976. p 219.

The Naughty Boy, and Other Stories. Boston: J. E. Tilton, n.d. p 128. Ill.

New Tales, 1843. Tr. Reginald Spink. Intro. Erik Dal. Ill. from many countries. Copenhagen: Høst & Søn, 1973. p 64. Ill. [A translation of *Nye Eventyr, 1844*.] [Three of the tales are reprinted from Everyman's Library, vol. 4.]

The Princess and the Pea. It's Absolutely True. Ill. Gustav Hjortlund. Odense: Skandinavisk Bogforlag, in cooperation with the H. C. Andersen House, 1977. p 28. Ill.

The Princess on the Pea, and Other Famous Stories. Ill. Jan Balet. New York: Parents' Magazine Press, 1962. Unp. Ill.

Puss-in-Boots, and Other Stories. By (Charles) Perrault and (H. C.) Andersen. Ill. Paul Durand and Gian Berto Vanni. Andersen stories tr. Tamara Alferoff. London: Paul Hamlyn, 1964. Feltham: Hamlyn, 1968. p 59. Ill. [Printed in Prague.]

Seven Stories by Hans Christian Andersen. Illustrated and retold by Eric Carle. New York: Watts, 1978. p 92. Ill.

Seven Tales. Tr. Eva Le Gallienne. Ill. Maurice Sendak. New York: Harper, 1959. p 127. Ill. Kingswood, England: World's Work, 1972. p 128. Ill. [Forewords by the translator and the illustrator.]

Seven Tales from Hans Christian Andersen. Tr. R. P. Keigwin. Ill. Vilhelm Pedersen and Lorenz Frølich. Odense: Flensted, 1961. p 72. Ill.

Six Fairy Tales by the Danish Writer Hans Christian Andersen. Published on the occasion of the 150th anniversary of his birth. British ed. tr. R. P. Keigwin. American ed. tr. Jean Hersholt. Ill. Vilhelm Pedersen. Ed. Svend Dahl and H. G. Topsøe-Jensen. Intro. Bo Grønbech. Epilogue Erik Dal. Copenhagen: Danish Ministry of State, Berlingske Bogtr. and the Committee for Danish Cultural Activities Abroad, 1955. p 72. Ill. [Contains: The Princess on the Pea, The Nightingale, The Ugly Duckling, The Fir Tree, The Little Match Girl, The Story of a Mother.]

The Snow Queen, and Other Stories. Retold by Jane Carruth. Ill. Benvenuti. London: Odhams Books, 1964. p 71. Ill. [Printed in Milan.] [Odhams Royal Fairy Tale Series.]

The Snow Queen and Other Stories. See *Dulac's The Snow Queen and Other Stories.*

The Snow Queen, and Other Tales. A new selection, ed., trans. and with an intro. by Pat Shaw Iversen. Ill. Sheila Greenwald. New York: New American Library, London: New English Library, 1966. p 318. Ill. [A Signet classic, CT334.]

The Snow Queen; and The Emperor's New Clothes. Ill. Philippe Degrave. Feltham: Hamlyn, 1970. p 189. Ill. [Gold star library.]

Stories by Hans Andersen. Retold by Shirley Dean. Ill. Hutchings. London: Robert J. Tyndall, Ltd., 1968. p 26. Ill. [Wonderful series, 1.] As *Stories from Hans Andersen.* London: Robert J. Tyndall, Ltd., 1973. p 25. Ill. [Star classics.]

Stories from Andersen. Ill. Pauline Hodder. London: Blackie, 1960, 1967. p 128. Ill. [Stories Old and New.]

Stories from Andersen. Ill. Constance Marshall. London: Blackie, 1967. p 124. Ill. [Contents: The Ugly Duckling, The Fir Tree, The Tinder Box, The Snow Queen.]

Stories from Hans Andersen. Retold by Shirley Goulden. Ill. Cremonini. London: W. H. Allen & Co., Sydney: Golden Press, 1960. p 28. Ill. [Printed in Milan.] [Junior Splendour Books no. 3.]

Stories from Hans Andersen. Ill. Edmund Dulac. New York: G. H. Doran, n.d. p 250. Ill. New York: Abaris Books, 1975. p 192. Ill.

Stories from Hans Christian Andersen. Stories compiled and retold by Mae Broadley. Ill. Janet and Anne Grahame-Johnstone. Manchester: World Distributors, 1968. New York: Platt & Munk, 1969. p 61. Ill.

Stories from Hans Christian Andersen. Selected and prefaced by Philippa Pearce. Ill. Pauline Baynes. London: Collins, 1972. p 181. Ill. [Classics for today.]

Tales. Tr. R. P. Keigwin. Ill. Gustav Hjortlund. Odense: Flensteds Forlag, 1971. p 96. Ill. [Contents: Little Ida's Flowers, The Little Mermaid, The Princess and the Pea, The Swineherd, Thumbelina, The Emperor's New Clothes, Dad's Always Right.]

Tales from Andersen. Tr. W. K. Holmes. Ill. Barbara Freeman. London: Blackie, 1950, 1963. New York: Arco Publishing Co., 1964. p 84. Ill. [American ed., Arco Juvenile Library.] [British ed., Enchanted World Library.] [Included in 1957 ed., *Tales from Andersen and Grimm.*]

Tales from Andersen. Written within the vocabulary of *New Method Reader 1* by Brian Heaton. Ill. Anne Reynolds. Harlow: Longmans, 1968. p 59. Ill. [New method supplementary reader, stage 1.]

Tales from Andersen and Grimm. Retold by W. K. Holmes. Ill. Barbara Freeman. London: Blackie, 1957. New York: Oceana Publications, 1958. p 160. Ill. [1950 edition, *Tales from Andersen.*] [1963 edition, also *Tales from Andersen.* p 84. Ill.]

Tales from Hans Andersen. Retold by Shirley Goulden. Ill. Maraja. London: W. H. Allen, 1956. New York: Grosset & Dunlap, 1957. p 62. Ill. [Printed in Milan.] [British ed., Splendour Books Series no. 2.]

Tales from Hans Andersen. The Ugly Duckling. Thumbelina. The Emperor's New Clothes. The Swineherd. London: Oldbourne Press, 1961. p 62. Ill. [Printed in Italy.]

Tales from Hans Andersen. Ill. Dennis Doherty. London: Rylee Ltd., 1969. p 42. Ill.

Tales from Hans Andersen. Simplified and brought within the 500 word vocabulary of the New Method Supplementary Readers, Stage 1 by Michael West and Brian Heaton. London: Longmans, 1977. p 52. Ill.

Tales from Hans Christian Andersen, as told by Katharine Carter. Ill. Joseph Smith. Racine, Wis.: Whitman Pub. Co., 1965. p 156. Ill. [A Whitman tween-age book.]

Tales of Grimm and Andersen. Selected by Frederick Jacobi, Jr. Intro. W. H. Auden. New York: Random House, 1952. p 767. [Modern Library Giant. 76.]

Tales the Moon Can Tell. Picture Book without Pictures. Tr. R. P. Keigwin. Intro. H. Topsøe-Jensen. Ill. Marlie Brande. Copenhagen: Berlingske Forlag, 1955. p 82. Ill. (Published on the occasion of Andersen's 150th birthday, April 2, 1955, by the Andersen Museum, Odense.)

Three Tales from Andersen. Tr. R. P. Keigwin. Ill. Gustav Hjortlund. Ed. Svend Larsen. New York: Macmillan, Odense: Flensted, 1958. p 50. Ill. [Contains: The Emperor's New Clothes, Simple Simon, It's Absolutely True.]

Thumbelina. The Princess and the Swineherd. The Shepherdess and the Chimney-sweep. Ill. René Cloke. London: Award, 1975. p 15. Ill.

Thumbelina and Other Fairy Tales. Intro. Isak Dinesen. Ill. Sandro Nardini and Ugo Fontana. New York and London: Macmillan, Milan: Fratelli Fabbri, 1962. p 44. Ill.

Thumbelina and Other Stories. London: Hamlyn, 1968. p 48. Ill.

Thumbkin, and Other Stories. Text by W. K. Holmes. Ill. Barbara C. Freeeman. London and Glasgow: Blackie & Son, 1951. p 46. Ill.

The Tinder-Box, and Other Stories. Text by W. K. Holmes. Ill. Barbara C. Freeman. London and Glasgow: Blackie & Son, 1951. p 46. Ill.

A Treasury of Grimm and Andersen. Ill. Doreen Baxter. London: Collins, 1956. p 128. Ill.

The Ugly Duck, and Other Tales. New York: James Miller, n.d. p 158. Ill. [Hans Andersen's Library.]

The Ugly Duckling, and Other Andersen Fairy Tales. Retold by Jane Carruth. London: Hamlyn, 1975. p 61. Ill. [Contents: The Ugly Duckling, The Snow Queen. Thumbelina, The Emperor's Nightingale. These adaptations originally published in *The Giant All-Colour Book of Fairy Tales*, 1971.]

The Ugly Duckling and Two Other Stories. A new English version by Lillian Moore. Ill. Trina Schart Hyman. New York: Scholastic Book Services, 1969, 1973. p 56. Ill.

The Wild Swans and Other Stories. London: Hamlyn, 1968. London: Ward Lock, 1970. p 46. Ill.

The Feather Duster: a fairy-tale musical, devised by Rumer Godden from the tales of Hans Christian Andersen. Music by Kai Normann Andersen. Book and lyrics by Rumer Godden. Libretto in English. Chicago: Dramatic Publishing Co., 1964. p 70. [Stories included are: Thumbelina, The Constant Tin Soldier, The Galoshes of Fortune, The Toad, the Beetle, the Rose and the Snail.]

34 **Little Plays from Andersen.** Ed. and dramatized by George Henry Holroyd. Ill. Branney Williams. London: George Philip & Son, 1963. p 57. Ill. [Plays from literature series.] [Contents: The Little Swineherd, The Tinder Box, Little Claus og Big Claus, The Emperor's New Clothes.]

5) **Individual Tales**
Tales are listed in order of publication under each title

Dad's Always Right, *Hvad Fatter gjør, det er altid det rigtige. Nye Eventyr og Historier,* 1861.
What the Good Man Does Is Always Right. Ill. Rick Schreiter. New York: Dial Press, 1968. p 32. Ill.
Dad's Always Right. Ill. Gustav Hjortlund. Odense: Skandinavisk Bogforlag, in cooperation with the H. C. Andersen House, 1977. p 28. Ill.

A Drop of Water. *Vanddraaben, Nye Eventyr,* 1848.
A Drop of Water. Tr. Reginald Spink. *Nor* vol. 13, no. 2 (March-April 1955) p 139.

The Emperor's New Clothes. *Keiserens nye Klæder, Eventyr fortalte for Børn,* 1837.
The Emperor's New Clothes. Tr. Jean Hersholt. Ill. Ervine Metzl. New York: Limited Editions Club, 1952. p 34. Ill.
The Emperor's New Clothes. Tr. Jean Hersholt. In *The Real Andersen* by Bo Grønbech. Copenhagen: Ministry of Foreign Affairs, 1952.
The Emperor's New Clothes. Tr. and ill. Erik Blegvad. New York: Harcourt, Brace & Co., 1959. p 32. Ill.
The Magic Suit. Retold by Elizabeth Rose from the story by Hans Andersen. Ill. Gerald Rose. London: Faber, 1966. p 32. Ill.
The Emperor's New Clothes. New York: Golden Press, 1966. London: Golden Pleasure, 1967. p 30. Ill.
The Emperor's New Clothes. Ill. Abe Gurvin. Katonah, N. Y.: Young Readers Press, 1968. Unp. Ill.
The Emperor's New Clothes. Tr. M. R. James. Ill. Birte Dietz. London: Kaye & Ward, 1969. New York: Van Nostrand Reinhold, 1971. p 30. Ill. [This translation originally published in 1930.]
The Emperor's New Clothes. London: Collins, 1969. p 16. Ill.

Emperor's New Clothes. Text adapted from Hans Christian Andersen and other sources by Jean Van Leeuwen. Ill. Jack and Irene Delano. York: Random House, 1971. London: Blackie, 1973. p 58. Ill.
The Emperor's New Clothes. New York: Scholastic Book Services, 1971.
The Emperor's New Clothes. Ill. Monika Laimgruber. London: Hamilton; Reading, Mass.: Addison-Wesley, 1973. p 19. Ill. [American ed. is An Addisonian Press Book.]
The Emperor's New Clothes. Ill. Fulvio Testa. London: Abelard Schuman, 1976. p 23. Ill. [This adaptation originally published in Zürich, 1974.]
The Emperor's New Clothes. Ill. Gustav Hjortlund. Odense: Skandinavisk Bogforlag, in cooperation with the H. C. Andersen House, 1977. p 28. Ill.
The Emperor's New Clothes. A new English version by Ruth Belov Gross. Ill. Jack Kent. New York: Four Winds Press, 1977. p 32. Ill.
The Emperor's New Clothes. New edition. Ill. Pamela B. Ford. Mahwah, N. J.: Troll Associates, 1978.
The Emperor's New Clothes. Retold by Ian Aitken. Ill. George Craig. Exeter: Wheaton, 1979. p 22. Ill.
The Emperor's New Clothes. London: Dent, 1979. p 32. [Tr. from the German edition, *Des Kaisers neue Kleider,* 1974.]
The Queen's New Dress. Adapted from a story by Hans Anderson (sic) by Ellen Evans. London: Paxton, 1952. p 8. [Paxton playlets series.]
The Emperor's New Clothes; a Satirical Ballad, based on the story by Hans Christian Andersen. Adapted by May Orrell. Ill. Charles Abbott. Boston: Bruce Humphries, 1954. p 22. Ill.
New Clothes for the Emperor. (A play for children). Loosely based on the story by H. Andersen. Adapted by Nicholas S. Gray. Ill. Joan Jefferson Farjeon. London: Oxford University Press, 1957. p 118. Ill.
The Emperor's New Clothes, a play for children in three acts. Adapted by Charlotte Barrows Chorpenning. New York: Samuel French, 1959. p 103.
The Emperor's New Clothes. Conception and construction of the puppets, Hannelore Wegener. Scenery and photographs, Hannelore Wegener and Adolf Schmidt. Niederweisa, Germany: Verlag K. Nitzsche, 1966. p 20. Ill. [Corrected by addition of a pasted-in slip to Whenton: Exeter, 1967.]
Emperor's New Clothes, Drama. Adapted by A. Thane. *Plays* vol 43 (October 1974) pp 59-68.

The Fir Tree. *Grantræet, Nye Eventyr,* 1845.

The Fir Tree. Ill. William F. M. Kay. Berkeley, Ca.: Lederer, Street & Zeus Co., printers, 1952. p 30. Ill.

The Fir Tree. Retold by Kashin Wheeler. Ill. Robert L. Anderson. New York: Dell Pub. Co., 1964. Unp. ill. [A Harlin Quist book.]

The Fir Tree. Tr. H. W. Dulcken. Ill. Nancy Ekholm Burkert. New York: Harper & Row, 1970. p 34. Ill.

The Fir Tree. Tr. M. R. James. Ill. Svend Otto S. London: Kaye & Ward, New York: Van Nostrand Reinhold, 1971. p 30. Ill. [This translation originally published in *Forty-two Stories,* 1968.]

The Flying Trunk, *Den flyvende Kuffert. Eventyr fortalte for Børn,* 1839.

The Flying Trunk. London: Collins, 1969. p 16. Ill.

Hans Clodhopper. *Klods-Hans, H. C. Andersen's Historier,* 1855.

Hulking Hans. Retold by Hakon Mielche. With photos and drawings. Copenhagen: Det Schønbergske Forlag, 1972. p 12. Ill.

Hans Clodhopper. Retold and ill. by Leon Shtainmets. Philadelphia, Pa.: J. B. Lippincott, 1975. p 25. Ill.

Simple Simon. Ill. Gustav Hjortlund. Odense: Skandinavisk Bogforlag, in cooperation with the H. C. Andersen House, 1977. p 28. Ill.

Jack the Numskull. Tr. David Hohnen. Ill. Dorte. Stenløse: KRT Products, 1977. [Famous Fairy Tales as Painting Books series.] [Reversible book with *The Steadfast Tin Soldier.*]

It's Absolutely True! *Det er ganske vist! Historier,* 1852.

It's Perfectly True! Tr. Reginald Spink. *DFOJ* vol. 14 (1954) pp 24-25.

It's Perfectly True. Tr. Paul Leysac. *AScL* pp 54-56.

The Jumping Match. *Springfyrene. Nye Eventyr,* 1845.

The Jumping Match. Ill. Gaynor Chapman. London: Hamilton, 1973. p 32. Ill.

The Jumper. Tr. W. A. and J. K. Cragie. London: Chatto & Vindus, n.d. p 4. Ill. [Broadsheet no. 6, in limited edition of 2850.]

Little Claus and Big Claus. *Lille Claus og store Claus. Eventyr fortalte for Børn,* 1835.

Little Claus and Big Claus. Ill. Helge Kühn-Nielsen. Copenhagen: Forlaget Tiden, 1955. p 113. Ill.

Great Claus and Little Claus. Ill. Rick Schreiter. London and New York: Grove Press, 1968. p 31. Ill.

Little Claus and Big Claus. Tr. M. R. James. Ill. Palle Bregnhøi. London: Kaye & Ward, 1970. New York: Van Nostrand Reinhold, 1971. p 24. Ill.

Little Claus and Big Claus. Ill. Gustav Hjortlund. Odense: Skandinavisk Bogforlag, in cooperation with the H. C. Andersen House, 1977. p 28. Ill.

Big Klaus and Little Klaus, a comedy of one act, of several continuous scenes, based on the story of the same name by Hans Christian Andersen. By Dean Wenstrom. Anchorage, Kentucky: Anchorage Press, 1966. p 48.

The Little Match Girl. *Den lille Pige med Svovlstikkerne. Dansk Folkekalender for 1846.* (dec. 1845) and *Nye Eventyr,* 1848.

The Little Match Girl. Manchester: World Distributors, 1966. p 16. Ill. [Classic fairy story books.]

The Little Match Girl. Ill. Blair Lent. Boston: Houghton Mifflin Co., 1968. p 43. Ill.

The Little Match Girl. Retold by Ruby Apsler. Ill. Kerman Kerman. Tel Aviv: Edrei-Sharon, 1972. p 15.

Allumette. By Toni Ungerer. With due respect to H. C. Andersen, the Grimm brothers and the Hon. Ambrose Bierce. New York: Parents Magazine Press, 1974. London: Methuen, 1975. p 32. Ill.

The Little Mermaid. *Den lille Havfrue. Eventyr fortalte for Børn,* 1837.

Den lille Havfrue. The Little Mermaid. Facsimile and Text. Ill. Vilh. Pedersen. Ed. Svend Larsen. Odense: H. C. Andersens Hus, 1951. p 124. [English text, pp 81-124.]

The Little Mermaid. Retold from Hans Andersen. Ill. Rie Cramer. London: Blackie, 1953. p 32. Ill. [Silver thimble series.]

The Little Mermaid: A Fairy Tale by Hans Christian Andersen. Tr. David Hohnen. Illustrations from different countries. Intro. Erik Dal. Copenhagen: Høst & Søn, 1959. 2nd rev. ed. 1960. 3rd ed. 1963. 4th rev. ed. 1964. 6th rev. ed. 1968. 8th ed. 1973. p 64. Ill.

The Little Mermaid. The fairy tale that was translated into 82 languages. Line drawings by twenty artists of world renown. The brewer who created the fairy tale in bronze. The most photographed girl in the world. Ed. Gert Munch. Tr. Jack Lind. Copenhagen: Forum (Branner og Korch), 1964. p 32. Ill.

The Little Mermaid. Retold by Marguerite R. Duffy. Ill. José Correas. Cleveland, Ohio:

36

World Pub. Co., 1966. Unp. Ill. [A Holly book.]

The Little Mermaid. New York: Golden Press, 1966. London: Golden Pleasure, 1967. p 30. Ill.

The Little Mermaid. Retold by Jane Carruth. Ill. Chihiro Iwasaki. Feltham: Hamlyn, 1969. p 33. Ill. [Round the year storybooks.]

The Little Mermaid. London: Collins, 1969. p 16. Ill.

The Little Mermaid. Tr. Eva Le Gallienne. Ill. Edward Frascinol. New York: Harper & Row, 1971. p 50. Ill.

The Little Mermaid. Her Story and the Fairy Tale. Text by Per Eilstrup. Text tr. Grethe Jantzen. Story tr. Lucie Duff Gordon. Copenhagen: Grønlund, 1972. p 60. Ill.

The Little Mermaid. Ill. Mária Zalibská. London: Hamlyn, 1973. p 59. Ill.

The Little Mermaid. Illustrations after W. Heath Robinson. Santa Barbara, Ca.: Bellerophon Books, 1976. p 48. Ill.

The Little Mermaid. A children's musical in two acts adapted from the tale of Hans Christian Andersen by Pat Hale. Music by Al Bahret. New York: New Plays for Children, 1968. Unp. [Mimeographed; music not included.]

The Lovers. *Kjærestefolkene, Nye Eventyr,* 1844.

The Lovers. In *Treasury of World Literature.* Ed. Dagobert D. Runes. New York: Philosophical Library, 1956. pp 28-30.

The Nightingale. *Nattergalen. Nye Eventyr,* 1844.

The Nightingale. Westport, Conn.: The Redcoat Press, 1954. p 35. Ill. [Limited ed. of 210.]

The Emperor and the Nightingale. Ill. Bill Sokol. New York: Pantheon Books, 1959. p 30. Ill.

The Nightingale. Ill. Harold Berson. Philadelphia: J. B. Lippincott, 1962. p 31. Ill.

The Nightingale. Franklin, New Hampshire: Hillside Press, 1964. p 67. Ill. [Numbered limited ed. of 350, each 60 mm. high.]

The Emperor's Nightingale. Tr. Gerda M. Andersen. Ill. Charles Brey. New York: Holt, Rinehart and Winston, 1965. p 42. Ill. [A Wise Owl book.]

The Nightingale. Tr. Eva Le Gallienne. Ill. Nancy Ekholm Burkert. New York: Harper & Row, 1965. London: Collins, 1967. p 33. Ill.

The Nightingale and the Emperor. Ill. Anne Marie Jauss. Irvington-on-Hudson, N. Y.: Harvey House, Inc., 1970. p 37. Ill.

The Emperor and the Nightingale. Ill. Jenny Thorne. London: Macdonald, 1971. p 30. Ill. [Macdonald fairy tales.]

The Nightingale. Tr. M. R. James. Ill. Kaj Beckman. London: Kaye & Ward, New York: Van Nostrand Reinhold, 1972. p 28. Ill. [Translation originally published in *Forty-two stories*, 1968.]

The Nightingale. Adapted by E. J. Pelgrave. Ill. Fulvio Testa. London & New York: Abelard-Schuman, 1974. p 24. Ill. 2nd ed. 1978.

The Nightingale. Ill. and designed by Kim Milnazik. Philadelphia: Moonlight Express, 1976. p 38. Ill. [Ltd. ed. of 60 copies.]

The Nightingale. Ill. Gustav Hjortlund. Odense: Skandinavisk Bogforlag, in cooperation with the H. C. Andersen House, 1977. p 28. Ill.

The Imperial Nightingale. (A play). Adapted from the story by H. C. Andersen by Nicholas S. Gray. Ill. Joan Jefferson Farjeon. London: Oxford Univ. Press, 1957. p 116. Ill.

The Nightingale and the Emperor. Adapted by Alfred Bradley. Songs by Alex Glasgow. London: Dobson, 1976. p 50, with music. [Theatre in education series.]

The Princess on the Pea. *Prindsessen paa Ærten, Eventyr fortalte for Børn,* 1853.

The Princess on the Pea. Tr. Reginald Spink. *DFOJ* vol. 15 (1955) p 21.

The Princess and the Pea. Adapted from Hans Christian Andersen. Ill. Anne Sellers Leaf. Chicago: Rand McNally, 1965. Unp. Ill.

The Real Princess. Ill. Tadasu Izawa and Shigemi Hijikata. New York: Grosset & Dunlap, 1971. p 18. Ill.

The Princess and the Pea. Tr. David Stoner. *ADL* pp 215-217.

The Princess and the Pea. Ill. Sarah Chamberlain. Easthampton, Mass.: Pennyroyal Press, 1974. p 10. Ill. in portfolio. [Limited ed. of 40 copies.]

The Princess on the Pea. In *Three Favorite Tales.* Book club ed. New York: Random House, 1975. [Disney's Wonderful World of Reading.]

The Princess and the Pea. Ill. Paul Galdone. New York: Seabury Press, 1978. Tadworth: World's Work, 1979. p 30. Ill.

Princess and the Pea, Dramatization of a Story by Hans Christian Andersen. Adapted by Lewis Mahlmann and D. C. Jones. *Plays* no. 32 (May 1973) pp 62, 73-78.

The Red Shoes. *De røde Skoe. Nye Eventyr,* 1845.

The Red Shoes. In *Story. An Introduction to Prose Fiction.* By Arthur Foff and Daniel

Knapp. Belmont, Ca.: Wadsworth Publishing Co., 1964. pp 24-28.

Red Shoes. Retold by Geraldine Kaye. Ill. Harry Toothill. London: Oxford University Press, 1971. p 32. Ill. [Oxford graded readers, junior level.]

The Red Shoes. A Two-act Play to Amuse Children. Based on the fairy tale by H. C. Andersen. Adapted by Robin Short. New York: Samuel French, 1956. p 74.

The Red Shoes. Dramatized by Hans Josef Schmidt. Chicago: Coach House Press, 1969. Copyright 1956. p 66. [Full length play series, no. 16.]

The Seven Dreams. *Ole Lukøie. Eventyr fortalte for Børn,* 1842.

The Seven Dreams. Retold by Jane Carruth. Ill. Teruyo Endo. Feltham: Hamlyn, 1969. p 47. Ill. [Storytime gift books.]

Willie Winkie. Tr. L. W. Kingsland. Ill. Kaj Beckman. London: Kaye & Ward, 1974. p 42. Ill. [Translation originally published in *Fairy Tales,* Oxford University Press, 1959.]

The Shadow. *Skyggen. Nye Eventyr,* 1847.

The Shadow. Tr. Jean Hersholt. In *The House of Fiction. An Anthology of the Short Story.* 2nd ed. New York: Charles Scribner's Sons, 1960. pp 56-64. [Translation from *The Complete Andersen,* 1949.]

The Shepherdess and the Chimneysweep. *Hyrdinden og Skorstensfeieren. Nye Eventyr,* 1845.

The Shepherdess and the Chimneysweep. Tr. M. R. James. Ill. Fleur Brofos Asmussen. London: Kaye and Ward, 1975. p 20. Ill.

The Shepherdess and the Chimneysweep. Ill. Monika Laimgruber. London: Hamish Hamilton, 1977. p 22. Ill. [Printed in Switzerland.]

The Shirt Collar. *Flipperne. Nye Eventyr,* 1848.

The Shirt Collar. Tr. Paul Leyssac. *AScL* pp 57-59.

The Snow Queen. (See also poem by that title). *Sneedronningen. Nye Eventyr,* 1845.

The Snow Queen. Retold and ill. Froukje van der Meer. London: Oxford Univ. Press, 1950. p 28. Ill.

The Snow Queen. Retold from Hans Andersen. Ill. Rie Cramer. London: Blackie, 1953. p 32. Ill. [Silver thimble series.]

The Snow Queen. New York: Golden Press, 1966. London: Golden Pleasure, 1967. p 30. Ill.

The Snow Queen. New edition. Based on the story by Hans Christian Andersen. Ed. Suria Magito and Rudolf Weil. New York: Theatre Arts Books, London: Heinemann Educational Books, 1967. p 85. Ill.

The Snow Queen, a Fairy Tale. In a new adaptation by Naomi Lewis. Ill. Toma Bogdanovic. New York: Scroll Press, 1968, c1967. London: Constable Young Books, 1968. p32. Ill.

The Snow Queen. London: Longmans Young Books, 1968. p 48. Ill.

The Snow Queen. Tr. R. P. Keigwin. Ill. June Atkin Corwin. New York: Atheneum, 1968. First Am. ed. p 95. Ill. [Copyright 1950.]

The Snow Queen. Ill. Pauline Hohly. London: Rylee Ltd., 1969. p 41. Ill.

The Snow Queen. Tr. R. P. Keigwin. Ill. Marcia Brown. New York: Charles Scribner's Sons, 1972. p 95. Ill.

The Snow Queen, a Story in Seven Parts. Tr. R. P. Keigwin. Papercuttings by Sonia Brandes. Odense: Flensted, 1975. p 46. Ill.

The Snow Queen. Adapted by Naomi Lewis. Ill. Errol le Cain. Harmondsworth: Kestrel Books, 1979. p 30. Ill. [This adaptation originally published in 1968.]

[The Snow Queen.] Frames of a Story. By Daphne Marlatt. Toronto: Ryerson Press, 1968. p 63. [A book-length poem based on Hans Christian Andersen's *The Snow Queen.*]

The Snow Queen . . . (a Play.). Based on the story by Hans Andersen. Adapted by Suria Magito and Rudolph Weil. Melbourne: William Heinemann, 1951. p 85.

The Snow Queen and the Goblin, dramatized by Martha Bennett King from the Hans Christian Andersen fairytale. Chicago: The Coach House Press, 1956. [The Coach House Press Play no. 7.]

The Snow Queen. A Musical Play in Two Acts. Books and lyrics, Winifred Palmer. Musical score adapted by King Palmer from the music of Edvard Grieg. London: Joseph Weinberger, 1969. p 34.

The Steadfast Tin Soldier. *Den standhaftige Tinsoldat. Eventyr fortalt for Børn,* 1838.

The Steadfast Tin Soldier. Tr. M. R. James. Ill. Marcia Brown. New York: Charles Scribner's Sons, 1953, 1964. p 28. Ill.

My Book of The Little Tin Soldier. Ill. Nardini. New York: Maxton Pub. Corp., London: Odhams Press, 1960. Unp. Ill. [Printed in Milano.] [An Odhams All-Colour Book.] [A Giant Maxton Book.]

38

The Steadfast Tin Soldier. Tr. Carl Malmburg. Woodcuts by Robert M. Quackenbush. New York: Holt, Rinehart & Winston, 1964. Unp. Ill.

The Little Tin Soldier. New York: Golden Press, 1966. London: Golden Pleasure, 1967. p 30. Ill.

The Little Lead Soldier. Retold by Adele J. Wright. Ill. Pablo Ramirez. Cleveland, Ohio: World Publishing Co., 1966. Unp. Ill. [A Holly book.]

The Brave Tin Soldier. Retold and ill. René Cloke. London: Dean, 1969. p 28. Ill. [A Dean gold medal book.]

The Steadfast Tin Soldier, a Story. Ill. Monika Laimgruber. New York: Atheneum; London: Hamilton, 1970. p 20. Ill.

The Toy Soldier. London: Ward Lock, 1971. p 18. Ill. [A Kingfisher colour book.]

The Tin Soldier. Retold by Geraldine Kaye. Ill. Douglas Hall. London: Oxford University Press, 1971. p 32. Ill. [Oxford graded readers, junior level.]

The Steadfast Tin Soldier. Tr. L. W. Kingsland. Ill. Kaj Beckman. London: Kaye and Ward, 1976. p 27. Ill. [Translation originally published in *Fairy Tales*, Oxford University Press, 1959.]

The Steadfast Tin Soldier. Tr. David Hohnen. Ill. Dorte. Stenløse: KRT Products, 1977. [Famous Fairy Tales as Painting Books series.] [Reversible book with *Jack the Numskull.*]

The Storks. *Storkene. Eventyr fortalte for Børn,* 1839.

The Storks. Ill. With old Danish illustrations. Aabenraa: Dirckinck-Holmfelds Antikvariat, 1959. p 16. Ill.

The Story of the Year. *Aarets Historie. Historier,* 1852.

The Story of the Year. Tr. Erik C. Haugaard. Ill. Kaj Beckman. London: Kaye & Ward, 1979. p 28. Ill. [This translation orig. pub. in the 1974 Gollancz collection.]

The Swineherd. *Svinedrengen. Eventyr fortalte for Børn,* 1842.

The Swineherd. Fredericia: A/S Ernst Voss Fabrik, 1953. p 16. Ill. [Danish and English text.]

The Swineherd. Tr. and ill. Erik Blegvad. New York: Harcourt, Brace and World, 1958. p 32. Ill.

The Princess and the Swineherd. Tr. M. R. James. Ill. Palle Bregnhøi. New York: Van Nostrand Reinhold, 1971. p 28. Ill.

The Swineherd. Retold by Hakon Mielche. With photos and drawings. Copenhagen: Det Schønbergske Forlag, 1972. p 12. Ill.

The Swineherd. Ill. Gustav Hjortlund. Odense: Skandinavisk Bogforlag, in cooperation with the H. C. Andersen House, 1977. p 28. Ill.

The Princess and the Swineherd. A Play for Children. Adapted by Nicholas S. Gray. Ill. Joan Jefferson Farjeon. With the score of a song. London: Oxford Univ. Press, 1952. p 104. Ill. With music.

A Thousand Years Hence. *Om Aartusinder. Fædrelandet,* 26. jan. 1852.

A Thousand Years Hence. Copenhagen: Bennett, 1952. p 6. Ill. [2 editions, one with cover legend *Happy New Year* and the other with *Welcome to Scandinavia.*]

Thousands of Years from Now; A Story Written in 1853. Tr. Jean Hersholt. Stockholm: Scandinavian Airlines System, 1952. p 6. Ill.

Across the Ocean on Wings of Steam. Tr. Reginald Spink. *American Book Collector* vol. 7, no. 4 (December 1956) p 3.

Thumbelina. *Tommelise. Eventyr fortalte for Børn,* 1835.

Tenggren's Thumbelina. Ill. Gustaf Tenggren. New York: Simon and Schuster, 1953. Unpag. Ill. [The Little Golden Library.] London: Golden Pleasure Books, 1965. p 24. Ill. [Happy time series no. 73.]

Thumbelina. Retold from Hans Andersen. Ill. Rie Cramer. London: Blackie, 1953. p 32. Ill. [Silver thimble series.]

Thumbelina. Tr. R. P. Keigwin. Ill. Adrienne Adams. New York: Charles Scribner's Sons, 1961. p 56. Ill.

Thumbelina. Ill. Marta Seitz and Carl Larsson. London: Litor Publishers, Montreal: Danny Books, 1961. [Printed in Helsingborg.]

My Book of Thumbelina. Retold by Jane Carruth. Ill. Giovetti, etc. London: Odhams Books, 1965. [Odhams All-Colour Books.]

Thumbelina. Retold by Marguerite R. Duffy. Ill. Pablo Ramirez. Cleveland, Ohio: World Pub. Co., 1965. Unp. Ill. [A Holly book.]

Thumbelina. New York: Golden Press, 1966. London: Golden Pleasure, 1967. p 30. Ill.

Thumbelina. Manchester: World Distributors, 1968. p 16. Ill. [Classic fairy story books.]

Thumbelina. London: L. Miller, 1968. p 32. Ill.

Thumbelina. Tr. M. R. James. Ill. Kaj Beckman. London: Kaye and Ward; New York: Van Nostrand Reinhold, 1973. p 42. Ill.

Thumbelina. Tr. M. R. James. Ill. Josef Paleček. London: Dobson, 1975. p 30.

Thumbelina. Ill. Linda Griffith. London: Chatto & Windus, 1976. Unpag. Ill. [A Peepshow book.]

Thumbelina. Ill. Gustav Hjortlund. Odense: Skandinavisk Bogforlag, in cooperation with the H. C. Andersen House, 1977. p 28. Ill.

Thumbelina. New edition. Ill. Christine W. Nigoghossian. Mahwah, N. J.: Troll Associates, 1978.

Thumbelina. Retold by Amy Ehrlich. Ill. Susan Jeffers. New York: The Dial Press, 1979. Unp. Ill.

Thumbelina. Ill. Elsa Beskow. London: Dent, 1979. p 32.

Thumbeline. Tr. Richard and Clara Winston. Ill. Lisbeth Zwerger. New York: William Morrow & Co., 1980. p 32. Ill. [Originally published in German, 1980.]

The Tinder Box. *Fyrtøiet. Eventyr fortalte for Børn,* 1835.

The Tinder-Box. Retold by Joan Cherry. Ill. Lucien Lowen. London: Polytint, 1954. p 17. Ill. [Printed in Vienna.] [Polytint Fairy Tales no. 2.]

The Tinderbox. Tr. David Hohnen. Vol. I of *With Kind Regards,* by David Hohnen. Copenhagen: Høst, 1957. p 38.

The Tinderbox. From the story by Hans Christian Andersen. Ill. Eva Johanna Rubin. London: Methuen, 1967. p 32. Ill. [Translated from an adaptation pub. in Berlin, 1964: *Das Feuerzeug.*]

The Tinder Box. Ill. Cyril Satorsky. Englewood Cliffs, N. J.: Prentice-Hall, 1970. p 31. Ill.

The Tinder Box. Ill. George Thompson. London: Macdonald, 1971. p 31. Ill. [Macdonald fairy tales.]

The Tinder Box. Retold by Leslie Alexander Hill. Ill. Richard Kennedy. London: Oxford University Press, 1972. p 32. Ill. [Oxford graded readers, junior level.]

The Tinderbox. Tr. M. R. James. Ill. Svend Otto S. Princeton: Van Nostrand Reinhold, 1971. London: Kaye & Ward, 1972. p 25. Ill.

The Tinder Box. Ill. Brychta. London: F. Watts, 1972. p 48. Ill.

The Tinderbox. Ill. Gustav Hjortlund. Odense: Skandinavisk Bogforlag, in cooperation with the H. C. Andersen House, 1977. p 26. Ill.

The Tinder-Box. A Play for Children. (Based on the tale by Hans Andersen.) Adapted by Nicholas S. Gray. Ill. Joan Jefferson Farjeon. With the tunes of the songs. London: Oxford University Press, 1951, 1956. p 113. Ill.

The Tinder Box, a play for children in two acts. Adapted by Alan Broadhurst. Anchorage, Kentucky: Children's Theatre Press, 1963. p 60. Ill.

Once upon a Tinderbox; Dramatization of a Story by Hans Christian Andersen. Adapted by Frances Mapp. *Plays* (November 1973) pp 48-54.

Twelve by the Mail. *Tolv med Posten. Nye Eventyr og Historier,* 1861.

Twelve by the Mail. Tr. Jean Hersholt. Ill. Fritz Kredel. New York: Limited Editions Club, 1956. [Broadside.]

Twelve by the Mail. Mindelheim, Germany: Three Kings Press, 1966. p 15. Ill. [50 copies, printed by hand.]

The Ugly Duckling. *Den grimme Ælling. Nye Eventyr,* 1844.

Ugly Duckling. In Friskey, Margaret: *Farm Friends, and Hans Christian Andersen's Ugly Duckling.* Ill. Pauline Adams and Phoebe Erickson. Chicago: Childrens Press, 1951.

The Ugly Duckling. Tr. R. P. Keigwin. Ill. Johannes Larsen. Copenhagen: Gyldendal; New York: Macmillan Co., 1955. London: Edmund Ward, 1956. p 55. Ill.

My Book of the Ugly Duckling. Ill. Maraja. New York: Maxton Pub. Corp., London: Odhams Press, 1960. [Printed in Milano.] [An Odhams All-Colour Book.] [A Giant Maxton Book.] [Also, in special format for teaching, London: Initial Teaching Publishing Co., 1964. Printed in Milan.]

The Ugly Duckling. Tr. Mrs. Edgar Lucas. Adapted and ill. Tony Palazzo. Garden City, N. Y.: Doubleday, 1962. Unp. Ill. [A Tony Palazzo nursery classic, adapted from the book *Hans Andersen's Fairy Tales.*]

The Ugly Duckling. Tr. R. P. Keigwin. Ill. Adrienne Adams. New York: Charles Scribner's Sons, 1965. Unp. Ill.

The Ugly Duckling. Retold by Jane Carruth. London: Odhams Books, 1966. [Printed in Bilbao.] [Odhams new adventure-reading picture storybooks.]

The Ugly Duckling. London: Kaye & Ward, 1967. p 54. Ill.

The Ugly Duckling. Text by Charlotte Kindrey. Ill. Osamu Tsukasa. Feltham: Hamlyn, 1968. p 33. Ill.

The Ugly Duckling. London: Collins, 1969. p 16. Ill.

The Ugly Duckling. Retold by Leslie Alexander Hill. Ill. Douglas Hall. London: Oxford University Press, 1971. p 16. Ill. [A Junior Level Reader.]

The Ugly Duckling. Ill. Tadasu Izawa and Shigemi Hijikata. New York: Grosset & Dunlap, 1971. p 20. Ill.

40   **The Ugly Duckling.** Tr. R. P. Keigwin. Ill. Toma
Bogdanovic. Slightly abridged by the editor.
New York: Scroll Press, 1971. p 30. Ill.
London: Blackie, 1972. [Full ed. of this trans.
is in *Fairy Tales by H. C. Andersen*, Odense,
1950-58.]
The Ugly Duckling. Adapted from the story by
Hans Christian Andersen. German transla-
tion ed. Phyllis Hoffman. Ill. Josef Paleček.
London and New York: Abelard-Schuman,
1972. p 32. Ill.
The Ugly Duckling. Ed. Arlene Noel. Retold
by Bonnie Nims. Kansas City, Mo.: Hallmark
Card Inc., 1973.
The Ugly Duckling. Tr. from the French ver-
sion. Ill. Lilian Obligado. London: Collins,
1977. p 18. Ill. [Starlight storybooks.] [Tr.
from *Le vilain petit canard*, 1977.]
The Ugly Duckling. Retold by Manuela Lazzara
Pittoni and Ester Piazza. Tr. from Italian by
Erica Propper. Ill. Roberto Molino. London:
Macdonald Educational, 1977. p 28. Ill.
[Macdonald favourites.] [Tr. from *Il brutto
anatroccolo*, 1974.]
The Ugly Duckling. Ill. Gustav Hjortlund.
Odense: Skandinavisk Bogforlag, in coopera-
tion with the H. C. Andersen House, 1977. p
28. Ill.
Ugly Duckling. New edition. Ill. Jennie Wil-
liams. Mahwah, N. J.: Troll Associates, 1978.
The Ugly Duckling. Tr. L. W. Kingsland. Ill.
Svend Otto S. London: Kaye & Ward, 1979.
The Ugly Duckling. Retold for easy reading by
Lynne Bradbury. Ill. Petula Stone. Loug-
borough: Ladybird Books, 1979. p 51. Ill.
[Ladybird easy reading books: well-loved
tales: grade 1.]
The Ugly Duckling. A Tale from Hans Chri-
stian Andersen retold and illustrated by
Lorinda Bryan Cauley. New York: Harcourt
Brace Jovanovich, 1979. Unp. Ill.
The Ugly Duckling. Ill. Harrison Weir. New
York: Leavitt & Allen, n.d. p 30. Ill.

The Wild Swans. *De vilde Svaner. Eventyr
fortalte for Børn*, 1838.
The Wild Swans. New York: Golden Press,
1966. London: Golden Pleasure, 1967. p 30.
Ill.
The Wild Swans. Tr. M. R. James. Ill. Marcia
Brown. New York: Charles Scribner's Sons,
1963. London: Longmans Young, 1969. p 80.
Ill.
The Wild Swans. Ill. Gillian Kenny. London:
Macdonald, 1971. p 31. [Macdonald fairy
tales.]

6) Books about Hans Christian Andersen

Andersen's Land. Catalogue of editions in the
Library of Congress and the Dallas Public
Library's Rare Books Collection. For an ex-
hibit held in October, 1964. Dallas: Dallas
Public Library, 1964. p 15.
Böök, Fredrik. **Hans Christian Andersen. A
Biography.** Tr. from the Swedish by George
C. Schoolfield. Norman: University of Okla-
homa Press, 1962. p 260. Ill. [Originally pub-
lished in 1938.]
**A Book on the Danish Writer Hans Christian
Andersen. His Life and Work.** Published on
the 150th anniversary of his birth. Ed. Svend
Dahl and H. G. Topsøe-Jensen. Tr. W. Glyn
Jones. Copenhagen: Danish Ministry of State
and the Committee for Danish Cultural Acti-
vities Abroad, 1955. p 222. Ill. [Contains:
Bomholt, Julius: Intro. Larsen, Svend: The
Life of Hans Christian Andersen. Rubow,
Paul V.: Idea and Form in Hans Christian
Andersen's Fairy Tales. Dal, Erik: Hans
Christian Andersen in Eighty Languages.
Woel, Cai M.: Hans Christian Andersen as an
Example for Writers.]
Bredsdorff, Elias. **Hans Andersen and Charles
Dickens. A Friendship and Its Dissolution.**
Copenhagen: Rosenkilde & Bagger, Cam-
bridge: W. Heffer & Sons, 1956. [Printed in
Copenhagen.] p 140. Ill. [Vol. 7 of the Angli-
stica Series.]
Bredsdorff, Elias. **Hans Christian Andersen;
the Story of His Life and Work 1805-1875.**
New York: Charles Scribner's Sons; London:
Phaidon Press Ltd., 1975. p 375. Ill.
Broby-Johansen, R., ed. **Hans Andersen's Co-
penhagen.** Photos and commentary by R.
Broby-Johansen. Drawings by Eiler Krag.
Texts by Hans Christian Andersen. Tr. Niels
Haislund and Helen Fogh. Copenhagen: Gyl-
dendal, 1963. p 48. Ill.
Brown, Marion (Marsh). **The Pauper Prince; A
Story of Hans Christian Andersen.** Los Ange-
les: Crescent Publications, 1973. p 119. Ill.
[Juvenile biography.]
**Catalog of the Jean Hersholt Collection of Hans
Christian Andersen;** original manuscripts,
letters, first editions, presentation copies, and
related materials. Intro. Frederik R. Goff.
Contains two articles by Jean Hersholt. Wash-
ington, D.C.: Library of Congress, 1954. p
97. Ill.
Collin, Hedvig. **Young Hans Christian Ander-
sen.** Ill. by the author. New York: Viking
Press, 1955. p 216. [A biography for children.]

Dreslov, Aksel. **A River - a Town - a Poet: A Walk together with Hans Christian Andersen.** Ill. William Hansen. Odense: Skandinavisk Bogforlag; Chester Springs, Pa: Dufour Editions, 1961. p 149. Ill.

Eilstrup, Per. **The Little Mermaid. Her Story and the Fairy Tale.** Tr. Grethe Jantzen. Includes story, tr. Lucie Duff Gordon. Copenhagen: Grønlund, 1972. 60 p. Ill.

Faaborg, N. L. **Hans Christian Andersen Portraits in Graphic Representation.** Copenhagen: The Royal Library, 1971. p 78. Ill.

Garst, Shannon. **Hans Christian Andersen. Fairy Tale Author.** Boston, Mass.: Houghton Mifflin, 1965. p 191. Ill.

Godden, Rumer. (Pseudonym for Margaret Rumer Haynes Dixon). **Hans Christian Andersen. A Great Life in Brief.** London: Hutchinson; New York: Alfred A. Knopf, 1955. p 192. [Great Lives in Brief series.]

Grønbech, Bo. **The Real Andersen. An Introduction and One of His Fairy-tales.** Intro. Jean Hersholt. Includes a trans. of *The Emperor's New Clothes* by Jean Hersholt. Copenhagen: Ministry of Foreign Affairs, 1952. p 12.

Hans Christian Andersen. Book of the Warner Bros. film starring Danny Kaye. London: Latimer House, 1953. p 58. Ill.

Hans Christian Andersen, 1805–1875–1975. Copenhagen: Ministry of Foreign Affairs, 1975. p 44. Ill.

Hans Christian Andersen, 1805 - 2. April - 1955. Catalogue of a Jubilee Exhibition held at the National Book League, London. Arranged in association with the Danish Government, in cooperation with the Royal Library, Copenhagen, and Dr. R. Klein. Organized by Elias Bredsdorff. Copenhagen: The Ministry of Foreign Affairs, for the National Book League, 1955. p 92. Ill.

Haugaard, Erik Christian. **Portrait of a Poet, Hans Christian Andersen and His Fairytales.** Lecture delivered March 5, 1973, as part of the 10th anniversary program of the Children's book section of the Library of Congress. Washington: Library of Congress, 1973. p 17.

Heltoft, Kjeld. **Hans Christian Andersen as an Artist.** Tr. Reginald Spink. Copenhagen: Royal Danish Ministry of Foreign Affairs, 1977. p 143. Ill.

Jacobsen, Hans Henrik. **A Visit to Funen with Hans Christian Andersen.** Odense: Skandinavisk Bogforlag, 1969. p 80. Ill. [Includes excerpts from Andersen's writings.]

Knudsen, Mogens. **Hans Andersen's Denmark Described in Pictures and Text.** Picture ed.

by Chr. Bang. Copenhagen: Illustrations-forlaget, 1950. New York: Bonniers, 1951. p 88. Ill.

Larsen, Svend. **Hans Christian Andersen. A Biography.** Tr. Mabel Dyrup. Odense: Flensted, 1953. p 164. Ill. Also 1958, 1961, 1967, 1971. [Originally published in Danish, 1949.] [Illustrated with photographs from Andersen's life.]

Manning-Sanders, Ruth. **The Story of Hans Andersen: Swan of Denmark.** Ill. Astrid Walford. 1949; rpt. New York: E. P. Dutton & Co.; London: Heinemann, 1966. p 230. Ill. [A biography for children.]

Marker, Frederick J. **Hans Christian Andersen and the Romantic Theatre. A Study of Stage Practices in the Prenaturalistic Scandinavian Theatre.** Toronto & Buffalo: University of Toronto Press, 1971. p 225. Ill.

Meynell, Esther Hallam (Moorehouse). **The Story of Hans Andersen.** 1924; rpt. New York: H. Schuman, 1950. p 135. Ill.

Montgomery, Elizabeth Rider. **Hans Christian Andersen, Immortal Storyteller.** Ill. Richard Lebenson. Champaign, Illinois: Garrard Publishing Co., 1968. p 144. Ill. [Written for children, reading level Grade 5. A Creative Arts Biography.]

Nielsen, Erling. **Hans Christian Andersen.** Tr. Reginald Spink. Copenhagen: Ministry of Foreign Affairs, 1963, 1967. p 48. Ill. [Profile no. 2.]

Pereslegina, E. V. **Hans Christian Andersen. A Bio-Bibliographical Index.** Text by E. V. Pereslegina. Bibliography by V. N. Stefanovitch. Ed. A. S. Pogodin. Moscow: Izdatelstvo Vsesoyuznity Palaty, 1961. p 113.

Reumert, Elith. **Hans Andersen the Man.** Tr. from Danish by Jessie Bröchner. Facsimile reprint of 1927 edition. Detroit: Tower Books, 1971. p 192. Ill.

Robb, Nesca Adeline. **Four in Exile: Critical Essays on Leopardi, Hans C. Andersen, Christina Rossetti, A. E. Housman.** Port Washington, N. Y.: Kennikat Press, 1969. p 158. [Rpt. of 1948 ed.]

Sadolin, Ebbe. **Hans Christian Andersen's Copenhagen, 1805-1875. A Walk in the Footsteps of the Fairy-tale Writer.** With Ebbe Sadolin, who has also done the illustrations. Copenhagen: The Tourist Association of Copenhagen, 1964. Unp.

Sasu-Timerman, Dorothea. **Hans Christian Andersen. Bibliography of the Works Translated into Romanian Which Are Published in Volume (1886-1965).** Bucharest: Institute for Cultural Relations with Foreign Countries, 1966. p 40.

42 Shanning, (Doris) Garst. **Hans Christian Andersen: Fairy Tale Author.** Ill. John Gretzer. Boston: Houghton Mifflin Co., 1965. p 191. Ill. [Novel-like biography written for children. A Piper Book.] [Contains a translation of *The Ugly Duckling,* pp 178-191.]

Spink, Reginald. **Hans Christian Andersen and His World.** New York: Putnam; London: Thames & Hudson, 1972. p 128. Ill. A biography of H. C. Andersen which incorporates 135 illustrations, some of which are rare.

Spink, Reginald. **Hans Christian Andersen. The Man & His Work.** Intro. Erik Dal. Copenhagen: Høst & Søn, 1972. p 64. Ill. 2nd. ed., 1978. p 64. Ill.

Spink, Reginald. **The Young Hans Andersen.** Ill. Anne Linton. New York: Roy; London: Max Parrish, 1962. p 143. Ill. [A novel-like biography for children. Famous Childhood series.]

Stirling, Monica. **The Wild Swan. The Life and Times of Hans Christian Andersen.** London: Collins; New York: Harcourt, Brace & World, 1965. p 384. Ill.

Toksvig, Signe. **The Life of Hans Christian Andersen.** New York: Kraus Reprint Co., 1969. p 289. Ill. [Photographic reproduction of original edition of 1934.]

Vinding, Ole. **A Conversation in Elysium with Hans Christian Andersen.** Intro. H. Topsøe-Jensen. Copenhagen: Rhodos, 1970. p 63. Ill. [Limited ed. of 500.] [*Samtale i Elysium med H. C. Andersen.* Danish-English text.]

Voss, Knud. **Poetical Ouverture or From Hans Christian Andersen's Childhood.** Tr. Jørgen Kornerup. Odense: A/S Hagen & Sørensen, Odense litografiske Anstalt, 1954. p 48. Ill. [*Poetisk Ouverture eller Af H. C. Andersens Barndom.*]

Wheeler, Opal. **Hans Andersen, Son of Denmark.** Ill. Henry C. Pitz. New York: E. P. Dutton, 1951. p 184. Ill. [A novel written for children.]

With Hans Christian Andersen as Our Guide through the Collections in Odense. Tr. Mabel Dyrup. Ill. Gustav Hjortlund. Odense: H. C. Andersens Hus and Munksgaard, 1957. 3rd ed. 1963. Reprinted 1973. p 50. Ill.

KNUD ANDERSEN (1890-1980)

Campanella. Tr. Lydia Cranfield. *CDPr* pp 186-188. [*Campanella,* short story from the collection *Morild,* 1932.]

Previous Translations:
The Brand of Sea.
Surf.
Phosphorescence, Three Sketches:
  Discard, Northeast, Sissy.
In the Grip of the Gale.

VITA ANDERSEN (b. 1944)

The Beautiful Room. Tr. Jannick Storm and Linda Lappin. *Modern Poetry in Translation* (New York) no. 33 (Spring 1978) p 9. [*Det smukke Rum,* poem from the collection *Tryghedsnarkomaner,* 1977.]

Good Breasts Are Necessary. Tr. Jannick Storm and Linda Lappin. *Modern Poetry in Translation* (New York) no. 33 (Spring 1978) pp 8-9. [*Der skal et godt Bryst til,* poem from the collection *Tryghedsnarkomaner,* 1977.]

To You Gudrun Brun. Tr. Jannick Storm and Linda Lappin. *Modern Poetry in Translation* (New York) no. 33 (Spring 1978) pp 7-8. [*Til dig Gudrun Brun,* poem from the collection *Tryghedsnarkomaner,* 1977.]

The Wound Eater. Tr. Jannick Storm and Linda Lappin. *Modern Poetry in Translation* (New York) no. 33 (Spring 1978) p 9. [*Sårspiseren,* poem from the collection *Tryghedsnarkomaner,* 1977.]

JOHANNES ANKER LARSEN (1874-1957)

The Philosopher's Stone. Tr. Arthur G. Chater. 1924; rpt. Garden City, N. Y.: The Waldorf Press, 1977. p 379. [*De Vises Sten,* novel, 1923.]

KRISTIAN AUGUST EMIL ARENTZEN (1823-1899)

Evening Prayer. Tr. S. D. Rodholm. *HoS* p 52. [*Jeg er træt og gaar til Ro,* hymn published in *Dansk Kirketidende,* 8. marts 1846, and in the collection *Digte,* 1854.]

BIRTHE ARNBAK (b. 1923)

Country Lass. Tr. H. Raphael. *LitR-Dk* p 74. [*Bondepige uden Slør*, poem from the collection *Skjulesteder*, 1955.]

Hope's My Enemy. Tr. Anne Born. *Orbis* (International Poetry Society, Derbeyshire) no. 35 (June 1979) p 28. [*Håbet er min Fjende*, poem from the collection *Jeg ser dig allevegne*, 1977.]

The Little Grey Cat. Tr. Anne Born. *Orbis* (International Poetry Society, Derbeyshire) no. 35 (June 1979) p 29. [*Den lille grå Kat*, poem from the collection *Jeg ser dig allevegne*, 1977.]

Two Big Faces. Tr. Anne Born. *Orbis* (International Poetry Society, Derbeyshire) no. 35 (June 1979) p 28. [*To store Ansigter i Træerne*, poem from the collection *Jeg ser dig allevegne*, 1977.]

CLAUS ARVESEN (1830-1917)

Forward and Homeward. Tr. S. D. Rodholm. *HoS* p 125. [*Fremad er Verdens vilde Røst*, hymn published in *Oplandenes Avis*, 1879, nr. 94.]

CARL CHRISTIAN BAGGER (1807-1846)

The Departure. Tr. Charles Wharton Stork. *SeBDV* pp 46-50. [*Bortreisen*, poem written in 1834, published in *Samlede Værker*, II, 1867.]

Previous Translations:

The English Captain.

JENS BAGGESEN (1764-1826)

My Childhood. Tr. R. P. Keigwin. *IDIWB* pp 23-27. [*Da jeg var lille*, poem, 1784.]

Works about Jens Baggesen

Bredsdorff, Thomas. **The Fox at Ploen. The Idea of Nature in a Major Work of Danish Eighteenth Century Literature, Jens Baggesen's »The Labyrinth«.** *Orbis Litt.* vol. 22 (1967) pp 241-251.

Henriksen, Aage. **Baggesen - The European.** *DFOJ* vol. 48 (1964) pp 17-20. Ill.

Previous Translations:

Infancy.
To My Country.
Elsa's Lay.
When I Was Little.
Childhood.
Ridder Oller (Sir Oller).
Extracts from »The Labyrinth«.
Agnete and the Mermaid.
Ridder Ro and Ridder Rap.
To My Native Land.
To My Father Land.
From »Holger the Dane«.

ESTRID BALSLEV (b. 1936)

Natura Natura and Rondo. Tr. Robert Fred Bell. *LitR-Dk* p 82. [*Natura, naturata* and *Rondo*, poems from the collection *Døgnfuga, Digt Cyklus*, 1966.]

HERMAN BANG (1857-1912)

Expelled from Germany. Tr. P. M. Mitchell and Kenneth H. Ober. *RG* pp 218-235. [*Udvist af Tyskland*, from *Ti Aar i Erindringer og Hændelser*, 1912.]

Franz Pander. Tr. P. M. Mitchell and Kenneth H. Ober. *RG* pp 197-217. [*Franz Pander*, short story from the collection *Excentriske Noveller*, 1885.]

Irene Holm. Tr. David Stoner. *ADL* pp 307-331. [*Irene Holm*, short story, 1890.]

You Shall Remember Me! Tr. William O. Makely. *ASR* vol. 61, no. 1 (Spring 1973) pp 62-67. [*Men du skal mindes mig* - short story from the collection *Sælsomme Fortællinger*, 1907.]

Previous Translations:

In Rosenborg Park.
Denied a Country.
The Pastor.
Ida Brandt.
Four Devils.
The Last Evening.
A Play and Some Poems.

44 Works about Herman Bang

Driver, Beverly R. **Herman Bang and Arthur Schnitzler. Modes of the Impressionist Narrative.** Ph. D. diss., Indiana University, 1970. [Diss. Abstr. 31:3543-A.] [Portions of the text are in German.]

Driver, Beverly R. **Herman Bang's Prose: The Narrative as Theatre.** *Mosaic* (Manitoba) vol. 4, no. 2 (1970) pp 79-89. [Issue on *Scandinavian Literature: Reality and Vision.*]

Hermannsen, Mogens. **Herman Bang.** *ASR*, vol. 45, no. 2 (June 1957) pp 170-172. Also in *American Book Collector* vol. 7 pp 22-23.

Jensen, Astrid and Jytte Jonker. **The Expectant Text. On Herman Bang's »Det hvide Hus« and »Det graa Hus«.** *Scandinavica* vol. 17, no. 2 (November 1978) pp 103-135.

THOMAS BARTHOLINUS (1616-1680)

Thomas Bartholin on the Burning of His Library, and on Medical Travel. Tr. Charles D. O'Malley. Lawrence, Kansas: Univ. of Kansas Libraries, 1961. p 101. [Univ. of Kansas Publications. Library Series no 9.]

JENS CHRISTIAN BAY (1871-1962)

A Kind Word. Tr. S. D. Rodholm. *HoS* p 169. [*Et venligt Ord*, poem published in *Sangbog for det danske Folk i Amerika*, 3rd ed., 1910.]

BODIL BECH (1889-1942)

In the Train. Tr. Charles Wharton Stork. *SeBDV* p 153. [*I Sporvognen*, poem from the collection *Granit og Dugg*, 1938.]

KNUTH BECKER (1891-1974)

The Show. Tr. J. F. S. Pearce. *CDPr* pp 189-205. [Chapter 20 of the novel *Det daglige Brød*, 1932.]

Works about Knuth Becker

Birket-Smith, Kjeld. **Knuth Becker.** *ASR* vol. 62, no. 3 (September 1974) pp 285-290.

HANS MARTIN BERG (b. 1926)

Two Worlds. Tr. H. R. Meyer. *ASR* vol. 53, no. 1 (March 1965) pp 73-77. [*Verdener*, short story, published in *Manden og Jorden. 13 Noveller af Unge danske Forfattere*, 1954.]

HARALD BERGSTEDT (1877-1965)

Before a Pair of Eyes. Tr. Martin S. Allwood. *TCScP* p 58. [*Foran et Par Øjne*, poem from the collection *Sange fra Provinsen*, vol. 4, 1921.]

»God's Grace« and The World War. Tr. Martin S. Allwood. *TCScP* p 57. [*»Guds Naade« og Verdenskrigen*, poem from the collection *Sange fra Provinsen*, vol. 4, 1921.]

Mr. Pin-Up. Tr. Martin S. Allwood. *TCScP* p 57. [*Hr. Klistermand*, poem from the collection *Sange fra Provinsen*, vol. 4, 1921.]

Nostalgia. Tr. Martin S. Allwood. *TCScP* p 57. [*Længsel*, poem from the collection *Sange fra Provinsen*, vol. 4, 1921.]

Primitive-Sophisticated. Tr. Martin S. Allwood. *TCScP* p 56. [*Primitiv-Raffineret*, poem from the collection *Sange fra Provinsen*, vol. 4, 1921.]

A Question. Tr. Martin S. Allwood. *TCScP* pp 57-58. [*Et Spørgsmaal*, poem from the collection *Sange fra Provinsen*, vol. 4, 1921.]

A Welling Spring. Tr. Martin S. Allwood. *TCScP* pp 56-57. [*Den levende Kilde*, poem from the collection *Sange fra Provinsen*, vol. 4, 1921.]

ANTON BERNTSEN (1873-1953)

My Neighbor. Tr. S. D. Rodholm. *HoS* p 150. [*Mi Nååbo, Pe Sme*, poem from the collection *Gjemm-Ævvel, Jyske Digte*, 1922.]

VILHELM BIRKEDAL (1809-1892)

I Saw Him in Childhood. Tr. P. C. Paulsen. *HinS* hymn no. 43. [*Jeg saa Ham*, poem published in *Dansk Kirketidende*, 1858.]

KARL BJARNHOF (1898-1980)

The Good Light. Tr. Naomi Walford. New York: Knopf and London: Methuen, 1960. p 264. [*Det gode Lys*, memoirs, 1957.]

The Stars Grow Pale. Tr. Naomi Walford. New York: Knopf and London: Methuen, 1958. p 282. Harmondsworth: Penguin, 1960. [Penguin Books no. 1430.] pb. p 267. [*Stjernerne blegner*, novel, 1956.] In braille: The Library of the Jewish Braille Institute of America, Inc.

HANS BJERREGAARD (b. 1907)

Humanity Outlawed. Tr. Martin S. Allwood. *TCScP* pp 98-99. [*Fredløse Menneskehed*, poem from the collection *Tusmørke efter Ragnarok*, 1946.]

THORKILD BJØRNVIG (b. 1918)

The Ballad of the Great Eastern. Tr. Ingvar Schousboe. *CDPo* pp 168-174. [*Balladen om Great Eastern*, poem from the collection *Figur og Ild*, 1959.]

The Big Blue Horses. Tr. George C. Schoolfield. *LitR-Dk* p 59. [*De store blaa Heste*, poem from the collection *Figur og Ild*, 1959.]

Cape Finisterre. Tr. George Schoolfield. *ASR* vol. 54, no. 1 (March 1966) p 61. [*Kap Finisterre*, poem from the collection *Figur og Ild*, 1959.]

Cypresses beneath a Night Sky. Tr. George C. Schoolfield. *LitR-Dk* p 61. [*Cypresser under natlig Himmel*, poem from the collection *Anubis*, 1955.]

The Dune Mirror. Tr. Anne Born. *Orbis* p 37. [*Klitspejlet*, poem from the collection *Figur og Ild*, 1959.]

Dysphorial Obituary. Tr. Ingvar Schousboe. *CDPo* pp 174-176. [*Pinlig Nekrolog*, poem from the collection *Vibrationer*, 1966.]

Epilogue to the Great Eastern. Tr. Anne Born. *Orbis* pp 38-39. [From *Balladen om Great Eastern*, poem from the collection *Figur og Ild*, 1959.]

Fragment. Tr. George C. Schoolfield. *LitR-Dk* pp 60-61. [*Fragment*, poem from the collection *Figur og Ild*, 1959.]

Jealousy. Tr. George C. Schoolfield. *ASR* vol. 54, no. 1 (March 1966) p 61. Also *ADL* p 588.

[*Jalousi*, poem from the collection *Anubis*, 1955.]

The Maple Tree. Tr. George C. Schoolfield. *LitR-Dk* pp 62-63. *ADL* pp 588-593. [*Ahorntræet*, poem from the collection *Figur og Ild*, 1959.]

Mask of Caesar. Tr. George C. Schoolfield. *LitR-Dk* p 63. [*Cæsarmaske*, poem from the collection *Anubis*, 1955.]

New Moon. Tr. George Schoolfield. *ASR* vol. 54, no. 1 (March 1966) p 60. [*Nymåne*, poem from the collection *Figur og Ild*, 1959.]

Owl. Tr. Robert Bly. *The Massachusetts Review* vol. 14 (Autumn 1973) p 745. [*Uglen*, poem from the collection *Anubis*, 1955.]

The Sycamore Tree. Tr. Anne Born. *Orbis* pp 39-40. [*Ahorntræet*, poem from the collection *Figur og Ild*, 1959.]

To the Fishermen Blockading the Grinddal. Tr. Nadia Christensen. Ill. Helene Brandt. *SR* vol. 64, no. 4 (December 1976) pp 54-55. [*Til Fiskerne som blokerer Grinddal*, poem from the collection *Delfinen: Miljødigte 1970-1975*, 1975.]

Too Much. Tr. George C. Schoolfield. *LitR-Dk* p 59. [*For meget*, poem from the collection *Figur og Ild*, 1959.]

The Tool. Tr. George Schoolfield. *ASR* vol. 54, no. 1 (March 1966) p 60. [*Værktøjet*, poem from the collection *Figur og Ild*, 1959.]

The Trees in the City. Tr. Nadia Christensen. Ill. Helene Brandt. *SR* vol. 64, no. 4 (December 1976) p 22. [*Træerne i Byen*, poem from *Delfinen: Miljødigte 1970-1975*, 1975.]

Tvind. Tr. Christina Danesen. *SR* vol. 66, no. 3 (September 1978) pp 44-45. [A shorter version of the poem *Tvind*, which appeared in *Politiken*, 2. april 1978.]

Your Eyes. Tr. Martin S. Allwood. *TCScP* pp 102-103. [*Dine Øjne*, poem from the collection *Stjernen bag Gavlen*, 1948.]

Previous Translations:

The Moon and the Good Darkness.

STEEN STEENSEN BLICHER (1782-1848)

Alas, How Changed! Tr. Hanna Astrup Larsen. *TS* pp 146-167. [*Ak, hvor forandret*, short story, 1828.]

Bird of Passage. Tr. S. D. Rodholm. *HoS* p 170. [*Præludium*, poem from the collection *Trækfuglene*, 1838.]

46

Brass-Jens. Tr. Hanna Astrup Larsen. *TS* pp 296-301. [*Messingjens,* short story from the collection *E Bindstouw,* 1842.]

The Diary of a Parish Clerk. Tr. Paula Hostrup-Jessen. Ill. with woodcuts by Povl Christensen. Intro. Søren Baggesen. Copenhagen: Hans Reitzel, 1967. p 61. Ill. [*Brudstykker af en Landsbydegns Dagbog,* novella, 1824.]

Diary of a Parish Clerk. Tr. Alexander Fenton. Epilogue Sigrid Undset. Etchings Jørgen C. Rasmussen. Herning: Poul Kristensen, 1976. p 114. Ill. [Edition included 200 numbered ed.] [*Brudstykker af en Landsbydegns Dagbog,* novella, 1824.]

From the Danish Peninsula. Poems and a Tale by Steen Steensen Blicher. Tr. R. P. Keigwin and Hanna Astrup Larsen. Foreword by Johannes Smith. Woodcuts by Erling Juhl. Copenhagen: Munksgaard, for the Tourist Association of Jutland, 1957. p 75. Ill. [Danish text for poems also included.] Individual poems listed separately under FtDP.

The Gamekeeper at Aunsbjerg. Tr. Hanna Astrup Larsen. *TS* pp 254-270. [*Skytten paa Aunsbjerg,* short story, 1839.]

Gypsy Life. Tr. Hanna Astrup Larsen. *TS* pp 202-219. [*Kjeltringliv,* short story, 1829.]

The Heather. Tr. Charles Wharton Stork. *SeBDV* p 42. Also *A Little Treasury* p 509. [Abbreviated version of *Forsang* to the song cycle *Jyllandsrejse i sex Døgn,* from the collection *Digte, Anden Deel,* 1817.]

From »Home-sickness«. Tr. R. P. Keigwin. *FtDP* p 23. [*Af Hjemve,* poem, 1814.]

The Hosier and His Daughter. Tr. Hanna Astrup Larsen. *TS* pp 220-236. [*Hosekræmmeren,* short story, 1829.]

The Journal of a Parish Clerk. Tr. Hanna Astrup Larsen. *ADL* pp 159-213. Also, *TS* pp 49-78. [*Brudstykker af en Landsbydegns Dagbog,* novella, 1824.]

The Jutlander. Tr. R. P. Keigwin. *IDIWB* p 37. [*Jyden,* poem published in *Aalborg Stiftstidende,* 11. maj 1849.] [Translated into dialect.]

The Jutlander. Tr. Charles Wharton Stork. *SeBDV* p 44. [*Jyden,* poem published in *Aalborg Stiftstidende,* 11. maj 1849.]

Marie. A Reminiscence from the Western Ocean. Tr. Hanna Astrup Larsen. *TS* pp 237-253. [*Marie, En Erindring fra Vesterhavet,* short story, 1836.]

My Home. Tr. R. P. Keigwin. *IDIWB* p 37. [*Kjær est du Fødeland,* stanzas 4 and 5 from *Hiemvee,* 1814.]

An Only Child. Tr. Hanna Astrup Larsen. *TS* pp 271-285. [*Eneste Barn,* short story, 1842.]

The Parson at Veilby. Tr. Hanna Astrup Larsen. *FtDP* pp 29-74. Also *TS* pp 168-201. [*Præsten i Veilby,* short story, 1829.]

Prelude to Birds of Passage. Tr. R. P. Keigwin. *FtDP* pp 25-27. [*Præludium - Trækfuglene,* poem, 1838.]

Prelude to Birds of Passage. Tr. Charles Wharton Stork. *SeBDV* pp 44-45. [*Præludium - Trækfuglene,* poem, 1838.]

The Robbers' Den. Tr. Hanna Astrup Larsen. *TS* pp 79-121. [*Røverstuen,* short story, 1827.]

Spring Song of the Young Skylark. (Stanzas). Tr. R. P. Keigwin. *IDIWB* p 35. [Abbreviated version of *Den unge Lærkes Foraarssang,* poem from the collection *Læsefrugter,* 1820.]

Tardy Awakening. Tr. Hanna Astrup Larsen. *TS* pp 122-145. [*Sildig Opvaagnen,* short story, 1828.]

Three Holiday Eves, A Story of Jutland Robbers. Tr. Hanna Astrup Larsen. *TS* pp 286-295. [*De tre Helligaftener, En jydsk Røverhistorie,* 1841.]

To Sorrow. Tr. R. P. Keigwin. *FtDP* pp 23-25. [*Til Sorgen,* poem, 1826.]

To Sorrow. Tr. Charles Wharton Stork. *SeBDV* p 43. [*Til Sorgen,* poem, 1826.]

Twelve Stories. Tr. Hanna Astrup Larsen. Intro. Sigrid Undset. 1945; rpt. Millwood, New York: Kraus Reprint Co., 1972. p 305. [Individual stories listed separately under *TS.*]

Previous Translations:

To Ingemann.
A Tale of Jutland.
Buhl.
Extracts from Stories (The Parsonage of Langebæk, Solholm, The Peasant Feast).
Esben.
From »At the Village Club«.
Jutlan' Booys is Wunnerf'l Tough.

Works about St. St. Blicher

Olwig, Kenneth. **Place, Society and the Individual in the Authorship of St. St. Blicher.** *Omkring Blicher, 1974.* Copenhagen: Gyldendal, 1974. pp 69-114.

KAREN BLIXEN
see ISAK DINESEN (pseud.)

ANDERS BODELSEN (b. 1927)

Anything Goes! Tr. John C. Pearce. *LitR-Dk* pp 87-95. [*Alt er tilladt*, short story from the collection *Drivhuset*, 1965.]

Consider the Verdict. Tr. Nadia Christensen. New York: Harper & Row, 1976. p 276. [A Harper novel of crime and punishment.] [*Bevisets Stilling*, novel, 1973.]

Freezing Down. Tr. Joan Tate. New York: Harper and Row, 1971. New York: Berkeley Medallion Book in the series *Berkeley International Science Fiction*, 1972. pb. p 159. [*Frysepunktet*, novel, 1969.] See also *Freezing Point*.

Freezing Point. Tr. Joan Tate. London: Michael Joseph, 1971. p 174. [*Frysepunktet*, novel, 1969.] See also *Freezing Down*.

Hit & Run, Run, Run. Tr. Carolyn Bly. London: Michael Joseph, 1970. Paperback ed., Harmondsworth: Penguin, 1971. p 219. [*Hændeligt Uheld*, novel, 1968.] See also *One Down*.

One Down. Tr. Carolyn Bly. London and New York: Harper & Row, 1970. Paperback ed., Popular Library Edition, 1972. p 278. [*Hændeligt Uheld*, novel, 1968.] See also *Hit & Run, Run, Run*.

Operation Cobra. Tr. Joan Tate. London: Pelham, 1976. p 140. [*Operation Cobra*, novel, 1975.]

Rama Sama. Tr. Nadia Christensen *ASR* vol. 61, no. 3 (September 1973) pp 273-275. [*Rama Sama*, short story from the collection by that name, 1967.]

The Silent Partner. Tr. David Hohnen. Harmondsworth: Penguin, 1978. p 221. [Penguin crime fiction.] [Tr. orig. pub. as *Think of a Number*, 1969] [*Tænk på et Tal*, novel, 1967.]

Straus. Tr. Nadia Christensen and Alexander Taylor. New York: Harper and Row, 1974. p 147. [A Harper Novel of Suspense.] [*Straus*, novel, 1971.]

Success. Tr. Paula Hostrup-Jessen. *DI* pp 192-260. [*Succes*, short story from the collection *Rama Sama*, 1967.]

Think of a Number. Tr. David Hohnen. London: Michael Joseph; New York: Harper and Row, 1969. p 186. [*Tænk paa et Tal*, mystery, 1967.]

Works about Anders Bodelsen

Grefe, Eric. **Anders Bodelsen.** *Scanorama* (Bromma) vol. 7, no. 5 (1978) pp 43-44. Ill.

CECIL BØDKER (b. 1927)   47

Adam's Rib. Tr. George C. Schoolfield. *LitR-Dk* pp 116-117. [*Adams Ribben*, poem from the collection *Luseblomster*, 1955.]

Almanac. Tr. Nadia Christensen. *Prism International* (Vancouver, B. C.) vol. 13, no. 2 (Winter 1973) pp 14-15. [*Kalender*, poem from the collection *I Vædderens Tegn*, 1968.]

The Bull, a Short Story. Tr. Nadia Christensen. *ASR* vol. 60, no. 2 (June 1972) pp 184-189. [*Tyren*, short story from the collection *Øjet*, 1961.]

Calendar. Tr. Nadia Christensen and Alexander Taylor. *CDPo* pp 222-223. Also *Books* p 27 (no trans. given). [*Kalender*, poem from the collection *I Vædderens Tegn*, 1968.]

The Companion. Tr. Tove Neville. *CDPo* pp 219-220. [*Følgesvenden*, poem from the collection *Anadyomene*, 1959.]

The Deaf'un's Door. Tr. Paula Hostrup-Jessen. *DI* pp 19-31. [*Døvens Dør*, short story from the collection *Øjet*, 1961.]

The Eye. Tr. Walter Foote. *LitR-Dk* pp 121-129. [*Øjet*, short story from the collection by that name, 1961.]

The Flute Notes of the Birds. Tr. Alexander Taylor. *ASR* vol. 59, no. 1 (March 1971) p 50. [*Fløjterne*, poem from the collection *Lytteposter*, 1960.]

Fury's Field. Tr. Nadia Christensen. *The Penguin Book of Women Poets*. London: Penguin, 1978. New York: Viking Press, 1979. p 236. [Poem from the collection *Fygende Heste*, 1956.]

Grass. Tr. Nadia Christensen. *Prism International* (Vancouver, B. C.) vol. 13, no. 2 (Winter 1973) p 13. [*Græs*, poem from the collection *Luseblomster*, 1955.]

Haste. Tr. Nadia Christensen. *Prism International* (Vancouver, B. C.) vol. 13, no. 2 (Winter 1973) p 11. [*Hastestemning*, poem from the collection *Luseblomster*, 1955.] [Incorrectly attributed to Inger Christensen.]

June Night. Tr. Nadia Christensen. *ASR* vol. 62, no. 2 (June 1974) p 166. Also *CDPo* pp 220-221. [*Juninat*, poem from the collection *Anadyomene*, 1959.]

Medusa. Tr. Robert Fred Bell and George C. Schoolfield. *LitR-Dk* p 120. [*Medusa*, poem from the collection *Luseblomster*, 1955.]

Ode to a Dead Cat. Tr. George C. Schoolfield. *LitR-Dk* p 119. [*Ode til en død Kat*, poem from the collection *Fygende Heste*, 1955.]

Sand. Tr. George C. Schoolfield. *LitR-Dk* pp 118-119. [*Sand*, poem from the collection *Luseblomster*, 1955.]

48

Self-portrait. Tr. Alexander Taylor. *CDPo* p 218. [*Selvportræt*, poem from the collection *Luseblomster*, 1955.]
Under the Sign of the Ram. Tr. Nadia Christensen. *CDPo* pp 221-222. [*I Vædderens Tegn*, poem from the collection of the same name, 1968.]
Vacation. Tr. George C. Schoolfield. *LitR-Dk* p 115. [*Ferie*, poem from the collection *Luseblomster*, 1955.]

LUDWIG BØDTCHER (1793-1874)

Footprints. Tr. Charles Wharton Stork. *SeBDV* pp 25-27. [*Fodsporet*, poem from *Portefeuillen*, 8. nov. 1840.]
Harvest Memory. Tr. S. Foster Damon. *BoDV* pp 85-86. [*Høstminde*, poem published in *Illustreret Tidende*, 27. aug., 1865.]
In the Spring. Tr. R. P. Keigwin. *IDIWB* p 47. [*I Foraaret*, poem from the collection *Digte*, 1867.]
Meeting with Bacchus. Tr. S. Foster Damon. *BoDV* pp 86-98. [*Mødet med Bacchus*, poem published in *Gæa, æsthetisk Aarbog*, published by P. L. Møller, 1846.]
What She Is. Tr. Charles Wharton Stork. *SeBDV* p 25. [*Hvordan hun er*, poem from the collection *Sidste Digte*, 1875.]

RASMUS ERIK BOE

Brief Writing. Glamsbjerg: Alf Boes Trykkeri, 1956. p 192. [Nonfiction about the period after 1945.]

ERIK BØGH (1822-1899)

The Snowstorm Is Sweeping. Tr. S. D. Rodholm. *HoS* p 151. [*Og Sneen den føg saa vide om Jord*, poem from the collection *Halvandet hundrede Viser*, 1892.]

NIELS BOHR (1885-1962)

Atomic Physics and Human Knowledge. *Lectures 1932-1957*. New York: John Wiley, 1958. p 101. [Essays.]

Essays, 1958-1962, on Atomic Physics and Human Knowledge. New York: John Wiley, 1964. p 100.
Unity of Knowledge. In *Great Essays by Nobel Prize Winners*. Ed. Leo Hamalian and Edmond L. Volpe. New York: The Noonday Press (Farrar, Straus & Cudahy), 1960. pp 230-248. [From *Unity of Knowledge*, an address delivered at a Columbia University conference in 1954.]

Works about Niels Bohr

See »Books about Denmark« section: Biography.

BO BOJESEN (b. 1923)

How to Be a Dane. Tr. James R. White. With the assistance of Erik Ruusunen. Intro. Poul Sørensen. Ill. Bo Bojesen. Copenhagen: Hans Reitzels Forlag, 1950. p 64. Ill. With *Meet the Danes* and *More about the Danes*. Tr. James R. White, Erik Ruusunen, Poul Sørensen. Copenhagen: Hans Reitzels Forlag, 1957. p 128. Ill. [*Dagligt Liv i Danmark*, humor, 1950.] [English-Danish-German-French text.]
Meet the Danes. With Poeten. (Pseud. for Poul Sørensen). Copenhagen: Hans Reitzel, 1951. p 48. Ill. [*Danskere her og der*, humor, 1951.] [See also *How to Be a Dane*, 1957 ed.]
More about the Danes. English texts by Erik Ruusunen. Intro. Knud Poulsen. Copenhagen: Hans Reitzel, 1953. p 48. Ill. [*Nyt Dagligliv*, humor 1953.] [See also *How to Be a Dane*, 1957 ed.]
Parade. English texts by Olaf Lindum. Copenhagen: Hans Reitzel, 1958. p 84. Ill. [Humor.]

EMIL BØNNELYCKE (1893-1953)

The Migrants. Tr. R. P. Keigwin. *TCScP* pp 51-52. [*Trækfuglene*, poem from the collection *Festerne*, 1918.]
My Soul. Tr. Charles Wharton Stork. *SeBDV* p 109. [*Min Sjæl*, poem from the collection *Taarer*, 1918.]

POUL BORCHSENIUS (b. 1897)

The Son of a Star. Tr. F. H. Lyon. London: George Allen & Unwin, 1960. p 223. [*Stjernesønnen*, 1952.]

POUL BORUM (b. 1934)

Against a Wall. Tr. Poul Borum. *CDPo* p 253. [*Mod en Mur*, poem from the collection *Dagslys*, 1966.]

The Black Picture. Tr. Poul Borum. *LR* p 7. Also *CDPo* p 254. [*Det sorte Billede*, poem from the collection *Kendsgerninger*, 1968.]

Chinese Myth. Tr. Poul Borum. *LR* p 8. [*Kinesisk Myte*, poem from the collection *Paa denne Side*, 1970.]

A Fierce Desire. Tr. Poul Borum. *CDPo* p 258. [*Et hårdt Begær*, poem from the collection *Denne Bog er en Drøm*, 1973.]

From Inside. Tr. Poul Borum. *LR* p 11. [*Indefra*, poem from the collection *I Live*, 1972.]

A Green Shed. Tr. Poul Borum. *CDPo* p 250. [*Et grønt Skur*, poem from the collection *Livslinier*, 1962.]

A Horse without a Rider. Tr. Poul Borum. *LR* p 12. [*En Hest uden Rytter*, poem from the collection *I Live*, 1972.]

The House. Tr. Poul Borum. *LR* pp 9-10. Also *CDPo* p 255. [*Huset*, poem from the collection *Den brændende By*, 1971.]

Madrigal. Tr. Poul Borum. *CDPo* p 257. [*Madrigal*, poem from the collection *I Live*, 1972.]

Now I Am. Tr. Poul Borum. *LR* pp 8-9. [*Nu er jeg*, poem from the collection *Paa denne Side*, 1970.]

Pictures from Reality. Tr. Poul Borum. *LR* pp 6-7. Also *CDPo* pp 251-252. [*Billeder fra Virkeligheden*, poem from the collection *Dagslys*, 1966.]

Poems. Tr. Robert Fred Bell. *LitR-Dk* pp 79-81. [Poems from *Livslinier*, 1962.]

Song before Death. Tr. Poul Borum. *LR* p 13. [*Sang før Døden*, poem from the collection *I Live*, 1972.]

A Train Is Passing. Tr. Poul Borum. *LR* p 5. Also *CDPo* p 251. [*Et Tog kører forbi*, poem from the collection *Livslinier*, 1962.]

Voices Disappear in the Air. Tr. Poul Borum. *LR* p 5. [*Stemmer forsvinder i Luften*, poem from the collection *Livslinier*, 1962.]

Waving. Tr. Poul Borum. *LR* p 5. [*Bølgende*, poem from the collection *Livslinier*, 1962.]

While the House Is Burning. Tr. Poul Borum. *LR* pp 10-11. Also *CDPo* p 256 and *Books* p 33. [*Mens Huset brænder*, poem from the collection *I Live*, 1972.]

World after World. Tr. Poul Borum. *LR* p 12. [*Verden efter Verden*, poem from the collection *I Live*, 1972.]

Your Lips, Your Tongue. Tr. Poul Borum. *CDPo* pp 258-259. [*Dine Læber, din Tunge*, poem from the collection *Sang til Dagens Glæde*, 1974.]

MORTEN BØRUP (ca. 1446-1526)

Spring Song. Tr. Lee Marshall. *ADL* pp 36-37. [*Veris Adventus*, poem in Latin.]

EDVARD BRANDES (1842-1927)

Previous Translations:

A Visit.

Works about Edvard Brandes

Marker, Frederick J. **Negation in the Blond Kingdom: The Theatre Criticism of Edvard Brandes.** *Educational Theatre Journal* (Columbia, Miss.) vol. 20, (1968) pp 506-515.

GEORG BRANDES (1842-1927)

Creative Spirits of the Nineteenth Century. Tr. Rasmus B. Anderson. 1923; rpt. Freeport, New York: Books for Libraries Press, 1967. p 478.

Ferdinand Lassalle. 1911; rpt. New York: Bergman, 1968; Westport, Conn.: Greenwood Press, 1970. p 230. [*Ferdinand Lassalle. En kritisk Fremstilling*, 1881.]

The French Romantics. [Vol. 5 of *Main Currents in 19th Century Literature*.] 1923; rpt. New York: Russell & Russell, 1966. p 390. [Russell & Russell Scholars' Classics, RP4.] [*Den romantiske Skole i Frankrig*, 1882.]

Friedrich Nietzsche. 1914; rpt. New York: Haskell, 1972. p 117. [*Friedrich Nietzsche*, essay in *Fremmede Personligheder*, 1889.]

Hellas. Travels in Greece. Authorized tr. by Jacob W. Hartmann. 1926; rpt. Freeport, New York: Books for Libraries Press, 1969. p 219. [*Hellas*, 1925.]

50 **Henrik Ibsen, A Critical Study.** With a 42 page essay on Björnstjerne Björnson. Tr. Jessie Muir and Mary Morison. 1899; rpt. New York: B. Blom, 1964. p 171.

Holberg and the Neo-classic Spirit. Tr. Evert Sprinchorn. *GScT* pp 537-547. [Excerpts from *Ludvig Holberg: Et Festskrift*, 1884.]

Impressions of Russia. Intro. Richard Pipes. Tr. Samuel C. Eastman. 1889; rpt. New York: Crowell, 1966, 1968. p 276. [*Indtryk fra Rusland*, 1888.]

The Infinitely Small and the Infinitely Great in Literature. Tr. David Stoner. *ADL* pp 263-287. [»*Det uendeligt Smaa*« og »*Det uendeligt Store*« *i Poesien*, essay from *Kritiker og Portraiter*, 1870.]

Lord Beaconsfield; A Study. Tr. Mrs. George Sturge. Intro. Salo W. Baron. 1880; rpt. New York: T. Y. Crowell Co., 1966, 1968. [*Benjamin Disraeli, Jarl af Beaconfield*, biography, 1878.]

Main Currents in 19th Century Literature. Tr. Diana White and Mary Morison. 1903-1905; rpt. New York: Russell & Russell, 1957-1966. Vols. 3-5. [*Hovedstrømninger i det 19. Aarhundredes Litteratur*, 6 vols., 1872-1890.] Individual vols. listed separately by title.

Main Currents in Nineteenth Century Literature. 1907 (ill. re-issue of 1901-1905 ed.); rpt. New York: Haskell House, 1975. 6 vols.

Michelangelo, His Life, His Times, His Era. Tr. and with foreword by Heinz Norden. New York: Frederick Ungar Publishing Co.: London: Constable & Co., 1963. p 428. [*Michelangelo*, biography, 1921.]

Naturalism in Nineteenth Century English Literature. (Vol. 4 of *Main Currents in 19th Century Literature*). New York: Russell & Russell, 1957. p 372. [Russell Scholars' Classics.] [*Naturalismen i England*, 1875.]

Reminiscences of My Childhood and Youth. 1906; rpt. New York: Arno Press, 1975. p 397. [The Modern Jewish Experience Series.] [*Barndom og første Ungdom*, vol. 1 of *Levned*, memoirs, 1905.]

Revolution and Reaction in Nineteenth Century French Literature. (Vol. 3 of *Main Currents in 19th Century Literature*). New York: Russell & Russell, 1960. p 300. [*Reactionen i Frankrig*, 1874.]

Voltaire. Tr. Otto Kruger and Pierce Butter. 1930; rpt. New York: Ungar, 1964. 2 vols. [*Voltaire*, biography, 1916-1917.]

Voltaire. Tr. John Butt. Baltimore, Md.: Penguin, 1964. pb. p 190.

William Shakespeare; A Critical Study. Tr. William Archer and Diana White. 1899; rpt. in 2 vols. New York: F. Ungar, 1963. [*William Shakespeare*, biography, 1895-1896.]

Previous Translations:

German Literature.
New Danish and Norwegian Poetry.
Eminent Authors of the Nineteenth Century.
Denmark and Germany.
Preface to Prince Kropotkin: Memoirs of a Revolutionist.
Nihilist Circles in Russia.
Poland. A Study of the Land. People and Literature.
Illustrated Cameos of Literature.
On Reading. An Essay.
Anatole France.
The World at War.
My American Colleagues.
Jesus, A Myth.
Life (February 4, 1902).
Wolfgang Goethe.
Russia - U.S.A. An Unpublished Letter.

Works about Georg Brandes

Asmundsson, Doris R. **America Meets Georg Brandes.** *SR* vol. 65, no. 1 (March 1977) pp 4-10.

Bredsdorff, Elias. **Georg Brandes as a Fictional Character in Some Danish Novels and Plays.** *SS* vol. 45, no. 1 (Winter 1973) pp 1-26.

Dyrenforth, Harald O. **Georg Brandes: 1842-1927.** *Educational Theater Journal* (Columbia, Miss.) vol. 15, no. 2 (1963) pp 143-150.

Hamer, Douglas. **The Gossip of Georg Brandes.** *Scandinavica* vol. 11, no. 1 (May 1972) pp 31-33. Also in *Notes and Queries* (Oxford) vol. 15, no. 11 (1968).

Larsen, Swen A. **Georg Brandes' Views on American Literature.** *SS* vol. 22, no. 4 (November 1950) pp 161-165.

Madsen, Børge Gedsø. **Georg Brandes' Criticism of »Niels Lyhne«.** *SS* vol. 38, no. 2 (May 1966) pp 124-130.

Møller Kristensen, Sven and Hans Hertel, eds. **The Activist Critic: Georg Brandes,** *Orbis Litterarum Supplement,* (Copenhagen), no. 5 (1980). Includes *Georg Brandes - a Bio-bibliographical Survey* by Per Dahl and John Mott.

Møller Kristensen, Sven. **Georg Brandes Research. A Survey.** *Scandinavica* vol. 3, no. 2 (Nov. 1964) pp 121-132.

Nolin, Bertil. **Georg Brandes.** Boston: Twayne Publishing Co., 1976. p 208. [World Authors Series.]

Ratner, Marc. **Georg Brandes and Hjalmar Hjort Boyesen.** *SS* vol. 33, no. 4 (1961) pp 218-230.

Schwab, Arnold T. **Georg Brandes and James Huneker: A Cosmopolitan Friendship.** *Modern Language Forum* vol. 38, nos. 3-4 (Sept.-Dec. 1953) pp 30-49.

Wellek, René. **The Lonely Dane: Georg Brandes.** In his *A History of Modern Criticism 1750-1950.* Vol. IV: *The Later Nineteenth Century.* New Haven, CT: Yale University Press, 1965. London: Jonathan Cape, 1966, 1970. pp 357-369, 606-610.

CARL JOAKIM BRANDT
(1817-1889)

Flowers in Spring. Tr. S. D. Rodholm. *HoS* pp 115-116. [*Nu Blomstertiden kommer*, published in *Salmebog for Kirke og Hjem*, 1885.]

Flowers of Spring. Tr. S. D. Rodholm. *HoS* pp 113-114. [*Nu Blomstertiden kommer*, published in *Salmebog for Kirke og Hjem*, 1885.]

God, Thou Opened. Tr. S. D. Rodholm. *HoS* p 38. Also *HinS* hymn no. 4. [*Gud, du som Lyset*, hymn, published in *Sange for den kristelige Folke-Skole*, 1874.]

JØRGEN GUSTAVA BRANDT
(b. 1929)

Advent. Tr. Anne Born. *Orbis* p 42. [*Advent*, poem from the collection *Dragespor*, 1957.]

Approaching Woman in a Landscape. Tr. J. G. Brandt and Alexander Taylor. *TaT* p 18. [*Kommende Kvinde i Landskab*, poem from the collection *Regnansigt*, 1976.]

Awakening II. Tr. Anne Born. *Orbis* p 42. [*Opvaagnen II*, poem from the collection *Dragespor*, 1957.]

Blue Night on the Hills. Tr. Karin Johansen. *Portland* p 99. [*Blå Nat på Højene*, poem from the collection *Her kunne Samtale føres*, 1978.]

Cerebus in the Storm. Tr. J. G. Brandt and Alexander Taylor. *TaT* pp 27-29. [*Kerubus i Stormen*, poem from the collection *Fragment af Imorgen*, 1960.]

Come Aboard. Tr. Alexander Taylor. *CDPo* p 186. [*Komme ombord*, poem from the collection *Regnansigt*, 1976.]

Come Aboard. Tr. J. G. Brandt and Alexander Taylor. *TaT* p 17. [*Komme ombord*, poem from the collection *Regnansigt*, 1976.]

Come On! Tr. J. G. Brandt and Alexander Taylor. *TaT* p 13. [*Kom så*, poem from the collection *De nødstedte Djævle er de værste*, 1972.]

Evident. Tr. Jørgen Gustava Brandt and Alexander Taylor. *CDPo* p 191. Also *TaT* p 15. [*Åbenbar*, poem from the collection *De nødstedte Djævle er de værste*, 1972.]

Face of Rain. Tr. J. G. Brandt and Alexander Taylor. *TaT* p 19. [*Regnansigt*, poem from the collection *Regnansigt*, 1976.]

The Finnish Sailor. Tr. Paula Hostrup-Jessen. *DI* pp 81-93. [*Den finske Sømand*, short story from the collection *Stof*, 1968.]

The House in Copenhagen. Tr. Jørgen Gustava Brandt and Alexander Taylor. *CDPo* pp 189-190. Also *TaT* pp 10-11. [*Huset i Byen*, poem from the collection *Fragment af Imorgen*, 1960.]

It Is the Bird in the Tree. Tr. Alexander Taylor. *CDPo* pp 192-193. [*Det er Fuglen i Træet*, poem from the collection *Der er Æg i mit Skæg*, 1966.]

It Is the Bird in the Tree. Tr. J. G. Brandt and Alexander Taylor. *TaT* pp 24-25. [*Det er Fuglen i Træet*, poem from the collection *Der er Æg i mit Skæg*, 1966.]

My Element. Tr. Alexander Taylor. *CDPo* p 187. [*Mit Es, (sidder på Terrassen i min Kurs på Stedet)*, poem from the collection *Der er Æg i mit Skæg*, 1966.]

My Element. Tr. J. G. Brandt and Alexander Taylor. *TaT* p 7. [*Mit Es, (sidder på Terrassen i min Kurs på Stedet)*, poem from the collection *Der er Æg i mit Skæg*, 1966.]

Night Hour of Suchness. Tr. Alexander Taylor. *CDPo* pp 187-188. [*Nattetime af Sådanhed*, poem from collection *Der er Æg i mit Skæg*, 1966.]

Night Hour of Suchness. Tr. J. G. Brandt and Alexander Taylor. *TaT* pp 8-9. [*Nattetime af Sådanhed*, poem from the collection *Der er Æg i mit Skæg*, 1966.]

On the Path. Tr. J. G. Brandt and Alexander Taylor. *TaT* p 30. [*På Stien*, poem from the collection *Regnansigt*, 1976.]

Out of Nothing You Come Walking. Tr. Alexander Taylor. *CDPo* p 191. [*Ud af intet kommer du gående*, poem from the collection *Ateliers. Anden Samling*, 1967.]

Out of Nothing You Come Walking. Tr. J. G. Brandt and Alexander Taylor. *TaT* p 14. [*Ud af intet kommer du gående*, poem from the collection *Ateliers. Anden Samling*, 1967.]

Patience. Tr. Alexander Taylor. *CDPo* p 190. [*Tålmod*, poem from the collection *I den høje Evighed lød et Bilhorn*, 1970.]

52 **Patience.** Tr. J. G. Brandt and Alexander Taylor. *TaT* p 31. [*Tålmod*, poem from the collection *I den høje Evighed lød et Bilhorn*, 1970.]

Phases. Tr. J. G. Brandt and Alexander Taylor. *TaT* p 12. [*Engang var Verdens Ende*, poem from the collection *Der er Æg i mit Skæg*, 1966.]

Safe and Sound. Tr. J. G. Brandt and Alexander Taylor. *TaT* pp 20-21. [*I god Behold*, poem from the collection *Her omkring*, 1974.]

Sound of the Bell. Tr. Alexander Taylor. *CDPo* pp 185-186. [*Klokkes Lyd*, poem from the collection *Ateliers. Anden Samling*, 1967.]

Sound of the Bell. Tr. J. G. Brandt and Alexander Taylor. *TaT* p 16. [*Klokkes Lyd*, poem from the collection *Ateliers. Anden Samling*, 1967.]

A Stroll on Amager's South Beach - Brief Repetitive Manoeuvre in a Precise Manner. Tr. John C. Pearce. *LitR-Dk* pp 55-58. [*En Spadseretur paa Amager Sydstrand: Lille Gentagelsesmanøvre i net Maner*, short story from the collection *Udflugter*, 1961.]

Tête à Tête. Tr. Jørgen Gustava Brandt and Alexander Taylor. Willimantic, CT: Curbstone Press, 1978. p 31. Individual poems listed separately under *TaT*.

There's a Sighing in the Leaves. Tr. J. G. Brandt and Alexander Taylor. *TaT* pp 22-23. [*Det suser i Løvet*, poem from the collection *I den høje Evighed lød et Bilhorn*, 1970.]

Under the Lamp. Tr. Anne Born. *Orbis* p 41. [*Under Lampen*, poem from the collection *Vendinger*, 1971.]

Unworriedness. Tr. Anne Born. *Orbis* p 42. [*Ubekymrethed*, poem from the collection *Regnansigt*, 1976.]

You. Tr. Alexander Taylor. *CDPo* p 189. [*Dig, (Så i dig)*, poem from the collection *Ateliers*, 1967.]

You. Tr. J. G. Brandt and Alexander Taylor. *TaT* p 26. [*Dig, (Så i dig)*, poem from the collection *Ateliers*, 1967.]

H. C. BRANNER (1903-1966)

Ariel. Tr. Vera Lindholm Vance. *TMoS* pp 192-211. [*Ariel*, short story from the collection by that name, 1963.]

At the End of August. Tr. Evelyn Heepe. *SotN* pp 35-50. [*Sidst i August*, short story from the collection *To Minutters Stilhed*, 1944.]

At the End of August. Tr. Victoria Nott. *ASR* vol. 54, no. 3 (September 1966) pp 281-287. [*Sidst i August*, short story from the collection *To Minutters Stilhed*, 1944.]

The Blue Parakeets. Tr. Vera Lindholm Vance. *TMoS* pp 75-92. Also *ADL* p 500-527. [*De blaa Undulater*, short story from the collection *Om lidt er vi borte*, 1939.]

A Child and a Mouse. Tr. Evelyn Heepe. *MoDA* pp 86-98. [*Et Barn og en Mus*, short story from the collection *Om lidt er vi borte*, 1939.]

The End of August. Tr. Victoria Nott. *ASR* vol. 54, no. 3 (Fall 1966) pp 281-287. [*Sidst i August*, short story from the collection *To Minutters Stilhed*, 1944.]

The End of August. Tr. Vera Lindholm Vance. *TMoS* pp 150-163. [*Sidst i August*, short story from the collection *To Minutters Stilhed*, 1944.]

Eva. Tr. Lydia Cranfield. *Nor* vol. 13, no. 1 (January-February 1955) pp 55-58. [Extract from *Historien om Børge*, novel, 1942.]

The First Morning. Tr. Vera Lindholm Vance. *TMoS* pp 131-149. [*Den første Morgen*, short story from the collection *To Minutters Stilhed*, 1944.]

Ingeborg. Tr. Vera Lindholm Vance. *TMoS* pp 22-28. [*Ingeborg*, short story from the collection *To Minutters Stilhed*, 1944.]

Iris. Tr. Vera Lindholm Vance. *TMoS* pp 56-74. [*Iris*, short story from the collection *Om lidt er vi borte*, 1939.]

The Judge. Tr. A. I. Roughton. *CDPl* pp 495-557. [*Søskende*, play, 1952.]

The Mistress. Tr. A. I. Roughton. New York: American Library, 1953. p 143. pb. [Signet Book 1056.] [Hardback ed. called *The Riding Master*.] [*Rytteren*, novel, 1947.]

No Man Knows the Night. Tr. A. I. Roughton. London: Secker & Warburg, 1958. p 301. Paperback: London: Brown, Watson, Ltd., 1966. p 318. [*Ingen kender Natten*, novel, 1955.]

The Pipe. Tr. Vera Lindholm Vance. *TMoS* pp 164-178. [*Shagpiben*, short story in the collection *To Minutters Stilhed*, 1944.]

Playing by the Beach. Tr. Vera Lindholm Vance. *TMoS* pp 106-130. [*Leg ved Stranden*, short story from the collection *Ariel*, 1963.]

Red Horses in the Snow. Tr. Vera Lindholm Vance. *TMoS* pp 93-105. [*Røde Heste i Sneen*, short story from the collection *To Minutters Stilhed*, 1944.]

The Riding Master. Tr. A. I. Roughton. London: Secker and Warburg; Toronto: S. J. R. Saunders & Co., 1951; New York: British Book Centre, 1952. p 195. [Also published in paperback as *The Mistress.*] [*Rytteren*, novel, 1947.]

The Ship. Tr. Vera Lindholm Vance. *TMoS* pp 1-21. [*Skibet*, short story from the collection *To Minutters Stilhed*, 1944.]

The Story of Börge. Tr. Kristi Planck. Intro. T. L. Markey. New York: Twayne Publishers, 1973. p 196. [Library of Scandinavian Literature no. 23.] [*Historien om Børge*, novel, 1942.]

Thermopylae. Tr. Pat Shaw. *MoNP1* pp 21-174. [*Thermopylæ*, play, 1958.]

The Three Musketeers. Tr. A. I. Roughton. *CDPr* pp 270-281. [*De tre Musketerer*, short story from the collection *To Minutters Stilhed*, 1944.]

The Three Musketeers. Tr. Vera Lindholm Vance. *TMoS* pp 39-55. [*De tre Musketerer*, short story from the collection *To Minutters Stilhed*, 1944.]

Two Minutes of Silence. Tr. Vera Lindholm Vance. Intro. by Richard Vowles. Madison, Wis.: The University of Wisconsin Press, 1966. [Nordic Translation Series, short story collection.] Individual stories listed separately under *TMoS.*

Two Minutes of Silence. Tr. Vera Lindholm Vance. *TMoS* pp 179-191. [*To Minutters Stilhed*, from the short story collection by that name, 1944.]

Previous Translations:

In a Little While We Shall Be Gone.
The Pipe.

Works about H. C. Branner

Dinesen, Isak. **H. C. Branner: The Riding Master.** Tr. P. M. Mitchell and W. D. Paden. *Daguerreotypes.* pp 157-194. [*H. C. Branner: Rytteren*, essay published in *Bazar*, 1958.]

Madsen, Børge Gedsø. **H. C. Branner: A Modern Humanist.** *ASR* vol. 47, no. 1 (March 1959) pp 39-45.

Markey, T. L. **H. C. Branner: An Encomium.** *Scandinavica* vol. 7, no. 1 (May 1968) pp 39-52.

Markey, Thomas L. **H. C. Branner.** Boston: Twayne Publishers. 1973. p 186.

Mishler, William. **The Theme of Reflection in H. C. Branner's »Ariel«.** SS vol. 47, no. 1 (Winter 1975) pp 42-51.

Vowles, Richard B. **Bergman, Branner and Off-stage Dying.** *SS* vol. 33, no. 1 (February 1961) pp 1-9.

JAN BREDSDORFF (b. 1942)

Ash. London: Anthony Blond, 1967. p 175. [Novel first published in English, 1967. Danish translation: *Støv*, 1967.]

To China and Back. New York: Pantheon Books, 1980. British ed., *Revolution There and Back.* London: Faber and Faber, 1980. p 208. Ill. [*Revolution tur/retur*, travel description, 1978.]

MARIE BREGENDAHL (1869-1940)

The Boundary. Tr. W. Glyn Jones. *CDPr* pp 41-48. [*Skellet*, short story from the collection *Med aabne Sind*, 1926.]

Previous Translations:

A Night of Death.
Hans Goul and His Kin.
Niels Hofman and Kirsten.

WILLY BREINHOLST (b. 1918)

Christmas in Denmark. Being a short account of the Danes' favorite festival, Christmas, sometimes called the feast of hearts. Tr. Peter Steen. Ill. Léon van Roy. Copenhagen: D.B.K., 1957. p 22. Ill. [As *Christmas in Scandinavia.* Ill. Erik Lind. Copenhagen: D.B.K., 1959. p 20. Ill.]

Meet the Vikings of Today. Being a brief and straightforward account of the past achievements of an ancient civilization. Ill. Léon. Copenhagen: Stig Vendelkær, 1977. p 39. Ill. Previously published by the author, 1971.

Nordic Problems. Ill. Léon van Roy. Copenhagen: Privately printed, 1965. [p 32.] Unp. Ill. [Not published in Danish.]

The North from A to Z. Ill. Léon van Roy. Copenhagen: C. Hellström & Co., 1963. p 32. Ill. [Not published in Danish.]

Scandinavian Vikings of Today. Being a brief and straight-forward account of the past achievements of an ancient civilisation, of its place on the globe in the present space age, together with an equally unceremonious analysis of the personal characteristics, faults and virtues of 15,000,000 present-day vikings. Ill. Léon van Roy. Copenhagen: Privately printed, 1961. p 24. [Not published in Danish.]

54 **Scandinavians - That's Us.** Some indisputable facts about the strange creatures who inhabit the countries of Hans Christian Andersen, the midnight sun and the smörgåsbord respectively. Tr. Peter Steen. Ill. Léon van Roy. Copenhagen: Privately printed, 1955-1971. pp 14-39. Copenhagen: Stig Vendelkær, 1977. p 39.

SUZANNE BRØGGER (b. 1944)

Deliver Us from Love. Tr. Thomas Teal. New York: Delacorte Press, 1976. London: Quartet Books, 1977. p 298. [*Fri os fra Kærligheden*, essays and short stories, 1973.]

HANS ADOLPH BRORSON (1694-1764)

Like Thousand Mountains. Tr. S. D. Rodholm. *HoS* pp 88-89. [*Den store hvide Flok vi se*, hymn from the collection *Svane-Sang*, 1765.]

Now Found Is the Fairest of Roses. Tr. J. C. Aaberg. *HinS* hymn no. 17. [*Den yndigste Rose er funden*, hymn from the collection *Troens rare Klenodie*, 1732.]

Thy Little Ones, O Savior Dear. Composite translation ed. Johannes Knudsen. *HinS* hymn no. 20. [*En liden Psalme for Børnene*. Hymn from the collection *Troens rare Klenodie*, 1732.]

Until the Day Breaks. Tr. R. P. Keigwin. *IDIWB* pp 13-15. [*Her vil ties, her vil bies*, poem, number 44 of *Svane-Sang*, 1765.]

Previous Translations:

Hymn of Praise.
The Providence of God.
The Nativity.
The Joy of Simeon.
The Divine Rose.
The Excellence of Grace.
Call to Repentance.
The World of God (Arise, All People of the Earth).
The Battle of Faith.
The Spiritual Reckoning.
Brotherly Love (The World's Huge Wilderness Behold).
The Fruits of Suffering.
The Joys of the Redeemer.

The Fatherland (Thy Kingdom Come, Thou God of Might).
Behold, They Stand in Robes of White.

HEÐIN BRÚ (pseud. for HANS JACOB JACOBSEN) (b. 1901) Faroese author

Emanuel. Tr. from the Faroese by Hedin Brønner. *FSS* pp 169-174. Also *ASR* vol. 55, no. 2 (June 1967) pp 178-181. [*Emanuel*, short story from the collection *Flókatrøll*, 1948.]

Lice. Tr. from the Faroese by Hedin Brønner. *FSS* pp 151-155. Also *ASR* vol. 59, no. 2 (June 1971) pp 166-169. [*Einbýli*, short story from the collection *Fjallaskuggin*, 2nd ed., 1967.]

The Long Darkness. Tr. from the Faroese by Hedin Brønner. *FSS* pp 190-205. [*Hin langa náttin*, short story from the collection *Flókatrøll*, 1948.]

Men of Letters. Tr. from the Faroese by Hedin Brønner. *FSS* pp 206-210. Also *ASR* vol. 59, no. 3 (September 1971) pp 291-293 and *Scanorama* (Scandinavian Airlines Flight Magazine) (April-May 1976). [Extract from the novel *Fastatøkur*, 1965.]

Old Halgir. Tr. from the Faroese by Hedin Brønner. *FSS* pp 156-161. Also *ASR* vol. 58, no. 2 (June 1970) pp 117-180 and *Faroe Isles Review* (June 1976). [*Halgir*, short story from the collection *Fjallaskuggin*, 1936.] [Danish translation in *Fjeldskyggen*, 1963.]

The Old Man and His Sons. Tr. from the Faroese and with an intro. by John F. West. New York: Paul S. Eriksson Inc., 1970. p 203. Ill. [*Feðgar á ferð (Fattigmandsære)*, novel, 1940.]

A Summons for the Blacksmith. Tr. from the Faroese by Hedin Brønner. *FSS* pp 175-189. [*Onnur hersøgan*, short story from the collection *Purkhus*, 1966.]

The White Church. Tr. from the Faroese by Hedin Brønner. *FSS* pp 162-168. Also *ASR* vol. 54, no. 4 (December 1966) pp 392-395. [*Tann hvita kirkjan*, short story from the collection *Flókatrøll*, 1948.]

Works about Heðin Brú

Brønner, Hedin. **Hedin Brú, Faroese Novelist.** *ASR* vol. 59, no. 4 (December 1971) pp 360-364.

Brønner, Hedin. **Three Faroese Novelists: An Appreciation of Jørgen-Frantz Jacobsen, William Heinesen and Hedin Brú.** New York: Twayne Publishers, 1973. p 140. [The Library of Scandinavian Studies Vol. 1.]

ERNST BRUUN OLSEN (b. 1923)

Bal i den Borgerlige (Resume with quotations from reviews in English and French). *World Theatre (Paris)* vol. 15, no. 5 (1966) p 448 (Technical Data: Denmark). [*Bal i den Borgerlige*, play, 1966.]
The Bookseller Cannot Sleep. Tr. Pat Shaw. *MoNP1* pp 179-259. [*Men Boghandleren kan ikke sove*, radio play, 1963.]

JOHANNES BUCHHOLTZ
(1882-1940)

Life's Great Moments. Tr. Lydia Cranfield. *CDPr* pp 135-139 [*Livets store Øjeblikke*, short story from the collection *De hvide Spurve*, 1944.]

Previous Translations:

Egholm and His God.
The Miracles of Clara van Haag.
The Devil Cheated out of a Soul.
Sixteen Christmas Qxen.
Cornelia's Conditions.
Secret Arrows.
Susanne.
The Saga of Frank Dover.

C. L. CHRISTENSEN

The Eternal Attempt. (Prose-Philosophy). New York: Privately printed by his widow, Henriette L. Christensen, 1955. [Poems and prose by a Danish emigrant to America who was known by the pseudonym Bror Enebo in Denmark.]

INGER CHRISTENSEN (b. 1935) 55

The Action: Continuities. Tr. Sheila LaFarge. *Portland* p 82. [*Handlingen: Kontinuiteter*, from the poetry collection *Det*, 1969.] [Danish text included.]
The Action: Symmetries. Tr. Sheila LaFarge. *Portland* p 85. [*Handlingen: Symmetrier*, from the poetry collection *Det*, 1969.] [Danish text included.]
Dawn. Tr. Nadia Christensen. *Mundus Artium* (Athens, Ohio) vol. 7, no. 2 (1974) p 105. [*Gry*, poem from the collection *Lys*, 1962.]
From **Det: The Action: Continuities 3.** Tr. Poul Borum. *LR* p 23. [*Handlingen: Kontinuiteter*, from the poetry collection *Det*, 1969.]
From **Det: The Stage: Symmetries 6, Transitivities 3, Transitivities 5, Connexities 5, Connexities 8, Variabilities 1, Variabilities 4, Variabilities 7, Variabilities 8, Universalities 2.** Tr. Poul Borum. *LR* p 17-23. [*Scenen*, from the poetry collection *Det*, 1969.]
From **Det: Variabilities.** Tr. Alexander Taylor. *LR* pp 23-26. Also *Occum Ridge Review* (Fall-Winter 1973) (South Willington, CT) pp 32-35. [Poetry from *Det*, 1969.]
Ephemerae. Tr. Nadia Christensen. *Prism International* (Vancouver, B. C.) vol. 13, no. 2 (Winter 1973) p 10. [*Forgængelighed*, poem from the collection *Lys*, 1962.]
I. Tr. Nadia Christensen. *Mundus Artium* (Athens, Ohio) vol. 7, no. 2 (1974) p 103. [*Jeg*, poem from the collection *Lys*, 1962.]
In the Wild Mountain Solitude. Tr. Alexander Taylor. *LR* pp 14-15. Also *CDPo* p 261. [*I Bjergenes vilde Ensomhed*, poem from the collection *Lys*, 1962.]
From: **It.** Tr. Sheila LaFarge. *CDPo* pp 262-266. [Selections from the poetry collection *Det*, 1969.]
Leaning Tenderly against the Night. Tr. Alexander Taylor. *LR* p 14. Also *CDPo* p 260. [*Læner mig ømt mod Natten*, poem from the collection *Lys*, 1962.]
Leaning Tenderly against the Night. Tr. Nadia Christensen. *Prism International* (Vancouver, B. C.) vol. 13, no. 2 (Winter 1973) p 9. [*Læner mig ømt mod Natten*, poem from the collection *Lys*, 1962.]
Like a Slate-gray Sea. Tr. Nadia Christensen. *Mundus Artium* (Athens, Ohio) vol. 7, no. 2 (1974). [*Som skifergråt Hav svæver*, (first line), poem from the collection *Lys*, 1962.]
Men's Voices. Tr. Nadia Christensen. *LR* p 16. [*Mændenes Stemmer*, poem from the collection *Lys*, 1962.]
Mutability. Tr. Nadia Christensen. *LR* p 17. [*Forgængelighed*, poem from the collection *Lys*, 1962.]

56 **The Scene: Transitivities.** Tr. Sheila LaFarge. *Portland* p 81. [*Scenen: Transitiviteter*, from the poetry collection *Det*, 1969.] [Danish text included.]

Sorrow. Tr. Nadia Christensen. *LR* p 15. Also *CDPo* p 262 and *Prism International* (Vancouver, B. C.) vol. 13, no. 2 (Winter 1973) p 12. [*Sorg*, poem from the collection *Lys*, 1962.] [Incorrectly attributed to Cecil Bødker in *Prism International*.]

The Text: Extensions. Tr. Sheila LaFarge. *Portland* p 79. [*Teksten: Extensioner*, from the poetry collection *Det*, 1969.] [Danish text included.]

The Text: Integrities. Tr. Sheila LaFarge. *Portland* p 83. [*Teksten: Integriteter*, from the poetry collection *Det*, 1969.] [Danish text included.]

The Text: Universalities. Tr. Sheila LaFarge. *Portland* p 84. [*Teksten: Universaliteter*, from the poetry collection *Det*, 1969.] [Danish text included.]

Under a City. Tr. Alexander Taylor. *LR* p 16. [*Under en By*, poem from the collection *Græs*, 1963.]

Variations. Tr. Alexander Taylor. *Trans-Pacific* (Yellow Springs, Ohio) vol. 2, no. 4 (1971) p 37. [Poetry from *Det*, 1969.]

You Walk beyond Me. Tr. Alexander Taylor. *Occum Ridge Review* (South Willington, CT) (Fall-Winter 1973) p 31. [*Du går forbi mig*, (first line), poem from the collection *Lys*, 1962.]

What Is My Dead Cracked Body. Tr. Nadia Christensen. *LR* p 14. Also *CDPo* p 261. [*Hvad er min døde sprukne Krop*, poem from collection *Lys*, 1962.]

LEIF E. CHRISTENSEN (b. 1924)

The Tempest. Tr. Paula Hostrup-Jessen. *DI* pp 68-80. [*Storm*, short story from the collection *Tyven i Tjørnsted*, 1951.]

NATHANIEL CHRISTENSEN

Thomas. New York: Vantage Press, 1959. p 218. [Novel by a Danish-born American writer.]

SVEN CLAUSEN (1893-1961)

The Bird of Contention. Tr. Peter and Ann Thornton. *CDP1* pp 17-40. [*Kivfuglen*, play, 1933.]

SOPHUS CLAUSSEN (1865-1931)

Abroad. Tr. Robert Silliman Hillyer. *BoDV* pp 161-162. [*Udenlands*, poem from the collection *Pilefløjter*, 1899.]

Abroad. Tr. Charles Wharton Stork. *SeBDV* p 92. [*Udenlands*, poem from the collection *Pilefløjter*, 1899.]

Anadyomene. Tr. Poul Borum. *CDPo* p 14. [*Anadyomene*, poem from the collection *Danske Vers*, 1912.]

Dreams. Tr. Martin S. Allwood. *TCScP* p 37. [*Drømme*, poem from the collection *Naturbørn*, 1887.]

The Flowing out into Infinity. Tr. Poul Borum. *CDPo* pp 17-18. [*Udløbet i Uendeligheden*, poem from the collection *Hvededynger*, 1930.]

Heroica. Tr. Poul Borum. *CDPo* p 16. [*Heroica*, poem from the collection *Heroica*, 1925.]

Imperia. Tr. Henry Meyer. *ADL* pp 579-581. [*Imperia*, poem from the collection *Danske Vers*, 1912.]

In an Orchard. Tr. Lee Marshall. *ADL* pp 577-579. [*I en Frugthave*, poem from the collection *Pilefløjter*, 1899.]

In an Orchard. Tr. Poul Borum. *CDPo* pp 12-13. [*I en Frugthave*, poem from the collection *Pilefløjter*, 1899.]

Look, I Met in a Street -. Tr. Poul Borum. *CDPo* p 15. [*Se, jeg mødte paa en Gade*, poem from the collection *Danske Vers*, 1912.]

Pan. Tr. Robert Silliman Hillyer. *BoDV* pp 162-164. [*Pan*, poem from the collection *Naturbørn*, 1887.]

With the Waiting. Tr. Martin S. Allwood. *TCScP* p 37. [*Hos de Ventende*, poem from the collection *Naturbørn*, 1887.]

Previous Translations:

Spring's Annunciation.

ROBERT CORYDON (b. 1924)

Chinese Brush. Tr. Tove Neville. *CDPo* pp 202-203. [*Kinesisk Pensel*, poem from the collection *Skrænten mod Havet*, 1955.]

Morning Slaughter. Tr. Christine Clifford. *Versuch* vol. 11 (1972) p 16. [*Morgen-slagtning*, poem from the collection *Fragtbrevet*, 1961.]

Nettles. Tr. Tove Neville. *CDPo* p 201. [*Nælder*, poem from the collection *Landskab med Huse*, 1953.]

Ocean Bridle. Tr. Nadia Christensen. *CDPo* p 205. [*Havbidsel,* poem from the collection *Ord til Havet,* 1968.]

Sea Poem. Tr. Robert Fred Bell. *LitR-DK* p 130. Also *CDPo* pp 200-201. [*Havdigt,* poem from the collection *Landskab med Huse,* 1953.]

Shout between Two Boats at Sea. Tr. Nadia Christensen. *CDPo* p 202. [*Raab mellem to Baade paa Havet,* poem from the collection *Landskab med Huse,* 1953.]

The Sign. Tr. Robert Fred Bell. *LitR-Dk* p 131. Also *CDPo* p 203. [*Tegnet,* poem from the collection *Krybet og Sommerfuglen,* 1958.]

Spacecraft R101. Tr. Tove Neville. *CDPo* pp 204-205. [*Luftskib R101,* poem from the collection *Cyklisten,* 1970.]

HANS DALSGAARD (1899-1970)
Faroese author

Nelson's Last Stand. Tr. from the Faroese by Hedin Brønner. *FSS* pp 57-66. [*Seinasta bragd Nelsons,* short story from the collection *Brøndur og Fátæk, Fljoð,* 1968.]

ALBERT DAM (1880-1972)

The Mandrake. Tr. Paula Hostrup-Jessen. *DI* pp 121-144. [*Alrune,* short story from the collection *Syv Skilderier,* 1962.]

ADAM DAN (pseud. for NIELS PEDERSEN) (1848-1931)

I Lift up the Banner of Hope Where I Go. Tr. S. D. Rodholm. *HinS* hymn no. 79. [*Fortrøstning (Jeg løfter mit Haab),* poem published in *Dannevirke,* 1889, and *Sangbog for det danske Folk i Amerika,* 3rd ed., 1910.]

Memory. Tr. S. D. Rodholm. *HoS* p 149. [*Hilsen til Moder (Saa langt, saa langt rækker Tanken frem,* poem published in *Sangbog for det danske Folk i Amerika,* ca. 1887.]

Thou Free and Rich and Noble Land. Tr. S. D. Rodholm. *HoS* pp 140-141. [*Du store, rige, frie Land,* poem published in *Sangbog for det danske Folk i America,* ca. 1887.]

ISAK DINESEN (pseud. for KAREN BLIXEN) (1885-1962)   57

Isak Dinesen wrote in English. Then she or others translated her writings into Danish. In most cases both versions were published simultaneously. Complete information on Danish edition is given only for titles that appeared separately. For detailed information see Liselotte Henriksen's bibliography.

Alexander and the Sybil. In Glenway Wescott, *Isak Dinesen tells a Tale. Harper's* (New York) March 1960 pp 69-70. [From the short story *Tales of Two Old Gentlemen,* 1957.]

Alkmene. *WT* pp 189-224.

Anecdotes of Destiny. New York: Random House; London: Michael Joseph, 1958. p 221. [*Skæbne-Anekdoter,* short stories, 1958. Individual stories listed separately under *AD.*]

Anecdotes of Destiny. New York: Vintage Books, 1974. London: University of Chicago Press, 1976. p 244.

The Angelic Avengers. Chicago and London: University of Chicago Press, 1975. p 304. [*Gengældelsens Veje,* novel written under pseudonym Pierre Andrézel, 1944.]

Anna. *CARNIVAL* pp 185-244. [Short story written in English in the early 1950s, published posthumously in *Efterladte Fortællinger,* 1975.]

Babette's Feast. *Ladies' Home Journal* (New York) June 1950 pp 34-35, 202-212. Also *AD* pp 23-68. [*Babettes Gæstebud,* short story tr. into Danish by Jørgen Claudi, 1952, and by the author, 1958.]

Babette's Feast. Finnish edition, specially adapted for the Finnish reader. Finnish vocabulary, synonyms, grammatical notes, idioms, etc. Helsinki: Otava, 1964. [Contains *Babette's Feast* and *The Ring,* 1950.]

Babette's Feast. The Ring. Norwegian edition. Specially adapted for the Norwegian reader. Norwegian vocabulary, synonyms, grammatical notes, idioms, etc. Printed in Finland. Oslo: Cappelen, 1965.]

Barua a Soldani. *Shadows on the Grass* pp 51-74.

Barua a Soldani. Letter from a King. *Esquire* (New York) December 1960 pp 99-102.

The Bear and the Kiss. Tr. P. M. Mitchell and W. D. Paden. *CARNIVAL* pp 284-326. [*Bjørnen og Kysset,* short story, written in 1958, published posthumously in *Efterladte Fortællinger,* 1975.]

The Blank Page. *LT* pp 125-131.

The Blue Eyes. *Ladies' Home Journal* (New York) January 1960 pp 38-39. [Oral version,

58

as told in the U.S., of the short story, *Peter and Rosa*, 1942.]

The Cardinal's First Tale. *LT* pp 9-35.

The Cardinal's Third Tale. *LT* pp 95-123.

Carnival. *CARNIVAL* pp 57-121. [Short story written in English in the late 1920s, published posthumously in *Efterladte Fortællinger*, 1975.]

Carnival: Entertainments and Posthumous Tales. Foreword by Frans Lasson. Chicago: The University of Chicago Press; London: Heinemann, 1977. p 338. [Most of these stories first appeared in Danish in *Efterladte Fortællinger*, 1975.] Individual stories listed separately under *Carnival*.

The Caryatids. An Unfinished Gothic Tale. *Ladies' Home Journal* (New York) November 1957 pp 64-65. [*Karyatiderne. En ufuldendt fantastisk Fortælling*, short story published in *Bonniers Litterära Magasin*, 7 (March 1938) pp 166-193, and *Sidste Fortællinger*, 1957.]

The Caryatids. An Unfinished Tale. *LT* pp 135-185.

The Cloak. *Ladies' Home Journal* (New York) May 1955 pp 52-53.

The Cloak. *LT* pp 37-58.

A Consolatory Tale. *WT* pp 287-313.

Converse at Night in Copenhagen. *LT* pp 375-405.

Copenhagen Season. *LT* pp 297-373.

A Country Tale. *Botteghe Oscure* (Rome) vol. XIX (Spring 1957) pp 367-417. Also *LT* pp 233-296 and *Ladies' Home Journal* (New York) March 1960 pp 52, 160-175.

Daguerreotypes. Tr. P. M. Mitchell and W. D. Paden. *Daguerreotypes* pp 16-63. [*Daguerreotypier*, essay, 1951.]

Daguerreotypes and Other Essays. Chicago: University of Chicago Press; London: William Heinemann, Ltd., 1979. p 229. Individual essays listed separately under *Daguerreotypes*.

The de Cats Family. Tr. P. M. Mitchell and W. D. Paden. *CARNIVAL* pp 1-28. [*Familien de Cats*, first printed in *Tilskueren*, 1909.]

The Deluge at Norderney. *SeGT* pp 1-79.

The Diver. *AD* pp 3-20.

The Dreamers. *SeGT* pp 271-355.

The Dreaming Child. *WT* pp 153-187. Also *CDPr* pp 140-166.

Echoes. *LT* pp 187-229. Also *Atlantic Monthly* (Boston) 100th Anniv. Issue, vol. 200, no. 5 (November 1957) pp 96-114.

Echoes from the Hills. *Shadows on the Grass* pp 107-149.

Ehrengard. New York: Random House; London: Michael Joseph, 1963. p 72. [*Ehrengard*, novellette tr. into Danish by Clara Svendsen, 1962.] [Published in condensed form as *The Secret of Rosenblad*, in 1962.]

Ehrengard. New York: Random House/Vintage Books, 1975. p 111. Ill. pb. Also London and Chicago: Univ. of Chicago Press, 1976. pb.

Essence of Africa. In *Country Matters*. Ed. Barbara Webster. Philadelphia and New York: J. B. Lippincott Co., 1959. pp 217-218. [Extract from *Out of Africa*.]

Farah. *Shadows on the Grass* pp 3-50. Also *Ladies' Home Journal* (New York) November 1960 pp 72-73, 116-122. [*Farah*, short story, published separately in 1950.]

The Fat Man. *CARNIVAL* pp 172-184. [Short story, published posthumously in *Hjemmet*, 1973, and in *Efterladte Fortællinger*, 1975.]

The Fish. *WT* pp 225-247.

Foreword to »The Fan. Viften«. Catalogue for an Exhibition. Copenhagen: Haandarbejdets Fremme, 1957. pp 7-12. [In Danish and English.]

A Fugitive Rests on the Farm. In Charles Muscatine and Marlene Griffith, eds., *First Person Singular*. New York: Knopf, 1973. pp 155-160. [From *Out of Africa*.]

The Ghost Horses. *Ladies' Home Journal* (New York) October 1951 pp 56-57. *CARNIVAL* pp 245-266.

The Great Gesture. *Shadows on the Grass* pp 77-106.

H. C. Branner: »The Riding Master«. Tr. P. M. Mitchell and W. D. Paden. *Daguerreotypes* pp 157-194. [*H. C. Branner: Rytteren*, essay published in *Bazar*, 1958.]

The Heroine. *WT* pp 69-88.

The Immortal Story. *Ladies' Home Journal* (New York) February 1953 pp 34-35, 91-108. Also *AD* pp 155-231.

Introduction. In Olive Schreiner, *The Story of an African Farm*. New York: Limited Edition Club, 1961. pp 5-12.

The Invincible Slave-owners. *WT* pp 125-151.

Kamante and Lulu. (Out of Africa). Ill. Edward Shenton. In *Reader's Digest Condensed Books* pp 321-352. New York: Reader's Digest, 1952. Also *Reader's Digest Condensed Books* pp 91-120. London: Reader's Digest, 1957. [Condensation of *Out of Africa*.]

Kitosch's Story. In Robert Scholes, ed., *Some Modern Writers*. New York: Oxford University Press, 1971. pp 138-141.

The Last Day. *CARNIVAL* pp 122-147. [*Den sidste Dag*, short story tr. into Danish by Clara Svendsen and published in *Politiken*, 26. and 30. marts, 2. april 1972 and *Efterladte Fortællinger*, 1975.]

Last Tales. New York: Random House; London: Putnam, 1957. p 408. New York: Random House/Vintage Books, 1975. London: University of Chicago Press, 1976. p 341. [*Sidste Fortællinger,* short stories, 1957.] Individual stories listed separately under *LT* (page nos. from 1957 ed.)

Last Tales. Abridged edition. London: Four Square Books, 1967. [Contains all *Last Tales* except *The Cardinal's First Tale, The Cardinal's Third Tale* and *Converse at Night in Copenhagen.*]

Letters from a Land at War. Tr. P. M. Mitchell and W. D. Paden. *Daguerreotypes* pp 88-137. [*Breve fra et Land i Krig,* essay first published in *Heretica,* 1948.]

The Monkey. *SeGT* pp 109-163.

Night Walk. *LT* pp 59-68.

The Nobleman's Wife. *Harper's Bazaar* (New York) November 1957 pp 139, 186. [Excerpt from the short story *Tales of Two Old Gentlemen.*]

Of Hidden Thoughts and of Heaven. *LT* pp 69-81.

The Old Chevalier. *SeGT* pp 81-107.

On Mottoes of My Life. A Speech before the American Academy of Arts and Letters, Jan. 28, 1959. *Proceedings of the American Academy of Arts and Letters and the National Institute of Arts and Letters.* (New York). Second Series, no. 10 (1960) pp 345-358. Also with a preface by Eigil Balling. Copenhagen: Ministry of Foreign Affairs, 1962. p 32, and in *Daguerreotypes* pp 1-15.

On Orthography. Tr. P. M. Mitchell and W. D. Paden. *Daguerreotypes* pp 142-156. [*Om Retskrivning,* essay published in *Politiken,* 23. and 24. marts 1938.]

Oration at a Bonfire, Fourteen Years Late. Tr. P. M. Mitchell and W. D. Paden. *Daguerreotypes* pp 64-87. [*En Baaltale med 14 Aars Forsinkelse,* essay published in *Det danske Magasin,* 1953.]

Out of Africa. 1937; rpt. London: Penguin Books, 1954. p 345. London: Jonathan Cape, 1964 and 1966. p 416. New York: Random House, 1970. New York: Vintage Books/Random House, 1972. p 389 pb. Harmondsworth: Penguin, 1979. p 329. [*Den afrikanske Farm,* memoirs, 1937.]

Out of Africa. Intro. Bernardine Kielty. New York: Modern Library, 1952. p 389. [Modern Library of the World's Best Books, no. 23.] [*Den afrikanske Farm,* memoirs, 1937.]

Out of Africa. By Karen Blixen. Intro. Elspeth Huxley. Ill. Peter Pendrey. London: The Folio Society, 1979. [*Den afrikanske Farm,* memoirs, 1937.]

Out of Africa. Intro. Alan Moorehead. New York: Time, 1963. [Time Reading Program.] [*Den afrikanske Farm,* memoirs, 1937.]

Out of Africa, Excerpt. *Holiday* vol. 23, no. 6 (June 1958) pp 165 ff.

The Parrot. *Argosy Short Story Magazine* (Edinburgh) October 1961, vol. 22, no. 10 pp 85-86. [Excerpt from *Out of Africa.*]

The Pearls. *WT* pp 105-124.

Peter and Rosa. *WT* pp 249-285.

The Poet. *SeGT* pp 357-420.

Preface. In H. C. Andersen, *Thumbelina and Other Fairy Tales.* New York and London: MacMillan, 1962.

The Proud Lady, Excerpt. *CARNIVAL* pp 267-283. [Short story, published posthumously in *Hjemmet,* 1974, and in *Efterladte Fortællinger,* 1975.]

Reunion with England. Tr. P. M. Mitchell and W. D. Paden. *Daguerreotypes* pp 138-141. [*Gensyn med England,* essay published in *En engelsk Bog. Tilegnet Kai Friis Møller,* 1948.]

The Revenge of Truth: A Marionette Comedy. In Donald Hannah's »*Isak Dinesen« and Karen Blixen: The Mask and the Reality.* London: Putnam, 1971. New York: Random House, 1972. pp 179-204.

Review of Sacheverell Sitwell's »Denmark«. *The Times* (London) May 6, 1956 p 5.

The Ring. *Ladies' Home Journal* (New York) July, 1950 pp 36-37, 120. Also *Harper's Bazaar* (New York) October 1958 pp 159, 207-208, and *AD* pp 235-244. [*Ringen,* short story from the collection *Skæbne-Anekdoter,* 1958.]

The Roads round Pisa. *SeGT* pp 165-216.

Rungstedlund: A Radio Address. Tr. P. M. Mitchell and W. D. Paden. *Daguerreotypes* pp 195-218. [*Rungstedlund,* essay published in *Hilsen til Otto Gelsted,* 1958.]

The Sailor-boy's Tale. *WT* pp 89-103.

Second Meeting. *CARNIVAL* pp 327-338. [Short story written in 1961, published posthumously in *Efterladte Fortællinger,* 1975.]

The Secret of Rosenblad. *Ladies' Home Journal* (New York) December, 1962 pp 51, 64-68, 98-102. [Condensation of *Ehrengard.*]

Seven Gothic Tales. London: Penguin, 1963. p 363. Also London: Putnam, 1969. With an introduction by Dorothy Canfield, New York: Vintage Books, 1972. p 420 pb. and St. Albans: Triad, 1979. p 352. [Short stories originally published in 1934. Introduction by Dorothy Canfield is from the original edition.] [*Syv fantastiske Fortællinger,* 1935.] Individual stories listed separately under *SeGT* (page nos. taken from 1934 ed.)

60 **Shadows on the Grass.** London: Michael Joseph, 1960. p 106. New York: Random House, 1961. p 149. Ill. New York: Vintage Books, 1974. pb. Also London: University of Chicago Press, 1976. pb. [*Skygger på Græsset*, short stories, 1960.] [Individual tales listed separately.]

Sorrow-Acre. *WT* pp 27-67. Also *ADL* pp 424-499 and in Robert Scholes, ed., *Some Modern Writers*. New York: Oxford Univ. Press, 1971. pp 142-171.

The Supper at Elsinore. *SeGT* pp 217-270.

Tale of Rungstedlund. *Vogue* (Boulder, Colorado) vol. 140 (November 1962) pp 132-135 ff. [Codensation of *Rungstedlund: En Radiotale*, radio speech given in Danish, 1958.]

Tales of Two Old Gentlemen. *LT* pp 83-93.

Tempests. *AD* pp 71-151.

Uncle Seneca. *CARNIVAL* pp 148-171. [Short story published as *The Uncertain Heiress* in *The Saturday Evening Post*, Dec. 10, 1949, pp 34-35, 112-121.]

Uncle Théodore. Tr. P. M. Mitchell and W. D. Paden. *CARNIVAL* pp 29-56. [*Onkel Théodore*, short story written 1909-1913, published posthumously in *Efterladte Fortællinger*, 1975.]

The Wild Came to the Aid of the Wild. In Robert Scholes, ed., *Some Modern Writers*. New York: Oxford University Press, 1971. pp 125-137. [From *Out of Africa*.]

The Wine of the Tetrarch. *The Atlantic Monthly* (Boston) vol. 204, no. 6 (December 1959) pp 125-130. Also in Ray, Cyril, ed. *The Complete Imbiber*. London: Vista Books, 1962. pp 58-67. [Excerpt from *Deluge at Norderney*, short story in the collection *Seven Gothic Tales*, as told in American recitals.]

Winter's Tales. New York: Dell, 1957. p 287. New York: Vintage Books/Random House, 1961. New York: Books for Libraries, 1972. London: University of Chicago Press, 1976. pb. [*Vinter-Eventyr*, short stories, 1942.] Individual tales listed separately under *WT*.

The Young Man with the Carnation. *WT* pp 1-26. [Short story written in English, 1942.]

Works about Isak Dinesen

Beard, Peter, ed. **Kamante. Longing for Darkness. Kamante's Tales from Out of Africa.** With original photographs and quotations from Isak Dinesen. Collected by Peter Beard. London and New York: Harbourt Brace Jovanovich, 1975. p 262. Ill.

Dinesen, Thomas. **My Sister, Isak Dinesen.** Tr. from Danish by Joan Tate. London: Michael Joseph, 1975. p 127. [*Tanne, Min Søster Karen Blixen*, 1974.]

Hannah, Donald. **»Isak Dinesen« and Karen Blixen: The Mask and the Reality.** London: Putnam, 1971. New York: Random House, 1972. p 218. Ill.

Henriksen, Liselotte. **Isak Dinesen: A Bibliography. Karen Blixen: En Bibliografi.** Copenhagen: Gyldendal, 1977. Annual supplement in *Blixeniana*, 1977-.

Johannesson, Eric O. **The World of Isak Dinesen.** Seattle: University of Washington Press, 1961. pp 168.

Jørgensen, Aage, ed. **Isak Dinesen, Storyteller.** Aarhus: Akademisk Boghandel, 1972. p 116. [10 essays by various authors.]

Langbaum, Robert. **The Gayety of Vision. A Study of Isak Dinesen's Art.** New York: Random House, London: Chatto and Windus, 1964. p 305.

Langbaum, Robert. **Isak Dinesen's Art. The Gayety of Vision.** Chicago and London: University of Chicago Press, 1975. [2nd ed. of *The Gayety of Vision*, 1964.]

Lasson, Frans, ed. **The Life and Destiny of Karen Blixen.** Collected and edited by Frans Lasson. Text and translation by Clara Svendsen. London: Michael Joseph, 1970. p 229. Ill. [*Karen Blixen. En Digterskæbne i Billeder*, 1969.]

Lasson, Frans, ed. **The Life and Destiny of Isak Dinesen.** Collected and edited by Frans Lassen. Text and translation by Clara Svendsen. New York: Random House, 1970. 2nd ed., London and Chicago: University of Chicago Press, 1976. p 229. Ill. [A Phoenix Edition.] [*Karen Blixen. En Digterskæbne i Billeder*, 1969.]

Migel, Parmenia. **Titania. The Biography of Isak Dinesen.** New York: Random House, 1967. p 327. Ill. London: Michael Joseph, 1968. p 256. Ill.

Svendsen, Clara, ed. **Isak Dinesen. A Memorial.** New York: Random House, 1964. p 209. [Contains 50 articles by various authors, not all in English.]

Trzebinski, Errol. **Silence Will Speak. A Study of the Life of Denys Finch Hatton and His Relationship with Karen Blixen.** London: Heinemann, 1977. p 348. Ill. Chicago: University of Chicago Press, 1978.

Whissen, Thomas Reed. **Isak Dinesen as Critic: A Study of the Critical Principles Contained in Her Major Works.** Ph. D. Dissertation, University of Cincinnati, 1969. p 184. [Diss. Abstr. 30, 1970.]

Whissen, Thomas R. **Isak Dinesen's Aesthetics.** London and Port Washington, N.Y.: Kennikat Press, 1973. p 130. [National University Publications: Series in Literary Criticism.]

THOMAS DINESEN (1892-1978)

Twilight on the Betzy. London: Putnam and Co., 1952. p 218. [*Syrenbusken*, novel, 1951.]

TOVE DITLEVSEN (1918-1976)

And It Was a Night. Tr. Martin S. Allwood. *MoDP* p 31. Also *TCScP* pp 91-92. [*Og det var en Nat*, poem from the collection *Blinkende Lygter*, 1947.]

Autumn. Tr. Nadia Christensen and Alexander Taylor. *Prism International* (Vancouver, B.C.) vol. 13, no. 2 (Winter 1973) p 17. [*Høst*, poem from the collection *Den hemmelige Rude*, 1961.]

The Dividing Line. Tr. Carol Gold. *SR* vol. 66, no. 2 (June 1978) pp 24-25. [*Skellet*, poem from the collection *De Voksne*, 1969.]

Divorce 1. Tr. Ann Freeman. *CDPo* pp 85-86. [*Skilsmisse 1*, poem from the collection *De Voksne*, 1969.]

Divorce 1. Tr. Lone and George Blecher. *SR* vol. 66, no. 2 (June 1978) pp 22-23. [*Skilsmisse 1*, poem from the collection *De Voksne*, 1969.]

Divorce 1. Tr. Anne Born. *Orbis* p 47. [*Skilsmisse 1*, poem from the collection *De Voksne*, 1969.]

Divorce 3. Tr. Ann Freemann. *CDPo* pp 90-91. [*Skilsmisse 3*, poem from the collection *De Voksne*, 1969.]

The Eternal Three. Tr. Martin S. Allwood, John Hollander and Inga Wilhelmsen Allwood. *MoDP* p 34. Also *TCScP* p 90. [*De evige tre*, poem from the collection *Lille Verden*, 1942.]

The Everlasting Three. Tr. Anne Born. *Orbis* pp 43-44. [*De evige tre*, poem from the collection *Lille Verden*, 1942.]

A Man's Love. Tr. Martin S. Allwood. *A Little Treasury* pp 512-513. [*En Mands Kærlighed*, poem from the collection *Blinkende Lygter*, 1947.]

Modus Operandi. Tr. Paula Hostrup-Jessen. *DI* pp 158-162. [*Måden*, short story from the collection *Den onde Lykke*, 1963.]

Morning. Tr. Nadia Christensen. *The Penguin Book of Women Poets.* London: Penguin, 1978. New York: Viking Press, 1979. pp 233-234. [*Morgenen er en Guds Gave*, poem from the collection *Det runde Værelse*, 1973.]

Mother Fear. Tr. Charles Wharton Stork. *SeBDV* p 146. [*Moderangst*, poem from the collection *Lille Verden*, 1942.]

A Mother's Anguish. Tr. Martin S. Allwood. *MoDP* p 32. Also *TCScP* pp 87-88. [*Moderangst*, poem from the collection *Lille Verden*, 1942.]

My Heart. Tr. Charles Wharton Stork. *SeBDV* p 147. [*Mit Hjerte*, poem included in the collection *Kærlighedsdigte*, 1949.]

The Old Folk. Tr. Nadia Christensen. *The Penguin Book of Women Poets.* London: Penguin, 1978. New York: Viking Press, 1979. p 235. [*De Gamle*, poem from the collection *Det runde Værelse*, 1973.]

Oranges. Tr. Carl Malmberg. *ASR* vol 51, no. 4 (December 1963) pp 427-431. [*Appelsiner*, short story from the collection *Dommeren*, 1948.]

Oranges. Tr. Ann and Peter Thornton. *CDPr* pp 353-357. [*Appelsiner*, short story from the collection *Dommeren*, 1948.]

The Parents. Tr. Anne Born. *Orbis* p 44. [*Forældrene*, poem from the collection *Den hemmelige Rude*, 1961.]

Prayer. Tr. Nadia Christensen. *Response* (Valparaiso, Ind.) vol. 14, no. 1 p 17. [*Bøn*, poem from the collection *Det runde Værelse*, 1973.]

The Round Room. Tr. Knud Mogensen. *CDPo* pp 88-89. [*Det runde Værelse*, poem from the collection by that name, 1973.]

Self-portrait 1. Tr. Ann Freeman. *CDPo* pp 92-93. Aslo *SR* vol. 66, no. 2 (June 1978) p 21, and *The Other Voice. Twentieth-Century Women's Poetry in Translation.* New York: W. W. Norton, 1976. p 27. [*Selvportræt 1*, poem from the collection *De Voksne*, 1969.]

Self-portrait 2. Tr. Ann Freeman. *The Other Voice. Twentieth-Century Women's Poetry in Translation.* New York: W. W. Norton, 1976. p 28. [*Selvportræt 2*, poem from the collection *De Voksne*, 1969.]

Self-portrait 2. Tr. Anne Born. *Orbis* p 46. [*Selvportræt 2*, poem from the collection *De Voksne*, 1969.]

Self-portrait 4. Tr. Ann Freemann. *CDPo* pp 93-94. [*Selvportræt 4*, poem from the collection *De Voksne*, 1969.]

The Snake in Paradise. Tr. Charles Wharton Stork. *SeBDV* p 148. Also *TCScP* pp 88-89. [*Slangen i Paradiset*, poem from collection *Pigesind*, 1939.]

62

Sunday. Tr. Knud Mogensen. *CDPo* pp 83-85. [*Søndag*, poem from the collection *Den hemmelige Rude*, 1961.]

To Grow Up. Tr. Mary Catherine Phinney. *LitR-Dk* pp 41-42. [*At vokse op*, poem from the collection *Den hemmelige Rude*, 1961.]

Visit. Tr. Christina Danesen. *SR* vol. 66, no. 2 (June 1978) pp 26-27. [*Besøg*, poem from the collection *Det runde Værelse*, 1973.]

When I Have Time. Tr. Anne Born. *Orbis* pp 44-46. [*Naar jeg faar Tid*, poem from the collection *De Voksne*, 1969.]

With No One. Tr. Nadia Christensen and Alexander Taylor. *Prism International* (Vancouver, B. C.) vol. 13, no. 2 (Winter 1973) p 16. [*Med ingen . .*, poem from the collection *De Voksne*, 1969.]

You Who Someone. Tr. Knud Mogensen. *CDPo* p 87. [*Du som ingen*, poem from the collection *Det runde Værelse*, 1973.]

Previous Translations:

Fear.
The Colony Garden.
The Blinking Lights.

HANS ANDREAS DJURHUUS
(1883-1951) Faroese author

Ocean Sang round Faroe Isles. Tr. R. P. Keigwin. *ASR* vol. 41, no. 3 (September 1953) p 232. [*Havið sang*, poem from the collection *Sjómannsrímur*, 1925.]

JENS HENDRIK OLIVER DJURHUUS (1881-1948)
Faroese author

Tova. Tr. Wayne O'Neil. *ASR* vol. 51, no. 2 (June 1963) p 182. [*Á halgum nattartima*, poem from the collection *Yrkingar*, 1914.]

AAGE DONS (b. 1903)

»Journey's End«. Tr. F. A. Rush. *CDPr* pp 282-291. [*»Alderstrøst«*, short story from the collection *Den gule Billedbog*, 1943.]

Where All Roads Meet. Tr. Evelyn Heepe. *MoDA* pp 102-124. [Extract from *Her mødes alle Veje*, novel, 1941.]

Previous Translations:

The Soldiers' Well.

HOLGER DRACHMANN
(1846-1908)

Amber. Tr. Charles Wharton Stork. *SeBDV* pp 61-62. Also *A Little Treasury* pp 510-511. [*Rav*, poem from the collection *Sange ved Havet*, 1877.]

Barcarolle. Tr. Robert Silliman Hillyer. *BoDV* pp 131-133. [*Rosenrøde Drømme*, poem from the collection *Ranker og Roser*, 1879.]

The Day When First I Saw Your Face. Tr. Robert Silliman Hillyer. *BoDV* pp 134-135. [*Den Dag, jeg første Gang dig saa*, poem from the collection *Sangenes Bog*, 1889.]

Dedication. Tr. Charles Wharton Stork. *SeBDV* pp 65-66. [Poem.]

Drink the Sweet Scent! Tr. Charles Wharton Stork. *SeBDV* pp 63-64. [Poem.]

I Hear in the Midnight. Tr. Robert Silliman Hillyer. *BoDV* pp 127-128. [*Jeg hører i Natten den vuggende*, poem from the collection *Sange ved Havet*, 1877.]

I Sit as I Have Always Sat. Tr. Charles Wharton Stork. *SeBDV* pp 64-65. [Part of the poem *Du retter tidt dit Øjepar*, from the collection *Ranker og Roser*, 1879.]

Improvisation on Board. Tr. R. S. Hillyer. *IDIWB* p 75. Also *BoDV* p 126. [*Improvisation om Bord*, poem the collection *Dæmpede Melodier*, 1875.]

Parting in Autumn. Tr. Charles Wharton Stork. *SeBDV* pp 60-61. [*Afsked i Høst*, poem from the collection *Sange ved Havet*, 1877.]

The Room Sank in Silence. Tr. Robert Silliman Hillyer. *BoDV* pp 130-131. [*Farlige Drømme*, poem the collection *Ranker og Roser*, 1879.]

Sakuntala. Tr. Robert Silliman Hillyer. *BoDV* pp 128-129. [*Sakuntala*, poem from the collection *Ranker og Roser*, 1879.]

Sakuntala. Tr. R. P. Keigwin. *IDIWB* pp 77-79. [*Sakuntala*, poem from the collection *Ranker og Roser*, 1879.]

There Wells Up Sound. Tr. Robert Silliman Hillyer. *BoDV* pp 133-134. [*Der vælder Lyd*, poem from the collection *Sangenes Bog*, 1889.]

Valborg Song. Tr. Robert Silliman Hillyer. *BoDV* pp 135-137. [*Valborgs-Sangen*, poem from the collection *Sangenes Bog*, 1889.]

Völund the Smith. Tr. Robert Silliman Hillyer. *BoDV* pp 137-138. [*Vølund*, poem from the collection *Sangenes Bog*, 1889.]

The Wild Red Wine. Tr. Charles Wharton Stork. *SeBDV* pp 62-63. [*Den røde vilde Vin*, poem from the collection *Sangenes Bog*, 1889.]

Previous Translations:

The Cruise of the »Wild Duck«, and Other Tales.
Paul and Virginia of a Northern Zone.
Robert Burns.
Nanna. A Story of Danish Love.
The MountainRuin.
New York.
The Ship-Rats.
Androcles and the Lion.
On the Atlantic.
Renaissance, Melodrama.
To August Strindberg.
The Dead Man's Boots.
Byron in Homespun.
These Proud Men and Who Are They.
The Fiddle.
A Ship in Church.
The Bumble Bee.

CARL EWALD (1856-1908)

The Battle of the Bees and Other Stories. Tr. and adapted from the Danish by Margaret Sperry. Ill. Lily R. Phillips. New York: Crane Russak, 1977. p 114. Ill. [Seven short stories about nature.]

My Little Boy. *J. L. News* (J. Lauritzen Lines, Copenhagen) no. 39 (1959) pp 19-20. [From *Min lille Dreng*, short novel, 1899.]

My Little Boy, My Big Girl. Tr. Beth Bolling. New York: Horizon Press, 1962. p 190. [*Min lille Dreng*, 1889, *Min store Pige*, 1904, two short novels.]

The Stone of the Mistletoe. Tr. Margaret Sperry. Copenhagen: Arnold Buscks Boghandel, 1951. p 22.

Previous Translations:

Two Legs, and Other Stories.
The Queen Bee, and Other Nature Stories.
The Old Room.
The Pond, and Other Stories.
The Four Seasons.
The Old Willow-Tree, and Other Stories.
The Old Post, and Other Nature Stories.
The Twelve Sisters, and Other Stories.

JOHANNES EWALD (1743-1781)   *63*

King Christian. Tr. H. W. Longfellow. *AScL* pp 41-42. [*Kong Kristian stod ved højen Mast*, poem from the tragedy *Fiskerne*, 1780, which has become the Danish national anthem.]

King Christian. (First and last verses). Tr. R. P. Keigwin. *IDIWB* pp 21-23. [*Kong Kristian stod ved højen Mast*, poem from the tragedy *Fiskerne*, 1780.]

Lament over the Dead Balder. Tr. George Borrow. *AScL* pp 42-43. [Poem from the tragedy *Balders Død*, 1775.]

Little Gunver. Tr. Charles Wharton Stork. *SeBDV* pp 3-4. Also *AScL* pp 44-45. [*Liden Gunver*, poem from the play *Fiskerne*, 1780.]

Ode to the Soul. Tr. John A. Dussinger. *ADL* pp 135-143. [*Til Sielen. En Ode*, poem, 1780.]

The Three Valkyries. Tr. Charles Wharton Stork. *SeBDV* pp 3-4. [*Over Bierg, over Dal*, (Tercet), poem from the tragedy *Balders Død*, 1775.]

Previous Translations:

From High the Seaman's Wearied Sight.
The Wishes.
Song.
Lament.
The Conqueror of Death.
The Death of Balder.
The Seaman.
The Eider-Goose.
Extract from »Life and Opinions«.

Works about Johannes Ewald

Carter, John Wayflete and Henry Graham Pollard. **The Mystery of »The Death of Balder« (by Johannes Ewald).** Oxford: B. H. Blackwell, 1969. p 21. Ill. [Working paper, no. 3.]

Greenway, John L. **The Two Worlds of Johannes Ewald: »Dyd« vs. Myth in »Balders Død«.** *Scandinavian Studies* vol. 42, no. 4 (November 1970) pp 394-409.

LECK FISCHER (1904-1956)

The King's Face. Tr. Eileen MacLeod. *CDPr* pp 292-296. [*Kongens Ansigt*, short story from a collection of the same name, 1943.]

The Mystery Tour. Tr. J. F. S. Pearce. *CDPl* pp 401-428. [*Selskabsrejsen*, play, 1949.]

64 OTTO FØNSS (1853-1922)

Shooting Stars. Tr. Charles Wharton Stork. *SeBDV* pp 72-73. [Poem.]

PETER FREUCHEN (1886-1957)

Adventures in the Arctic. Ed. Dagmar Freuchen. Canada: Copp Clark Publishing Co.; New York: Julian Messner, 1960. p 383. Ill. [Excerpts from the earlier works of Peter Freuchen, especially *Arctic Adventure.*]

The Arctic Year. By P. Freuchen and Finn Salomonsen. New York: G. P. Putnam's Sons, 1958. London: Jonathan Cape, 1959. p 438. Ill.

A Front Moves North. Tr. Lydia Cranfield. *Nor* vol. 8, no. 3 (May-June 1950) pp 145-152. [Article.]

I Sailed with Rasmussen. Tr. Arnold Andersen. New York: Julian Messner, 1958. p 224. Ill. [Story of Peter Freuchen's friendship with Knud Rasmussen and a tribute to him.]

Ice Floes and Flaming Water. A True Adventure in Melville Bay. Tr. Johan Hambro. New York: Julian Messner, 1954. p 242. London: Victor Gollancz, 1955. p 251. London: Landsborough Publications, 1959. p 221. [Landsborough ed., Four Square Book no. 138.]

Ivalu. The Eskimo Wife. Tr. James Juztis and Edward Price Ehrlich. New York: AMS Press, 1975. p 332. [Originally published in 1936.]

The Law of Larion. Tr. Evelyn Ramsden. New York: McGraw-Hill Book Co., 1952. London: Evans Bros., 1954. p 313. London: Transworld Publishers, 1956. p 380. [Transworld ed., Corgi Books no. G178.] [*Larions Lov*, novel, 1948.]

The Legend of Daniel Williams. New York: Julian Messner, 1956. London: Robert Hale, 1958. p 256.

Men of the Frozen North. Ed. and with a preface by Dagmar Freuchen. Canada: Nelson, Foster and Scott; Cleveland and New York: World Publishing Co., 1962. p 315.

The Peter Freuchen Reader. New York: Julian Messner, 1965. [Includes selections from *Vagrant Viking, Book of the Seven Seas, Arctic Adventure, Eskimo.*]

Peter Freuchen's Book of the Eskimos. Ed. and with a preface by Dagmar Freuchen. Canada: Nelson, Foster and Scott; Cleveland and New York: World Publishing Co., 1961. London: Arthur Barker, 1962. p 441. Ill. New York: Fawcett Crest, 1969.

Peter Freuchen's Book of the Seven Seas. By P. Freuchen with David Loth. New York: Messner, 1957. p 512. London: Jonathan Cape, 1958. p 512. Ill. New York: Simon and Schuster, 1968. Garden City, N.Y.: Nelson, Doubleday, 1958. [Best-in-Books series.]

The Sea Tyrant. Tr. Edwin Bjorkman. Abridged ed. New York: Pyramid Books, 1953. p 158. Also New York: Paperback Library, 1962. p 224.

The Story of the Remarkable Man Who Married a Fox. Tr. John Poole. *CDPr* p 179-185. [*Historien om en mærkelig Mand, som giftede sig med en Ræv*, short story from the collection *Eskimofortællinger*, 1944.]

Vagrant Viking: My Life and Adventures. Tr. Johan Hambro. New York: Julian Messner, 1953. London: Victor Gollancz, 1954. p 422. London: Pan Books, 1958. p 379. [Pan Books no. X18.]

Previous Translations:

The Sea Tyrant.
Eskimo.
Arctic Adventure. My Life in the Frozen North.
It's All Adventure.

Works about Peter Freuchen

Norman, Carl. **Peter Freuchen.** *Nor* vol. 16, no. 1 (January-February 1958) p 49.

KAI FRIIS MØLLER (1888-1960)

Song of the Figurehead. Tr. Charles Wharton Stork. *SeBDV* pp 111-114. [*Galionsfigurens Sang*, poem from the collection *Digte*, 1910.]

Previous Translations:

In an Autumn Rose Garden.
When Kipling's »Mandalay« Was a National Anthem.

H. GABRIELSEN

I Love the Sunset Hour of Rest. Tr. S. D. Rodholm. *HoS* p 48. [*Jeg elsker Aftenstundens Fred*, poem written in 1891, published in *Den dansk-amerikanske Højskolesangbog*, 1901.

CHARLES GANDRUP (1847-1911)

Happiness. Tr. S. D. Rodholm. *HoS* p 126. Also *HinS* hymn no. 82. [*Lykken er ikke Gods eller Guld*, poem written 1907, published in *Danmarks Melodier*, 1912.]

OTTO GELSTED (1888-1968)

April 9th. Tr. R. P. Keigwin. *TCScP* pp 54-55. [*Den niende April*, poem from the collection *De danske Strande*, 1940.]
Carriage Ride. Tr. Nadia Christensen. *CDPo* p 27. [*Køretur*, poem from the collection *Jomfru Gloriant*, 1923.]
A Drive. Tr. Charles Wharton Stork. *SeBDV* pp 115-116. [*Køretur*, poem from the collection *Jomfru Gloriant*, 1923.]
The Ninth of April. Tr. Charles Wharton Stork. *SeBDV* p 115. [*Den niende April*, poem from the collection *De danske Strande*, 1940.]
Poem. Tr. Isak Dinesen. In Isak Dinesen, *Shadows on the Grass*. London: Michael Joseph, 1960. New York: Random House, 1961. pp 102-103. [3 stanzas from the poetry collection *Aldrig var Dagen så lys*, 1959.]
The Show Boat. Tr. R. P. Keigwin. *TCScP* pp 52-54. Also *CDPo* pp 28-30. [*Reklameskibet*, poem from the collection *Jomfru Gloriant*, 1923.]

Previous Translations:

A Visit.
Danish Art Today.

JUL. CHR. GERSON (1811-1894)

A Little Nis. Tr. S. D. Rodholm. *HoS* p 179. [*Den største Mand*, poem from the collection *Digte for Børn*, 1845.]

ROLF GJEDSTED (b. 1947)

Dawn. Tr. Rolf Gjedsted. *CDPo* p 311. [*Gry*, poem from the collection *Trodsige Bekendelser*, 1972.]
Insanity. Tr. Rolf Gjedsted. *CDPo* p 312. [*Galskab*, poem from the collection *Saturnalia*, 1974.]

Old Water. Tr. Rolf Gjedsted. *CDPo* p 310. [*Gammelt Vand*, poem from the collection *Trodsige Bekendelser*, 1972.]
Rain. Tr. Rolf Gjedsted. *CDPo* p 311. [*Regn*, poem from the collection *Skønhedsreservatet*, 1973.]
Salt. Tr. Rolf Gjedsted. *CDPo* p 312. [*Salt*, poem from the collection *Saturnalia*, 1974.]

65

KARL GJELLERUP (1857-1919)

Love Rides the Lion. Tr. Charles Wharton Stork. *SeBDV* pp 82-83. [*Amors Løveridt*, poem from the collection *Min Kjærligheds Bog*, 1889.]
O, Let Me Kiss. Tr. Charles Wharton Stork. *SeBDV* p 83. [Poem.]
A Pair. Tr. Charles Wharton Stork. *SeBDV* p 84. [*Et Par*, poem from *Min Kjærligheds Bog*, 1889.]

Previous Translations:

The Pilgrim Kamanita.
Minna.

MEÏR GOLDSCHMIDT (1819-1887)

The Battle of Marengo. Tr. P. M. Mitchell and Kenneth H. Ober. *RG* pp 25-33. [From *Livs Erindringer og Resultater*, 1877.]
Bewitched, Based on a Legend. Tr. Kenneth Ober. *ADL* pp 243-261. [*Bjergtagen, Efter et Sagn*, novel, 1868.]
Maser: An Episode from Simon Levi's Life. Tr. P. M. Mitchell and Kenneth H. Ober. *RG* pp 34-76. [*Maser*, short story from *Smaa Fortællinger*, 1868.]

Previous Translations:

The Jew of Denmark. [En Jøde.]
Homeless, or, A Poet's Inner Life.
The Heir.
The Society of Virtue at Rome.
The Flying Mail.
Henrik and Rosalie.
Avromche Nightingale.

66 Works about Meïr Goldschmidt

Møller, Kai Friis. **Denmark at the 1851 Exhibition - and the Festival. The Conversion of Meïr Goldschmidt.** *Denmark. A Monthly Review of Anglo-Danish Relations* (November 1951) pp 1-2 and 13-15.

Ober, Kenneth H. **Meir Goldschmidt.** Boston: Twayne, 1976. p 146. [World Authors series.]

Ober, Kenneth H. **Meir Goldschmidt as a Writer of English.** *Orbis Litterarum* (Copenhagen) vol. 29 (1974) pp 231-244.

VILHELM GREGERSEN (1848-1929)

Christmas Snow. Tr. S. D. Rodholm. *HoS* p 101. Also *HinS* hymn no. 25. [*Sne, Sne, dejlige Julesne!* poem published in *Danmarks Melodibog*, v. 5, 1932.]

Our Father Has Light in His Window. Tr. J. C. Aaberg. *HinS* hymn no. 66. [*Vor Fader har Lys i sit Vindue,* poem from the collection, *Paa Vejen hjem*, 1895.]

There Is Something Inspiring. Tr. S. D. Rodholm. *HoS* pp 99-100. [*Der er noget i Luften*, poem from the collection *Vintergæk*, 1911.]

ELSA GRESS (b. 1919)

Ditto Daughter? *PW* pp 69-114. [Play written and first published in English. Later published in Danish as *Ditto Datter, en Fantasi*, in *Dæmoniske Damer og andre Figurer*, 1979.]

Philoctetes Wounded and Other Plays. Glumsø, Denmark: Decenter, 1969. p 168 ill. Individual plays listed separately under *PW*.

Philoctetes Wounded. *PW* pp 5-68. [Play written and first published in English. Later published in Danish as *Den sårede Filoktet*, in *Dæmoniske Damer og andre Figurer*, 1979.]

Revolt. Tr. Nadia Christensen. *ASR* vol. 62, no. 3 (September 1974) pp 298-301. [*Oprør*, short story from the anthology *Pejlemærker*, 1951.]

3:3 = 3. *PW* pp 115-168. [Play written and published in English.]

Previous Translations:

Waiting.

VILHELM GRØNBECH (1873-1948)

Religious Currents in the Nineteenth Century. Tr. P. M. Mitchell and W. D. Paden. Lawrence: University of Kansas Press, 1964. p 201. [*Religiøse Strømninger i det nittende Aarhundrede*, 1922.]

Works about Vilhelm Grønbech

Mitchell, P. M. **Vilhelm Grønbech, Synthesist.** *SS* vol. 38, no. 4 (November 1966) pp 318--330.

Mitchell, P. M. **Vilhelm Grønbech.** Boston: Twayne, 1978. p 162. [World Authors series no. 397.]

NICOLAI FREDERIK SEVERIN GRUNDTVIG (1783-1872)

About Folk-Life and Dr. Rudelbach. Tr. Johannes Knudsen. *SW-Gr* pp 44-48. [Essay, 1848.]

All Saints' Day. Tr. Enok Mortensen. *SW-Gr* pp 88-93. [Sermon, 1839.]

As Temple Walls Anew Were Rising. Tr. Johannes Knudsen. *HinS* hymn no. 58. [*Foragter ei de ringe Dage,* hymn from the collection *Sang-Værk* I, 1837.]

The Awakening in the Church. Tr. S. D. Rodholm. *HoS* pp 76-77. [*Herren han har besøgt sit Folk,* hymn from the collection *Sang-Værk* I, 1837.]

A Babe Is Born in Bethlehem. Tr. J. C. Aaberg. *HinS* hymn no. 16. [*Jule-Sang for christne Børn,* poem published in *Nyeste Skilderie af Kjøbenhavn,* 23. dec. 1820.]

Baptismal Hymn. Tr. S. D. Rodholm. *HoS* p 72. [*O, lad din Aand,* hymn from the collection *Sang-Værk* I, 1837.]

Basic Christian Teachings. The Christian Signs of Life. Tr. Johannes Knudsen. *SW-Gr* pp 54-63. [Essay from *Den christelige Børnelærdom,* 1855-61.]

Basic Christian Teachings. The Christian, the Spiritual, and the Eternal Life. Tr. Johannes Knudsen. *SW-Gr* pp 64-73. [Essay from *Den christelige Børnelærdom,* 1855-61.]

Basic Christian Teachings. The Christianity of the New Testament. Tr. Johannes Knudsen. *SW-Gr* pp 49-53. [Essay from *Den christelige Børnelærdom,* 1855-61.]

Basic Christian Teachings. The Innate and the Reborn Humanity. Tr. Johannes Knudsen. *SW-Gr* pp 74-79. [Essay from *Den christelige Børnelærdom,* 1855-61.]

Basic Christian Teachings. The Word of Eternal Life from the Mouth of the Lord to the Church. Tr. Johannes Knudsen. *SW-Gr* pp 80-81. [Essay from *Den christelige Børnelærdom*, 1855-61.]

Blossom as a Rose. Tr. S. D. Rodholm. *HoS* pp 62-63. [*Blomstre som en Rosengaard*, hymn published in the collection *Sang-Værk* I, 1837.]

Blossom Shall the Wilderness. Tr. Søren D. Rodholm. First verse rev. Johannes Knudsen. *SW-Gr* pp 108-111. Also *HinS* hymn no. 14. [*Blomstre som en Rosengaard*, poem published in the collection *Sang-Værk* I, 1837.]

Bright and Glorious Is the Sky. Tr. J. C. Aaberg. *HinS* hymn no. 15. [*Dejlig er den Himmel blaa*, poem from the collection *Kvædlinger*, 1815.]

Childhood Churchbell, for the Joy You Brought Me. Tr. Johannes Knudsen. *HinS* hymn no. 55. [*Kirkeklokke*, hymn published in *Dansk Kirketidende*, 19. okt. 1845.]

Christ Arose in Glory. Tr. Ingvard M. Andersen. *HinS* hymn no. 40. [*Christ stod op af Døde*, hymn from the collection *Sang-Værk* I, 1837.]

The Christmas Chimes, so Bold and Blest. Tr. Johannes Knudsen. *HinS* hymn no. 19. [*Det kimer nu til Julefest*, poem published in *Nyeste Skilderie af Kjøbenhavn*, 23. dec. 1817.]

Christus Liberator. Tr. S. D. Rodholm. *HoS* p 110. [*Tvang til Tro er Snak i Taaget*, hymn from the collection *Sang-Værk* I, 1837.]

The Church Bell. Tr. Lise-Lone Marker. *ADL* pp 155-157. [*Kirkeklokke*, hymn published in *Dansk Kirketidende*, 19. okt. 1845.]

The Church-bell. Tr. R. P. Keigwin. *IDIWB* pp 39-41. [*Kirkeklokke*, hymn published in *Dansk Kirketjeneste*, 19. okt. 1845.]

The Churchbell. Tr. S. D. Rodholm. *HoS* pp 80-81. [*Kirkeklokke*, hymn published in *Dansk Kirketidende*, 19. okt. 1845.]

Cradling Children in His Arm. Tr. Johannes Knudsen. *HinS* hymn no. 59. [*Herren strækker ud sin Arm*, hymn from the collection *Sang-Værk* I, 1837.]

The Danish High School. Tr. Johannes Knudsen. *SW-Gr* pp 160-165. [Essay, 1847.]

Dare We Yet Recall the Tender . . . Tr. Johannes Knudsen. *SW-Gr* pp 133-134. Also *HinS* hymn no. 57. [*Tør end Nogen ihukomme*, poem published in *Theologisk Maanedsskrift*, III, 1825.]

The Day. Tr. S. D. Rodholm. *HoS* pp 57-58. [*Den signede Dag*, hymn from the collection *Danske Høitids-Psalmer*, 1826.]

Day Song. Tr. S. Foster Damon. *BoDV* pp 55-57. [*Den signede Dag*, poem from the collection *Danske Høitids-Psalmer*, 1826.]

Denmark's Consolation. Tr. S. Foster Damon. *BoDV* pp 50-51. [*Danmarks Trøst (Langt højere Bjerge)*, poem published in *Sange til den 10de April, 1820*, ed. R. Nyerup, 1820.]

Dreams and Reality. Tr. S. D. Rodholm. *HoS* pp 111-112. [*Tør end Nogen ihukomme*, poem published in *Theologisk Maanedsskrift*, III, 1825.]

Easter. Tr. S. D. Rodholm. *HoS* p 87. [*Som Foraars-Solen morgenrød*, hymn published in *Psalmer til den stille Uge og Paasken*, 1846.]

Echo of the Lay of Bjarke. Tr. Lise-Lone Marker. *ADL* p 155. [First stanza of *Bjarkemaalets Efterklang (Soel er oppe)*, poem published in *Danne-Virke*, 3, 1817.]

8th Sunday after Trinity. Tr. Enok Mortensen. *SW-Gr* pp 108-111. [Sermon, 1855.]

18th Sunday after Trinity. Tr. Enok Mortensen. *SW-Gr* pp 94-99. [Sermon, 1845.]

Evening Prayer. Tr. S. D. Rodholm. *HoS* p 49. [*Søde Gud, din Engleskare*, prayer first published in *Kvædlinger*, 1815, final version in *Sang-Værk* IV, 1875.]

Fair beyond Telling. Tr. Jens C. Aaberg. Tr. rev. Johannes Knudsen. *SW-Gr* pp 124-125. Also *HinS* hymn no. 29. [Hymn.]

Faith, Hope, and Love. Tr. S. D. Rodholm. *HoS* p 91. [*O, Kristelighed*, hymn published in *Historiske Psalmer og Riim*, ed. L. C. Hagen, 1832.]

Folk-Life and Christianity. Tr. Johannes Knudsen. *SW-Gr* pp 37-43. [Essay, 1847.]

4th Sunday after Easter. Tr. Enok Mortensen. *SW-Gr* pp 112-116. [Sermon, 1855.]

God Planted a Garden from East to West. Tr. Johannes Knudsen. *HinS* hymn no. 108. [*Gud planted en Have fra Øst til Vest*, hymn from the collection *Sang-Værk* II, 1839-41.]

God's Angels of Joy, We Welcome You. Tr. and adapted by Johannes Knudsen. *SW-Gr* pp 137-138. Also *HinS* hymn no. 18. [*Velkommen igjen, Guds Engle smaa*, poem from the collection *Christelige Prædikener eller Søndags-Bog*, III, 1830.]

God's Blessing Falling on the Earth. Tr. Johannes Knudsen. *SW-Gr* p 140. Also *HinS* hymn no. 65. [*Velsignelse, al Jordens Tarv*, hymn from the collection *Kirkelig Samler*, 8, 1862.]

God's Little Child, What Troubles Thee? Tr. Jens C. Aaberg. *SW-Gr* pp 136-137. Also *HinS* hymn no. 56. [*Lille Guds Barn*, poem published in *Nytaarsgave*, ed. Ernst Trier, 1870.]

God's People Receive. Tr. Søren D. Rodholm. Tr. rev. Johannes Knudsen. *SW-Gr* pp 123-124. Also *HinS* hymn no. 52. [Hymn based on *O, deilige Land*, published in *Historiske Salmer og Riim*, ed. L. C. Hagen, 1832.]

68

God's Word Is Our Great Heritage. Tr. Johannes Knudsen. *SW-Gr* pp 139-140. Also *HinS* hymn no. 70. [*Guds Ord, det er vort Arvegods,* st. 5 of *Guds Kirke er vor Klippe-Borg,* hymn from the collection *Sang-Værk* I, 1837.]

Golden Light of Morning Bright. Tr. Fred C. M. Hansen. *HinS* hymn no. 5. [*Morgenstund har Guld i Mund,* hymn from the collection *Fest-Psalmer,* 1853.]

Good Friday. Tr. Enok Mortensen. *SW-Gr* pp 104-107. [Sermon, 1855.]

Grant Me, God, the Gift of Singing. Tr. Johannes Knudsen. *SW-Gr* pp 132-133. Also *HinS* hymn no. 26. [*Giv mig, Gud, en Psalme-Tunge,* hymn from the collection *Sang-Værk* I, 1837.]

The Harrowing of Hell. Tr. S. Foster Damon. *BoDV* pp 51-55. [*I Kveld blev der banket paa Helvedes Port,* hymn from the collection *Sang-Værk* I, 1837.]

Harvest Hymn. Tr. S. D. Rodholm. *HoS* pp 82-83. [*Høst-Sang,* 1844.]

Holy Spirit, Still Our Sorrow. Tr. Jens C. Aaberg. *SW-Gr* pp 131-132. Also *HinS* hymn no. 48. [*Kom, Gud Helligaand,* poem from the collection *Sang-Værk* I, 1837.]

Human First. Tr. S. D. Rodholm. *HoS* pp 121-122. [Adaptation of *Ingen har Guldtaarer fældet,* poem from the collection *Christendommens Syvstjerne,* 1860.]

I Was a Lad Keeping Watch o'er the Sheep. Tr. Johannes Knudsen. *HinS* hymn no. 90.

In Our Midst God's Kingdom Liveth. Tr. Johannes Knudsen. *SW-Gr* pp 126-127. Also *HinS* hymn no. 54. [Hymn.]

In the Warmth of Sunlight the Plants Unfold. Tr. Johannes Knudsen. *SW-Gr* pp 143-144. Also *HinS* hymn no. 76. [Hymn.]

Inscription on the Monument in Odde Churchyard to the 62 from the Crew of the Prince Christian Who Fell in the Battle of Zealand's Odde, March 22nd 1808. Tr. R. P. Keigwin. *IDIWB* p 41. [*Indskriften paa Monumentet paa Oddens Kirkegaard for de 62 af Prinds Kristian's Besætning, som faldt i Kampen ved Sjællands Odde den 22. Marts 1808.*]

Introduction to »Nordic Mythology«. Tr. Johannes Knudsen. *SW-Gr* pp 20-36. [Essay, 1832.]

King Pharaoh Was Quite a Wicked Old Man. Tr. Johannes Knudsen. *HinS* hymn no. 89. [*Moses og Pharao,* poem from the collection *Sang-Værk* II, 1839.]

The Land of the Living. Tr. John Jepson Egglishaw. *Nor* vol. 10, no. 2 (March-April 1952) pp 124-125. [*De Levendes Land,* poem written ca. 1824, published in its final version in *Poetiske Skrifter,* V, 1883.]

The Last Farewell to Life on Earth. Tr. Johannes Knudsen. *SW-Gr* pp 138-139. [Hymn.]

A Letter concerning the Folk High School to Peter Larsen Skræppenborg in Dons. Tr. Johannes Knudsen. *SW-Gr* pp 171-175. [Letter, 1848.]

Lullaby. Tr. R. P. Keigwin. *IDIWB* p 43. [*Aandelig Vugge-Vise,* poem from the collection *Psalmer og Sange til Julen,* comp. by J. F. og R. Th. Fenger, 1845.]

Man First and then Christian. Tr. Johannes Knudsen. *SW-Gr* pp 140-141. [*Menneske først og christen saa,* poem written in 1837 and published in *Salmer og Aandelige Sange,* 5, 1881.]

Most Wondrous Is of All on Earth. Tr. Jean Fraser. *SW-Gr* pp 125-126. Also in *Cantate Domino.* Geneva, Switzerland: World Student Christian Federation, 1951. [Hymn.]

Niels Ebbesen. Tr. Charles Wharton Stork. *SeBDV* pp 6-9. [*Niels Ebbesen,* poem, *En ganske ny Vise om den mandhaftige jyske Ridder . . .,* poem published separately in 1839.]

A Nordic University. Tr. Ernest D. Nielsen. *SW-Gr* pp 176-180. [Essay, 1837.]

O Day Full of Grace, Which We Behold. Tr. Carl Døving. Last verse tr. Johannes Knudsen. *SW-Gr* pp 121-122. [*Den signede Dag,* hymn from the collection *Danske Høitids-Psalmer,* 1826.]

O Holy Spirit, Come, We Pray. Adapted by N. F. S. Grundtvig from Martin Luther. Tr. P. C. Paulsen. *SW-Gr* pp 129-130. [*Nu bede vi den Hellig-Aand,* hymn from the collection *Sang-Værk* I, 1837.]

Palm Sunday. Tr. Enok Mortensen. *SW-Gr* pp 100-103. [Sermon, 1855.]

A Plain and Active Joyful Life on Earth. Tr. Johannes Knudsen. *SW-Gr* pp 141-142. Also *HinS* hymn no. 75. [*Et jævnt og muntert, virksomt Liv paa Jord,* poem published in *Brage og Idun* IV, 1841; expanded version in *Sange for den kristelige Folke-Skole,* 1874.]

Relentlessly the Human Story. Tr. Johannes Knudsen. *SW-Gr* pp 142-143. Also *HinS* hymn no. 88. [Hymn.]

The Response of the Church. Tr. Johannes Knudsen. *SW-Gr* pp 11-19. [Essay, 1825.]

The School for Life. Tr. Ernest D. Nielsen. *SW-Gr* pp 151-157 [Essay, 1838.]

Selected Writings. Ed. and intro. Johannes Knudsen. Tr. Johannes Knudsen, Enok Mortensen, Ernest D. Nielsen. Philadelphia: Fortress Press, 1976. p 184. Individual writings listed separately under *SW-Gr.*

Simplicity of Love. Tr. S. D. Rodholm. *HoS* p 162. [*Et jævnt og muntert, virksomt Liv paa*

Jord, poem published in *Brage og Idun*, IV, 1841; expanded version in *Sange for den kristelige Folke-Skole*, 1874.]

Sleep, My Child. Tr. S. D. Rodholm. *HoS* pp 50-51. [*Sov sødt, Barnlille*, hymn published in *Psalmer og Sange til Julen*, 1845.]

The Speech before the Constitutional Assembly. Tr. Ernest D. Nielsen. *SW-Gr* pp 166-170. [Speech, 1848.]

Spirit of God, Sent from Heaven Abroad. Tr. Johannes Knudsen. *SW-Gr* pp 128-129. Also *HinS* hymn no. 45. [Hymn.]

Spirit Who Unites in Love. Tr. S. D. Rodholm. *HoS* p 69. [*Kærligheds og Sandheds Aand*, hymn from the collection *Sang-Værk* I, 1837.]

The Sun Now Shines in All Its Splendor. Tr. S. D. Rodholm. *SW-Gr* pp 127-128. Also *HoS* pp 59-60, and *HinS* hymn no. 44. [*I al sin Glands nu straaler Solen*, hymn from the collection *Fest-Psalmer*, 5. udg., 1853.]

Thinking of a Faithful Friend. Tr. S. D. Rodholm. *HoS* p 73. [*Mindes vi en fuldtro Ven*, hymn from the collection *Sang-Værk* I, 1837.]

This Is the Day Which the Lord Has Given. Tr. J. C. Aaberg. *HinS* hymn no. 28. [*Denne er Dagen, som Herren har gjort*, hymn from the collection *Sang-Værk* I, 1837.]

Throughout the Years the Church Does Stand. Tr. Carl Døving. First line altered. *SW-Gr* pp 122-123. Also *HinS* hymn no. 51. [*Kirken, den er et gammelt Huus*, hymn from the collection *Sang-Værk* I, 1837.]

Trust. Tr. S. D. Rodholm. *HoS* p 94. Also *HinS* hymn no. 69. [*Alt staar i Guds Faderhaand*, poem published in *Dansk Kirketidende*, 7. sept.1856.]

Welcome Here, New Year of Grace. Tr. Ingvard M. Andersen. *HinS* hymn no. 50. [*Vær Velkommen, Herrens Aar*, poem published separately 2. dec. 1849, and in the collection *Sang-Værk* IV, 1875.]

The Word. Tr. and adaption S. D. Rodholm. *HoS* p 61. [Hymn.]

Worship the Lord and Remember His Kindness. Tr. and adaptation S. D. Rodholm. *HinS* hymn no. 27. [*Lovsynger Herren*, hymn from the collection *Sang-Værk* I, 1837.]

Zechariah 4. (As Temple Walls Anew Were Rising). Tr. Johannes Knudsen. *SW-Gr* pp 134-135. [*Foragter ei de ringe Dage*, hymn from the collection *Sang-Værk* I, 1837.]

Previous Translations:

Bibliotheca Anglo-Saxonica.
Song of Praise.
Faith, Hope and Charity.

Autumn.
Sabbath Morn.
Baptism.
Jesus Stretches Forth His Hand.
Our Mothertongue.
Long Hast Thou Stood, O Church of God.
Love is Life's True Crown and Glory.
Suffer the Children to Come to Me.
The Lord is in His Holy Place.

Works about N. F. S. Grundtvig

Allchin, A. M. **Grundtvig's Translations from the Greek.** *The Eastern Churches Quarterly* (St. Augustine's Abbey, Ramsgate) vol. 14 (1961-62) pp 28-44.

Allchin, A. M. **The Hymns of N. F. S. Grundtvig.** *The Eastern Churches Quarterly* (St. Augustine's Abbey, Ramsgate) vol. 12 (1959) pp 129-143.

Bredsdorff, Elias. **Grundtvig in Cambridge.** *Nor* vol. 10, no. 2 (March-April 1952) pp 114-123.

Fain, E. F. **Nationalist Origins of the Folk High School: The Romantic Visions of N. F. S. Grundtvig.** *British Journal of Educational Studies*, vol. 19 (Fall 1971) pp 70-90.

Grattan, Hartley. **Meaning of Grundtvig: Skill plus Culture.** *Antioch Review* vol. 18, no. 1 (1958) pp 78-86.

Grundtvig Studier 1973. Copenhagen: Danske Boghandleres Kommissionsanstalt, 1973. [Contains the following articles in English: Bjerre, Sv. Erik: *Grundtvig, the Danish Folk High School, and the Developing Countries.* Ehnevid, Tord: *The Dominant Peoples in History according to Grundtvig and Hegel.* Harbsmeier, Götz: *Grundtvig and Germany.* Thaning, Kaj: *Grundtvig, an Introduction.*]

Høirup, Henning. **Grundtvig and Kierkegaard: Their Views of the Church.** *Theology Today* (Princeton, N. J.) vol. 12, no. 3 (1955) pp 328-342. Also in *Grundtvig Studier 1956* pp 7-20.

Jones, Llewellyn. **Grundtvig as a Scandinavian Precursor of Humanism.** *Humanist* (Schenectady, N. Y.) vol. 13, no. 1 (January-February 1953) pp 34-36.

Jones, Llewellyn. **Kierkegaard or Grundtvig?** *Christian Century* (Chicago) vol. 69 (1952), no. 20 pp 588-589; no. 23 pp 674-675.

Knudsen, Johannes. **Danish Rebel. A Study of N. F. S. Grundtvig.** Philadelphia, Pa.: Muhlenberg Press, 1955. p 242.

Knudsen, Johannes. **Grundtvig and American Theology Today.** *Lutheran World* vol. 1, no. 4 (1954-1955) pp 277-287.

70

Knudsen, Johannes. **Grundtvig and Mythology.** *Lutheran Quarterly* (Gettysburg, Pa.) vol. 6, no. 4 (1954) pp 299-309.

Knudsen, Johannes. **Grundtvig Research.** *Lutheran Quarterly* (Gettysburg, Pa.) vol. 5, no. 2 (1953) p 167.

Knudsen, Johannes. **Grundtvig's Educational Writings.** *SW-Gr* pp 147-150.

Knudsen, Johannes. **Grundtvig's Hymns and Poetry.** *SW-Gr* pp 119-121.

Knudsen, Johannes. **Revelation and Man according to N. F. S. Grundtvig.** *Lutheran Quarterly* (Gettysburg, Pa.) vol. 10, no. 3 (1958) pp 217-225.

Koch, Hal. **Grundtvig.** Tr. from the Danish and with intro. and notes by Llewellyn Jones. Yellow Springs, Ohio: Antioch Press, 1952. p 231.

Lindhardt, Poul Georg. **Grundtvig. An Introduction.** London: Society for Promoting Christian Knowledge, 1951. p 141.

Mortensen, Enok. **N. F. S. Grundtvig as a Preacher.** *SW-Gr* pp 85-87.

Nauman, St. Elmo H., Jr. **The Social Philosophies of Søren Kierkegaard and Nicolai Frederik Severin Grundtvig.** Ph. D. diss., Boston University, 1969. (p 224). [Diss. Abstr. 30/05-A, p 2081.]

Nielsen, Ernest D. **N. F. S. Grundtvig: An American Study.** Rock Island. Ill.: Augustana Press, 1955. p 173.

Nielsen, Ernest D. **N. F. S. Grundtvig on Luther.** In *Interpreters of Luther, Essays in Honor of Wilhelm Pauck.* Ed. Jaroslav Pelikan. Philadelphia: Fortress Press, 1968. pp 159-186.

Rush, F. Aubrey. **Letters from England: Grundtvig Writes Home.** *Nor* vol. 11, no. 4 (July-Aug. 1953) pp 263-270.

Thaning, Kaj. **Man First . .** *DFOJ* vol. 48 (1964) pp 29-33.

Thaning, Kaj. **N. F. S. Grundtvig.** Tr. David Hohnen. Copenhagen: Det danske Selskab, 1972. p 180. Ill.

GUNNAR GUNNARSSON (1889-1975)
Icelandic author who wrote in Danish

The Black Cliffs. Tr. from the Danish by Cecil Wood. Intro. Richard Ringler. Madison: University of Wisconsin Press, 1967. p 222. [*Svartfugl,* historical novel, 1929.]

A Slumbering Castle in Ruins. Tr. Brad Marples. *Versuch* vol. 18 (1979) p 22. [*En slumrende Borgruin,* poem from the collection *Digte,* 1911.]

JØRGEN HALCK (b. 1915)

The Small Flag. Tr. Patricia Cardew Wood. London: Jonathan Cape, 1960. p 200. [*Sejrens Sønner,* novel, 1953.]

SØREN HALLAR (1887-1950)

Denmark Speaks. Tr. Charles Wharton Stork. *SeBDV* pp 129-130. [*Danmark-Sangen,* poem from the collection *Vers,* 1943.]

ANNE CHAPLIN HANSEN (b. 1924)

A Canticle of Love. Tr. R. P. Keigwin. *Nor* vol. 14, no. 4 (July-August 1956) pp 270-275. [*Kærlighedens Højsang,* short story from the collection *Olivenlunde,* 1956.]

The Christmas Wood. Tr. R. P. Keigwin. *Nor* vol. 11, no. 6 (November-December 1953) pp 417-422. [Short story.]

EVA HEMMER HANSEN (b. 1913)

Scandal in Troy; A Compelling Story of Helen of Troy. Tr. Dorothy F. Grimm and Sven O. Karell. New York: Popular Library, 1957. p 126. [*Skandale i Troja,* novel, 1954.]

MADS HANSEN (1834-1880)

I Am a Tiller of the Soil. Tr. J. C. Aaberg. *HinS* Song no. 96. [*Jeg er en simpel Bondemand,* poem from the collection *Sange,* 1867.]

MARTIN A. HANSEN (1909-1955)

Against the Wind. Stories by Martin A. Hansen. Tr. and intro. H. Wayne Schow. New York: Frederick Ungar Publishing Co., 1979. p 273. Individual stories listed separately under *AtW.*

The Birds. Tr. H. Wayne Schow. *AtW* pp 104-126. [*Fuglene,* short story from the collection *Agerhønen,* 1947.]

The Birds. Tr. R. P. Keigwin. *CDPr* pp 331-351. [*Fuglene,* short story from the collection *Agerhønen,* 1947.]

The Book. Tr. H. Wayne Schow. *AtW* pp 31-39. [*Bogen*, short story from the collection *Agerhønen*, 1947.]

The Book. Tr. Lydia Cranfield. *Nor* vol. 10, no. 3 (May-June 1952) pp 192-197. [*Bogen*, short story from the collection *Agerhønen*, 1947.]

The Book. Tr. Villy Sørensen and Anne Born. Copenhagen: The Wind-flower Press, 1978. p 19. [Ltd. ed. of 526 copies, 500 numbered.] [*Bogen*, short story in the collection *Agerhønen*, 1947.]

The Countenance. Tr. Niels Lyhne Jensen and James McFarlane. *Nor* vol. 13, no. 5 (September-October 1955) pp 328-333. [*Aasynet*, short story from the collection *Konkyljen*, 1955.]

Daniel. Tr. H. Wayne Schow. *AtW* pp 146-159. [*Daniel*, short story from the collection *Konkyljen*, 1955.]

Easter Bells. Tr. H. Wayne Schow. *AtW* pp 207-273. [*Paaskeklokken*, short story from the collection *Tornebusken*, 1946.]

The Gardener, the Beast, and the Child. Tr. Hallberg Hallmundsson. *AScL* pp 87-95. [*Gartneren, Dyret og Barnet*, short story from the posthumous collection *Efterslæt*, 1959.]

Haavn. Tr. H. Wayne Schow. *AtW* pp 160-193. [*Haavn*, short story from the collection *Konkyljen*, 1955.]

The Harvest Feast. Tr. H. Wayne Schow. *AtW* pp 127-145. [*Høstgildet*, short story from the collection *Agerhønen*, 1947.]

Harvest Feast. Tr. Evelyn Heepe. In *New World Writing*. 8th Mentor Selection. U.S.A.: The New American Library of World Literature, Inc., October 1955. pp 100-125. [*Høstgildet*, short story from the collection *Agerhønen*, 1947.]

The Just. Tr. H. Wayne Schow. *AtW* pp 79-103. [*Den Retfærdige*, short story from the collection *Konkyljen*, 1955.]

Letter to a Beginner. Tr. P. M. Mitchell. *The Literary Review* (Fairleigh Dickinson University, N. J.) vol. 6 (Summer 1963) pp 431-440. [*Brev til en Begynder*, essay published in *Vindrosen*, nr. 4, oktober 1955.]

The Liar. Tr. John Jepson Egglishaw. London: J. M. Dent & Sons, Ltd., 1954. Also with an introduction by Elias Bredsdorff, New York: Twayne Publishers and the American-Scandinavian Foundation, 1969. p 205. [1969 ed., The Library of Scandinavian Literature no. 5.] [*Løgneren*, novel, 1950.]

Lucky Kristoffer. Tr. John Jepson Egglishaw. Intro. Niels Ingwersen. New York: Twayne Publishers and The American-Scandinavian Foundation, 1974. p 371. [The Library of Scandinavian Literature, no. 25.] [*Lykkelige Kristoffer*, novel, 1945.]

March Night. Tr. H. Wayne Schow. *AtW* pp 194-206. [*Martsnat*, short story from the collection *Agerhønen*, 1947.]

March Night. Tr. Lydia Cranfield. *Nor* vol. 8, no. 1 (January-February 1950) pp 54-60. [*Martsnat*, short story from the collection *Agerhønen*, 1947.]

The Master Stonecutter Builds a Danish Parish Church. Tr. John Christianson. *ASR* vol. 50, no. 4 (December 1962) pp 362-372. Ill.

The Morning Hour. Tr. H. Wayne Schow. *AtW* pp 40-49. [*Morgenstunden*, short story from the collection *Agerhønen*, 1947.]

The Morning Hour. Tr. Martha Lepawsky. *LitR-DK* pp 31-39. [*Morgenstunden*, short story from the collection *Agerhønen*, 1947.]

The Owl. Tr. H. Wayne Schow. *AtW* pp 21-30. [*Uglen*, short story from the collection *Agerhønen*, 1947.]

The Paradise Apples. Tr. Marion Marzolf. *ASR* vol. 52, no. 1 (March 1964) pp 72-78. [*Paradisæblerne*, short story from the collection *Paradisæblerne og andre Historier*, 1953.]

Paradise Apples. Tr. Faith Ingwersen. *ADL* pp 529-547. [*Paradisæblerne*, short story from the collection *Paradisæblerne og andre Historier*, 1953.]

The Partridge. Tr. H. Wayne Schow. *AtW* pp 15-20. [*Agerhønen*, short story from the collection by that name, 1947.]

The Partridge. Tr. Erik J. Friis. *ASR* vol. 43, no. 4 (December 1955) pp 383-386. [*Agerhønen*, short story from the collection by that name, 1947.]

Sacrifice. Tr. H. Wayne Schow. *AtW* pp 53-70. [*Offer*, short story from the collection *Agerhønen*, 1947.]

Sacrifice. Tr. Evelyn Heepe. *SotN* pp 51-75. [*Offer*, short story from the collection *Agerhønen*, 1947.]

The Soldier and the Girl. Tr. H. Wayne Schow. *AtW* pp 71-78. [*Soldaten og Pigen*, short story from the collection *Agerhønen*, 1947.]

The Soldier and the Girl. A Short Story. Tr. James E. Anderson. *ASR* vol. 60, no. 1. (March 1972) pp 63-67. [*Soldaten og Pigen*, short story from the collection *Agerhønen*, 1947.]

The Soldier and the Girl. Tr. Richard B. Vowles. *Accent. A Quarterly of New Literature* (Urbana, Illinois) vol. 17, no. 1 (Winter 1957) pp 36-42. [*Soldaten og Pigen*, short story from the collection *Agerhønen*, 1947.]

Wind, Weather and Men's Minds. *DFOJ* no. 12 (June 1954) pp 1-3. Also *ASR* vol. 42, no. 4 (December 1954) pp 325-328. [*Dansk Klima og dansk Folkekarakter*, essay, 1954.]

72   Works about Martin A. Hansen

Fleisher, Frederic. **Martin A. Hansen (1909-1955).** *Books Abroad* (Norman, Oklahoma) vol. 30, no. 1 (1956) pp 35-36.

Ingwersen, Faith and Niels Ingwersen. **Martin A. Hansen.** Boston: Twayne Publishers, 1976. p 197. [Twayne's World Authors Series. 419.]

Ingwersen, Faith. **The Truthful Liars: A Comparative Analysis of Knut Hamsum's »Mysterier« and Martin A. Hansen's »Løgneren«.** Ph. D. Diss., Univ. of Chicago, 1974.

Koefoed, H. A. **Martin A. Hansen.** *Nor* vol. 13, no. 5 (September-October 1955) pp 322-327.

Printz-Påhlson, Göran. **»The Liar«. The Paradox of Fictional Communication in Martin A. Hansen.** *SS* vol. 36, no. 4 (November 1964) pp 263-280. Rpt. in *Omkring Løgneren.* Ed. Ole Wivel. Copenhagen: Hans Reitzels Forlag, 1971. pp 186-206.

Schow, H. Wayne. **Kierkegaardian Perspectives in Martin A. Hansen's »The Liar«.** In *Critique: Studies in Modern Fiction* (Atlanta, Georgia) vol. 15, no. 3 (1974) pp 53-65.

Vowles, Richard B. **Martin A. Hansen and the Uses of the Past.** *Nor* vol. 16, no. 2 (March-April 1958) pp 135-141. Also *ASR* vol. 46, no. 1 (March 1958) pp 33-40 and in *Omkring Løgneren.* Ed. Ole Wivel. Copenhagen: Hans Reitzels Forlag, 1971. pp 101-104.

Vowles, Richard B. **Martin A. Hansen: Danish Craftsman and Mystic.** *Accent. A Quarterly of New Literature* (Urbana, Illinois) vol. 17, no. 1 (Winter 1957) pp 43-44.

UFFE HARDER (b. 1930)

An Assignment on Icarus. Tr. Uffe Harder and Alexander Taylor. *CDPo* pp 215-216. [*En Fristil om Ikaros,* poem from the collection *Sort på hvidt,* 1968.]

Behind the Borders. Tr. Robert Fred Bell. *LitR-Dk* p 78. [*Bag Grænserne,* poem from the collection *Sprængte Diger,* 1954.]

Conditions. Tr. Uffe Harder and Alexander Taylor. *CDPo* p 217. [*Vilkår,* poem from the collection *I disse Dage,* 1971.]

Cycling. Tr. Uffe Harder and Alexander Taylor. *CDPo* pp 211-212. [*På Cycle,* poem from the collection *Positioner,* 1964.]

The Days Sink through Me. Tr. Uffe Harder and Alexander Taylor. *Portland* p 96. [*Dagene synker igennem mig,* poem from the collection *Verden som om,* 1979.] [Danish text included.]

Deep Quiet with Snow. Tr. Uffe Harder and Alexander Taylor. *CDPo* p 214. [*Dyb Tavshed med Sne,* poem from the collection *Sort på hvidt,* 1968.]

Factors. Tr. Uffe Harder and Alexander Taylor. *CDPo* p 212. [*Faktorer,* poem from the collection *Positioner,* 1964.]

Object. Tr. Uffe Harder and Alexander Taylor. *CDPo* pp 213-214. [*Genstand,* poem from the collection *Sort på hvidt,* 1968.]

To Reach Out for Pen and Paper. Tr. Uffe Harder and Alexander Taylor. *CDPo* p 213. [*Række ud efter Pen og Papir,* poem from the collection *Sort på hvidt,* 1968.]

THORKILD HANSEN (b. 1927)

Arabia Felix. The Danish Expedition of 1761-1767. Tr. James and Kathleen McFarlane. London: William Collins Sons & Co., Ltd.; New York: Harper & Row, 1964. p 381. Ill. [*Det lykkelige Arabien,* novel, 1962.]

North West to Hudson Bay. Tr. James McFarlane and John Lynch. London: William Collins Sons & Co. Ltd., 1970. p 348. Ill. [Abridged trans. of *Jens Munk,* novel, 1965.] See also *The Way to Hudson Bay - The Life and Times of Jens Munk.*

The Way to Hudson Bay - The Life and Times of Jens Munk. Tr. James McFarlane and John Lynch. New York: Helen and Kurt Wolff Books and Harcourt, Brace & World, Inc., 1970. p 348. Ill. [Abridged trans. of *Jens Munk,* novel, 1965.]

SVEN HASSEL (pseud. for WILLY ARBING) (b. 1917)
Also writes under Sven Hazel

Assignment Gestapo. Tr. Jean Ure. London: Corgi, 1971. London: Allison & Busby, 1976. p 347. [*Gestapo,* novel, 1963.] [Tr. from the French ed., *Camarades de front,* 1965.]

Blitzfreeze. London: Corgi, 1975. p 358. [*Jeg så dem dø,* novel, 1973.]

The Bloody Road to Death. Tr. Tim Bowie. London: Corgi, 1977. p 316. London: Allison & Busby, 1979. p 317. [*Glemt af Gud,* novel, 1976.]

Comrades of War. London: Corgi, 1977. p 316. [*Frontkammerater,* novel, 1960.]

Court Martial. Tr. Tim Bowie. London: Corgi, 1979. London: Severn House, 1980. p 319. [*Krigsret,* novel, 1978.]

The Legion of the Damned. Tr. Maurice Michael. London: George Allen & Unwin; New York: Farrar, Straus & Cudahy, 1957. p 297. London: Pan Books, 1959. p 249. London: Corgi, 1976. p 284. [*De Fordømtes Legion*, novel based on the author's experiences in a German penal regiment, 1953.]

Liquidate Paris. London: Corgi, 1977. p 285. [*Likvider Paris!*, novel, 1967.]

March Battalion. Tr. from the French by Jean Ure. London: Corgi, 1970. p 220. [*Marchbataillon*, novel, 1962.]

Monte Cassino. London: Transworld Publishers, 1969. p 253. [*Monte Cassino*, novel, 1965.]

Reign of Hell. London: Corgi, 1973. p 269. [*Kommando Reichsführer Himmler*, novel, 1971.]

S. S. General. Tr. from the French by Jean Ure. London: Corgi, 1972. p 285. London: Allison & Busby, 1977. p 286. [*SS-generalen*, novel, 1969.] [Translated from French version, *Général SS*, 1970.]

Wheels of Terror. Tr. Inger O'Hanlon. London: Souvenir Press, 1960. p 287. London: Transworld Publishers (Corgi Books), 1961. p 351. London: Corgi, 1977. p 351. [*Døden på Larvefødder*, novel, 1958.]

CARSTEN HAUCH (1790-1872)

From »**Confession**«. Tr. Charles Wharton Stork. *SeBDV* p 52. [Abbreviated version of *Bekiendelse*, poem from the collection *Lyriske Digte*, 1842.]

Consolation in Adversity. Tr. S. Foster Damon. *BoDV* pp 46-47. [*Trøst i Modgang*, poem from the collection *Lyriske Digte og Romancer*, 1861.]

Home. Tr. S. Foster Damon. *BoDV* pp 45-46. [*Hjem*, poem from *Robert Fulton*, 1853.]

The Pleiades at Midnight. Tr. S. Foster Damon. *BoDV* pp 47-48. [*Pleiaderne ved Midnat*, poem from the collection *Lyriske Digte og Romancer*, 1861.]

When o'er the Fields. Tr. Charles Wharton Stork. *SeBDV* p 51. [*Sang af Hamadryaden*, poem from the collection *Dramatiske Værker*, III, 1830.]

The Wild Hunt. Tr. S. Foster Damon. *BoDV* pp 42-45. [*Den vilde Jagt*, from ballad-cycle *Valdemar Atterdag, et romantisk Digt*, poem from the collection *Lyriske Digte og Romancer*, 1861.]

Previous Translations:

The Song of Agnes.
Robert Fulton; an Historical Novel.
Oehlenschläger.
When down the Stream the Swan Is Softly Gliding.
The Wild Hunt.
The Song of Poland.

POUL HAUTON

Evening Fantasy. Tr. P. F. Jacobsen. Ill. Mads Stage. Copenhagen: the Author, 1955. p 60. [Essays.]

Resignation. Ill. Gaston. Copenhagen: Martin, 1952. p 28. Ill. [Danish-English text.]

JOHAN LUDVIG HEIBERG (1791-1860)

Barcarole. Tr. Charles Wharton Stork. *SeBDV* p 24. [*Barcarole (Lette Bølge! naar du blaaner)*, from the *Prindsesse Isabella*, 1829.]

No. Tr. Donald Elwin Malmgren. Ph. D. Diss., University of Denver, 1972. [*Nei*, play, 1836.]

Seven Sleepers Day. Tr. Donald Elwin Malmgren. Ph. D. Diss., University of Denver, 1972. [*Syvsoverdag*, play, 1840.]

A Soul after Death. Tr. Donald Elwin Malmgren. Ph. D. Diss., University of Denver, 1972. [*En Sjæl efter Døden*, play, 1841.]

Previous Translations:

The Sun Had Sunk beneath the Sea.
Extract from »Protestantism in Nature«.
Songs from »Elfinhill«: Bride of the Elfin King. Summernight's Festival.
Hunter's Nightsong.

Works about Johan Ludvig Heiberg

Fenger, Henning. **The Heibergs.** Tr. and ed. Frederick J. Marker. Boston: Twayne Publishing Co., 1971.

Malmgren, Donald Elwin. **A Translation from the Danish of Three Plays by Johan Ludvig Heiberg (1791-1860).** Ph. D. Diss., University of Denver, 1972. [Diss. Abstr. 3064-A.]

74 PIET HEIN (b. 1905)

Also writes under Kumbel Kumbell

Analysis of Omnipotence. Tr. by the author. *TCScP* p 84. [*Almægtighed*, poem from the collection *Vers i Verdensrummet*, 1941.]

The Case for Obscurity. *Orbis.* [Poem written in English.]

Consolation Grook. *CDPo* p 103. [Poem written in English, from the collection *Grooks 1*, 1966.]

Conversation on the Road. Tr. Martin S. Allwood and Piet Hein. *TCScP* p 86. [*Samtale paa Vejen*, poem from the collection *Gruk*, bd. 2, 1942.]

The Common Well. *CDPo* p 98. [Poem written in English, from the collection *Grooks 4*, 1972.]

Dedication. Tr. Charles Wharton Stork. *SeBDV* p 155. [*Tilegnelse*, poem from the collection *Vers i Verdensrummet*, 1941.]

Grooks. Two Poems. *Brigham Young University Studies* (Provo, Utah) vol. 11, no 1 (1970) p 32.

Grooks 1. With the assistance of Jens Arup. Copenhagen: Borgen; Cambridge, Mass.: M. I. T. Press, 1966. Garden City, N. Y.: Doubleday; London: Hodder Paperbacks; Toronto: General Publishing, 1969. p 53. Ill. 2nd ed. Copenhagen: Borgen, 1970. [Short poems in English.]

Grooks 2. With the assistance of Jens Arup. Copenhagen: Borgen, 1968. Garden City, N. Y.: Doubleday; Toronto: General Publishing, 1969. p 53. Ill. 2nd ed. Copenhagen: Borgen, 1974. [See also *More Grooks.*] [Short poems in English, 1968.]

Grooks 3. With the assistance of Jens Arup. Copenhagen: Borgen; Garden City, N. Y.: Doubleday; Toronto: General Publishing, 1970. p 53. Ill. [See also *Still More Grooks.*] [Short poems in English, 1970.]

Grooks 4. With the assistance of Jens Arup. Copenhagen: Borgen; Garden City, N. Y.: Doubleday; Toronto: General Publishing, 1972. p 59. Ill. [See also *Motes and Beams.*] [Short poems in English, 1972.]

Grooks 5. With the assistance of Jens Arup. Copenhagen: Borgen; Garden City, N. Y.: Doubleday; Toronto: General Publishing, 1973. p 53. Ill. [See also *Mist and Moonshine.*] [Short poems in English, 1973.]

Grooks in Music. Words by Piet Hein with the assistance of Jens Arup. Music by Svend Asmussen. Copenhagen: Borgens Forlag, 1971. p 40. Ill.

Hamlet Anno Domini. *CDPo* p 95. [From the opening poem *Heirs to the Air*, written in English, for the international aeronautical conference in 1960. In the collection *Du skal plante et Træ*, 1960.]

Han havde ikke Tid. Tr. Emily Helling. *Versuch* vol. 17 (1978) p 20. [*Han havde ikke Tid*, poem from the collection *Gruk*, bd. 18, 1961.]

Hint and Suggestion. *CDPo* p 101. [Poem written in English, from the collection *Grooks 1*, 1966.]

Imagination and Fancy. *Orbis* [Poem written in English.]

Like a Tall, Stout Beechtree-Springthoughts. Tr. Kris Westfahl. *Versuch* vol. 14 (1975) p 14. [*Som et stort, tungt Bøgetræ. Løvspringstemning*, poem from the collection *Gruk*, bd. 11, 1954.]

Literary Gruk. Tr. Martin S. Allwood, Piet Hein and John Hollander. *MoDP* p 24. Also *TCScP* p 85. [*Litterært Gruk*, poem from the collection *Gruk*, bd. 2, 1942.]

Literary Gruk. Tr. Piet Hein, Stephen Schwartz and Martin S. Allwood. *A Little Treasury* pp 511-512. [*Litterært Gruk*, poem from the collection *Gruk*, bd. 2, 1942.]

Losing Face. *CDPo* p 99. [Poem written in English, from the collection *Grooks 1*, 1966.]

Majority Rule. *CDPo* pp 96-97. [Poem written in English, from the collection *Grooks 1*, 1966.]

Man's Communication to Man. Boston, 1968. p 28. [Alexander Graham Bell Lecture, 8.]

The Me above the Me. *CDPo* p 97. [Poem written in English, from the collection *Grooks 2*, 1968.]

Meeting the Eye. *Orbis* [Poem written in English.]

Mist and Moonshine: Grooks 5. With the assistance of Jens Arup. London: Basil Blackwell, 1973. [*Grooks 5*, short poems in English, 1973.]

Moral Gruk. Tr. Martin S. Allwood, Piet Hein and John Hollander. *TCScP* p 85. [*Moralsk Gruk*, poem from the collection *Gruk*, bd. 2, 1942.]

More Grooks. With the assistance of Jens Arup. Cambridge, Mass.: M. I. T. Press, 1969. London: Hodder Paperbacks, 1969. p 53. Ill. [*Grooks 2*, short poems in English, 1968.]

Motes and Beams: Grooks 4. With the assistance of Jens Arup. London: Basil Blackwell, 1973. [*Grooks 4*, short poems in English, 1972.]

Noble Funerals Arranged. Tr. Martin S. Allwood. *MoDP* p 26. Also *TCScP* p 85. [*Nobel Bisættelse besørges*, poem from the collection *Gruk*, bd. 2, 1942.]

Patriotic Summer. Tr. Martin S. Allwood and Piet Hein. *MoDP* p 28. Also *TCScP* p 86. [*Den nationale Sommer*, poem from the collection *Gruk*, bd. 2, 1942.]

The Prophet. To Niels Bohr. Tr. Robert Hillyer. *ASR* vol. 38, no. 1 (March 1950) p 45. [*Niels Bohr*, poem from *Vers af denne Verden*, 1948.]

The Road to Wisdom. *CDPo* p 100. [Poem written in English, from the collection *Grooks 1*, 1966.]

Runway Runes. (Short Grooks I). With the assistance of Jens Arup. Copenhagen: Borgen, 1968. p 55. Ill. 2nd ed. 1970. 3rd ed. 1973. p 54. Ill.

Spring Fever. Tr. Lori Nielsen. *Versuch* vol. 14 (1975) p 20. [*I Foraarssol*, poem from the collection *Gruk*, bd. 3, 1942.]

Still More Grooks. With the assistance of Jens Arup. London: Hodder Paperbacks, 1970. p 57. Ill. [*Grooks 3*, short poems in English, 1970.]

Summer Cloud. Tr. Lisa Sorensen. *Versuch* vol. 16 (1977) p 27. [*Sommersky*, poem from the collection *Gruk*, bd. 11, 1954.]

To Be. Tr. Pat Knuth. *Versuch* vol. 14 (1975) p 28. [*At være*, poem from the collection *Vers i Verdensrummet*, 1941.]

The True Defence. *CDPo* p 102. [Poem written in English, from the collection *Grooks 1*, 1966.]

Ved en Pen. Tr. Emily Helling. *Versuch* vol. 17 (1978) pp 19-20. [*Ved en Pen*, poem from the collection *Gruk*, bd. 18, 1961.]

Previous Translations:

We Shall Build a Bridge.

Works about Piet Hein

Quality Translator Wanted. *DFOJ* no. 47 (1964) p 33.

JENS PAULI HEINESEN (b. 1932)
Faroese author

Gestur. Tr. from the Faroese by Heðin Brønner. *FSS* pp 262-267. [*Gestur*, short story from the collection by that name, 1967.]

The Last of the Liquor. A Short Story. Tr. from the Faroese by Heðin Brønner. *ASR* vol. 60, no. 3 (September 1972) pp 291-295. [*Siðasti frísø ludagur*, short story from the collection *I aldag arðinum*, 1971.]

Little Frants Vilhelm. Tr. from the Faroese by Hedin Brønner. *FFS* 253-261. [*Litli Frants Vilhelm*, short story from the collection *Gestur*, 1967.]

WILLIAM HEINESEN (b. 1900)
Faroese author who writes in Danish

The Adept. Tr. Anne Born. *Modern Poetry in Translation* (London) (1979/80). [*Adepten*, poem from the collection *Den dunkle Sol*, 1936.]

Arctis. Selected Poems, 1921-1972. Tr. and intro. Anne Born. Findhorn, Forres, Morayshire: The Thule Press, 1980. p 56.

The Ascension of J. H. O. Djurhuus, Poet. Tr. Kurt Hansen. *CDPo* pp 41-43. [*Digteren J. H. O. Djurhuus's Himmelfart*, poem from the collection *Panorama med Regnbue*, 1972.]

Belsmand. A Short Story. Tr. Donald K. Watkins. *ASR* vol. 59, no. 4 (Winter 1971) pp 399-406. [*Belsmanden*, short story from *Det fortryllede Lys*, 1957.]

The Celestial Journey. Tr. Hedin Brønner. *ASR* vol. 59, no. 1 (March 1971) pp 55-57. Also *FSS* pp 145-148. [*Himmelfarten*, short story from the collection *Gamaliels Besættelse*, 1960.]

Dancing Poplar Seeds. Tr. Anne Born. *Modern Poetry in Translation* (London) (1979/80). [*Dansende Poppelfrø*, poem from the collection *Panorama med Regnbue*, 1972.]

A Dream. Tr. Dennis Preston. *Versuch* vol. 17 (1978) p 5. [*Drøm*, poem from the collection *Højbjergning ved Havet*, 1924.]

The Faroe Islands. By Gérard Franceschi and William Heinesen. Copenhagen: Rhodos, 1971. p 183. Ill.

The Faroe Islanders' Saga. By George Johnston. Drawings by William Heinesen. Ottawa: Oberon Press, 1975. p 144. Ill.

The Flies. Tr. Hedin Brønner. *New Directions Anthology* (New York) no. 38 (1979). [*Fluerne*, short story from the collection *Kur mod onde Ånder*, 1967.]

Gamaliel's Bewitchment. Tr. Hedin Brønner. *FSS* pp 69-92. [*Gamaliels Besættelse*, short story from the collection by that name, 1961.]

Hymnus Amoris. Tr. Ingvar Schousboe. *CDPo* pp 37-39. [*Hymnus Amoris*, poem from the collection *Hymne og Harmsang*, 1961.]

In the Madman's Garden. Tr. Hedin Brønner. *FSS* pp 93-105. [*Den gale Mands Have*, short story from the collection *Gamaliels Besættelse*, 1961.]

The Kingdom of the Earth. Tr. and intro. Hedin Brønner. Boston: Twayne Publishers, 1974. p 171. [*Moder Syvstjerne*, novel, 1952.]

The Knife. Tr. Hedin Brønner. *FSS* pp 128-144. [*Kniven*, short story from the collection *Don Juan fra Tranhuset*, 1970.]

The Lost Musicians. Tr. Erik J. Friis. Intro. Hedin Brønner. New York: The American-

75

76

Scandinavian Foundation and Twayne Publishers, 1971. p 364. Also pb. ed., New York: Hippocrene Books, 1972. [Library of Scandinavian Literature series.] [*De fortabte Spillemænd*, novel, 1950.]

The Night of the Gryla. Tr. Hedin Brønner, *New Directions Anthology* (New York) no. 40 (April 1980). [*Grylen*, short story from the collection *Det fortryllede Lys*, 1957.]

The Night of the Storm. Tr. Hedin Brønner. *FSS* pp 117-127. [*Stormnatten*, short story from the collection *Det fortryllede Lys*, 1957.]

On Being Faroese. *DJ* Special Faroe Island Issue, 1971 pp 17-20. Also *ASR* vol. 60, no. 2 (June 1972) pp 137-143.

Rain in Leningrad. Tr. Alexander Taylor. *CDPo* p 40. [*Regn i Leningrad*, poem from the collection *Panorama med Regnbue*, 1972.]

The Smoking Mirror. Tr. Hedin Brønner. *FSS* pp 106-116. [*Det rygende Spejl*, short story from the collection *Gamaliels Besættelse*, 1961.]

The Winged Darkness. Tr. Hedin Brønner. *SS* vol. 49, no. 2 (Spring 1977) pp 165-172. [*Det vingede Mørke*, short story from the collection *Det fortryllede Lys*, 1957.]

Previous Translations:

Niels Peter.

Works about William Heinesen

Brønner, Hedin. **Three Faroese Novelists: An Appreciation of Jørgen-Frantz Jacobsen, William Heinesen and Hedin Bru.** New York: Twayne Publishers, 1973. p 140. [The Library of Scandinavian Studies vol. 1.]

Brønner, Hedin. **William Heinesen: Faroese Voice - Danish Pen.** *ASR* vol. 61, no. 2 (Summer 1973) pp 142-154.

In Love with the Life Force. *Times Literary Supplement*, no. 3,704 (2 March 1973) p 245.

Jones, W. Glyn. **Faroe and Cosmos. An Inaugural Lecture Delivered before the University of Newcastle on Tuesday, 5 February 1974.** Newcastle upon Tyne: University of Newcastle, 1974. p 18.

Jones, W. Glyn. **»Noatun« and the Collective Novel.** *SS* vol. 41, no. 3 (August 1969) pp 217-230.

Jones, W. Glyn. **William Heinesen.** New York: Twayne Publishers, 1974. p 201.

Jones, W. Glyn. **William Heinesen and the Myth of Conflict.** *Scandinavica* vol. 9, no. 2 (November 1970) pp 81-94.

Jones, W. Glyn. **William Heinesen's »Tårnet ved Verdens Ende«: A Restatement and an Extension.** *SS* vol. 50 (1978) pp 19-30.

GRETHE HELTBERG (b. 1911)

Happiness. Tr. Charles Wharton Stork. *SeBDV* p 150. [*Og der var mig, der drømte om*, poem from the collection *Døden og Foraaret*, 1943.]

Sand. Tr. H. G. Leach. *ASR* vol. 39, no. 2 (June 1951) p 154. [*Sand*, poem from the collection *Testamente*, 1945.]

To My Son. Tr. Robert Hillyer. *ASR* vol. 39, no. 3 (September 1951) p 197. [*Til min Søn*, poem from the collection *Testamente*, 1945.]

The Word. Tr. Robert Hillyer. *ASR* vol. 39, no. 4 (December 1951) p 295. [*Ordet*, poem from the collection *Døden og Foraaret*, 1943.]

AGNES HENNINGSEN (1868-1962)

Spring. Tr. Ann and Peter Thornton. *CDPr* pp 48-57. [An extract from Chapter 1 of *Kærlighedens Aarstider*, novel, 1927.]

HARALD HERDAL (1900-1978)

The Tin Boxes. Tr. J. F. S. Pearce. *CDPr* pp 251-256. [*Blikdaaserne*, short story from the collection *Bisser og andre Fortællinger*, 1948.]

Previous Tranlations:

Spring Day by a City Lake.
The Tree in Isted Street.

HENRIK HERTZ (1798-1870)

The Meeting. Tr. R. P. Keigwin. *IDIWB* p 53. [*Mødet*, poem no. 4 in the song cycle *Sommerliv*, 1845.]

Queen Dagmar. Tr. S. D. Rodholm. *HoS* p 133. [*Fra fjerne Lande kom hun*, poem from the play *Svanehammen*, 1841.]

Previous Translations:

King René's Daughter.

KAREN HILDEBRANDT (1899-1948)

Romance. Tr. Charles Wharton Stork. *SeBDV* p 152. [*Romantik,* poem from the collection *Til en Ven,* 1937.]

KAJ HIMMELSTRUP (b. 1927)

Welcome to Dallas, Mr. Kennedy. Tr. Christine Hauch. London: Calder and Boyars, 1971. p 64. [*Velkommen til Dallas, Hr. Kennedy,* play, 1967.]

KNUD HJORTØ (1869-1932)

The Tailor's Summer. Tr. J. F. S. Pearce. *CDPr* pp 58-66. [*Jens Skrædders Sommer,* short story from the collection *Kringelveje,* 1929.]

POUL HOFFMANN (b. 1928)
Also spelled Hoffman

The Brazen Serpent. Tr. David Hohnen. Philadelphia: Fortress Press, 1964. p 288. [*Kobberslangen (Moses III),* novel, 1958.]
The Burning Bush. Tr. David Hohnen. The Moses Trilogy vol. 1. Philadelphia: Muhlenberg Press, 1961. p 325. [*Den brændende Tornebusk (Moses I),* novel, 1956.]
The Eternal Fire. Tr. David Hohnen. The Moses Trilogy vol. 2. Philadelphia: Muhlenberg Press, 1962. p 432. [*Den evige Ild (Moses II),* novel, 1957.]
The Fleeing Follower. Tr. Bernard H. J. Habel. Minneapolis, Mn.: Augsburg Publishing House, 1962. p 144.

ULF HOFFMANN (b. 1905)

I Hear. Tr. Martin S. Allwood. *TCScP* p 82. [*Jeg hører Maager skrige,* poem from the collection *Sejle, se og synge,* 1941.]

PER HØJHOLT (b. 1928)

A 5-pinnate Leaf. Tr. Poul Borum. *CDPo* p 196. [*Et femfliget Blad,* poem from the collection *Min Hånd 66,* 1966.]

Frosty Night. Tr. Poul Borum. *CDPo* p 197. [*Frostnat,* poem from the collection *Min Hånd 66,* 1966.]
M/S Nelly in Countersound. Tr. Nadia Christensen and Alexander Taylor. *CDPo* pp 194-195. [*M/S Nelly i Modlyd,* poem from the collection *Poetens Hoved,* 1963.]
November. Tr. Nadia Christensen. *CDPo* p 194. [*November,* poem from the collection *Poetens Hoved,* 1963.]
Outside. Tr. Nadia Christensen. *CDPo* p 195. [*Udenfor,* poem from the collection *Min Hånd 66,* 1966.]
The Poet H. Tr. Poul Borum. *CDPo* p 197. [*Poeten H,* poem from the collection *Min Hånd 66,* 1966.]
So and so Many Larks. Tr. Nadia Christensen and Alexander Taylor. In *The Wormwood Review* (Stockton, Ca.) no. 48 (1972) p 122. Also *CDPo* p 196. [*Så og så mange Lærker,* poem from the collection *Min Hånd 66,* 1966.]
Turbo 4. Tr. Tove Neville. *CDPo* pp 198-199. [*Turbo 4,* poem from the collection *Turbo,* 1968.]

KAI HOLBERG (1877-1932)

My Love. Tr. Charles Wharton Stork. *SeBDV* p 154. [*Min Kærlighed til dig er som en Palme,* poem from the collection *Udvalgte Digte,* 1927.]

LUDVIG HOLBERG (1684-1754)

The Arabian Powder. Tr. Henry Alexander. *SeOPl* pp 53-79. [*Det arabiske Pulver,* comedy, 1724.]
The Arabian Powder. Tr. Reginald Spink. *TC* pp 39-64. [*Det arabiske Pulver,* comedy, 1724.]
Barney Brae or the Wee Mountainy Farmer That Got Changed. Tr. G. V. C. Young. Belfast: Young, 1972. p 83. [*Jeppe paa Bjerget,* play, 1723.]
The Changed Bridegroom. Tr. Henry Alexander. *SeOPl* pp 187-205. [*Den forvandlede Brudgom,* comedy for actresses alone, 1753.]
The Christmas Party. *AScL* pp 24-40. [*Julestuen,* comedy, 1724.]
The Christmas Party. Tr. Henry Alexander. *SeOPl* pp 81-102. [*Julestuen,* comedy, 1724.]
Diderich the Terrible. Tr. Henry Alexander. *SeOPl* pp 103-132. [*Diderich Menschenskræk,* comedy, 1724.]

78

Four Plays by Holberg. Tr. Henry Alexander. Intro. Oscar James Campbell, Jr. 1946; rpt. New York: Kraus Reprint Co., 1971. p 202. Individual plays listed separately under *FP1-H.*

The Fussy Man. Tr. Henry Alexander. *FP1-H* pp 1-61. [*Den Stundesløse*, play, 1723.]

The Healing Spring. Tr. Reginald Spink. *TC* pp 65-91. [*Kilderejsen*, comedy, 1725.]

Jeppe of the Hill. Tr. Oscar James Campbell and Frederic Schenk. *ADL* pp 93-115. [*Jeppe paa Bjerget*, play, 1723.]

Jeppe of the Hill. Tr. Oscar James Campbell. With an introduction. *GScT* pp 33-75. [*Jeppe paa Bjerget*, play, 1723.]

The Journey of Niels Klim to the World Underground. Based on the 1742 English translation. Intro. and ed. James I. McNelis, Jr. Lincoln: University of Nebraska Press, 1960. p 236. [A Bison Book.] [*Nicolai Klimii iter subterraneum*, comedy written in Latin, 1741.]

A Journey to the World Underground. New York: Garland, 1974. p 324. [Facsim. ed. of the 1st English ed., 1742.][*Nicolai Klimii iter subterraneum*, comedy written in Latin, 1741.]

Ludvig Holberg's Memories: An Eighteenth-century Danish Contribution to International Understanding. Ed. Stewart E. Fraser. Leiden: E. J. Brill, 1970. p 289. Ill.

The Masked Ladies. Tr. Henry Alexander. *FP1-H* pp 63-97. [*De Usynlige*, play, 1725.]

Masquerades. Tr. Henry Alexander. *FP1-H* pp 149-202. [*Maskarade*, play, 1724.]

Master Gert Westphaler, or The Talkative Barber. Tr. Henry Alexander. *SeOPI* pp 19-51. [*Mester Gert Westphaler*, comedy, 1722.]

Moral Thoughts, Book I, Epigram 5. Tr. P. M. Mitchell. *ADL* pp 117-133. [*Moralske Tanker, Libr. I, Epigram 5*, essay, 1744.]

Niels Klim. Being an incomplete translation by Thomas De Quincey . . . now edited from the manuscript by S. Musgrove. Auckland: Auckland University College, 1953. p 37. [Bulletin no. 42.]

On the Effects of Inflation. Tr. P. M. Mitchell. *ASR* vol. 40, no. 2 (June 1952) pp 132-133. [*Epistel 371*, essay.]

The Peasant in Pawn. Tr. Henry Alexander. *SeOPI* pp 133-163. [*Den pantsatte Bonde-dreng*, comedy, 1724.]

Peder Paars. Tr. Bergliot Stromsoe. Intro. Børge Gedsø Madsen. With illustrations from the 1772 edition. Lincoln, Nebraska: The University of Nebraska Press and the American-Scandinavian Foundation, 1962. p 193. Ill. [*Peder Paars*, mock-heroic poem, 1719-1720.]

Quislimiri, or The Inequality of Wages. Tr. P. M. Mitchell. *ASR* vol. 40, no. 1 (March 1952) pp 27-29. [*Epistel 79*, essay, 1748-1754.]

Selected Essays of Ludvig Holberg. Tr., and with intro. and notes by P. M. Mitchell. Lawrence: University of Kansas Press, 1955. p 166. [49 essays from *Epistler*, I-V, 1748-1754.]

Seven One-Act Plays. Tr. Henry Alexander. Intro. Svend Kragh-Jacobsen. New York: The American-Scandinavian Foundation and Princeton University Press, 1950. p 205. Rpt. Millwood, New York: Kraus Reprint Co., 1972. Individual plays listed separately under *SeOPI.*

The Talkative Barber. See **Master Gert Westphaler.**

Sganarel's Journey to the Land of the Philosophers. Tr. Henry Alexander. *SeOPI* pp 165-186. [*Sganarels Rejse til det filosofiske Land*, comedy, 1751.]

Three Comedies. Tr. and intro. Reginald Spink. London: William Heineman; New York: Theatre Arts Books, 1957. p 91. [The Drama Library.] Individual plays listed separately under *TC.*

The Transformed Peasant. Tr. Reginald Spink. *TC* pp 7-38. [*Jeppe paa Bjerget*, play, 1723.]

The Weathercock. Tr. Henry Alexander. *FP1-H* pp 99-148. [*Den Vægelsindede*, play, 1722.]

Previous Translations:

An Introduction to Universal History.
The History of Norway, from the Union of Calmar.
Extracts from »Don Ranudo«.
The Babbling Barber.
Erasmus Montanus.
The Blue-Apron Statesman.
Henry and Pernilla.
Captain Bombastus Thunderton. [Diderich Menschen-Skræk.]
The Political Tinker.
A Letter by Holberg concerning Cromwell.

Works about Ludvig Holberg

Argetsinger, Gerald S. **The Dramaturgy of Ludvig Holberg's Comedies.** Bowling Green, Ohio: Bowling Green State University Press, 1975.

Beyer, Harald. **Holberg and Bergen.** *Nor* vol. 11, no. 2 (March-April 1953) pp 96-98.

Billeskov Jansen, F. J. **Ludvig Holberg.** Tr. David Stoner. Boston: Twayne Publishing Co., 1974. p 134.

Billeskov Jansen, F. J. **Ludvig Holberg and Some French Thinkers.** In *Scandinavian Studies; Essays presented to Dr. Henry Goddard Leach.* Seattle: University of Washington Press for the American-Scandinavian Foundation, 1965. pp 153-169.

Brandes, Georg. **Holberg and the Neo-classic Spirit.** Tr. Evert Sprinchorn. In his *The Genius of the Scandinavian Theater.* New York: Mentor Books - The New American Library of World Lit., 1964. pp 537-547. [Excerpts from *Ludvig Holberg: Et Festskrift,* 1884.]

Campbell, James Oscar. **The Comedies of Holberg.** 1914, rpt. New York and London: Benjamin Blom, 1968. p 363.

Harthan, J. P. **Holberg and Oxford.** *Nor* vol. 8, no. 1 (Jan.-Feb. 1950) pp 26-30.

Koefoed, H. A. **Holberg's Humour and Humanity. Was Holberg Moralist or Humorist - or Both?** *Denmark. A Monthly Review of Anglo-Danish Relations* (London) (March 1954) pp 8, 13.

Lundqvist, Anne S. **Ludvig Holberg and Molière: Imitation or Constructive Emulation?** In *Molière and the Commonwealth of Letters: Patrimony & Posterity.* Ed. Roger Johnson [et al.] Jackson, Mississippi: University Press of Mississippi, 1975. pp 245-251.

Møller, Kai Friis. **Holberg - A Great European.** *DFOJ* no. 10 (1954) pp 1-6. Also *ASR* vol. 42, no. 2 (June 1954) pp 145-152.

Muinzer, L. A. **Holberg and Modern Sensibility: A Study of »The Political Tinker«.** *The Newman Review* (Belfast) vol. 3 (1971) pp 9-16.

AGNETE HOLK

The Straggler. Tr. Antony Hinton. London: Arco Publications, 1955. p 272. [*Et Vildskud,* novel, 1941.]
See also *Strange Friends.*

Strange Friends. Tr. Anthony Hinton. New York: Pyramid Books, 1955. p 190. [*Et Vildskud,* novel, 1941.]

MORGEN HOLM (pseud. for NINA THOMSEN)

I, a Sailor. New York: Dell, 1969. London: Mayflower, 1970. p 203. [*Jeg - en Sømand,* erotic novel, 1966.]

SIV HOLM (pseud. for NINA THOMSEN)

I, a Woman. Tr. J. W. Brown. New York: Dell; London: Mayflower-Dell, 1967. (Also 1970, 1973). p 220. [*Jeg - en Kvinde,* erotic novel, 1961.]

I, a Woman, Part II. New York: Dell Books, 1969. London: New English Library, 1970. [*Jeg - en Kvinde, 2. del,* erotic novel, 1963.]

STIIG HOLM (pseud. for IVAN STRANGE) (b. 1935)

I, a Lover. New York: Dell, 1968. p 154. London: New English Library, 1969. p 127. [*Jeg - en Elsker,* erotic novel, 1965.]

SUSANNE HOLM (pseud.)

I, Susanne. St. Albans: Mayflower, 1974. New York: Dell, 1972. p 128. [*Jeg - en Elskerinde,* erotic novel, 1967.]

SVEN HOLM (b. 1940)

The Execution. Tr. Alexander Taylor. *Zone* (New York) (1980). [*Henrettelsen,* short story from the collection *Den store Fjende,* 1961.]

Love 1 & 2 - Erotic Tales from Scandinavia. Edited by Sven Holm. Tr. Maurice Michael. Ill. with photographs from the Danish film *Darling Playthings.* New York: Grove Press, 1969. [*Sengeheste 1* and *Sengeheste 2.*] [Also includes stories from *Kärlek 1* and *Kärlek 2* by Bengt Anderberg.]

Miss Urst Visits the Deer Park. Tr. Paula Hostrup-Jessen. *DI* pp 236-246. [*Frk. Urst i Dyrehaven,* short story from the collection *Nedstyrtningen,* 1963.]

The Plant. Tr. Leonie Marx. *Mundus Artium* (Athens, Ohio) vol. 8, no. 2 (1975) p 14. [*Planten,* short story from the collection *Nedstyrtningen,* 1963.]

The Poet. Tr. Walter Foote. *LitR-Dk* pp 67-73. [*Digteren,* short story from the collection *Den store Fjende,* 1961.]

Termush. Tr. Sylvia Clayton. London: Faber & Faber, Ltd., 1969. p 110. [*Termush, Atlanterhavskysten,* novel, 1967.]

80 **SVERRE HOLM (pseud. for GEORG GJEDDE or GEORGJEDDE) (b. 1913)**

I, a Man. Tr. J. W. B. London: Mayflower, 1978. p 223. [*Jeg, en Mand*, novel 1965.]

TINE HOLM (pseud. for TINE SCHMEDES) (b. 1946)

I, a Teenager. London: Mayflower, 1972. p 126. [*Jeg - en Pige*, novel, 1967.]

KNUD HOLST (b. 1936)

The Pumpkins, Tr. Paula Hostrup-Jessen. *DI* pp 163-176. [*Græskarrene*, short story from the collection *Dyret*, 1963.]

LUDVIG HOLSTEIN (1864-1946)

Ah, Look, My Friend. Tr. Robert Silliman Hillyer. *BoDV* pp 147-148. [*Aa, se dog Veninde*, poem included in the collection *Udvalgte Digte*, 1953.]

Apple Blossoms. Tr. Charles Wharton Stork. *SeBDV* p 85. Also *TCScP* p 38. [*Æbleblomst*, poem from the collection *Digte*, 1895.]

Autumn. Tr. Gwen Rasmussen. *Versuch* vol. 17 (1978) p 22. [*Efteråret*, poem.]

Father, the Swans Fly Away. Tr. Robert Silliman Hillyer. *BoDV* pp 149-150. [*Fa'er, hvor flyver Svanerne hen?*, poem included in the collection *Udvalgte Digte*, 1953.]

Father, Where Do the Wild Swans Go? Tr. Charles Wharton Stork. *IDIWB* p 85 and *SeBDV* p 88. [*Fa'er, hvor flyverne Svanerne hen?*, poem included in the collection *Udvalgte Digte*, 1953.]

Forth, My Gallant Honey-Bees! Tr. Charles Wharton Stork. *SeBDV* pp 86-87. [*Alle mine Honningbi'r*, poem included in the collection *Udvalgte Digte*, 1953.]

Sunlight in the Room. Tr. Robert Silliman Hillyer. *BoDV* pp 148-149. [*Solskin i Stuen*, poem included in the collection *Udvalgte Digte*, 1953.]

Thou Lovely One Far Distant. Tr. Charles Wharton Stork. *SeBDV* p 85. [*Langt borte*, poem from the collection *Løv*, 1915.]

JENS CHRISTIAN HOSTRUP (1818-1892)

Christmas Consolation. Tr. S. D. Rodholm. *HoS* p 106. [*Julebudet til dem, der bygge*, hymn published in *Ude og Hjemme*, vol. 5, no. 221 (25. dec. 1881).]

The Women of the North. Tr. Charles Wharton Stork. *SeBDV* p 59. [*Nordens Kvinde*, poem from the collection *Sange og Digte fra tredive År*, 1872.]

KARSTEN HOYDAL (b. 1912)
Faroese author

Christmas Courtship. A Short Story. Tr. from the Faroese by Hedin Brønner. *ASR* vol. 60, no. 4 (December 1972) pp 420-424. [*Ójavnt er bytt*, short story from the collection *Leikapettið*, 1971.]

Summer Eve at »Rockall«. Tr. from the Faroese by Hedin Brønner. *FSS* pp 247-250. [*Summarkvøld við »Rockall«*, short story published in the magazine *Varðin*, 1939.]

BERNHARD SEVERIN INGEMANN (1789-1872)

As Wide as the Skies Is Thy Love, O My God! Tr. P. C. Paulsen. *HinS* hymn nr. 30. [*Den Miskundelige*, hymn published in *Samlede Skrifter*, IV, bd. 7, 1845.]

Be with Us. Tr. S. D. Rodholm. *HoS* p 40. Also *HinS* hymn nr. 9. [*Bliv hos os naar Dagen hælder*, poem from the collection *Syv Aftensange*, 1838.]

Beauty around Us. Tr. S. D. Rodholm. *HoS* p 95. Also *HinS* hymn nr. 71. [*Pilgrimssang*, published in *Dansk Kirketidende*, 8. sept. 1850.]

The Castle in the West. Tr. R. P. Keigwin. *IDIWB* p 45. [*Der staar et Slot i Vesterled*, poem from the collection *Syv Aftensange*, 1838.]

Cheer Up! Tr. S. D. Rodholm. *Hos* p 109. [*I Snee staar Urt og Busk i Skjul*, poem published in *Huldregaverne*, 1831.]

Christmas Is Here with Joy Untold. Tr. D. G. M. Bach. *HinS* hymn nr. 21. [*Børnenes Julesang (Julen har bragt)*, poem from the collection *Folkedands-Viser og blandede Digte*, 1842.]

Dannebrog. (The Danish Flag). Tr. Charles Wharton Stork. *SeBDV* p 10. [Abbreviated version of *Til Dannebroge*, poem from *Julegave*, 1816. Also known by first line, *Vift stolt på Codans Bølge*.]

Evening Song. Tr. Robert Silliman Hillyer. *BoDV* pp 59-60. [*Der staar et Slot i Vesterled*, poem from the collection *Syv Aftensange*, 1838.]

Evening Song. Tr. S. D. Rodholm. *HoS* pp 42-43. [*I fjerne Kirketaarne hist*, poem from the collection *Syv Aftensange*, 1838.]

Evening Song. Tr. Robert Silliman Hillyer. *BoDV* p 60. [*Den skønne Jordens Sol gik ned*, poem from the collection *Syv Aftensange*, 1838.]

Evening Song. Tr. Robert Silliman Hillyer. *BoDV* p 61. [*Den store, stille Nat gaar frem*, poem from the collection *Syv Aftensange*, 1838.]

The Great and Skillful Master. Tr. S. D. Rodholm. *HoS* p 66. [*Mesteren kommer*, hymn from the collection *Høimesse-Psalmer til Kirkeaarets Helligdage*, 1843.]

Holger Danske's Arms. Tr. Robert Silliman Hillyer. *BoDV* pp 61-62. [*I alle de Riger og Lande*, from *Holger Danske*, ballad cycle, 1837.]

Lovely the Earth Is. Tr. Charles Wharton Stork. *SeBDV* p 13. [*Pilgrimssang*, poem from *Dansk Kirketidende*, 8. sept. 1850, nr. 257.]

Morning Song. Tr. Robert Silliman Hillyer. *BoDV* pp 58-59. [*I Østen stiger Solen op*, poem from the collection *Morgensange*, 1837.]

Now Peace Descends. Tr. S. D. Rodholm. *HoS* p 41. Also *HinS* hymn nr. 8. [*Aftensang*, poem published in *Harpen* vol. 4, no. 1 (1823).]

The Snow Lies Heavy on the Hedge. Tr. S. D. Rodholm. *HinS* hymn nr. 22. [*I Snee staar Urt og Busk i Skjul*, poem published in *Huldregaverne*, 1831.]

The Two Days. Tr. Charles Wharton Stork. *SeBDV* pp 10-13. [*De to Dage*, poem from the collection *Folkedands-Viser og blandede Digte*, 1842.]

Previous Translations:

To a Girl Beloved.
The Dancing Fleeting One.
The Wishes.
The Wooer.
The Mermaid.
The Instructress.
Song (Whither? O Whither, What Doth It Avail).
Song (When the Last Golden Ray).
Waldemar, Surnamed Seir; or The Victorious.
King Eric and the Outlaws, or the Throne, the Church and the People in the Thirteenth Century.

Progress of Axel Hwide.
The Aspen.
Dame Martha's Fountain.
From »Massaniello«: Massaniello, Mad, in the Church-Yard.
The Childhood of King Erik Menved. An Historical Romance.
Extracts from »Holger Danske«:
Holger on the Warrior Cairn;
Holger's Song on Life.
The Secret Witness.
The Doomed House.
The Death Ship.
The Aged Rabbi.
All Souls' Day.
Unity and Progress: »Through the Night of Doubt and Sorrow«.
The True Comfort (When My Nearest Friends Forsake).
The Tears of Jesus (Jesus Weeps while Laughs the World).
Christ, King and Judge.
Tidings or Salvation (Rise, Sinner from the Slumber).
Grace Abounding (In Earth Is Tribulation Great).
The Pilgrimage of the Soul.
Morning.
Lines (»Up! the Sun's Rays Are Calling Thee«).
Charles the Fifth's Song in His Coffin.
The Boy and the Mermaid.
O Blessed the Soul.
As Gold by Fire Is Tested.

BENJAMIN JACOBSEN (b. 1915)

»Oh Sir, You've Shot Her!« Recollections of a Copenhagen Childhood. Tr. Estrid Bannister. Ill. Des Asmussen. Intro. Victor Borge. London: Jonathan Cape, 1958. New York: G. P. Putnam's Sons, 1959. p 192 [*Midt i en Klunketid*, humorous memoirs, 1955.]

JENS PETER JACOBSEN (1847-1885)

Apparition. Tr. S. Foster Damon. *BoDV* pp 122-123. [*Nævner min Tanke dig*, poem from the collection *Digte og Udkast*, 1886.]

Arabesque. For a Sketch by Michelangelo. Tr. George C. Schoolfield. *ADL* pp 569-575. [*Arabesk. Til en Haandtegning af Michel Angelo*, poem from the collection *Digte og Udkast*, 1886.]

82

An Arabesque. Tr. S. Foster Damon. *BoDV* pp 118-120. [*En Arabesk*, poem from the collection *Digte og Udkast*, 1886.]

An Arabesque. Tr. John Jepson Egglishaw. *Nor* vol. 9, no. 6 (Nov.-Dec. 1951) p 425. [*En Arabesk*, poem from the collection *Digte og Udkast*, 1886.]

Death in Bergamo. Tr. Henry Meyer. *ADL* pp 289-305. [*Pesten i Bergamo*, short story from the collection *Mogens og andre Noveller*, 1882.]

Dream! Tr. Charles Wharton Stork. *SeBDV* p 67. [*Drøm*, poem from the song cycle *Hervert Sperring*, from the collection *Digte og Udkast*, 1886.]

Genre Picture. Tr. S. Foster Damon. *BoDV* p 124. [*Genrebillede*, poem first published in *Fra Fjeld og Dal*, ed. by Greensteen, 1875.]

Genre-picture. Tr. Paul Selver. *IDIWB* p 81. [*Genrebillede*, poem first published in *Fra Fjeld og Dal*, ed. by Greensteen, 1875.]

In the Moonlight. Tr. Charles Wharton Stork. *SeBDV* p 67. [*O naar Maanens Straaler milde spille*, (first line), poem from the second *Gurresang*, 1868-1869.]

Irmeline Rose. Tr. Charles Wharton Stork. *SeBDV* pp 69-70. [*Irmelin Rose*, poem from the collection *Digte og Udkast*, 1886.]

Landscape. Tr. R. P. Keigwin. *IDIWB* pp 79-81. [*Landskab*, poem from the collection *Digte og Udkast*, 1886.]

The Last Hours of Ulrik Christian. Tr. Hanna Astrup Larsen. *AScL* pp 60-69. [Excerpt from the novel *Marie Grubbe*, 1876.]

Marie Grubbe. Tr. Hanna Astrup Larsen. Revised and with intro. by Robert Raphael. 2nd revised edition. Boston: Twayne Publishing Co., 1975. p 261. [*Marie Grubbe*, novel, 1876.]

Marie Grubbe: A Lady of the Seventeenth Century. Tr. Hanna Astrup Larsen. New York: American-Scandinavian Foundation, 1952. [*Marie Grubbe*, novel, 1876.]

Mrs. Fonss. Tr. Anna Grabow. In *Mogens, and Other Stories.* Intro. O. F. Theis. 1921 ed., rpt. Freeport, N.Y.: Books for Libraries Press, 1972. pp 119-150. [*Fru Fønss*, short story from the collection *Mogens og andre Noveller*, 1882.]

Mogens. Tr. Anna Grabow. In *Mogens, and Other Stories.* Intro. O. F. Theis. 1921 ed., rpt. Freeport, N.Y.: Books for Libraries Press, 1972. pp 15-84. [*Mogens*, short story, first published in *Nyt dansk Maanedsskrift* 3 (1871-72), and later in *Mogens og andre Noveller*, 1882.]

Mogens. Tr. P. M. Mitchell and Kenneth H. Ober. *RG* pp 79-129. [*Mogens*, short story

first published in *Nyt dansk Maanedsskrift* 3, (1871-72), and later in *Mogens og andre Noveller*, 1882.]

The Moment Inexpressible. Tr. Charles Wharton Stork. *SeBDV* pp 68-69. [*Navnløs*, poem from the collection *Digte og Udkast*, 1886.]

Niels Lyhne. Tr. Hanna Astrup Larsen. Intro. Børge Gedsø Madsen. 1919; rpt. New York: Twayne Publishers and The American-Scandinavian Foundation, 1967. p 244. [The Library of Scandinavian Literature, vol. 2.] [*Niels Lyhne*, novel, 1880.]

Niels Lyhne, (condensed). In *Masterplots*, vol. III. Ed. Frank N. Magill. New York: The Salem Press, 1952. [*Niels Lyhne*, novel, 1880.]

Night Piece. Tr. S. Foster Damon. *BoDV* p 123. [*Har Dagen sanket al sin Sorg*, poem from the collection *Digte og Udkast*, 1886.]

No More than a Dream. Tr. Charles Wharton Stork. *SeBDV* pp 67-68. [*Der hjælper ej Drømme*, poem from the collection *Digte og Udkast*, 1886.]

The Plague at Bergamo. Tr. Anna Grabow. In *Mogens, and Other Stories.* Intro. O. F. Theis. 1921 ed., rpt. Freeport, N. Y.: Books for Libraries Press, 1972. pp 87-102. [*Pesten i Bergamo*, short story from the collection *Mogens og andre Noveller*, 1882.]

The Plague at Bergamo. In *Treasury of World Literature.* Ed. Dagobert D. Runes. New York: Philosophical Library, 1956. pp 623-629. [*Pesten i Bergamo*, short story from the collection *Mogens og andre Noveller*, 1882.]

Scarlet Roses. Tr. S. Foster Damon. *BoDV* pp 124-125. [*Det bødes der for*, poem from the collection *Digte og Udkast*, 1886.]

Silken Shoe upon Golden Last. Tr. Charles Wharton Stork. *SeBDV* p 69. [*Silkesko over gylden Læst*, poem from the collection *Digte og Udkast*, 1886.]

There Should Have Been Roses. Tr. Anna Grabow. In *Mogens, and Other Stories.* Intro. O. F. Theis. 1921 ed., rpt. Freeport, N. Y.: Books for Libraries Press, 1972. pp 105-115. [*Der burde have været Roser*, short story from the collection *Mogens og andre Noveller*, 1882.]

There Should Have Been Roses. Tr. Peter H. Salus. *ASR* vol. 55, no. 4 (December 1967) pp 393-396. [*Der burde have været Roser*, short story from the collection *Mogens og andre Noveller*, 1882.]

Valdemar's Complaint over His Murdered Mistress. Tr. S. Foster Damon. *BoDV* pp 120-121. [*Herre, ved du hvad du gjorde?* the seventh *Gurresang*, 1868-1869.]

The Wood Whispers with Tove's Voice. Tr. S. Foster Damon. *BoDV* pp 121-122. [From *Den vilde Jagt*, the eighth *Gurresang*, 1868-1869.]

Previous Tranlations:

Poems.
Our Earth is Rocked.
Two Worlds.
Go on, My Boat, Go On.
So Do the Seraphim.
Ever Unending and Changeless.
Let Me Not Die.
For Garlanding My Picture.

Works about J. P. Jacobsen

Arestad, Sverre. **J. P. Jacobsen's »Niels Lyhne«.** In *Scandinavian Studies: Essays Presented to Dr. Henry Goddard Leach.* Seattle: University of Washington Press for the American-Scandinavian Foundation, 1965. pp 202-212.

Bergholz, Harry. **»Miss Julie«. Strindberg's Response to J. P. Jacobsen's »Fru Marie Grubbe«.** *Scandinavica* vol. 11, no. 1 (May 1972) pp 13-19.

Gustafson, Alrik. **J. P. Jacobsen.** In his *Six Scandinavian Novelists.* 1940; rpt. Minneapolis: University of Minnesota Press and the American-Scandinavian Foundation, 1968. New York: Biblo & Tannen, 1969. pp 73-122.

Ingwersen, Niels. **Problematic Protagonists: Marie Grubbe and Niels Lyhne.** In Weinstock, John M. and Robert T. Rovinsky, eds.: *The Hero in Scandinavian Literature from Peer Gynt to the Present.* Austin and London: University of Texas Press, 1975. pp 39-61.

Jensen, Niels Lyhne. **Jens Peter Jacobsen.** Boston: Twayne, 1980. p 187. (Twayne World Authors Series, 573.)

Madsen, Børge Gedsø. **Georg Brandes' Criticism of »Niels Lyhne«.** *SS* vol. 38, no. 2 (May 1966) pp 124-130.

Madsen, Børge Gedsø. **Influences from J. P. Jacobsen and Sigbjörn Obstfelder on Rainer Maria Rilke's »Die Aufzeichnungen des Malte Laurids Brigge«.** *SS* vol. 26, no. 3 (August 1954) pp 105-114.

Madsen, Børge Gedsø. **J. P. Jacobsen Reconsidered.** *ASR* vol. 50, no. 3 (September 1962) pp 272-279.

Palmer, Christopher. **J. P. Jacobsen and Schoenberg.** *Denmark* (London) no. 157 (Autumn 1971) pp 13-15. Ill.

Palmer, Christopher. **Schoenberg, Jacobsen and the Gurrelieder.** *Musical Opinion* 96 (August 1973) pp 557-9.

Schoolfield, George C. **Stefan George's Translations of Jens Peter Jacobsen.** *Kentucky Foreign Language Quarterly* (Lexington, Kentucky) vol. 10, no. 1 (1963) pp 31-40.

Stanford, Derek. **That Great, Great Writer.** *Nor* vol. 13, no. 1 (Jan.-Feb. 1955) pp 65-67.

JØRGEN-FRANTZ JACOBSEN (1900-1938)
Faroese author who wrote in Danish

The Farthest Shore. In Elkjær-Hansen, Niels: *The Faroe Islands.* Copenhagen: Royal Danish Ministry of Foreign Affairs, 1965. p 40.

Previous Translations:

Barbara.

Works about Jørgen-Frantz Jacobsen

Brønner, Hedin. **Jørgen-Frantz Jacobsen and Barbara.** *ASR* vol. 61, no. 1 (Spring 1973) pp 39-45.

Brønner, Hedin. **Three Faroese Novelists: An Appreciation of Jørgen-Frantz Jacobsen, William Heinesen and Hedin Brú.** New York: Twayne Publishers, 1973. p 140. (The Library of Scandinavian Studies vol. 1.)

Matras, Chr. **Jørgen-Frantz Jacobsen. Writer and Friend.** *Føroyar. Welcome to the Faroes* (Rungsted Kyst, Denmark) vol. 9 (1975) pp 91-97.

FRANK JÆGER (1926-1977)

The Afternoon of the Faun in the Park. Tr. Poul Borum. *CDPo* p 179. [*Faunens Eftermiddag i Parken*, poem from the collection *Morgenens Trompet*, 1949.]

But in September. Tr. Poul Borum. *CDPo* pp 180-181. [*Men i September*, poem from the collection *Tyren*, 1953.]

Children Sing like This. Tr. Poul Borum. *CDPo* p 184. [*Saadan synger Børn*, poem from the collection *Idylia*, 1967.]

84 **Cinna, the Poet.** Tr. Anne Born. *Orbis* pp 48-49. [*Cinna, Poeten*, poem from the collection *Cinna og andre Digte*, 1959.]

The Devil's Instrument. Tr. Maureen Neiiendam. Ill. Ib Spang Olsen. *DFOJ* vol. 47 (1964) pp 20-23. [*Djævelens Instrument*, short story from the collection *Den unge Jægers Lidelser*, 1953.]

The Devil's Instrument. Tr. Paula Hostrup-Jessen. *DI* pp 7-18. [*Djævelens Instrument*, short story from the collection *Den unge Jægers Lidelser*, 1953.]

Goodbye Tut. Tr. Martin S. Allwood. *MoDP* pp 46-47. [*Farvel Tut*, poem from the collection *Digte 1948-1950*, 1951.]

Handshake for Tony. Tr. Martin S. Allwood. *TCScP* pp 104-105. [*Haandslag til Tony*, poem from the collection *Digte 1948-1950*, 1951.]

Lover. Tr. Poul Borum. *CDPo* pp 181-182. [*Elsker*, poem from the collection *Havkarlens Sange*, 1956.]

My Evening Prayer. Tr. Anne Born. *Orbis* p 49. [*Min Aftenbøn*, poem from the collection *Tyren*, 1953.]

Neighbor to the Sea. Ill. Ib Andersen. *DFOJ* no. 64 (1968) pp 26-28.

Ophelia Restored. Tr. Anne Born. *Orbis* pp 49-50. [*Den genfundne Ophelia*, poem from the collection *De fem Aarstider*, 1950.]

Sidenius in Esbjerg. Tr. Alexander Taylor. *Contemporary Literature in Translation* (Vancouver, B.C.) no. 9 (Winter 1970) p 22. [*Sidenius i Esbjerg*, poem from the collection *Cinna og andre Digte*, 1959.]

Sidenius in Esbjerg. Tr. Poul Borum. *CDPo* p 183. [*Sidenius i Esbjerg*, poem from the collection *Cinna og andre Digte*, 1959.]

Small Sun. Tr. Poul Borum. *CDPo* p 180. [*Liden Sol*, poem from the collection *Tyren*, 1953.]

Sonnet CLV. Tr. Anne Born. *Orbis* p 49. [*Sonet CLV*, poem from the collection *Cinna og andre Digte*, 1959.]

Sunday in September. Tr. Poul Borum. *CDPo* p 177. [*Søndag i September*, poem from the collection *Dydige Digte*, 1948.]

Susanne after Bathing. Tr. Nadia Christensen. Ill. John Nielsen. *SR* vol. 64, no. 3 (September 1976) pp 44-47. [Short story from the collection *Alvilda*, 1969.]

To a Sensitive Girl Friend. Tr. Poul Borum. *CDPo* p 178. [*Til en følsom Veninde*, poem from the collection *Dydige Digte*, 1948.]

Winter's Tale. Tr. John C. Pearce. *LitR-Dk* p 75. [*Vintereventyr*, poem from the collection *Tyren*, 1953.]

Works about Frank Jæger

Hugus, Frank. **The Dilemma of the Artist in Selected Prose Works of Frank Jaeger.** *SS* vol. 47, no. 1 (Winter 1975) pp 52-65.

JESPER JENSEN (b. 1931)

Board and Lodging. (Resume with quotations of reviews in English and French). *World Theatre* (Paris) vol. 14, no. 1 (1965) p 97 (Technical Data: Denmark). [*Diskret ophold*, play by Jesper Jensen and Klaus Rifbjerg, 1964.]

JOHANNES V. JENSEN (1873-1950)

A. Conradsen. Tr. Ronald Bathgate. *WR* pp 116-133. [*A. Conradsen*, myth, 1930.]

A Koy. Tr. Marion L. Nielsen. *Dk-JVJ* pp 20-36. [*A Koy*, short story from the collection *Lille Ahasverus*, vol. II of *Eksotiske Noveller*, 1909.]

Agony and Literature (The Wisdom Tooth). Tr. B. E. Juel-Jensen. *Oxford Medical School Gazette* (Oxford) vol. 26 (197-) pp 37-39. Ill. [*Visdomstanden*, from *Gyldendals Julebog*, 1944.]

Among the Birds. Tr. Evelyn Heepe. *MoDA* pp 15-28. [*Hos Fuglene*, short story originally published in *Berlingske Tidende*, 4. april 1926 and later in the collection *Ved Livets Bred*.]

At Lunch. Tr. Alexander Taylor. *CDPo* pp 19-22. [*Ved Frokosten*, poem from the collection *Digte*, 1906.]

At Memphis Station. Tr. Alexander Taylor. *CDPo* pp 23-26. [*Paa Memphis Station*, poem from the collection *Digte*, 1906.]

At Memphis Station. Tr. S. Foster Damon. *TCScP* pp 44-47. Also *BoDV* pp 165-168. [*Paa Memphis Station*, poem from the collection *Digte*, 1906.]

The Banks of Life. Tr. Lydia Cranfield. *WR* pp 86-100. [*Ved Livets Bred* -, short story originally published in *Berlingske Tidendes Julenummer*, 20. dec. 1925 and later in the collection *Ved Livets Bred og andre Myter*, *Myter*, vol. IV, 1928.]

A Bathing Girl. Tr. Charles Wharton Stork. *SeBDV* pp 98-99. [*Stev, nr. 7*, poem in the novel *Columbus*, 1921.]

The Blind Girl. Tr. Robert Silliman Hillyer. *BoDV* pp 172-174. [Poem published as *Den blinde Merete* in *Illustreret Tidende*, 1903, and as *Den blinde Pige* in *Digte*, 1906.]

Columbus. Tr. Robert Silliman Hillyer. *BoDV* pp 176-179. [*Columbus*, poem from the collection *Digte*, 1906.]

Columbus. Tr. Evelyn Neepe. *Nor* vol. 8, no. 6 (Nov.-Dec. 1950) pp 411-412. [*Columbus*, poem from the collection *Digte*, 1906.]

Columbus. Tr. Murray Brown. *SR* vol. 63, no. 2 (June 1975) pp 8-10. [*Columbus*, poem from the collection *Digte*, 1906.]

The Cornfield. Tr. Ronald Bathgate. *WR* pp 148-153. [*Kornmarken*, myth, 1932.]

Dance of Death. *Western Humanities Review* (Utah) vol. 4, no. 2 (Spring 1950) pp 116-119. [Included in Marion L. Nielsen's article on Johannes V. Jensen.] [*Knokkelmanden*, myth from the collection *Myter og Jagter*, 1907.]

The Danish Coast-line Is Bright with Smiles. Tr. Johannes Knudsen. *HinS* song nr. 92. [*Hvor smiler fager den danske Kyst*, poem published in *Social-Demokraten*, 19. juli 1925.]

Danse Macabre. Tr. Ronald Bathgate. *WR* pp 71-76. [*Knokkelmanden*, myth from the collection *Myter og Jagter*, 1907.]

Dedication. *The Bridge* (Junction City, Oregon) no. 3 (1979) p 14. [*Tilegnelse*, poem from the collection *Skovene*, 1904.]

Denmark Song. Tr. Charles Wharton Stork. *SeBDV* pp 96-97. [*Danmarkssangen*, poem from the collection *Verdens Lys*, 1926.]

Denmark's Johannes V. Jensen. Tr. and intro. Marion L. Nielsen. Logan: Utah State Agricultural College, 1955. p 45. [Utah State Agricultural College Monograph series, vol. III, no. 1.] Individual stories listed separately under *Dk-JVJ*.

Did They Catch the Ferry? Tr. Lydia Cranfield. *AScL* pp 81-86. *Nor*, vol. 11, no. 5 (Sept.-Oct. 1953) pp 343-346. *WR* pp 101-108. [*Nåede de Færgen?*, short story originally published in *Social-Demokraten*, 24. dec. 1925.]

The Duet. *Nor* vol. 14, no. 6 (Nov.-Dec. 1956) pp 413-415. [*Knokkelmanden*, myth from the collection *Myter og Jagter*, 1907.] [See also *Dance of Death*. Same translation.]

The Eagle and the Serpent. In *Great Essays by Nobel Prize Winners.* Ed. Leo Hamalian and Edmond L. Volpe. New York: The Noonday Press (Farrar, Straus & Cudahy), 1960. pp 189-204. [Extract from *Den lange Rejse*, book 2 (1908-1922), translation of 1923.]

Fujiyama. Tr. Elias Bredsdorff. *CDPr* pp 91-92. [*Fusijama*, myth from *Myter og Jagter*, 1907.]

Fujiyama. Tr. Marion L. Nielsen. *Western Humanities Review* vol. 4, no. 2 (1950) pp 111-119. Also *Dk-JVJ* pp 19-20. [*Fusijama*, myth from *Myter og Jagter*, 1907.]

The Greatest Sorrow. Tr. Ronald Bathgate. *WR* pp 51-57. [*Den største Sorg*, myth, 1931.]

In the Indian Ocean. Tr. Marion L. Nielsen. *Dk-JVJ* pp 36-40. [*I det indiske Hav*, myth published in *Aarbog*, 1916.]

Kirsten's Last Journey. Tr. Lee Marshall. *ADL* pp 360-379. [*Kirstens sidste Rejse*, short story published in *Julealbum*, 1901, and in *Nye Himmerlandshistorier*, 1904.]

Kirsten's Last Journey. Tr. Marion L. Nielsen *Dk-JVJ* pp 10-19. [*Kirstens sidste Rejse*, short story published in *Julealbum*, 1901, and in *Nye Himmerlandshistorier*, 1904.]

The Light Nights. Tr. Marion L. Nielsen. *Dk-JVJ* pp 40-45. [*De lyse Nætter*, from *Midsommerbrev*, in *Politiken*, 22. juni 1943, also published in *Myter*, vol. 2. 1960.]

From The Long Journey. Tr. A. C. Chater. In *Nobel Parade.* Selection by Winners of the Award for Literature. Ed. Helen M. McDonnel. Glenview, Ill.: Scott, Foresman & Co., 1975. pp 253-269. [From the 1923 translation of *Den lange Rejse*, 1908-1922.]

Lost Forests. Tr. Henry Commager. *Nobel Prize Reader* pp 431-436. [Trans. first pub. 1928.] [*De forsvundne Skove*, short story from the collection *Intermezzo*, 1899.]

The Monsoon. Tr. Carl Nesjar. *Nor* vol. 9, no. 1 (Jan.-Feb. 1951) pp 52-56. [*Monsunen*, short story from the collection *Lille Ahasverus*, 1909.]

The Moon City. Tr. Lee M. Hollander. *The Literary Review* (Fairleigh Dickinson University, New Jersey) vol. 12, no. 3 (Spring 1969) pp 360-366. [*Maanebyen*, short story first published in *Berlingske Tidendes Julenummer*, 1926, and included in the collection *Ved Livets Bred og andre Myter*, *Myter*, vol. IV, 1928.]

Mother's Song. Tr. S. Foster Damon. *BoDV* pp 175-176. [*Moderens Sang*, poem from the collection *Digte*, 1906.]

Norwegian Journey. Tr. A. J. Poole. *Nor* vol. 13, no. 5 (Sept.-Oct. 1955) pp 337-338. [*Med Skyds*, travel description, 1901. Included in *Myter og Jagter*, 1907.]

The Old Clock. Tr. Ronald Bathgate. *Nor* vol. 16, no. 6 (Nov.-Dec. 1958) pp 408-409. Also *WR* pp 69-70. [*Det gamle Ur*, myth from *Myter og Jagter*, 1907.]

The Old Troll. Tr. F. A. Rush. *Denmark: A Monthly Review of Anglo-Danish Relations* (London) (Jan. 1950) p 7. [*Den gamle Trold*, myth from the collection *Myter*, 1912.]

86

Olivia Marianne. Tr. Evelyn Heepe. *SotN* pp 13-17. [*Olivia Marianne*, myth, 1915.]

Olivia Marianne. Tr. C. A. Bodelsen. *Nor* vol. 16, no. 6 (Nov.-Dec. 1958) pp 404-408. Also *WR* pp 77-85. [*Olivia Marianne*, myth, 1915.]

Our Lady. Tr. Ronald Bathgate. *WR* pp 37-50. (A chapter from the novel *Christofer Columbus*, 1921.]

Peace on Earth, Goodwill to Men. Tr. R. H. Bathgate. *CDPr* pp 85-90. [*Julefred*, short story from the collection *Himmerlandshistorier*, 1900.]

Potowatomi's Daughter. Tr. Ronald Bathgate. *WR* pp 134-147. [*Potowatomis Datter*, myth, 1905.]

Prayer of the Pantheist. Tr. Gertrude B. Longbrake. *ASR* vol. 39, no. 4 (Dec. 1951) p 319. [Poem.]

The Red Tree. Tr. S. Foster Damon. *BoDV* pp 169-171. [*Det røde Træ*, poem from the collection *Digte*, 1906.]

The Red Tree. Tr. Charles Wharton Stork. *TCScP* pp 43-44. [*Det røde Træ*, poem from the collection *Digte*, 1906.]

A Sailor's Watch Is Lone and Long. Tr. Martin S. Allwood and Roger Roe. *ScSoB* p 8. [*Sømandsvise (En Sømand har sin Enegang)*, song from *Aarets Højtider*, 1925.]

The Sleepers. Tr. L. S. Hanson. *ASR* vol. 38, no. 4 (Dec. 1950) pp 355-362. [*Syvsoverne*, short story from the collection *Nye Himmerlandshistorier*, 1904.]

Song of England. Tr. R. P. Keigwin. *TCScP* pp 42-43. [*Englands-sangen*, song from *Aarets Højtider*, 1925.]

Steen Steensen Blicher. Tr. R. P. Keigwin. *FtDP* pp 19-21. [*Steen Steensen Blicher*, poem on the occasion of his 150th birthday, 1932.]

The Trio. Tr. C. A. Bodelsen. *WR* pp 18-36. [*Trioen*, introduction to an unwritten novel, 1922.]

The Wandering Girl. Tr. Robert Silliman Hillyer. *BoDV* p 172. Also *TCScP* pp 47-48. [*Pigen der vandrer*, poem from the collection *Digte*, 1906.]

The Waving Rye. Intro. C. A. Bodelsen. Tr. C. A. Bodelsen, Ronald Bathgate and Lydia Cranfield. Copenhagen: Gyldendal, 1958; New York: American-Scandinavian Foundation, 1959. [14 short stories.] Individual stories listed separately under *WR*.

The Waving Rye. Tr. Ronald Bathgate. *Nor* vol. 16, no. 6 (Nov.-Dec. 1958) pp 401-404. *WR* pp 11-17. [*Rugen bølger*, short story originally published in *Politiken*, 16. juni 1911.]

The Windmill. Tr. Ronald Bathgate. *WR* pp 58-68. [*Møllen*, short story originally published in *Politiken*, 21. marts 1941.]

Yellow Tulips. Tr. Ronald Bathgate. *WR* pp 109-115. [*Gule Tulipaner*, myth, 1916.]

Previous Translations:

The Knifegrinder.
Bo'l.
Ane and the Cow.
The Long Journey.
The Maiden.
Hamlet.
The English Style. In the History of Sports.
Fall of the King.
The Heart.
The Ladybug.
The Kingfisher.
The Jutland Wind.
The Danish Homestead.
The Border of Life.
Cecil - a Himmerland Tale.
Denmark's Christmas Gnome.
Garden Colonies in Danmark.

Works about Johannes V. Jensen

Friis, Oluf. **Johannes V. Jensen.** *Scandinavica* vol. 1, no. 2 (Nov. 1962) pp 114-123.

Madsen, Børge Gedsø. **»Lavt Land« and Its Debt to »Himmerlandshistorier«.** *SS* vol. 31, no. 3 (Aug. 1959) pp 121-128.

Nielsen, Marion L. **Denmark and the Wide World: Johannes V. Jensen.** *Western Humanities Review* vol. 4, no. 2 (1950) pp 111-119.

Rush, F. A. **A Tribute to Johannes V. Jensen.** *Nor* vol. 9, no. 1 (Jan.-Feb. 1951) pp 32-36.

Wiehl, Inga Wolfsberg. **Johannes V. Jensen's Concept of America.** Ph. D. diss., Seattle: University of Washington, 1967.

Wiehl, Inga. **Johannes V. Jensen's Discovery of America.** *The Bridge* (Junction City, Oregon) no. 3 (1979) pp 5-14.

Wiehl, Inga. **Johannes V. Jensen's »Myte« and James Joyce's Epiphany; a Study of »Potowatomi's Daughter«.** *Orbis litt.* no. 23 (1968) pp 225-232.

NIELS JENSEN (b. 1927)

Days of Courage. A Medieval Adventure. Tr. Oliver Stallybrass. New York: Harcourt Brace Jovanovich, 1973. p 188. [*Da Landet lå øde*, novel, 1971.]

When the Land Lay Waste. Tr. Oliver Stallybrass. London: Methuen, 1973. pp 174. [*Da Landet lå øde*, novel, 1971.]

P. A. JENSEN

My Mother. Tr. S. D. Rodholm. *HoS* p 180. [*Hvem tog mig først i sin kærlige Favn*, poem published in *Den dansk-amerikanske Højskolesangbog*, 2. udg., 1907.]

THIT JENSEN (1876-1957)

The Knights of Rind Welcome a Kinsman. Tr. Ann R. Born. *CDPr* pp 93-99. [*De Rinds Knaber hylder Blod af deres Blod*, chapter 6 of the novel *Af Blod er du kommet*, 1928.]

HANS LYNGBY JEPSEN (b. 1920)

The Blackbird. Tr. Paula Hostrup-Jessen. *DI* pp 42-51. [*Solsorten*, short story from the collection *Der er Lys*, 1968.]

The Blackbird. Tr. David Stoner. Ill. Axel Andersen. *ASR* vol. 56, no. 1 (March 1968) pp 60-65. [*Solsorten*, short story from the collection *Der er Lys*, 1968.]

Jezabel and the Shoemaker. Tr. Maureen Neiiendam. *Nor* vol. 12, no. 4 (July-Aug. 1954) pp 273-279. [*Jezabel og Skomageren*, short story from the collection *I Kærlighed og andre Noveller*, 1959.]

Jezebel and the Shoemaker. Tr. Eva Schweizer Vogel. *ASR* vol. 57, no. 3 (Sept. 1969) pp 283-288. [*Jezabel og Skomageren*, short story from the collection *I Kærlighed og andre Noveller*, 1959.]

MARTIN JOENSEN (1902-1966)
Faroese author

The »Man« on Board. Tr. from the Faroese by Hedin Brønner. *FFS* pp 213-224. [*Maðurin umborð*, short story from the collection *Útrák*, 1949.]

To Be a Dentist. Tr. from the Faroese by Hedin Brønner. *FSS* pp 225-237. [*Tanntongin*, short story from the collection *Útrák*, 1949.]

ILJITSCH JOHANNSEN (1925-1957)

Still Life. Tr. Elizabeth Byrd. *MoDP* pp 40-43. [*Nature morte*, poem from the collection by that name, 1950.]

JOHANNES JØRGENSEN (1866-1956)

Autumn Dream. Tr. Robert Silliman Hillyer. *BoDV* pp 143-144. [*Høstdrøm*, poem from the collection *Bekendelse*, 1894.]

Confession. Tr. Robert Silliman Hillyer. *BoDV* pp 145-146. [*Bekendelse*, poem from the collection by the same name, 1894.]

The Legend of My Life. Tr. Evelyn Heepe. *MoDA* pp 24-44. [Selection from *Mit Livs Legende*, memoirs, 1916-28.]

Meseemed There Called--. Tr. Charles Wharton Stork. *SeBDV* p 77. [*Manon (V)*, *(Det er som kaldte i Natten)*, song cycle from the collection *Lyrik*, 1904. Original version called *Ellen (V)* in the collection *Stemninger*, 1892.]

The Plants Stand Silent round Me. Tr. Robert Silliman Hillyer. *BoDV* p 144. Also *TCScP* p 38. [*Jeg sidder blandt stille Planter (ForaarsEvangelium, XI)*, poem from the collection *Bekendelse*, 1894.]

St. Bridget of Sweden. Tr. Ingeborg Lund. London: Longmans, Green & Co., 1954. 2 vols. [*Den Hellige Birgitta af Vadstena*, saint's life, 1941-43.]

St. Peter and Mordecai. Tr. Ann R. Born. *CDPr* pp 20-28. [*Sanct Peder og Mardochai*, short story from the collection *Joachims Hjemkomst*, 1933.]

The Tread from Above. Tr. Lydia Cranfield. *Nor* vol. 14, no. 4 (July-August 1956) pp 258-259. [*Traaden ovenfra*, short story from the collection *Lignelser*, 1898.]

'Twas at the Bridal Time of Flowers. Tr. Charles Wharton Stork. *SeBDV* p 76. [*Manon (VI) (Det var ved Knopbrudstide)*, song cycle from the collection *Lyrik*, 1904.]

Previous Translations:

Pilgrim Walks in Franciscan Italy.
St. Francis of Assisi. A Biography.
Lourdes.
False Witness.
The War Pilgrim.
Jörgensen. An Autobiography. [**Mit Livs Legende.**]
Don Bosco.
Saint Catherine of Siena.

88 Works about Johannes Jørgensen

Jensen, Niels Lyhne. **Johannes Jørgensen.** *Nor* vol. 14, no. 4 (July-Aug. 1956) pp 255-258.

Jones, W. Glyn. **The Early Novels of Jørgensen.** *SS* vol. 36, no. 2 (May 1964) pp 103-117.

Jones, W. Glyn. **Johannes Jørgensen.** Boston: Twayne, 1969. p 183. [Twayne World Authors Series.]

Jones, W. Glyn. **Johannes Jørgensen and His Apologetics.** *SS* vol. 32, no. 1 (Feb. 1960) pp 27-36.

Jones, W. Glyn. **Johannes Jørgensen in the Centenary of His Birth.** *Scandinavica* vol. 5, no. 2 (Nov. 1966) pp 100-110.

Jones, W. Glyn. **Some Personal Aspects of Johannes Jørgensen's Prose.** *Modern Language Review* vol. 55 (1960) pp 399-410.

Nugent, Robert. **Jørgensen's Devotional Verse: A Contemporary Act of Faith.** *Renascence Magazine* (Milwaukee, Wisconsin) vol. 15, no. 2 (1963) pp 79-81.

AXEL JUEL (1883-1948)

Joy, Sorrow and Happiness. Tr. Charles Wharton Stork. *SeBDV* p 110. [*Glæden, Sorgen og Lykken*, poem from the collection *De første Blomster*, 1909.]

STEN KAALØ (b. 1945)

For Ever. Tr. Linda Tagliaferro. *CDPo* pp 313-315. [*For Ever*, poem from the collection *Til Folk i Byen*, 1971.]

Recollection. Tr. Linda Tagliaferro. *CDPo* p 319. [*Erindring*, poem from the collection *Sidste Forår*, 1973.]

Run. Tr. Linda Tagliaferro. *CDPo* p 318. [*Løbetur*, poem from the collection *Sidste Forår*, 1973.]

You Sit Out There, Peeing. Tr. Linda Tagliaferro. *CDPo* pp 316-317. [*Der ude sidder du og tisser*, poem from the collection *Sidste Forår*, 1973.]

HANS VILHELM KAALUND (1818-1885)

Everyday Life. Tr. S. D. Rodholm. *HoS* pp 123-124. [*Paa det Jevne!* poem from the collection *En Eftervaar*, 3. opl., 1882.]

In a Sunny Nook. Tr. Charles Wharton Stork. *SeBDV* pp 56-57. [*I en Solskinskrog*, poem included in the collection *Samlede Digtninge*, 1920.]

Previous Translations:

The Goldfishes.
The Rattle.
The Critic.

GUDMUND KAMBAN (1888-1945)
Icelandic author who wrote in Danish

We Murderers. A play in three acts. Tr. Einar Haugen. Intro. Donald E. Askey. Madison: University of Wisconsin Press, 1970. p 74. [Nordic Translation Series.] [*Vi Mordere*, play, 1920.]

CHRISTIAN KAMPMANN (b. 1939)

Absence. Tr. Paula Hostrup-Jessen. *DI* pp 177-186. [*Fravær*, short story from the collection *Ly*, 1965.]

HARALD KIDDE (1878-1918)

The Lost Son. Tr. V. Elizabeth Balfour-Browne. *CDPr* pp 100-119. [*Den fortabte Søn*, short story from the collection *Vandringer*, 1920.]

The Obol. Tr. P. M. Mitchell. *Nor* vol. 13, no. 4 (July-August 1955) pp 275-278. [*Obolen*, short story from the collection *Luftslotte*, 1904.]

SØREN KIERKEGAARD (1813-1855)

Armed Neutrality. An Open Letter. Selections from His (K's) Journals and Papers. Ed., tr. and with intro. by Howard V. and Edna H. Hong. Background essay and commentary by Gregor Malantschuk. Bloomington: Indiana University Press, 1968. p 179. [*Den bevæbnede Neutralitet; Foranlediget ved en Ytring af Dr. Rudelbach mig betræffende*, in *Fædrelandet*, 31. jan. 1851.]

Christian Discourses. The Lilies of the Field and the Birds of the Air. Three Discourses at the Communion on Fridays. Intro. and tr. Walter Lowrie. 1939; rpt. New York & London: Oxford University Press, 1952. p 389. New York: Galaxy, 1961. p 407. Princeton: Princeton University Press, 1971. [*Lilien på Marken og Fuglen under Himlen. Tre gudelige Taler,* 1849.]

The Concept of Anxiety. A Simple Psychologically Orienting Deliberation on the Dogmatic Issue of Hereditary Sin. Ed., tr. and with intro. and notes by Reidar Thomte in collaboration with Albert B. Anderson. Princeton, N. J., Princeton University Press, 1980. p 304. [Kierkegaard's Writings, VIII.] [*Begrebet Angest,* 1844.]

The Concept of Dread. Tr. and with notes and intro. by Walter Lowrie. 2nd ed. Tr. revised by H. A. Johnson. Princeton: Princeton University Press, 1957, 1964, 1967. p 154. Also New York: Harper, 1959. pb. [1st ed. 1944.] [*Begrebet Angest,* 1844.] See also *The Concept of Anxiety.*

The Concept of Irony, with Constant Reference to Socrates. Tr. and with notes and intro. by Lee M. Capel. London: Collins; New York: Harper & Row, 1966. p 442. [*Om Begrebet Ironi med stadigt Hensyn til Socrates,* 1841.]

Concluding Unscientific Postscript. Tr. David F. Swenson, completed after his death and provided with intro. and notes by Walter Lowrie. 1941; rpt. Princeton: Princeton University Press for The American-Scandinavian Foundation, 1953, 1960. p 571. [*Afsluttende uvidenskabelig Efterskrift,* 1846.]

From **Concluding Unscientific Postscript.** In *The Search for Being; Essays from Kierkegaard to Sartre on the Problem of Existence.* Tr. and ed. by Jean T. Wilde and William Kimmel. Intro. by William Kimmel. Preface: Martin D'Arcy. New York: Twayne Pub., 1962. pp 52-96. [*Afsluttende uvidenskabelig Efterskrift,* 1846.]

Crisis in the Life of an Actress, and Other Essays on Drama. Tr. and with notes and intro. by Stephen Crites. London: Collins; New York: Harper & Row, 1967. p 154. [*Krisen og en Krise i en Skuespillerindes Liv,* in *Fædrelandet,* 24.-27. juli 1848.]

Diary. Ed. Peter P. Rohde. Tr. Gerda M. Andersen. New York: Philosophical Library; Toronto: Copp, 1960. London: Peter Owen, 1961. p 225. [American ed., the Wisdom Library. 75.] [239 selections from Kierkegaard's *Papirer,* 1836-1855.]

Diary of a Seducer. Tr. and intro. Gerd Gillhoff. New York: Ungar Publishing Co., 1966,

1969. London: Elek, 1969. p 181. [*Forførerens Dagbog = Enten - Eller, Første Deel,* 1843.]

The Difficulty of Being Christian. Ed. and intro. by Jacques Colette. Tr. Ralph M. McInerny and Leo Turcotte. Notre Dame, Indiana: University of Notre Dame Press, 1968. p 311. [Tr. to English from the French translation, *La difficulté d'être chrétien.*] [Includes selections from the works and papers of Søren Kierkegaard. Many of the text translations taken from other English editions.]

Edifying Discourses. Tr. David F. and Lillian M. Swenson. 2 vol. pb. 1943-5; rpt. Minneapolis: Augsburg, 1962. [*Opbyggelige Taler,* essays, 1843-1852.]

Edifying Discourses; A Selection. Tr. David F. and Lillian M. Swenson. Ed. and intro. Paul L. Holmer. New York: Harper, 1958. p 284. London and Glasgow: Collins, 1962. p 253. [Harper Torchbooks. The Cloister Library.]

Either/Or. Volume 1 tr. David F. and Lillian M. Swenson. Volume 2 tr. Walter Lowrie. Revisions and intro. by Howard A. Johnson. Garden City, N. Y.: Doubleday, 1959. Also Princeton, N.J.: Princeton University Press, 1971. 2 vols. [Doubleday ed. Anchor Books A181ab.] [*Enten - Eller,* 1843.]

Farce Is Far More Serious (a Fragment from »Repetition«). Tr. Louis Mackey. *Yale French Studies* no. 14 (1955) pp 3-9. [From *Gjentagelsen,* 1843.]

Fear and Trembling, a Dialectical Lyric. Tr. and with intro. and notes by Walter Lowrie. 1941; rpt. Princeton: Princeton University Press, 1952, 1968. Garden City, N. Y.: Doubleday, 1954. p 278. [Anchor Books A30.] [*Frygt og Bæven, Dialektisk Lyrik af Johannes de Silentio,* 1843.]

For Self-examination and Judge for Yourselves! and Three Discourses, 1851. Tr. Walter Lowrie. 1944; rpt. Princeton: Princeton University Press, 1968. p 501 pb. [*Til Selvprøvelse, Samtiden anbefalet,* 1851, and *Dømmer selv!,* 1852.]

For Self-examination, Recommended for the Times. Tr. Edna and Howard Hong. Minneapolis: Augsburg Publishing House, 1965. [*Til Selvprøvelse, Samtiden anbefalet,* 1851.]

The Gospel of Our Sufferings. Christian Discourses, Being the Third Part of Edifying Discourses in a Different Vein, Published in 1847 in Copenhagen. Tr. A. S. Aldworth and W. S. Ferrie. London: James Clarke, 1955. p 150. Also Grand Rapids: Erdmans, 1964. [*Lidelsernes Evangelium, (Opbyggelige Taler i forskjellig Aand,* III*),* 1847.]

90

Is There Such a Thing as a Teleological Suspension of the Ethical? (excerpt from *Fear and Trembling*). In Bronstein, D. J. and H. M. Schulweis, eds. *Approaches to the Philosophy of Religion*. New York: Prentice-Hall, 1954. pp 86-91.

Johannes Climacus, or De Omnibus Dubitandum Est, and a Sermon. Tr., and with an assessment, by T. H. Croxall. London: A. & C. Black; Stanford, Ca.: Stanford University Press, 1958. p 196. [A library of modern religious thought.] [*Johannes Climacus, eller De Omnibus dubitandum est* written 1842-43, published posthumously in *Papirer*, v. 4, 1912.]

The Journals of Søren Kierkegaard. A selection ed. and tr. Alexander Dru. 1938; rpt. London and New York: Oxford University Press, 1951. London: Collins, 1958. p 254. As Journals. New York: Harper; London: Oxford University Press, 1959. p 254 pb. Gloucester, Mass.: Peter Smith, 1959. hb. [Harper Torchbooks. The Cloister Library.]

Kierkegaard. Selected and intro. W. H. Auden. London: Cassell, 1955. p 184.
See also American edition, *The Living Thoughts of Kierkegaard.*

A Kierkegaard Anthology. Ed. Robert Bretall. 1946, rpt. Princeton: Princeton University Press, 1951, 1956. Also New York: Modern Library, 1959. p 494. [Modern Library of the World's Best Books.]

The Kierkegaard Papers. Tr., intro. and afterword by Howard V. Hong. *Tri-Quarterly* (Evanston, Ill.] No. 16 (1969) pp 100-123. [Selection from *Papirer*, 1909-48.]

Kierkegaard's Attack upon »Christendom« 1854-1855. Tr. and intro. Walter J. Lowrie. 1944, rpt. Boston: Beacon Press, 1956. Princeton, N.J.: Princeton University Press, 1968. p 303 p.b. [Beacon Paperback no. 28.]

The Last Years; Selections from the Journals 1853-1855. Tr. and ed. Ronald Gregor Smith. London: Collins, 1965, 1968. New York: Harper and Row, 1965. p 383. [*Efterladte Papirer*, 1869-81.]

Letters and Documents. Princeton, N.J.: Princeton University Press, 1978. p 518.

The Living Thoughts of Kierkegaard, presented by W. H. Auden. New York: D. McKay Co., 1952. Also Bloomington, Indiana: Indiana University Press, 1952, 1963. p 225. [The Living Thoughts series.]
See also British edition *Kierkegaard*. Selected and Introd. W. H. Auden.

Meditations from Kierkegaard. Tr. and ed. T. H. Croxall. Philadelphia: Westminster Press; London: J. Nisbet, 1955. Printed in Norwood,

Mass. p 165. [Devotional selections from *Papirer*, 1909-48.]

On Authority and Revelation: The Book on Adler; or A Cycle of Ethico-Religious Essays. Intro., notes and tr. by Walter Lowrie. Princeton, N.J.: Princeton University Press; London: Oxford University Press, 1955. p 205. With an intro. by Frederick Sontag. New York: Harper & Row, 1966. p 205. [Harper Torchbooks. The Cloister Library.] [Written in 1847, published in *Papirer*, v. 7 II, 1916.]

On Danish Soil. Ill. Arne Ungermann. *DFOJ* no. 17 (1955) p 15. [Excerpt from *Stadier paa Livets Vei*, 1845.]

On His Mission (selection from *Concluding Unscientific Postscript*). In Kaufmann, Walter. *Existentialism from Dostoevsky to Sartre*. New York: World Publishing Co., 1956. London: Thames & Hudson, 1957. pp 84-85. [Meridian books.]

On His »Mode of Existence« (selection from *The Point of View*). In Kaufmann, Walter. *Existentialism from Dostoevsky to Sartre*. New York: World Publishing Co., 1956. London: Thames & Hudson, 1957. pp 86-92. [Meridian books.]

On His Works (selection from *The Point of View*). In Kaufmann, Walter. *Existentialism from Dostoevsky to Sartre*. New York: World Publishing Co., 1956. London: Thames & Hudson, 1957. pp 85-86. [Meridian books.]

Parables of Kierkegaard. Ed. and intro. Thomas C. Oden. Princeton, N.J.: Princeton University Press, 1978. p 186. Ill.

Philosophical Fragtments; or, A Fragtment of Philosophy, by Johannes Climacus (pseud.) . . . Responsible for Publication: S. Kierkegaard. Originally tr. and with intro. by David F. Swenson. New intro. and commentary by Niels Thulstrup. Tr. rev. and commentary tr. by Howard V. Hong. 1936; rpt. Princeton: Princeton University Press, 1962, 1967. p 260. [*Philosophiske Smuler*, 1844.]

The Point of View for My Work as an Author; a Report to History, and Related Writings. Tr. and ed., and with notes by Walter Lowrie. Newly ed. and with a preface by Benjamin Nelson. New York: Harper, 1962. p 170.

The Point of View, etc., including the Point of View for My Work as an Author. Two Notes about the Individual and on My Work as an Author. Tr. and with notes and intro. by Walter Lowrie. 1939; rpt. New York and London: Oxford University Press, 1950. p 174. [*Om min Forfatter-Virksomhed*, 1851.]

Prayer. *Theology Today* no. 13 (Jan. 1957) pp 447-448.

The Prayers of Kierkegaard. Ed. with an interpretation of his life and thought by Perry D. LeFevre. Chicago & London: University of Chicago Press, 1956, 1963. p 244.

Prayers of Kierkegaard; for Mixed Chorus, Soprano Solo, and Orchestra, with Incidental Solos for Tenor and Alto Solo ad libitum, op. 30. Music by Samuel Barber. New York: G. Schirmer, 1954. p 45. [Piano Partitur.]

The Present Age and Of the Difference between a Genius and an Apostle. Tr. Alexander Dru. Intro. Walter Kaufmann. New York: Harper & Row, 1962. p 108. Tr. and intro. Alexander Dru. London: Collins, 1962. p 129. [Harper Torchbooks. The Cloister Library.] [Published in 1940 as The Present Age and Two Minor Ethico-religious Treaties.] [Two essays, the first from En litterair Anmeldelse. To Tidsaldre, 1846, and the other from Skriftprøver - Bogen om Adler, written 1847, published in Papirer, v. 7 II, 1916.]

The Professor. In Huszar, G. B., ed. The Intellectuals. Glencoe. Ill. Free Press, 1960. pp 117-118.

Purify Your Hearts! A Discourse for a Special Occasion, the First of Three Edifying Discourses in a Different Vein, Published in 1847. Tr. A. S. Aldworth and W. S. Ferrie. New York: Irving Ravin, 1950. p 179. [Opbyggelige Taler i forskjellig Aand, I, 1847.]

Purity of Heart Is to Will One Thing; Spiritual Preparation for the Office of Confession. Tr. and intro. by Douglas V. Steere. New York: Harper & Row, 1956. London: Collins, 1961. p 192. [Rev. ed. originally published 1948 (first ed. 1938).] [Harper Torchbooks. The Cloister Library.] [Opbyggelige Taler i forskjellig Aand, I, 1847.]

Repetition, and an Essay in Experimental Psychology. Tr. and with intro. and notes by Walter Lowrie. 1941, rpt. New York: Harper & Row, 1964. p 212. [Harper Torchbooks. The Cloister Library.] [Gjentagelsen, 1843.]

The Seducer. A Play in Two Acts Adapted from »Diary of the Seducer« by S. Kierkegaard. By Myfanwy Piper. London: Gerald Duckworth & Co., 1958. p 87.

Selections from the Writings of Kierkegaard. Rev. ed. Tr. L. M. Hollander. New York and Toronto: Doubleday; London: Mayflower, 1960. p 259. [Anchor Books A-210.]

The Sickness unto Death. Tr. and intro. Walter Lowrie. 1941; rpt. Princeton, N. J.: Princeton University Press, 1951. New York: Anchor Books, 1954. [Sygdommen til Døden, 1849.]

The Sickness unto Death. A Christian Psychological Exposition for Upbuilding and Awakening. Ed., tr. and with intro. and notes by Howard V. Hong and Edna H. Hong. Princeton, N. J.: Princeton University Press, 1980. p 224. [Kierkegaard's Writings, XIX.] [Sygdommen til Døden, 1849.]

Søren Kierkegaard's Journals and Papers. Tr. and ed. Howard V. Hong and Edna H. Hong, asst. by Gregor Malantschuk. Intro. Howard A. Johnson. Bloomington & London: Indiana University Press, 1967-1978. Vols. 1-7. [From Papirer, 1909-48.]

Stages of Life's Way. Tr. Walter Lowrie. Intro. Paul Sponheim. New York: Schocken Books, 1967. p 472 [Facsimile of 1940 edition.] [Stadier paa Livets Vei, 1845.]

That Individual. (Selection from The Point of View.). In Kaufmann, Walter. Existentialism from Dostoevsky to Sartre. New York: World Publishing Co., 1956. London: Thames & Hudson, 1957. pp 92-99. [Meridian books.]

Training in Christianity and the Edifying Discourse Which »Accompanied« It, by Søren Kierkegaard. Tr. and with intro. and notes by Walter Lowrie. 1941; rpt. Princeton: Princeton University Press, 1952, 1957. p 275. [Indøvelse i Christendom, 1850.]

Two Ages. The Age of Revolution and the Present Age. A Literary Review. Princeton, N. J.: Princeton University Press, 1978. p 187. [En litterair Anmeldelse. To Tidsaldre, 1846.]

What Does It Mean to Doubt. Cross Currents no. 4 (1954) pp 367-373. [From De Omnibus dubitandum est published posthumously in Papirer, 4, 1912.]

What It Is to Become a Christian. (Excerpt from Concluding Unscientific Postscript). In Bronstein, D. J. and H. M. Schulweis, eds. Approaches to the Philosophy of Religion. New York: Prentice-Hall, 1954. pp 91-98.

The Witness of Kierkegaard: Selected Writings on How to Become a Christian. Ed. Charles Michalson. New York: Association Press, 1960. p 127. [An Association Press reflection book.]

Works of Love; Some Christian Reflections in the Form of Discourses. Tr. Howard and Edna Hong. New York: Harper; London: Collins, 1962, 1964. p 383. [Kjærlighedens Gjerninger, 1847.]

Works about Søren Kierkegaard

Allen, Kenneth Ralph. Identity and the Individual: Personhood in the Thought of Erik Erikson and of Søren Kierkegaard. Ph. D.

92

diss., Boston University, 1967. (p 294). [Diss. Abstr. 28/05-A, p 1885.]

Anderson, Barbara. **Kierkegaard: A Fiction.** Syracuse, N. Y.: Syracuse Univ. Press, 1974. p 155.

Anderson, Raymond Eugene. **Kierkegaard's Theory of Communication.** Ph. D. diss., University of Minnesota, 1959.

Ansbro, John Joseph. **Kierkegaard's Critique of Hegel - An Interpretation.** Ph. D. diss., Fordham University, 1964. (p 356). [Diss. Abstr. 25/06, p 3615.]

Arbaugh, George E. and George B. **Kierkegaard's Authorship; A Guide to the Writings of Kierkegaard.** Rock Island, Ill.: Augustana College Library, 1967. Also London: Allan & Unwin, 1968, p 431.

Bain, John, A. **Sören Kierkegaard. His Life and Religious Teaching.** 1935; rpt. New York: Kraus Reprint Co., 1971. p 160.

Barrett, William. **Irrational Man. A Study in Existential Philosophy.** New York: Doubleday, 1958. p 278. [Doubleday Anchor books.]

Beauchamp, Richard Arthur. **Passion and Prudence: A Study of Kierkegaard's Ethics.** Ph. D. diss., Duke University, 1970. (p 290). [Diss. Abstr. 32/03-A, p 1605.]

Bedell, George Chester. **Kierkegaard and Faulkner: Modalities of Existence.** Ph. D. diss., Duke University, 1969. (p 344). [Diss. Abstr. 30/11-A, p 5056.]

Bedell, George C. **Kierkegaard and Faulkner: Modalities of Existence.** Baton Rouge: Louisiana State University Press, 1972.

Berberelly, John, Jr. **Soren Kierkegaard's Criticism of Hegelian Philosophy.** M. A. thesis, Columbia University, 1951.

Bjarnason, Loftur L. **Categories of Soren Kierkegaard's Thought in the Life and Writings of A. Strindberg.** Ph. D. diss., Stanford University, 1951. [*Abstracts of Dissertations* (Stanford University), 26:144-146 (1950-1951).]

Bonifazi, Conrad. **Christendom Attacked: A Comparison of Kierkegaard and Nietzsche.** London: Rockliff, 1953. p 190.

Bragstad, W. R. **Søren Kierkegaard's Case of Paradox: A Comparative Study.** Ph. D. thesis, University of Edinburgh, 1976.

Brandt, Frithiof. **Søren Kierkegaard 1813-1855. His Life - His Works.** Tr. Anne R. Born. Copenhagen: Det danske Selskab and Press and Information Department of the Danish Foreign Office, 1963. p 120. [Danes of the Present and Past.]

Brown, James. **Kierkegaard, Heidegger, Buber and Barth: Subject and Object in Modern Theology.** New York: Collier, 1962. p 192. [The Croall lectures.] Originally published as *Subject and Object in Modern Theology. The Croall Lectures Given in the University of Edinburgh 1953.* London: SCM Press; New York: Macmillan, 1955. p 214.

Burgess, Andrew John. **The Concept of Passionate Faith: Kierkegaard and Analytical Philosophy of Mind.** Ph. D. diss., Yale University, 1969. (p 250). [Diss. Abstr. 31/03-A, p 1319.]

Bykhovskii, Bernard. **Kierkegaard.** Tr. Henry F. Mins. Amsterdam: Grüner, 1977. p 122. [Philosophical Currents, v. 16.]

Cain, David William. **Reckoning with Kierkegaard: Christian Faith and Dramatic Literature.** Ph. D. diss., Princeton University, 1976. (p 325). [Diss. Abstr. 37/04-A, p 2240.]

Campbell, Charles Ray. **The Attack from Behind: Irony and Søren Kierkegaard's Dialectic of Communication.** Ph. D. diss., Syracuse University, 1973. (p 345). [Diss. Abstr. 34/10-A, p 6696.]

Carnell, Edward John. **The Burden of Søren Kierkegaard.** Grand Rapids, Michigan: William B. Eerdmans Publishing Co., 1965. p 174.

Chakma, N. K. **Kierkegaard and Sartre: Study of Individual Freedom in Existentialsm.** Ph. D. thesis, University of Dundee, 1973-1974.

Cherbonnier, Phyllis. **The Preservation of the Individual in the Thoughts of Nietzsche and Kierkegaard.** M. A. thesis, Columbia University, 1950.

Chervin, Ronda De Sola. **The Process of Conversion in the Philosophy of Søren Kierkegaard.** Ph. D. diss., Fordham University, 1967. (p 209). [Diss. Abstr. 28/10-A, p 4207.]

Christopherson, Myrvin Frederick. **Søren Kierkegaard's Dialectic of Communication: An Approach to the Communication of Existential Knowledge.** Ph. D. diss., Purdue University, 1965. (p 298). [Diss. Abstr., 27/01-A, p 271.]

Clive, Geoffrey H. **The Connection between Ethics and Religion in Kant, Kierkegaard and Bradley.** Ph. D. diss., Harvard University, 1953.

Cole, James Preston. **Kierkegaard's Concept of Dread, with Constant Reference to Sigmund Freud.** Ph. D. diss., Drew University, 1964. (p 361). [Diss. Abstr. 25/05, p 3136.]

Cole, J. Preston. **The Problematic Self in Kierkegaard and Freud.** New Haven, Conn.: Yale Univ. Press, 1971. p 244.

Collins, James. **The Mind of Kierkegaard.** Chicago: Henry Regnery Co., 1953. London: Secker & Warburg, 1954. p 304.

Congleton, Ann. **Spinoza, Kierkegaard, and the Eternal Particular.** Ph. D. diss., Yale University, 1962.

Copp, John Dixon. **The Concept of the Soul in Kierkegaard and Freud.** Ph. D. diss., Boston University, 1953. (p 286).

Crites, Stephen D. **In the Twilight of Christendom; Hegel vs. Kierkegaard on Faith and History.** Chambersburg, Pa.: American Academy of Religion, 1972. p 109.

Croxall, T. H., ed. **Glimpses and Impressions of Kierkegaard.** Selected and trans. by T. H. Croxall. London: J. Nisbet & Co., Ltd., 1959. p 134. Ill.

Croxall, T. H. **Kierkegaard Commentary.** London: J. Nisbeth; New York: Harper, 1956. p 263. Ill.

Croxall, T. H. **Kierkegaard Studies: With Special Reference to (a) The Bible, (b) Our Own Age.** Foreword by Lord Linsay of Birker. 1948; rpt. New York: Roy Publishers, 1956. p 227.

Crumbine, Nancy Jay. **The Same River Twice: A Critique of the Place of Eros in the Philosophy of Kierkegaard.** Ph. D. diss., The Pennsylvania State University, 1972. (p 191). [Diss. Abstr. 33/12-A, p 6962.]

Cutting, Patricia Morrison. **The Possibility of Being-with-others for Kierkegaard's Individual (Den Enkelte).** Ph. D. diss., The University of New Mexico, 1976. (p 240). [Diss. Abstr. 37/05-A, p 2939.]

Daane, James. **Kierkegaard's Concept of the Moment: An Investigation into the Time-eternity Concept of Søren Kierkegaard.** Th. D. diss., Princeton Theological Seminary, 1974. (p 192). [Diss. Abstr. 35/04-A, p 2379.]

Daise, Benjamin. **Kierkegaard's Pseudonymous Works.** Ph. D. diss., University of Texas (Austin), 1973. (p 216). [Diss. Abstr. 34/09-A, p 6040.]

Despland, Michael Samuel. **The Idea of Divine Education: A Study in the Ethical and the Religious as Organizing Themes for the Interpretation of the Life of the Self in Kant, Schleiermacher, and Kierkegaard.** Ph. D. diss., Harvard University, 1966.

Dewey, Bradley Rau. **The Imitation of Christ in the Thought of Søren Kierkegaard.** Ph. D. diss., Yale University, 1964. (p 357). [Diss. Abstr. 30/01-A. p 380.]

Dewey, Bradley Rau. **The New Obedience: Kierkegaard on Imitating Christ.** Foreword by Paul L. Holmer. Washington: Corpus Books, 1968. p 247. [Corpus Books.]

Deyoung, Quintin R. **A Study of Contemporary Christian Existential Theology (Kierkegaard and Tillich) and Modern Dynamic Psychology (Freud and Sullivan) concerning Guilt Feelings.** Ph. D. diss., University of Southern California, 1959. (p 329). [Diss. Abstr. 20/05, p 1883.]

Diem, Hermann. **Kierkegaard: An Introduction.** Tr. from the German by David Green. Richmond: John Knox Press, 1967. p 124.

Diem, Hermann. **Kierkegaard's Dialectic of Existence.** Tr. from the German by Harold Knight. Edinburgh: Oliver & Boyd, 1959. p 217. [*Die Existenzdialektik von Sören Kierkegaard,* 1950.]

Donnelly, John Joseph Patrick. **Soren Kierkegaard's »Teleological Suspension of the Ethical«: A Reinterpretation.** Ph. D. diss., Brown University, 1970. (p 168). [Diss. Abstr. 32/01-A, p 483.]

Donohue, Kevin E. **Reflection and Faith in Soren Kierkegaard.** Ph. D. diss., The Catholic University of America, 1973. (p 264). [Diss. Abstr. 33/12-A, p 6963.]

Doyle, Harry William Osmond. **Ethical Implications of Truth according to Søren Kierkegaard.** M. A. thesis, University of Toronto, 1965.

Duncan, Elmer Hubert. **Kierkegaard and Value Theory: A Study of the Three Spheres of Existence.** Ph. D. diss., University of Cincinnati, 1962. (p 136). [Diss. Abstr. 23/06, p 2171.]

Duncan, Elmer H. **Sören Kierkegaard.** Waco, Texas: Word Books, 1976. p 155.

Dunne, Mary Rachel. **Kierkegaard and Socratic Ignorance: A Study of the Task of a Philosopher in Relation to Christianity.** Ph. D. diss., University of Notre Dame, 1970. (p 356). [Diss. Abstr. 31/09-A, p 4835.]

Dupré Louis. **Kierkegaard as Theologian: The Dialectic of Christian Existence.** London and New York: Sheed & Ward, 1963. p 229.

Eller, Vernard. **Kierkegaard and Radical Discipleship: A New Perspective.** Princeton: Princeton University Press; London: Oxford University Press, 1968. p 445.

Eller, Vernard Marion. **A Protestant's Protestant: Kierkegaard from a New Perspective.** Th. D. diss., Pacific School of Religion, 1964. (p 451). [Diss. Abstr. 25/06, p 3719.]

Elrod, John W. **Being and Existence in Kierkegaard's Pseudonymous Works.** Princeton: Princeton Univ. Press, 1975. p 271.

Elrod, John William. **An Interpretation of Søren Kierkegaard's Concept of the Self in the Pseudonymous Corpus.** Ph. D. diss., Columbia University, 1972. (p 412). [Diss. Abstr. 37/01-A, p 404.]

Eriksson, Vincent Erik. **A Critical Exposition of the Argument of Kierkegaard's Philosophical Fragtments and Concluding Unscientific Postscript.** M. A. thesis, University of Saskatchewan, 1964.

Evans, Charles Stephens. **Subjective Justifica-**

94

tions of Religious Belief: A Comparative Study of Kant, Kierkegaard, and James. Ph. D. diss., Yale University, 1974. (p 285). [Diss. Abstr. 35/07-A, p 4611.]

Fackre, Gabriel Joseph. A Comparison and Critique of the Interpretations of Dehumanization in the Thought of Soren Kierkegaard and Karl Marx. Ph. D. diss., University of Chicago, 1962.

Fitzpatrick, T. Mallary, Jr. An Interpretation of the Thought of Soren Kierkegaard: with Special Regard for the Problem of Method. Ph. D. diss., University of Chicago, 1969.

Flottorp, Haakon. Kierkegaard and Norway. A Study in »Inwardness« in History with Illustrative Examples from Religion, Literature, and Philosophy. Ph. D. diss., Columbia University, 1955. (p 345). [Diss. Abstr. 15/05, p 890.]

Friedman, Rudolph. Kierkegaard. Norfolk, Conn.: New Directions, 1950. p 68. [Direction 15.]

Garelick, Herbert M. The Anti-Christianity of Kierkegaard. A Study of the »Concluding Unscientific Postscript«. The Hague: Martinus Nijhoff, 1965. New York: Humanities Press, 1966. p 73.

Gates, John A. Christendom Revisited: A Kierkegaardian View of the Church Today. Philadelphia: Westminster Press, 1963. p 176.

Gates, John Alexander. The Life and Thought of Kierkegaard for Everyman. London: Hodder and Stoughton, 1961. p 155. Philadelphia: Westminster Press, 1960. p 172.

George, Arapura Ghevarghese. The First Sphere: A Study in Kierkegaardian Aesthetics. Bombay & New York: Asia Publishing House, 1965. p 80.

Gerry, Rev. Joseph, O.S.B. Kierkegaard: The Problem of Transcendence; An Interpretation of the Stages. Ph. D. diss., Fordham University, 1959. (p 123).

Gill, Jerry H., ed. Essays on Kierkegaard. Minneapolis: Burgess Publishing Co., 1969. p 197.

Gilmartin, Thomas V. Soul-sickness: A Comparison of William James and Søren Kierkegaard. Th. D. diss., Graduate Theological Union, 1974. (p 321). [Diss. Abstr. 36/10-A, p 6763.]

Goicoechea, David L. The Equivalence of the Existential and the Religious in Kierkegaard. Ph. D. diss., Loyola University of Chicago, 1972.

Goodenough, Thomas Wright. The Social Relevance of Kierkegaard's Ethical Stage. M. A. thesis, University of Alberta, 1966.

Gosselin, Gilles Robert. Faith and the Credo quia absurdum in Kierkegaard. M. A. thesis, University of Toronto, 1964.

Gottlieb, Roger S. »The Existing Individual and the Will-to-power«. A Comparison of Kierkegaard's and Nietzsche's Answers to the Question: What Is It to Make a Transition from One Value System to Another? Ph. D. diss., Brandeis University, 1975. (p 365). [Diss. Abstr. 36/05-A, p 2894.]

Grimsley, Ronald. Søren Kierkegaard: A Biographical Introduction. London: Studio Vista; New York: Charles Scribner's Sons, 1973. p 127.

Grimsley, Ronald. Søren Kierkegaard and French Literature - Eight Comparative Studies. Cardiff: Univ. of Wales Press, 1966. p 171.

Guthrie, George Paul. Kierkegaard's Corrective of Liberal Theology. D. B. thesis, University of Chicago, 1954.

Gwaltney, Marilyn Ethel. The Concept of Alienation in Kierkegaard. Ph. D. diss., State University of New York at Buffalo, 1976. (p 171). [Diss. Abstr. 37/08-A, p 5181.]

Haecker, Theodor. Kierkegaard the Cripple. Tr. from German by C. van O. Bruyn. Intro. Alexander Dru. New York: Philosophical Library, 1950. p 53. [Der Buckel Kierkegaards, 1947.]

Halevi, Jacob. A Critique of Martin Buber's Interpretation of Soren Kierkegaard. Ph. D. diss., Hebrew Union College, 1960.

Hamilton, Kenneth. The Promise of Kierkegaard. Philadelphia: J. B. Lippincott, 1969. p 116.

Hamilton, Lester I. The Existential Dialectic in the Writings of Soren Aabye Kierkegaard. M. A. thesis, University of Kentucky, 1951.

Hamilton, Wayne Bruce. Soren Kierkegaard's Conception of Temporality. Ph. D. diss., McGill University, 1972. [Diss. Abstr. 33/06-A, p 2977.]

Hamrick, William Spencer. Soren Kierkegaard's Category of the Distinct Individual. Ph. D. diss., Union Theological Seminary in Virginia, 1962.

Hanna, Thomas L. The Lyrical Existentialists: The Common Voice of Kierkegaard, Nietzsche and Camus. Ph. D. diss., University of Chicago, 1959. (p 135).

Hansen, Olaf. The Problem of Alienation and Reconciliation: A Comparative Study of Marx and Kierkegaard in the Light of Hegel's Formulation of the Problem. Th. D. diss., Princeton Theological Seminary, 1956. (p 449). [Diss. Abstr. 35/07-A, p 4680.]

Harcourt, H. R. **The Significance of Socrates for the Thought of Kierkegaard.** Ph. D. thesis, University of Edinburgh, 1957-1958.

Harper, Ralph. **The Seventh Solitude: Man's Isolation in Kierkegaard, Dostoevsky and Nietzsche.** Baltimore: Johns Hopkins University Press, 1965. p 153. [Later published as *The Seventh Solitude: Metaphysical Homelessness in Kierkegaard, Dostoevsky and Nietzsche.* Baltimore: Johns Hopkins University Press, 1967. p 153 pb.]

Heinecken, Martin J. **The Moment before God.** Philadelphia: Muhlenberg Press, 1956. p 386.

Heis, Robert. **Hegel, Kierkegaard and Marx.** New York: Delacorte, 1975.

Helm, Adelbert J. **Soren Kierkegaard and the Church; A Problem in Christian Strategy.** M. A. thesis, Vanderbilt University, 1953.

Henriksen, Aage. **Methods and Results of Kierkegaard Studies in Scandinavia. A Historical and Critical Survey.** Copenhagen: Publications of the Kierkegaard Society and Munksgaard, 1951. p 160.

Himmelstrup, Jens. **Søren Kierkegaard: International Bibliography.** Asst. by Kjeld Birket-Smith. Copenhagen: Nyt Nordisk Forlag, 1962. p 222. [Preface and headings in Danish and English.]

Hitchcock, John Lathron. **A Comparison of 'Complementarity' in Quantum Physics with Analogous Structures in Kierkegaard's Philosophical Writings, from a Jungian Point of View.** Ph. D. diss., Graduate Theological Union, 1975. (p 363). [Diss. Abstr. 36/10-A, p 6764.]

Hohlenberg, Johannes. **Sören Kierkegaard.** Tr. from Danish by T. H. Croxall. 1940, rpt. New York: Pantheon Books, 1953. p 321. London: Routledge & Kegan Paul Ltd., 1954. p 321. Ill. New York: Octagon Books, 1978.

Hossain, Shahana. **Ethical Teachings of Kierkegaard and Sartre; A Comparative Study.** M. A. thesis, University of Alberta, 1966.

Hubben, William. **Four Prophets of Our Destiny: Kierkegard, Dostoevsky, Nietzsche, Kafka,** New York: Macmillan, 1952. p 170.

Hughes, Roderick P., III. **The Notion of the Ethical in Kierkegaard.** Ph. D. diss., University of Notre Dame, 1973. (p 307). [Diss. Abstr. 33/11-A, p 6398.]

Hultgran, Lawrence Drew. **The Problem of Religious Consciousness in Kierkegaard's Thought.** Nashville, Tennessee: Vanderbilt University, 1976. (p 489). [Diss. Abstr. 38/02-A, p 845.]

Humphries, Hugh Will. **Søren Kierkegaard's Concept of Sanctification.** Ph. D. diss., New York University, 1962. (p 249). [Diss. Abstr. 23/03, p 1096.]

Hunsinger, George. **Kierkegaard, Heidegger, and the Concept of Death.** Stanford, Ca.: Leland Stanford Jr. University, 1969. p 87. [Stanford honors essay in humanities, no. 12.]

Johnson, Howard A. and Thulstrup, Niels, eds. **A Kierkegaard Critique: An International Selection of Essays Interpreting Kierkegaard.** New York: Harper & Bros., 1962. p 311. Gateway Edition. Chicago: Henry Regnery Co., 1967.

Johnson, Ralph Henry. **The Concept of Existence in »Concluding Unscientific Postscript«.** The Hague: Martinus Nijhoff, 1972.

Jolivet, Regis. **Introduction to Kierkegaard.** Tr. from the French by W. H. Barber. London: Frederick Muller; Toronto: S. J. Saunders, 1950. New York: E. P. Dutton, 1951. p 233. [*Introduction à Kierkegaard.*]

Jones, Charles Edwin. **The Theory of Truth as Subjectivity in Kierkegaard, Compared with Theories of Truth in Blanshard and Ayer.** Ph. D. diss., University of Arkansas, 1973. (p 190). [Diss. Abstr. 34/05-A, p 2699.)

Jones, Jere Jene. **On the Distinction between Religiousness »A« and Religiousness »B« in the »Concluding Unscientific Postscript« of Soren Kierkegaard.** Ph. D. diss., The University of Nebraska, Lincoln, 1971. (p 256). [Diss. Abstr. 32/02-A, p 1017.]

Jones, Ozro T., Jr. **The Meaning of the »Moment« in Existential Encounter according to Kierkegaard.** S. T. D. diss., Temple University, 1962. (p 196). [Diss. Abstr. 26/10, p 6197.]

Jørgensen, Aage. **Søren Kierkegaard: An International Bibliography 1961-1970.** Århus: Akademisk Boghandel, 1971. p 99.

Kaltreider, Kurt. **The Self, Existence and Despair in Kierkegaard: A Secular Interpretation.** Ph. D. diss., The University of Tennessee, 1977. (p 209). [Diss. Abstr. 38/07-A, p 4211.]

Kates, Roberta Louise. **The Problem of Inter-human and Divine-human Relations in the Philosophies of Buber and Kierkegaard.** M. A. thesis, University of Toronto, 1963.

Keane, Ellen Marie. **The Equation of Subjectivity and Truth in Kierkegaard's »Postscript«.** Ph. D. diss., University of Notre Dame, 1965. (p 188). [Diss. Abstr. 26/09, p 5485.]

Kern, Edith G. **Existential Thought and Fictional Technique: Kierkegaard, Sartre, Beckett.** New Haven, Conn.: Yale University Press, 1970. p 262.

Khan, Abrahim Habibulla. **The Treatment of the Theme of Suffering in Kierkegaard's Works.** Ph. D. diss., McGill University, 1973. [Diss. Abstr. 34/12-A, p 7823.]

96

Khan, Theodore A. R. **A Critique of Kierke-gaard's Category of the Individual Based on His Philosophico-religious View of Man.** Ph. D. diss., New York University, 1962. (p 417). [Diss. Abstr. 24/02, p 778.]

King, Joseph Norman Baxter. **Kierkegaard's Doctrine of the Three Stages.** M. A. thesis, University of Toronto, 1962.

Kleinman, Jaquline Agnew. **Public Private - The Education of Soren Kierkegaard.** Ph. D. diss., The Ohio State University, 1971. (p 174). [Diss. Abstr. 32/07-A, p 4064.]

Klemke, E. D. **Studies in the Philosophy of Kierkegaard.** The Hague: Nijhoff, 1976. p 79.

Koller, Kerry Joseph. **Christianity and Philosophy according to Kierkegaard's Johannes Climacus.** Ph. D. diss., University of Notre Dame, 1975. (p 196). [Diss. Abstr. 36/03-A, p 1582.]

Kristensen, Juhl-Bagge. **The Relevance of Soren Kierkegaard's Existentialism to a Philosophy of Education.** Ph. D. diss., State University of New York at Buffalo, 1971.

Larson, Curtis Walter. **A Comparison of the Views of Paul and Kierkegaard on Christian Suffering.** Ph. D. diss., Yale University, 1953.

Lawson, Lewis. ed. **Kierkegaard's Presence in Contemporary American Life: Essays from Various Disciplines.** Ed. and with notes and intro. by Lewis Lawson. Metuchen, N.J.: Scarecrow Press, 1971. p 299.

Letswaart, Willem L. **Kierkegaard's Concept of Faith.** Ph. D. diss., Princeton Theological Seminary, 1952. (p 175).

Likins, Majorie Harjes. **The Concept of Self-hood in Freud and Kierkegaard.** Ph. D diss., Columbia University, 1963. (p 210). [Diss. Abstr. 26/03, p 1805.]

Lin, Tian-min. **Paradox in the Thought of Søren Kierkegaard.** Ph. D. diss., Boston University, 1969. (p 241). [Diss. Abstr. 30/05-A, p. 2133.]

Link, Mae M. **Kierkegaard's Way to America: A Study in the Dissemination of His Thought.** Ph. D. diss., The American University, 1951.

Loder, James Edwin. **The Nature of Religious Consciousness in the Writings of Freud and Kierkegaard: A Theoretical Study in the Correlation of Religious and Psychiatric Concepts.** Ph. D. diss., Harvard University, 1962.

Lowrie, Walter. **Kierkegaard.** 1938, rpt. New York: Harper and Bros., 1962. Single volume in hardcover ed., 2 vol. in pb. Gloucester, Mass.: Smith, 1970. 2 vols. p 640. Ill. [Harper Torchbooks. The Cloister Library pb. ed.]

Lowrie, Walter. **A Short Life of Kierkegaard.** Garden City, N. Y.: Doubleday, 1961. p 226. [Anchor Books no. A273.]

McCarthy, Vincent A. **The Meaning and Dialectic of Moods in Kierkegaard.** Ph. D. diss., Stanford University, 1974. (p 339). [Diss. Abstr. 35/06-A, p 3871.]

McCarthy, Vincent A. **The Phenomenology of Moods in Kierkegaard.** The Hague: Nijhoff, 1978. p 169.

McDonald, N. M. **The Aggressive Freedom: A Comparative Study in Karl Marx and Søren Kierkegaard.** M. A. thesis, University of Bath, 1974-1975.

McInerny, Ralph. **The Existential Dialectic of Søren Kierkegaard.** Ph. D. diss., Université Laval (Canada), 1954.

McInerny, Ralph Matthew. **A Thomistic Evaluation of the Philosophy of Soren Kierkegaard.** M. A. thesis, University of Minnesota, 1952.

Macken, Louis. **Kierkegaard: A Kind of Poet.** Philadelphia: University of Pennsylvania Press, 1971. p 340.

Mackey, Louis H. **The Nature and the End of the Ethical Life according to Kierkegaard.** Ph. D. diss., Yale University, 1954.

McKinnon, Alastair. **The Kierkegaard Indices.** Vol. I: Kierkegaard in Translation. Leiden: Brill, 1970.

McKnight, T. J. **Hegel's Philosophy of History and Kierkegaard's Criticisms.** M. Litt. thesis, University of Edinburgh, 1968-1969.

McLane, Henry Earl, Jr. **Kierkegaard's Use of the Category of Repetition: An Attempt to Discern the Structure and Unity of His Thought.** Ph. D. diss., Yale University, 1961.

McLaughlin, Wayman Bernard. **The Relation between Hegel and Kierkegaard.** Ph. D. diss., Boston University, 1958. (p 346). [Diss. Abstr. 19/07, p 1788.]

Madden, Myron C. **The Contribution of Søren Kierkegaard to a Christian Psychology.** Ph. D. diss., The Southern Baptist Theological Seminary, 1950. (p 176).

Magel, Charles R. **An Analysis of Kierkegaard's Philosophic Categories.** Ph. D. diss., University of Minnesota, 1960. (p 314). [Diss. Abstr. 21/11, p 3488.]

Malantschuk, Gregor. **Kierkegaard's Thought.** Ed. and tr. from Danish by Howard V. and Edna H. Hong. Princeton: Princeton University Press, 1971. p 388. [Dialektik og Eksistens hos Søren Kierkegaard, 1968.]

Malantschuk, Gregor. **Kierkegaard's Way to the Truth; an Introduction to the Authorship of Søren Kierkegaard.** Tr. from Danish by Mary Michelsen. Preface by Howard V. Hong. Minneapolis: Augsburg Publishing House, 1963. p 126.

Manheimer, Ronald J. **Kierkegaard and the Education of Historical Consciousness.** Ph. D. diss., University of California, Santa Cruz, 1973. (p 390). [Diss. Abstr. 35/02-A, p 1163.]

Manheimer, Ronald J. **Kierkegaard as Educator.** Berkeley: University of California Press, 1977. p 218.

Marsh, James Leonard. **Hegel and Kierkegaard: A Dialectical and Existential Contrast.** Ph. D. diss., Northwestern University, 1971. (p 129). [Diss. Abstr. 32/06-A, p. 3371.]

Martin, George Arthur. **An Interpretive Principle for Understanding Kierkegaard.** Ph. D. diss., University of Notre Dame, 1969. (p 244). [Diss. Abstr. 30/05-A, p 2079.]

Martin, Harold Victor. **Kierkegaard: The Melancholy Dane.** New York: Philosophical Library; London: Epworth Press, 1950. p 119. [Philosopher's Library no. 3.]

Martin, Harold Victor. **The Wings of Faith. A Consideration of the Nature and Meaning of Christian Faith in the Light of the Work of Søren Kierkegaard.** Forewood by Dr. Lovell Cocks. London: Lutterworth Press, 1950. p 131. New York: Philosophical Library, 1951.

Marxer, Charles Gordon. **Irrationalism in Kierkegaard's Philosophy of Religion.** Phil. M. thesis, University of Toronto, 1968.

Matthis, Michael James. **Kierkegaard and the Problem of Community.** Ph. D. diss., Fordham University, 1977. (p 277). [Diss. Abstr. 38/01-A, p 322.]

Miller, Libuse Lukas. **In Search of the Self: The Individual in the Thought of Kierkegaard.** Philadelphia: Muhlenberg Press, 1962. p 317.

Miller, Samuel H., ed. **Kierkegaard Centennial Issue.** *Andover Newton Bulletin* (Boston) vol. 47, no. 3 (February 1955) p 39.

Milne, Gretchen Elizabeth. **Søren Kierkegaard: A Philosophy by Indirection.** Ph. D. diss., The University of Texas at Austin, 1964. (p 247). [Diss. Abstr. 25/05, p 3034.]

Minear, Paul S. and Paul S. Morimoto. **Kierkegaard and the Bible. An Index.** Princeton, N. J.: Princeton Theological Seminary, 1953. p 36.

Mitchell, J. H. **Some Aspects of the Problem of Guilt with Special Reference to Kafka, Kierkegaard and Dostoevsky.** Ph. D. thesis, University of Edinburgh, 1957-1958.

Moore, Robert B. **Kierkegaard's Conception of Truth.** M. A. thesis, University of Minnesota, 1958.

Moore, Stanley Raymond. **The Social Implications of the Category of the Single One in the Thought of Søren Kierkegaard.** Ph. D. diss., Drew University, 1964. (p 312). [Diss. Abstr. 25/08, p 4843.]

Mueller, Robert William. **A Critical Examination of Martin Buber's Criticisms of Søren Kierkegaard.** Ph. D. diss., Purdue University, 1974. (p 228). [Diss. Abstr. 35/06-A, p 3816.]

Mulholland, Royal William. **A Study of Søren Kierkegaard's Interpretation of the Christian Experience as It Relates to the Meaning of Christian Higher Education.** Ph. D. diss., University of Illinois, 1967. p 317. [Microfilm order no. 68-8178.]

Muska, Rudolph Charles. **Antithetical Religious Conceptions in Kierkegaard and Spinoza.** Ph. D. diss., Michigan State University, 1960. (p 173). [Diss. Abstr. 21/11, p 3489.]

Nauman, St. Elmo H., Jr. **The Social Philosophies of Søren Kierkegaard and Nicolai Frederik Severin Grundtvig.** Ph. D. diss., Boston University, 1969. (p 224). [Diss. Abstr. 30/05-A, p 2081.]

Nielsen, Edith Ortmann and Niels Thulstrup. **Søren Kierkegaard. Bidrag til en Bibliografi. Contributions towards a Bibliography.** Copenhagen: Munksgaard, 1951. p 96.

Nissen, Lowell Allen. **Kierkegaard on Humor.** M. A. thesis, University of Minnesota, 1958.

Nordentoft, Kresten. **Kierkegaard's Psychology.** Pittsburgh, Pa.: Duquesne University Press, 1978. p 408.

Norton, R. W. **The Concepts of the Tragic of Soren Kierkegaard and Miguel de Unamuno.** M. A. thesis, University of Illinois, 1952.

Ohara, Shin. **Kierkegaard's Authorship Considered as an Ethical Argument.** Ph. D. diss., Harvard University, 1966. (p 387). [Diss. Abstr. 27/12-A, p 4301.]

Oliver, Richard Lester. **Schelling and Kierkegaard: Experimentations in Moral Autonomy.** Ph. D. diss., The University of Oklahoma, 1977. (p 184). [Diss. Abstr. 38/04-A, p 2175.]

O'Neill, Kevin David. **Kierkegaard's Attempt at a Balanced Philosophy of Religion.** Ph. D. diss., Yale University, 1967. (p 271). [Diss. Abstr. 28/10-A, p 4215.]

Oppenheim, Michael David. **Soren Kierkegaard and Franz Rosenzweig: The Movement from Philosophy to Religion.** Ph. D. diss., University of California, Santa Barbara, 1976. (p 384). [Diss. Abstr. 37/09-A, p 5898.]

Paley, Alan L. **Søren Kierkegaard: Philosopher and Existentialist.** Charlotteville, N. Y.: SamHar Press, 1972. p 32.

Parrill, Lloyd Ellison. **The Concept of Humor in the Pseudonymous Works of Søren Kierkegaard.** Ph. D. diss., Drew University, 1975. (p 296). [Diss. Abstr. 36/06-A. p 3772.]

Peck, William Dayton. **On Autonomy: The Primacy of the Subject in Kant and Kierke-**

98   **gaard.** Ph. D. diss., Yale University, 1974. (p
297). [Diss. Abstr. 35/05-A, p 3063.]

Peiros, Sherri. **Kierkegaardian Parody.** Ph. D.
diss., University of California, Santa Cruz,
1974. (p 205). [Diss. Abstr. 35/12-A, p 7964.]

Pelikan, Jaroslav. **From Luther to Kierkegaard.
A Study in the History of Theology.** St.
Louis: Concordia Publishing House, 1950. p
171.

Penn, William Y., Jr. **Kierkegaard: A Study in
Faith and Reason.** Ph. D. diss., The Universi-
ty of Texas at Austin, 1976. (p 224). [Diss.
Abstr. 37/05-A, p 2948.]

Perkins, Robert. **Existence and Aesthetics:
Some Kierkegaardian Themes.** M. A. thesis,
Indiana University, 1959.

Perkins, Robert Lee. **Kierkegaard and Hegel:
The Dialectical Structure of Kierkegaard's
Ethical Thought.** Ph. D. diss., Indiana Uni-
versity, 1965. (p 316). [Diss. Abstr. 26/05-
A, p 2809.]

Perkins, Robert L. **Søren Kierkegaard.** Richmond, Va.: John Knox Press; London: Lutterworth Press, 1969. p 46. pb. [Makers of
Contemporary Theology series.]

Petersen, Bengt Edv. **Philosopher and Comba-
tant.** A talk given in the Anglo-Danish Society, Students' Section, London. August, 1955.
Drawings by Hakon Spliid. Copenhagen: privately printed, 1955. p 16.

Plekon, Michael Paul. **Kierkegaard: Diagnosis
and Disease. An Excavation in Modern Consciousness.** New Brunswick, N.J.: Rutgers
University, 1977. p 405.

Pojman, Louis Paul. **The Dialectic of Freedom
in the Thought of Soren Kierkegaard.** Th. D.
diss., Union Theological Seminary in the City
of New York, 1972. (p 287). [Diss. Abstr.
33/02-A, p 8200.]

Pojman, L. P. **Faith and Reason in the Thought
of Kierkegaard.** D. Phil. thesis, Oxford University, 1977.

Pojman, Louis P. **Kierkegaard as Philosopher.**
Swindon: Waterleaf Press, 1978. p 34.

Pomerleau, Wayne Paul. **Perspectives on Faith
and Reason: Studies in the Religious Philosophies of Kant, Hegel & Kierkegaard.** Ph. D.
diss., Northwestern University, 1977. (p
266). [Diss. Abstr. 38/09-A, 5531.]

Price, George. **The Narrow Pass. A Study of
Kierkegaard's Concept of Man.** London:
Hutchinson, 1963. p 224.

Quinn, Wylie Savalas, III. **Kierkegaard and
Wittgenstein: The »Religious« as a »Form of
Life«.** Ph. D. diss., Duke University, 1976. (p
222). [Diss. Abstr. 37/12-A, p 7804.]

Read, Lawrence McKim. **Hegel and Kierkegaard: A Study in Antithetical Concepts of**

the Incarnation. Ph. D. diss., Columbia University, 1967. (p 212). [Diss. Abstr.   28/
05-A, p 1852.]

Reed, Walter L. **Meditations on the Hero: Narrative Form in Carlyle, Kierkegaard, and
Melville.** Ph. D. diss., Yale University, 1969.
(p 315). [Diss. Abstr. vol. 31/03-A, p 1288.]

Refsell, Lloyd. **Kierkegaard's Understanding of
Luther.** Ph. D. diss., Jewish Theological Seminary of America, 1964.

Rohde, K. P., ed. **The Auctioneer's Sales Re-
cord of the Library of Søren Kierkegaard.
With an Essay on Søren Kierkegaard as a
Collector of Books.** Copenhagen: The Royal
Library, 1967. p 183. [Danish-English text.]

Rohde, Peter P. **Søren Kierkegaard: The Danish Philosopher.** Copenhagen: The Press
Dept., Ministry of Foreign Affairs, 1955. p
21.

Rohde, Peter P. **Søren Kierkegaard. An Introduction to his Life and Philosophy.** Tr. from
the Danish and with foreword by Alan Moray
Williams. London: George Allen and Unwin;
New York: Humanities Press, 1963. p 164.

Rohde, Peter P. **Søren Kierkegaard. The Father
of Existentialism.** Tr. Reginald Spink. Copenhagen: Ministry of Foreign Affairs, 1963. p
24. 2nd ed. 1969. p 22 [Profiles - Denmark
series, no. 1.]

Roos, Heinrich, S. J. **Søren Kierkegaard and
Catholicism.** Tr. from Danish by Richard M.
Brackett, S. J. Westminster, Maryland: The
Newman Press, 1954. p 62. [Originally a
lecture delivered before the Kierkegaard So-
ciety in Copenhagen.]

Rose, A. P. **The 'Instant' and 'Contemporanei-
ty' in the Philosophy of Søren Kierkegaard.**
M. A. thesis, University of Manchester, 1973-
1974.

Salladay, Susan. **A Study of the Nature and
Function of Religious Language in Relation
to Kierkegaard's Theories of Subjective
Truth and Indirect Communication.** Ph. D.
diss., Boston College, 1974. (p 204).   [Diss.
Abstr. 35/02-A, p 1166.]

Sandok, Theresa H. **Kierkegaard on Irony and
Humor.** Ph. D. diss., University of Notre Dame, 1975. (p 251). [Diss. Abstr. 36/03-A, p
1586.]

Schaepman, P. M. **The Philosophy of Existence
(Kierkegaard, Nietzsche, Sartre, and Heidegger).** M. A. thesis, University College (London), 1958.

Schrag, Calvin. **Kierkegaard and Heidegger:
The Ontology of Human Finitude.** Chicago:
Northwestern Univ. Press, 1961.

Schrag, Calvin Orville. **The Problem of Existence: Kierkegaard's Descriptive Analysis of the**

Self and Heidegger's Phenomenological Ontology of 'Dasein'. Ph. D. diss., Harvard University, 1957.

Schuelke, Gertrude Luise. **Kierkegaard and Rilke: A Study in Relationships.** Ph. D. diss., Stanford University, 1950. [*Abstracts of Dissertations* (Stanford), 26:151-153 (1950-1951.)]

Schwandt, Jack Allen. **Alienation and Reconciliation in the Works of Soren Kierkegaard.** M. A. thesis, University of Minnesota, 1959.

Seat, Leroy Kay. **The Meaning of »Paradox«: A Study of the Use of the Word »Paradox« in Contemporary Theological and Philosophical Writings with Special Reference to Søren Kierkegaard.** Th. D. diss., Southern Baptist Theological Seminary, 1967. (p 351). [Diss. Abstr. vol. 27/11-A, p 3927.]

Seymour, Betty Jean. **The Dyer's Hand: Kierkegaardian Perspectives on Person, Word, and Art Re-discovered in W. H. Auden.** Ph. D. diss., Duke University, 1975. (p 155). [Diss. Abstr. 36/07-A, p 4583.]

Shearson, William Arrindell. **The Notion of Encounter in Existentialist Metaphysics: An Inquiry into the Nature and Structure of Existential Knowledge in Kierkegaard, Sartre, and Buber.** Ph. D. diss., University of Toronto, 1970. [Diss. Abstr. 32/06-A, p 3374.]

Sherwood, Vance Robert, Jr. **Kierkegaard's Attack on the Church: Images of Ministry to the Church.** D. Div., Vanderbilt University Divinity School, 1972. (p 182). [Diss. Abstr. 33/04-A, p 1828.]

Shestov, Lev. **Kierkegaard and the Existential Philosophy.** Tr. Elinor Hewitt. Athens, Ohio: Ohio University Press, 1969. p 314 [Originally published as *Kierkegaard et la philosophie existentielle*, 1936, under author's French name, Léon Chestov.]

Shmuëli, Adi. **Kierkegaard and Consciousness.** Tr. Naomi Handelman. Foreword by Paul L. Holmer. Princeton: Princeton University Press, 1971. p 202.

Sikes, Walter W. **On Becoming Truth: An Introduction to the Life and Thought of Søren Kierkegaard.** St. Louis: Bethany Press, 1968. p 190.

Silver, Jeffrey Howard. **Kierkegaard's Psychology of Health & Alienation.** Ph. D. diss., Graduate Theological Union, 1978. (p 147). [Diss. Abstr. 39/06-A, p 3650.]

Simons, P. M. **Kierkegaard on Choice: A Critique.** M. A. thesis, University of Manchester, 1972-1973.

Sivertsen, Eddie. **Faith and Reason in Søren Kierkegaard's Philosophy of Religion.** Ph. D.

diss., Northern Baptist Theological Seminary, 1953.

Sjursen, Harold P. **Kierkegaard: The Individual and the Public. A Study in the Problem of Essential Communication.** Ph. D. diss., New School for Social Research, 1974. (p 283). [Diss. Abstr. 35/10-A, p 6764.]

Smit, Harvey. **Kierkegaard's Pilgrimage of Man.** Grand Rapids: William B. Eerdmans Publishing Co., 1965. p 193.

Smith, Joel Robert. **The Dialectic Selfhood in the Works of Soren Kierkegaard.** Ph. D. diss., Vanderbilt University, 1977. (p 198). [Diss. Abstr. 38/03-A, p 1456.]

Smith, Kenneth Ray. **Dialectical Conceptions of the Spirit: Hegel, Kierkegaard, and Nietzsche.** Ph. D. diss., Yale University, 1972. (p 239). [Diss. Abstr. 33/07-A, p 3720.]

Soneson, Joseph Melburn. **The Individual: A Comparison of the Philosophical Anthropologies of Soren Kierkegaard and Alfred North Whitehead with Theological Implications.** Pd. D. diss., University of Chicago, 1969.

Soper, William Wayne. **The Self and Its World in Ralph Barton Perry, Edgar Sheffield Brightman, Jean-Paul Sartre and Søren Kierkegaard.** Ph. D. diss., Boston University, 1962. (p 563). [Diss. Abstr. 23/03, p 1042.]

Søren Kierkegaard Number. *The American Book Collector.* (Chicago) vol. XII, no. 4 (1961) p 32. Ill.

Sponheim, Paul Ronald. **The Christological Formulations of Schleiermacher and Kierkegaard in Relation to Fundamental Options Discernible in Divergent Strands in Their Discussion of God and Man.** Ph. D. diss., University of Chicago, 1961.

Sponheim, Paul R. **Kierkegaard on Christ and Christian Coherence.** London: S. C. M. Press; New York: Harper & Row, 1968. p 322.

Stack, George J. **Kierkegaard's Existential Ethics.** University, Alabama: University of Alabama Press, 1977. p 237. [Studies in the humanities.]

Stack, George J. **On Kierkegaard: Philosophical Fragments.** Nyborg, Dk.: F. Løkkes Forlag; Atlantic Highlands, N. J.: Humanities Press, 1976. p 127.

Start, Lester J. **Kierkegaard and Hegel.** Ph. D. diss., Syracuse University, 1953.

Stavrides, Maria M. **The Concept of Existence in Kierkegaard and Heidegger.** Ph. D. diss., Columbia University, 1952. (p 205). [Diss. Abstr. 12:641 (1952).]

Stendahl, Brita. **Søren Kierkegaard.** Boston: Twayne Publishers, 1976. p 235.

Stevens, Eldon Lloyd. **Kierkegaard's Categories of Existence.** Ph. D. diss., University of

100   Colorado, 1964. (p 283). [Diss. Abstr. 26/09, p 5487.]

Stevens, Eldon Lloyd. **The Kierkegaardian Concept of History: an Analysis of the Thought of Kierkegaard as It Is Related to the Meaning of History.** M. A. thesis, University of Minnesota, 1950.

Stines, James William. **Phenomenology of Language in the Thought of Søren Kierkegaard.** Ph. D. diss., Duke University, 1970. (p 279). [Diss. Abstr. 31/11-A, p 6152.]

Suber, Peter Dain. **Kierkegaard's Concept of Irony Especially in Relation to Freedom, Personality and Dialectic.** Ph. D. diss., Northwestern University, 1978.

Sugerman, Shirley Greene. **Sin and Madness. A Study in the Self in Søren Kierkegaard and Ronald D. Laing.** Ph. D. diss., Drew University, 1970. (p 321). [Diss. Abstr. 31/06-A, p 3029.]

Sullivan, Frank Russell, Jr. **Faith and Reason in Kierkegaard.** Ph. D. diss., Boston University Graduate School, 1973. (p 185). [Diss. Abstr. 34/04-A, p 1976.]

Survin, V. **Pascal and Kierkegaard: Their Understanding of Man and the Human Condition.** M. A. thesis, University of Bath, 1974-1975.

Swenson, David F. **Something about Kierkegaard.** Ed. Lillian Marvin Swenson. Revised ed. Minneapolis: Augsburg Publishing House, 1956. [First pub. 1941, rev. ed. first pub. 1945.]

Taylor, Douglas Randolph. **The Aesthetic Methodology of Søren Kierkegaard's Pseudonymous Works.** Ph. D. diss., The Florida State University, 1977. (p 328). [Diss. Abstr. 38/05-A, p 2854.]

Taylor, Lewis Jerome, Jr. **The Becoming of the Self in the Writings of Walker Percy: A Kierkegaardian Analysis.** Ph. D. diss., Duke University, 1972. (p 349). [Diss. Abstr. 33/03, p 1224.]

Taylor, Mark C. **Kierkegaard's Pseudonymous Authorship: A Study of Time and the Self.** Princeton, Princeton Univ. Press, 1975. (p 391).

Taylor, Mark C. **Time and Self: A Study of Søren Kierkegaard's Pseudonymous Authorship.** Ph. D. diss., Harvard University, 1973.

Tescher, George Albert. **The Relation of Man to Transcendence in the Philosophy of Kierkegaard.** Ph. D. diss., New School for Social Recearch, 1975. (p 251). [Diss. Abstr. 36/09-A, p 6152.]

Thomas, John Heywood. **Subjectivity and Paradox.** Oxford: Basil Blackwell, 1957. p 174.

Thomasson, James William. **Concepts: Their Role, Criteria and Correction in the Thought of Søren A. Kierkegaard.** Ph. D. diss., Yale University, 1968. (p 303). [Diss. Abstr. 29:11.]

Thompson, Josiah. **Kierkegaard.** New York: Alfred A. Knopf, 1973. London: Victor Gollancz, 1974. pp 312.

Thompson, Josiah, ed. **Kierkegaard: A Collection of Critical Essays.** Anchor Books Edition. Garden City, N. Y.: Doubleday, 1972. p 464. [Modern Studies in Philosophy Series.]

Thompson, Josiah Donald, Jr. **The Lonely Labyrinth: A Study in the Pseudonymous Works of Søren Kierkegaard, 1843-1846.** Ph. D. diss., Yale University, 1964.

Thompson, Josiah. **The Lonely Labyrinth: Kierkegaard's Pseudonymous Works.** Foreword by George K. Plochman. London: Feffer & Simons, Inc.; Carbondale: Southern Illinois Univ. Press, 1967. p 242.

Thomte, Reidar. **Kierkegaard's Philosophy of Religion.** New York: Greenwood Press, 1969. p 228.

Thulstrup, Marie Mikulová, ed. **The Sources of Depths of Faith in Kierkegaard.** Copenhagen: Reitzel, 1978. p 180.

Thulstrup, Niels and Marie Mikulová Thulstrup, eds. **Kierkegaard's View of Christianity.** Copenhagen: Reitzel, 1978. p 193.

Toettcher, R. W. **Kierkegaard and Sartre: A Comparison of the Conception of Freedom of Two Existential Philosophers.** M. A. thesis, Birkbeck College (Great Britain), 1963-1964.

Trentman, John Allen. **Kierkegaard's Interpretation of the Socratic-Ethical Theory.** M. A. thesis, University of Minnesota, 1958.

Tweedie, Donald F. **The Significance of Dread in the Thought of Kierkegaard and Heidegger.** Ph. D. diss., Boston University, 1954. (p 234). [Diss. Abstr., vol. 37, p 604.]

Underwood, Byron Edward. **Kierkegaard's Category of the Concrete Individual.** Ph. D. diss., Harvard University, 1966.

Ussher, Percy Arland. **Journey through Dread. On Kierkegaard, Heidegger and Sartre.** London: Finlayson, 1955. p 160. Ill. rpt. New York: Biblo & Tannen, 1968. p 160.

Utterback, Sylvia Walsh. **Kierkegaard's Dialectic of Christian Existence.** Ph. D. diss., Emory University, 1975. (p 373). [Diss. Abstr. 36/05-A, p 2914.]

Van Roekel, Joseph G. **Decisive Christianity in the Authorship of Søren Kierkegaard.** Ph. D. diss., The Southern Baptist Theological Seminary, 1954.

Waitkus, Werner. **Kierkegaard's Concept of Dread.** B. D. thesis, St. Stephen's College (Edmonton, Alberta, Canada), 1968.

Waring, E. **Kierkegaard and Modern Ethics.** M. Litt. thesis, Cambridge University, 1953-1954.

Warner, D. H. J. **The Dialectic of Existence in Kierkegaard, with Particular Reference to Socrates.** B. Litt. thesis, Oxford University, 1954-1955.

Weiland, J. Sperna. **Philosophy of Existence and Christianity. Kierkegaard's and Jasper's Thoughts on Christianity.** Assen (The Netherlands): Van Gorcum & Co., 1951. p 144.

Wells, William Walter, III. **The Influence of Kierkegaard on the Theology of Karl Barth.** Ph. D. diss., Syracuse University, 1970. (p 294). [Diss. Abstr. 32/01-A, p 531.]

White, Carol Jean. **Time and Temporality in the Existential Thought of Kierkegaard and Heidegger.** Ph. D. diss., University of California, Berkeley, 1976. (p 369). [Diss. 38/02-A, p 853.]

White, Willie. **Faith and Existence: A Study in Aquinas and Kierkegaard.** Ph. D. diss., University of Chicago, 1966.

Williams, Joan Leona. **Søren Kierkegaard - Who Is the Philosophical Man?** M. A. thesis, University of Toronto, 1965.

Wolf, Herbert C. **Kierkegaard and Bultmann: The Quest of the Historical Jesus.** Minneapolis: Augsburg Publishing House, 1965. p 100.

Wyschogrod, Michael. **Kierkegaard and Heidegger; The Ontology of Existence.** Ph. D. diss., Columbia University, 1954. London: Routledge & K. Paul, 1954. p 156.

Zuidema, Sytse Ulbe. **Kierkegaard.** Tr. from the Dutch by David H. Freeman. Philadelphia: Presbyterian and Reformed Publishing Co., 1960. p 57. [International Library of Philosophy and Theology, Modern Thinkers series.]

THOMAS KINGO (1634-1703)

Admiral Niels Juel's Epitaph. Tr. R. P. Keigwin. *IDIWB* p 9. [*Gravskriften for Admiral Niels Juel*, or *Paa-Skriffter udi Niels Juels Epitaphio*, poem below the bust at his grave in Holmens Church, Copenhagen, 1697.]

Come Holy Spirit, Truth Divine. Tr. S. D. Rodholm. *HoS* p 65. Also *HinS* hymn nr. 47. [*Nu nærmer sig vor Pintze-Fest*, hymn from the collection *Ny Kirke-Psalme-Bog*, 1699.]

The Dawn from Mountain Crest. Tr. P. C. Paulsen and Johannes Knudsen. *HinS* hymn nr. 3. [*Nu rinder Solen op af Østerlide*, hymn from the collection *Aandelige Siunge-koors Første Part*, 1674.]

Everyone Has His Destiny. Tr. John A. Dussinger. *ADL* pp 87-91. [*Hver har sin Skæbne*,] hymn from the collection *Aandelige Siunge-koors Anden Part*, 1681.]

Like the Golden Sun Ascending. Tr. J. C. Aaberg. *HinS* hymn nr. 39. [*Som dend Gyldne Sool frembryder*, hymn from the collection *Vinter-Parten*, 1689.]

Lord Jesus Christ, Receive Me Now. Tr. J. C. Aaberg. *HinS* hymn nr. 62. [*O Jesu, paa din Alterfood*, hymn from the collection *Aandelige Siunge-koors Anden Part*, 1681.]

Morning Song. Tr. R. P. Keigwin. *AScL* p 23. Also *IDIWB* p 11. [*Dend siette Morgen-sang*,] poem from *Aandelige Siunge-koors Første Part*, 1674.]

O Dearest Lord, Receive from Me. Tr. J. C. Aaberg. *HinS* hymn nr. 61. [*O Jesu, Søde Jesu*, hymn from the collection *Vinter-Parten*, 1689.]

Sorrow and Gladness Together Go Wending. Tr. William and Mary Howitt. *AScl* pp 21-23. [*Sorrig og Glæde de vandre tilhaabe*, or *Hver har sin Skæbne*, hymn from *Aandelige Siunge-koors Anden Part*, 1681.]

Previous Translations:

Of the Seven Words on the Cross.
The Nativity.
The Transfiguration.
The Resurrection.
Trial and Faith.
The Nazareth of the Soul.
Evening.
Ordination of Pastors.
Grace before Meal (Before Us Our Repast Is Spread).
Grace after Meal (Now Is Ended Our Repast).
Hymn of the Sick (O, God, my God, How Long Shall I).

HANS KIRK (1898-1962)

The Birth of a New Era. Tr. Marianne Helweg. *CDPr* pp 243-250. [Extract from the novel *Daglejerne*, 1936.]

Exiled. Tr. Lydia Cranfield. *Nor* vol. 14, no. 2 (March-April 1956) pp 126-133. [*Landsforvist*, memoirs, from the collection *Skyggespil*, 1953.]

102 PER KIRKEBY (b. 1938)

From: **Explanations of Pictures.** Tr. Poul Borum. *CDPo* pp 282-283. [From the poetry collection *Billedforklaringer*, 1968.]
From: **Jüngling auf der Wanderschaft.** Tr. Poul Borum. *CDPo* pp 284, 285. [From the poetry collection *Jüngling auf der Wanderschaft*, 1970.]
From: **2 Poems.** Tr. Poul Borum. *CDPo* pp 286-287. [From the poetry collection *2 digte*, 1973.]

MOGENS KLITGAARD (1906-1945)

The English Bombardment of Copenhagen in 1807. Tr. J. F. S. Pearce. *CDPr* pp 300-301. [Extract from the novel *De røde Fjer*, 1940.]
The Nineteen Thirties. Tr. J. F. S. Pearce. *CDPr* pp 302-314. [Extract from the novel *Der sidder en Mand i en Sporvogn*, 1937.]

ERIK KNUDSEN (b. 1922)

Bourgeois All at Sea. Tr. Kurt Hansen. *CDPo* p 147. [*Bourgeois i Vildrede*, poem from the collection *Babylon marcherer*, 1970.]
The Eve of St. Bartholomew. Tr. Martin S. Allwood. *TCScP* pp 94-95. [*Bartholomeusnat*, poem from the collection *Blomsten og Sværdet*, 1948.]
The Flower and the Sword. Tr. Alexander Taylor. *CDPo* p 142. [*Blomsten og Sværdet*, poem from the collection by the same name, 1949.]
It's Time. (Gustaf Munch-Petersen in Memoriam). Tr. Phillip Marshall. *LitR-Dk* p 19. [*Det er pa Tide*, poem from the collection *Minotauros*, 1955.]
My Heart Cries. Tr. Martin S. Allwood. *TCScP* pp 93-94. [*Mit Hjerte raaber*, poem from the collection *Blomsten og Sværdet*, 1948.]
My Lundbye Ecstasy. Tr. Alexander Taylor. *CDPo* p 141. [*Min Lundbyerus*, poem from the collection *Dobbelte Dage*, 1945.]
Nik, Nik, Nikolaj. (Resume with quotations of reviews in English and French). *World Theatre* (Paris) vol. 15, nos. 3-4 (1966) p 330 (Technical Data: Denmark). [*Nik, Nik, Nikolaj*, play, 1966.]
Non Scholae. Tr. Kurt Hansen. *CDPo* pp 143-145. [*Non Scholæ*, poem from the collection *Sensation og Stilhed*, 1958.]

The Representatives. Tr. Kurt Hansen, *CDPo* pp 146-147. Also *Books* p 16 (no trans. given). [*Repræsentanterne*, poem from the collection *Babylon marcherer*, 1970.]
Shall We . . .? Tr. H. Raphael. *LitR-Dk* p 20. [*Skal vi aflægge en Visit*, poem, part of *Anfægtelser 1946* from the collection *Til en ukendt Gud*, 1947.]
To Complete. Tr. Martin S. Allwood. *MoDP* pp 38-39. [*At fuldende er at begrænse*, (first line), poem from the collection *Til en ukendt Gud*, 1947.]
When I Walk in the Wood. Tr. Martin S. Allwood. *TCScP* p 93. [*Naar jeg gaar i Skoven*, poem from the collection *Digte 1945-58*.]

JAKOB KNUDSEN (1858-1917)

Heavy Murky Clouds of Night. Tr. Johannes Knudsen. *HinS* hymn nr 7. [*Tunge, mørke Natteskyer*, poem published in *Tidens Strøm*, VII, 10 (5. december 1890) and in the collection *Digte*, 1938.]
Indomitability. Tr. V. Elizabeth Balbour-Browne. *CDPr* pp 9-16. [*Sejglivethed*, short story from the collection *Jyder*, 1915-1917.]
Morning. Tr. S. D. Rodholm. *HoS* pp 36-37. Also *HinS* hymn nr. 2. [*Se, nu stiger Solen*, poem published in *Højskolebladet*, 20. marts 1891.]

Works about Jakob Knudsen

Jones, W. Glyn. **»Det forjættede Land« and »Fremskridt« as Social Novels. A Comparison.** *SS* vol. 37, no. 1 (February 1965) pp 77-90.

JOHANNES KNUDSEN (b. 1902)
Danish-American church historian

Come, Let Us Forward Go. *HinS* hymn nr. 101.
The Farmer's Furrow Breaks the Sod. *HinS* hymn nr. 63.
God in His Word Brought the World to Creation. *HinS* hymn nr. 35.
In the Mists of Beginning God's Almighty Act. *HinS* hymn nr. 32.
The Past is People Who Lived Their Day. *HinS* hymn nr. 83.
The Word Was with God. *HinS* hymn nr. 33.
The World of the Christ. *HinS* hymn nr. 34.

TOM KRISTENSEN (1893-1974)

Born Again. Tr. Martin S. Allwood and Grant Keener. *TCScP* pp 63-64. [*Genfødt*, poem from the collection *Den syngende Busk*, 1949.]

Diminuendo. Tr. Charles Wharton Stork. *SeBDV* p. 141. Also in *TCScP* pp 62-63. [*Diminuendo*, poem from the collection *En Fribytters Ord*, 1932, originally published in the novel *Hærværk*, 1930.]

The Disaster. Tr. Lydia Cranfield. *CDPr* pp 205-212. [*Ulykken*, short story from the collection *Vindrosen*, 1934.]

The Execution. Tr. Poul Borum. *CDPo* pp 31-33. [*Henrettelsen*, poem from the collection *Paafuglefjeren*, 1922.]

Fear. Tr. Carl Malmberg. *CDPo* p 35. [*Angst*, poem published in the novel *Hærværk*, 1930.]

Grass. Tr. Poul Borum. *CDPo* p 34. *Græs*, poem from the collection *Verdslige Sange*, 1927.]

Havoc. Tr. Carl Malmberg. Intro. Børge Gedsø Madsen. Madison, Wisconsin: University of Wisconsin Press, 1968. p 427. [*Hærværk*, novel, 1930.]

In a Japanese Railway Carriage. Tr. Evelyn Heepe. *MoDA* pp 129-137. [*I en japansk Kupé*, short story from the collection *Vindrosen*, 1934.]

It's Knud Who Is Dead. Tr. Poul Borum. *CDPo* p 36. [*Det er Knud, som er død*, poem from the collection *Mod den yderste Rand*, 1936.]

The Slow Spring. Tr. Martin S. Allwood and Knud Mogensen. *MoDP* p 12. Also *TCScP* p 61. [*Det langsomme Forår*, poem written in 1940 and published in the collection *Med disse Øjne*, 1973.]

The Vanished Faces. Tr. Evelyn Heepe. *MoDA* pp 138-144. [*De forsvundne Ansigter*, short story from the collection *Vindrosen*, 1934.]

What Is War? Tr. Lydia Cranfield. *Nor* vol. 9, no. 6 (November-December 1951) pp 415-424. [*Hvad er Krigen*, short story from the collection *Hvad er Heta?*, 1946.]

Works about Tom Kristensen

Byram, Michael. **The Reality of Tom Kristensen's »Hærværk«.** *Scandinavica* (London) vol. 15, no. 1 (May 1976) pp 28-37.

Byram, Michael. **Tom Kristensen's »Livets Arabesk« Seen as a Political Gesture.** *Scandinavica* vol. 16, no. 2 (November 1977) pp 109-118.

Jones, W. Glyn. **Tom Kristensen at Eighty.** *Denmark* (London) no. 164 (1973) pp 7-8. Ill.

JENS KRUUSE (1908-1978)

Madness at Oradour. Tr. Carl Malmberg. London: Secker & Warburg, 1969. p 179. [*Som Vanvid, Oradour-sur-Glane*, historic novel, 1967.]

See also *War for an Afternoon*.

War for an Afternoon. Tr. Carl Malmberg. New York: Pantheon Books, 1968. p 146 [*Som Vanvid, Oradour-sur-Glane*, historic novel, 1967.]

PAUL LA COUR (1902-1956)

Aphorisms. *LitR-Dk* pp 20, 30, 39, 40, 53, 65, 131. [Aphorisms taken from *Fragmenter af en Dagbog*, 1948.]

Faint Horn-sound of Summer. Tr. Poul Borum. *CDPo* p 48. [*Sommerens bløde Hornlyd*, poem from the collection *Efterladte Digte*, 1957.]

Happiness. Tr. Frederick Fleischer. *Nor* vol. 12, no. 5 (September-October 1954) p 312. [*I Dag er jeg fuld af Ømhed*, (first line), poem from the collection *Mellem Bark og Ved*, 1950.]

Peloponnesian Nights. Tr. Poul Borum. *CDPo* pp 47-48. [*Peloponnesiske Aftner*, poem from the collection *Efterladte Digte*, 1957.]

She Could Not Fall. Tr. Poul Borum. *CDPo* p 45. [*Hun kunne ikke falde*, poem from the collection *Mellem Bark og Ved*, 1950.]

That Day. Tr. Charles Wharton Stork. *SeBDV* pp 142-143. Also *TCScP* pp 76-77. [*Kan du huske disse Dage*, poem from the collection *Regn over Verden*, 1933.]

Threshold. Tr. Poul Borum. *CDPo* p 46. [*Tærskel*, poem from the collection *Mellem Bark og Ved*, 1950.]

The Tree. Tr. Poul Borum. *CDPo* p 46. [*Træet*, poem from the collection *Mellem Bark og Ved*, 1950.]

The Unforeseen. Tr. Poul Borum. *CDPo* p 44. [*Det Uforudsete*, poem from the collection *Levende Vande*, 1946.]

TAGE LA COUR (b. 1915)

The Murder Book: An Illustrated History of the Detective Story. By Tage La Cour and Harald Mogensen. Tr. Roy Duffell. London: Allen & Unwin, 1971. p 191. Ill. [*Mordbogen*, 1969.]

The Murder of Santa Claus. Tr. Paul Ib Liebe. Ill. Lars Bo. Denmark: Privately printed, 1954. p 20. Ill. [Murder mystery.]

104 THOR LANGE (1851-1915)

Alas, You Birchtree. Tr. Marie Rasmussen. *Versuch* vol. 18 (1979) p 9. [*Ak, du Birketræ*, poem from the collection *Nogle Folkeviser*, 1878.]

To Tell How I Love You. Tr. Charles Wharton Stork. *SeBDV* p 80. [*Jeg tør ingen betro*, poem included in *Udvalgte Digte*, 1915.]

Were I a Lark So Gay. Tr. Charles Wharton Stork. *SeBDV* pp 80-81. [*Folkevise (Var jeg en Lærke graa)* poem included in *Udvalgte Digte*, 1915.]

Previous Translations:

Folksong (I Gather Two Frozen Branches).
Sunset [Aftenrøde].
Why? A Danish Version of an Old Russian Folksong.
Oh, I Possess Pretty Fingers Small.

EMIL LANGE-MÜLLER
(1849-1881)

Summer Lightning - -. Tr. Charles Wharton Stork. *SeBDV* p 71. [Poem.]

P. E. LANGE-MÜLLER (1850-1926)

Wishing. Tr. S. D. Rodholm. *HoS* p 146. [*Kornmodsglansen ved Midnat*, serenade written and composed 1879.]

MARIANNE LARSEN (b. 1951)

Anonymous I, II. *CDPo* p 329. [*Anonym I, II*, poem written in English from the collection *Cinderella*, 1974.]

Now I Am Gone. Tr. Poul Borum. *CDPo* pp 323-324. [*Nu er jeg borte*, poem from the collection *Overstregslyd*, 1972.]

Serial Dream. Tr. Poul Borum. *CDPo* pp 325-326. [*Seriel Drøm*, poem from the collection *Ravage*, 1973.]

Seven-year-old Girls. Tr. Poul Borum. *CDPo* p 330. [*Syvårspiger*, poem from the collection *Cinderella*, 1974.]

Sick Women in the Park. Tr. Poul Borum. *CDPo* pp 324-325. [*De syge Koner i Parken*, poem from the collection *Ravage*, 1973.]

Today. Tr. Poul Borum. *CDPo* pp 326-327. [*I Dag*, poem from the collection *Billedtekster*, 1974.]

Unknown Person. Tr. Poul Borum. *CDPo* p 328. [*Ukendt Person*, poem from the collection *Billedtekster*, 1974.]

THØGER LARSEN (1875-1928)

At the Circus. Tr. R. P. Keigwin. *TCScP* pp 50-51. [*I Cirkus*, poem from the collection *Dagene*, 1905.]

The Danish Summer. Tr. R. P. Keigwin. *IDIWB* pp 101-103 and *TCScP* pp 49-50. Also *J. L. News* (J. Lauritzen Lines, Copenhagen) no. 44 (1961) p 17. [*Den danske Sommer*, poem from the collection *Slægternes Træ*, 1914.]

Summer. Tr. Charles Wharton Stork. *SeBDV* p 108. [*Sommer*, poem from the collection *Jord*, 1904.]

Previous Translations:

Celestial Neighbours.

MARCUS LAUESEN (1907—1975)

Francisca. Tr. John Poole. *CDPr* pp 315-325. [*Francisca*, short story from the collection *Glædens Dag*, 1933.]

Previous Translations:

Waiting for a Ship.
The Very Beautiful Days.
Two Stories: Wanja, the Red House.

PETER LAUGESEN (b. 1942)

From: **Catatonia.** Tr. Poul Borum. *CDPo* pp 305-306. [From the poetry collection *Katatonien*, 1970.]

From: **Divine Innocence.** Tr. Poul Borum. *CDPo* p 309. [From the poetry collection *Guds Ord fra Landet*, 1974.]

From: **I Can Hear You Singing.** Tr. Poul Borum. *CDPo* p 308. [From the poetry collection *Jeg kan høre dig synge*, 1973.]

From: **It Is only a Paper Moon.** Tr. Poul Borum. *CDPo* p 307. [From the poetry collection *Det er kun en Måne af Papir*, 1973.]

Manuscript 4th Version. Tr. Poul Borum. *CDPo* pp 302-303. [*Manuskript fjerde Version*, poem from the collection *Landskab*, 1967.]

November Piece. Tr. Poul Borum. *CDPo* p 303. [*Novemberstykke*, poem from the collection *Landskab*, 1967.]

From: **Writing.** Tr. Poul Borum. *CDPo* pp 304-305. [From the poetry collection *Skrift*, 1968.]

PALLE LAURING (b. 1909)

The Roman. Tr. Reginald Spink. London: Museum Press, 1956. p 224. [*Vitellius*, novel, 1944.]

EDVARD LEMBCKE (1815-1857)

Our Mother-tongue. Tr. R. P. Keigwin. *IDIWB* pp 71-73. [*Vort Modersmaal*, poem written in 1859, printed in *Digte og Sange*, 1870.]

HANS JØRGEN LEMBOURN (b. 1923)

The Best of All Worlds, or What Voltaire Never Knew. Tr. Evelyn Ramsden. Ill. Gunvor Ovden Edwards. London: Jonathan Cape Ltd., 1960. New York: G. P. Putnam's Sons, 1961. p 192. Ill. [*Grev Frederik eller Den bedste af alle Verdener*, novel, 1958.]

Forty Days with Marilyn. London: Hutchinson, 1979. p. 214. [*40 Dage med Marilyn*, novel, 1977.]

PETER LEMCKE

The Little Ole. Tr. S. D. Rodholm. *HoS* p 173. Also *HinS* song nr. 106. [*Den lille Ole*, children's song.]

LEONORA CHRISTINA (1621-1698)

The Captive Countess Leonora Christina's Memory of Woe. Tr. F. E. Bunnett. *ADL* pp 51-65. [*Den Fangne Grefwinne Leonorae Christinae Jammers Minde*, autobiography, c. 1685.]

JØRGEN LETH (b. 1937)

My Vietnam Poem. Tr. Else Mathiessen and Alexander Taylor. *CDPo* pp 234-235. [*Mit Vietnamdigt*, poem from the collection *Lykken i Ingenmandsland*, 1967.]

Tales, Number 15. Tr. Else Mathiessen and Alexander Taylor. *CDPo* pp 239-241. [*Eventyret, No. 15*, poem from the collection *Eventyret om den sædvanlige Udsigt*, 1971.]

Tales, Number 10. Tr. Else Mathiessen and Alexander Taylor. *CDPo* pp 237-238. [*Eventyret, No. 10*, poem from the collection *Eventyret om den sædvanlige Udsigt*, 1971.]

There Is Always Music through the Walls. Tr. Else Mathiessen and Alexander Taylor. *CDPo* p 236. [*Der er altid Musik gennem Væggene*, poem from the collection *Glatte hårdtpumpede Puder*, 1969.]

LOUIS LEVY (1875-1940)

The Swallow's Flight. Tr. Martin S. Allwood and Sanford Kaufman. *TCScP* p 56. [*Svalens Flugt*, poem from the collection *De 150 Børnerim*, 1931.]

»LILITH« (pseud.)

Revenge. By »Lilith«, an anonymous Danish woman. Tr. Nadia Christensen. *SR* vol. 65, no. 3 (September 1977) p 39. [Poem from the collection *Poesibogen -- Kvindeord og Kvindebilleder*, 1974.]

JANNIK LINDBÆK (1862-1909)

Christmas Eve. Tr. S. D. Rodholm. *HoS* p 103. [*Nu kimer Klokkerne sammen*, poem from the collection *Digte*, 1911.]

KELVIN LINDEMANN (b. 1911)

The Red Umbrellas. Tr. by the author. New York: Appleton-Century-Croft, 1955. p 214. London: Methuen & Co., 1956. p 175. [*En Aften i Kolera-Aaret*, historical novel, 1953.]

Previous Translations:

The House with the Green Tree.

106 JENS LOCHER (1889-1952)

Tea for Three. Tr. anonymously, revised by P. N. Furbank and Elias Bredsdorff. *CDPl* pp 327-400. [*Tre maa man være*, play, 1943.]

BIØRN CHRISTIAN LUND (1738-1809)

O Jesus, in My Heart Instill. Rev. N. F. S. Grundtvig. Tr. J. C. Aaberg. *HinS* hymn nr. 42. [*Min Jesus, lad mit Hjerte faa*, hymn from the collection *Jesu Bruds Glæde...*, 1764.]

HENRIK LUND (ENDALEEQQAMIK) (1875-1948)
Greenlandic author

Nunarput -- Our Country. The Eskimo National Anthem of Greenland. Translated from the Danish version by Martin S. Allwood. Danish translation by W. Thalbitzer. *TCScP* pp 105-106.

KNUD LUNDBERG (b. 1920)

The Olympic Hope: A Story from the Olympic Games, 1996. Tr. Eiler Hansen and William Luscombe. London: S. Paul, 1958. p 172. [*Det olympiske Håb*, novel, 1955.]

HULDA LÜTKEN (1896-1946)

I Am Perishing Now. Tr. Kevin Kennedy. *Versuch* vol. 18 (1979) p 21. [*Jeg går til grunde nu*, poem from the collection *Grædende Latter*, 1944.]

Mammon. Tr. Martin S. Allwood. *TCScP* pp 74-76. [*Mammon*, poem from the collection *Grædende Latter*, 1944.]

Megalomania. Tr. Martin S. Allwood. *MoDP* pp 16-17. Also *TCScP* p 74. [*Storhedsvanvid*, poem from the collection *Grædende Latter*, 1944.]

The Moon Mother. Tr. Nadia Chistensen. *CDPo* pp 60-61. [*Maanemoderen*, poem from the collection *Klode i Drift*, 1951.]

INGEBORG MADSEN

Christmas. Tr. S. D. Rodholm. *HoS* p 102. Also *HinS* hymn nr. 24. [*Det tindrer af Sne paa Vej og Sti.*]

SVEND ÅGE MADSEN (b. 1937)

Here. Tr. Leonie Marx. *SS* vol. 49, no. 2 (Spring 1977) pp 138-142. [*Hist*, short story from the collection *Texter fra Slutningen af 60'erne*, 1969.]

The Judge. Tr. Christine Hauch. *New Writers II*. London: Calder and Boyars, 1974. pp 17-18. [*Dommeren*, short story from the collection *Otte Gange Orphan*, 1965.]

The Judge. Tr. Paula Hostrup-Jessen. *DI* p 213-222. [*Dommeren*, short story from the collection *Otte Gange Orphan*, 1965.]

Schizophrenic Pictures. Tr. Leonie Marx. *Mundus Artium* (Athens, Ohio) vol. 8, no. 2 (1975) pp 21-23. [Experimental prose from *Otte Gange Orphan*, 1965.]

IVAN MALINOVSKI (b. 1926)

Agricultural Poem. Tr. Carl King. *CrS* pp 31-32. [*Landbrugspoem*, poem from the collection *Åbne Digte*, 1963.

Bert's Own Blend. Tr. Carl King. *CrS* pp 33-34. [*Stykkeskriverens egen Blanding*, poem from the collection *Åbne Digte*, 1963.]

Critique of Child Slayers. Tr. Carl King. *CrS* p 70. Also *CDPo* p 161. [*Kritik af Børnenes Banemænd*, poem from the collection *Kritik af Tavsheden*, 1974.]

Critique of Defeatism. Tr. Carl King. *CrS* p 75. Also *CDPo* p 163. [*Kritik af Defaitismen*, poem from the collection *Kritik af Tavsheden*, 1974.]

Critique of Distraction. Tr. Dave Nelson. *CrS* p 66. [*Kritik af Distraktionen*, poem from the collection *Kritik af Tavsheden*, 1974.]

Critique of Everyone Who Should Have Gone Home to Bed Long Ago. Tr. Jonathan Schwartz. *CrS* p 67. [*Kritik af alle dem der forlængst skulle være gået hjem i Seng*, poem from the collection *Kritik af Tavsheden*, 1974.]

Critique of Freedom. Tr. Carl King. *CrS* p 71. Also *CDPo* p 161. [*Kritik af Friheden*, poem from the collection *Kritik af Tavsheden*, 1974.]

Critique of Long-suffering. Tr. Carl King. *CrS* p 73. Also *CDPo* p 162. [*Kritik af Langmodigheden*, poem from the collection *Kritik af Tavsheden*, 1974.]

Critique of Myself. Tr. Carl King. *CrS* p 69. Also *CDPo* p 160 and *Books* p 4 (no trans. given). [*Kritik af mit selv*, poem from the collection *Kritik af Tavsheden*, 1974.]

Critique of Personal Sorrow. Tr. Carl King. *CrS* p 68. [*Kritik af den personlige Sorg*, poem from the collection *Kritik af Tavsheden*, 1974.]

Critique of Reason. Tr. Carl King. *CrS* p 72. Also *CDPo* p 161. [*Kritik af Fornuften*, poem from the collection *Kritik af Tavsheden*, 1974.]

Critique of Silence. Tr. Carl King. *CrS* p 74. Also *CDPo* p 162. [*Kritik af Tavsheden*, poem from the collection by the same name, 1974.]

Critique of Silence. Selected Poems. Copenhagen: Gyldendal, 1977. p 78. Individual poems listed separately under *CrS*.

Critique of the Way of the World. Tr. Carl King. *CrS* p 65. Also *CDPo* p 160. [*Kritik af Verdens Gang*, poem from the collection *Kritik af Tavsheden*, 1974.]

Demonstration. Tr. Carl King. *CrS* p 26. Also *CDPo* p 159. [*Demonstration*, poem from the collection *Åbne Digte*, 1963.]

Deserter from the War They Call Society. Tr. Carl King. *CrS* pp 47-49. [*Desertør fra den Krig de kalder Samfundet*, poem from the collection *Leve som var der en Fremtid og et Haab*, 1968.]

Disjecta Membra. Tr. Carl King. *CrS* p 9. [*Disjecta Membra*, poem from the collection *Galgenfrist*, 1958.]

The End of the White Panther. Tr. Nana Mansour. *CrS* p 50. [*Den hvide Panters Endeligt*, poem from the collection *Leve som var der en Fremtid og et Haab*, 1968.]

(43). Tr. Martin S. Allwood. *TCScP* p 104. [*43 (Stakkels forvildede Korstog)*, poem from the collection *De tabte Slag*, 1947.]

Gnat Song. Tr. Nana Mansour. *CrS* p 13. [*Myggesang*, poem from the collection *Galgenfrist*, 1958.]

He Who Comes from the World. Tr. Nadia Christensen. *LR* pp 29-30. [*Han som kommer fra Verden*, poem from the collection *Leve som var der en Fremtid og et Haab*, 1968.]

In Memory of a Summer. Tr. Nadia Christensen. *LR* p 31. Also *CrS* p 12. [*Til Minde om en Sommer*, poem from the collection *Galgenfrist*, 1958.]

The Land Which Is. Tr. Nadia Christensen. *LR* pp 31-33. Also *CrS* pp 55-57. [*Landet som er*, poem from the collection *Misnøje til Skade for Mandstugten*, 1969.]

Lapidary Landscapes. Tr. Nadia Christensen and Alexander Taylor. *LR* p 37. [*Lapidariske Landskaber i-iv*, poem from the collection *Galgenfrist*, 1958.]

Love Poem I-II. Tr. Nadia Christensen. *LR* pp 38-39. Also *CrS* pp 10-11 and *CDPo* pp 155-157. [*Kærlighedsdigt I-II*, poem from the collection *Galgenfrist*, 1958.]

Lumumba's Murderers. Tr. Dave Nelson. *CrS* pp 29-30. [*Lumumbas Mordere*, poem from the collection *Åbne Digte*, 1963.]

Open Poem to Franco. Tr. Dee Ann Dokken. *Versuch* vol. 11 (1972) p 18. [*Åbent Digt til Franco*, poem from the collection *Åbne Digte*, 1963.]

Open Poem to God. Tr. Carl King. *CrS* pp 27-28. [*Åbent Digt til Vorherre*, poem from the collection *Åbne Digte*, 1963.]

The Petrol Heart. Tr. Carl King. *CrS* pp 35-36. Also *CDPo* pp 157-158. [*Benzinhjertet*, poem from the collection *Åbne Digte*, 1963.]

Poem above the Clouds in May. Tr. Nadia Christensen. *LR* pp 28-29. Also *CrS* p 51. [*Digt over Skyerne i Maj*, poem from the collection *Leve som var der en Fremtid og et Haab*, 1968.]

Praise of the Black Panther. Tr. Jack Spots. *CrS* pp 61-62. [*Prolog*, poem published in *Ekstra-Bladet*, 13. juni 1970.]

Silent Movie. Tr. Nomi Erteschik and Jay Birdsong. *CrS* pp 21-22. [*Stumfilm*, poem from the collection *Romerske Bassiner*, 1963.]

Soliloquies. Tr. Nadia Christensen and Alexander Taylor. *LR* pp 33-36. Also *CrS* pp 14-17. [*Enetaler*, poem from the collection *Galgenfrist*, 1958.]

(37). Tr. Martin S. Allwood. *MoDP* pp 44-45. [*37 (Du døde som alle de andre)*, poem from the collection *De tabte Slag*, 1947.]

To Stand. Tr. Carl King. *CrS* p 25. [*At stå*, poem from the collection *Åbne Digte*, 1963.]

To the Distant Love. Tr. Nadia Christensen. *LR* pp 27-28. [*Til den fjerne Elskede*, poem from the collection *Galgenfrist*, 1958.]

Twenty Three Short Poems. Tr. Carl King, Nadia Christensen, Alexander Taylor and Nana Mansour. *CrS* pp 39-44. [Selections from the collection *Poetomatic*, 1965.]

Two Sections from »Poetomatic.« Tr. Nadia Christensen. *LR* p 36. [From *Poetomatic*, 1965.]

VILHELM MALLING (1846-1912)

Christmas Bells. Tr. S. D. Rodholm. *HoS* p 105. Also *HinS* hymn nr. 23. [*Hører du Kirkeklokkerne ringe.*]

108 IB MELCHIOR

The Haigerloch Project. New York: Harper & Row, 1977. p 317. [War novel written by a Dane in English.]
The Marcus Device. New York: Harper & Row, 1980. p 270. [Novel written in English.]
Order of Battle. New York: Harper & Row, 1972. p 304. [Novel written in English.]
Sleeper Agent. New York: Harper & Row, 1975. p 299. [Novel written in English.]
The Watchdogs of Abaddan. New York: Harper & Row, 1979. p 384. [Novel written in English.]

TOVE MEYER (1913-1972)

I Have Three Pearls. Tr. Charles Wharton Stork. *SeBDV* p 151. [*Jeg har tre Perler*, poem from the collection *Skygger på Jorden*, 1943.]
In a Garden Back Home. Tr. Linda Tagliaferro. *CDPo* pp 79-82. [*I en Have derhjemme*, poem from the collection *Drømte Digte*, 1952.]

KARIN MICHAËLIS (1872-1950)

The First Party. Tr. Ann and Peter Thornton, *CDPr* pp 81-84. [*Det første Selskab*, extract from the novel cycle *Vidunderlige Verden*, 1924-1930.]

Previous Translations:

Little Troll.

SOPHUS MICHAËLIS (1865-1932)

Night. Tr. Charles Wharton Stork. *SeBDV* pp 93-94. [Poem.]
The Smile. Tr. Charles Wharton Stork. *SeBDV* p 93. [Poem.]
Villa Borghese. Tr. Charles Wharton Stork. *SeBDV* pp 94-95. [*Villa Borghese*, poem from the collection *Romersk Foraar*, 1921.]

CHRISTIAN K. F. MOLBECH (1821-1888)

Freya's Star. Tr. Charles Wharton Stork. *SeBDV* pp 28-29. [*Freias Stjerne*, poem from the collection *Dæmring*, 1852.]

It Is So Joyous When Two Can Share. Tr. Thorvald Hansen. *HinS* hymn nr. 86. [*Sølvbryllupssang*, poem from the collection *Efterladte Digte*, 1880.]

Previous Translations:

Pleasure and Friendship.

HANS MØLBJERG (b. 1915)

Going to Church. Tr. Martin S. Allwood. *TCScP* p 86. [*Kirkegang*, poem from the collection *Mod nye Maal*, 1946.]

FLEMMING QUIST MØLLER (b. 1942)

The Generation That Tripped over its Own Feet at the Start. Tr. Stephen Schwartz. Copenhagen: Hans Reitzel, 1966. p 64. Ill. [*Generationen, der jokkede sig selv over Tæerne i Starten*, satire, 1966.] [Danish-English text.]
A Pleasure Journey. Cartoons by Flemming Quist Møller. Tr. Stephen Schwartz. Copenhagen Hans Reitzels Forlag, 1965. p 64. Ill. [*En Lystrejse*, satire, 1965.] [Danish-English text.]

POUL MARTIN MØLLER (1794-1838)

The Fair Unknown. Tr. Charles Wharton Stork. *SeBDV* pp 35-36. [*Den Ubekjendte*, poem published posthumously in *Efterladte Skrifter*, III, 1843.]
Joy over Denmark. Tr. Robert Silliman Hillyer. *BoDV* pp 63-65. [*Glæde over Danmark*, poem published in *Tilskueren*, 1823.]
The Master among the Rioters. Tr. S. Foster Damon. *BoDV* pp 67-78. [*Kunstneren mellem Oprørerne*, poem published in *Nytaarsgave fra danske Digtere*, 1838.]
The Old Pedant. Tr. S. Foster Damon. *BoDV* pp 65-67. [*En gammel Pedant*, from *Scener i Rosenborg Slotshave*, published posthumously in *Efterladte Skrifter*, I, 1839.]
Spring Song. Tr. R. P. Keigwin. *IDIWB* pp 49-51. [*Aprilvise*, poem published first in *Kjøbenhavns Morgenblad*, nr. 49, 1825.]

Works about Poul Martin Møller

Jones, W. Glyn. **Søren Kierkegaard and Poul Martin Møller.** *The Modern Language Review* (Cambridge) vol. 60, no. 1 (January 1965) pp 73-82.

VIGGO F. MØLLER (1887-1955)

Thus Speaks the Wise Father. Tr. Martin S. Allwood. *TCScP* pp 55-56. [*Saaledes taler den kloge Fader,* poem from the collection *Venlige Vers,* 1947.]

GUSTAF MUNCH-PETERSEN (1912-1938)

Apprenticeship. Tr. Carl Nesjar and Martin S. Allwood. *MoDP* pp 20-21. [*Læreår,* poem from the collection *Det nøgne Menneske,* 1932.]

At the Bottom. *CDPo* p 72. [Poem, written in English, first published in the collection *Samlede Skrifter II,* 1967.]

The Certainty. *CDPo* p 76. [Poem, written in English, first published in the collection *Samlede Skrifter II,* 1967.]

Do Not Speak to Me. Tr. Martin S. Allwood. *TCScP* p 83. [*Tal ikke til mig,* poem from the collection *Det underste Land,* 1933.]

Early Morning. *Udvalgte Digte.* Copenhagen: Gyldendal, 1962. p 83. [Poem written in English, 1934-35, first published in 1962.]

Etching. Tr. Poul Borum. *CDPo* p 77. [*Rids,* poem from the collection *Nitten Digte,* 1937.]

Fishing Hamlet. Tr. Nadia Christensen and Erik Hansen. *CDPo* p 77. [*Fiskerleje,* poem from the collection *Nitten Digte,* 1937.]

God of All Nature. *Udvalgte Digte.* Copenhagen: Gyldendal, 1962. p 77. Also *LitR-Dk* p 143. [Poem, written in English, 1934-35, first published in 1962.]

In the Glade. *Udvalgte Digte.* Copenhagen: Gyldendal, 1962. p 79. [Poem written in English, 1934-35, first published in 1962.]

The Land Below. Tr. Poul Borum. *CDPo* pp 70-71. [*Det underste Land,* poem from the collection by that name, 1933.]

A Little Song. *CDPo* p 74. [Poem, written in English, first published in the collection *Samlede Skrifter II,* 1967.]

March. Tr. James S. Aber. *Versuch* vol. 17 (1978) p 3. [*Marts,* poem from the collection *Nitten Digte,* 1937.]

March. Tr. Poul Borum. *CDPo* p 78. [*Marts,* poem from the collection *Nitten Digte,* 1937.]

My Evening Has Come. *Udvalgte Digte.* Copenhagen: Gyldendal, 1962. pp 85-86. [Poem written in English, 1934-35, first published in 1962.]

Portrait. *Udvalgte Digte.* Copenhagen: Gyldendal, 1962. p 78. Also *CDPo* p 74. [Poem, written in English, 1934-35, first published in 1962.]

Prayer. Tr. Carl Nesjar and Martin S. Allwood. *TCScP* p 84. [*Bøn,* poem from the collection *Nitten Digte,* 1937.]

Proposal. *Udvalgte Digte.* Copenhagen: Gyldendal, 1962. pp 80-81. [Poem written in English, 1934-35, first published in 1962.]

Song of the Council. *CDPo* p 75. [Poem, written in English, first published in the collection *Samlede Skrifter II,* 1967.]

The Special Miracle. *CDPo* p 73. [Poem, written in English, first published in the collection *Samlede Skrifter II,* 1967.]

Thought. Tr. Carl Nesjar. *TCScP* p 84. [*Tanke,* poem first published in the collection *Udvalgte Digte,* 1962.]

The Time Has Come. *LitR-Dk* p 142. [Poem, written in English, first published in *Samlede Skrifter II,* 1967.]

To My Parents. Tr. Phillip Marshall. *LitR-Dk* p 17. [*Til mine Forældre,* poem from the collection *Det nøgne Menneske,* 1932.]

To One. Tr. Carl Nesjar and Martin S. Allwood. *A Little Treasury* p 512. [*Til en,* poem from the collection *Det nøgne Menneske,* 1932.]

To the Earth. *Udvalgte Digte.* Copenhagen: Gyldendal, 1962. p 84. [Poem written in English, 1934-35, first published in 1962.]

Tune. *Udvalgte Digte.* Copenhagen: Gyldendal, 1962. p 82. [Poem written in English, 1934-35, first published in 1962.]

Winter. Tr. Nadia Christensen and Erik Hansen. *CDPo* p 78. [*Vinter,* poem from the collection *Nitten Digte,* 1937.]

KAJ MUNK (1898-1944)

Before Cannae. Tr. R. P. Keigwin. *FPI* pp 261-272. Also *ADL* pp 548-567. [*Før Cannæ,* play, 1942.]

Being Danish. Tr. Charles Wharton Stork. *SeBDV* pp 120-121. [*Dansk at være,* poem from the collection *Sværg det, Drenge,* 1945.]

The Blue Anemone. Tr. R. P. Keigwin. *IDIWB* pp 107-109. [*Den blaa Anemone,* poem in the collection by the same name, 1943.]

110 **But It's Not Like Him!** Tr. Evelyn Heepe. *SotN* pp 18-34. [*Det ligner jo ikke*, short story published in *Nationaltidende*, 16.-17. sept. 1940.]

Cant. Tr. R. P. Keigwin. *FPl* pp 149-208. *Cant*, play, 1931.]

Easter. Tr. R. P. Keigwin. *TCScP* pp 60-61. [*Paaske*, poem from the collection *Himmel og Jord*, 1938.]

Egelykke. Tr. Llewellyn Jones. In *Modern Scandinavian Plays* pp 97-171. New York: American-Scandinavian Foundation and Liveright Pub. Corp., 1954. [*Egelykke*, play, 1940.]

Five Plays. Tr. R. P. Keigwin. Intro. by R. P. Keigwin. New York: American-Scandinavian Foundation, 1953, 1964. Also Copenhagen: Nyt Nordisk Forlag - Arnold Busck, 1964. Individual plays listed separately under *FPl*.

The Flowers of Nazareth. Tr. Charles Wharton Stork. *SeBDV* pp 122-128. [Poem.]

For Shame! Tr. Charles Wharton Stork. *SeBDV* p 119. [*Gør dem til Skamme*, poem from the collection *Sværg det, Drenge*, 1945.]

He Sits at the Melting-Pot. Tr. R. P. Keigwin. *FPl* pp 215-260. [*Han sidder ved Smeltediglen*, play, 1938.]

Herod the King. Tr. R. P. Keigwin. *CDPl* pp 41-104. Also *FPl* pp 27-86. [*En Idealist*, play, 1923.]

The Honorable Justices. Tr. R. P. Keigwin. *Nor* vol. 10, no. 2 (March-April 1952) pp 85-95. [*De Herrer Dommere*, play published in Gyldendal's Christmas annual *Juleroser*, 1942.]

An Idealist (Herod the King). Tr. Evelyn Heepe. *MoDA* pp 156-164. [A slightly abridged edition of the 1938 version of the play *En Idealist*.]

A Little Baby Is Christened at Iver's. Tr. R. P. Keigwin. *CDPr* pp 238-242. [*Et bitte Barn bliver døbt hos Ivers*, short story from the collection *Himmel og Jord*, 1938.]

Niels Ebbesen. Tr. Hanna Astrup Larsen. *ScPlTC* (2nd series) pp 171-221. [*Niels Ebbesen*, play, 1942.]

No Appeasement. Tr. Charles Wharton Stork. *SeBDV* p 118. [*Ikke Forlig*, poem from the collection *Sværg det, Drenge*, 1945.]

A Row on the Lake. Tr. R. P. Keigwin. *Nor* vol. 12, no. 1 (January-February 1954) pp 50-52. [Essay, 1936.]

Spring Comes So Gently. Tr. Evelyn Heepe. *MoDA* pp 149-155. [First chapter of *Foraaret saa sagte kommer*, memoirs, 1942.]

To the King. Tr. Charles Wharton Stork. *SeBDV* p 117. [*Til Kongen*, poem from the collection *Sværg det, Drenge*, 1945.]

The Word. Tr. Evelyn Heepe. *MoDA* pp 165-170. [Act III of *Ordet*, play, 1925.]

The Word. Tr. R. P. Keigwin. *FPl* pp 91-148. [*Ordet*, play, 1925.]

Previous Translations:

Anti-Christian Germany.
The Cost of Truth.
Day of Prayer and Penitence.
John and Jesus.
To King Christian.
Four Sermons.
By the Waters of Babylon.
Master Almighty, Who Fillest the Whole of Creation.
The Church at Vedersø.
Kærlighed. Act III.
The Death of Ewald.

Works about Kaj Munk

Arestad, Sverre. **Kaj Munk as a Dramatist (1898-1944.)** *SS* vol. 26, no. 4 (November 1954) pp 151-176.

Harcourt, Canon Melville. **Kaj Munk.** In Harcourt, C. Melville. *Portraits of Destiny*. New York: Sheed & Ward, 1966, 1969. pp 1-47. Ill.

Keigwin, R. P. **Kaj Munk and the Theatre. New Book on the Plays.** *Denmark. A Monthly Review of Anglo-Danish Relations* (London) (January 1954) pp 10-11.

Madsen, Børge Gedsø. **Bjørnstjerne Bjørnson's »Beyond Human Power« and Kaj Munk's »The Word«.** *Modern Drama* (Lawrence, Kansas) vol. 3, no. 1 (1960) pp 30-36.

Ree, Kirsten. **A Notable New Film.** *DFOJ* no. 15 (1955) pp 26-27. [About the film *The Word*.]

Spink, Reginald. **A Review of Kaj Munk's »Five Plays«.** *DFOJ* vol. 11 (1954) p 11.

JØRGEN NASH (b. 1920)

Bird Song. Ill. Asger Jorn. *CDPo p 129*. [Poem, written in English, from the collection *Stavrim og Sonetter*, 1960.]

Dreams Come True Sometimes. *CDPo p 127*. [Poem, written in English, from the collection *Det naturlige Smil*, 1965.]

Let Us Sing of the Paradise Earth. Tr. Poul Borum. *CDPo* pp 125-126. [*Lad os synge om Paradiset Jorden*, poem from the collection *Vredens Sange*, 1951.]

Partying and Parting. Tr. H. Raphael. *LitR-Dk* p 66. [*Stævne og Hævnemødet*, poem from the collection *Salvi Dylvo*, 1945.]

Quiet. Tr. H. Raphael. *LitR-Dk* p 66. [*Stilheders Sang*, poem from the collection *Salvi Dylvo*, 1945.]

Some People Don't Like Bacon. *CDPo* p 130. [Poem, written in English, from the collection *Sweden and Their Immigrants*, 1975.]

Song of Silence. Tr. Poul Borum. *CDPo* pp 124-125. [*Stilhedens Sang*, poem from the collection *Salvi Dylvo*, 1945.]

Whoring Song. Tr. Martin S. Allwood. *MoDP* pp 30-31. Also *TCScP* pp 101-102. [*Horehymne*, poem from the collection *Leve Livet*, 1948.]

World Youth. *CDPo* p 128. [Poem, written in English, from the collection *I denne Transistorsommer*, 1967.]

MARTIN ANDERSEN NEXØ (1869-1954)

Adrift. Tr. W. Glyn Jones. *CDPr* pp 67-80. [*Flyvende Sommer*, short story from the collection *Af Dybets Lovsang*, 1908.]

Ditte: Girl Alive; Daughter of Man; Towards the Stars. 3 vol. in one. 1931; rpt. Gloucester, Mass.: Peter Smith, 1963. [*Ditte Menneskebarn*, novel, 1917-1921.]

Gossamer. Tr. David Stoner. *ADL* pp 381-407. [*Flyvende Sommer*, short story from the collection *Af Dybets Lovsang*, 1908.]

The Passengers of the Empty Seats. Tr. Hallberg Hallmundsson. *AScL* pp 75-80. [*De tomme Pladsers Passagerer*, short story from the collection *Muldskud*, 1905.]

Pelle the Conqueror. Tr. Jesse Muir and Bernard Miall. 1913; rpt. New York: P. Smith, 1950. p 587. 2nd ed. Intro. Otto Jespersen. Gloucester, Mass.: Peter Smith, 1963. 2 volumes. [*Pelle Erobreren*, novel, 1906-1910.]

Pelle the Conqueror's Boyhood. Tr. Jesse Muir. Fully revised and abridged by Patricia Crampton. London: New English Library, 1963. p 196. [Four Square Classics.]

Reminiscences. Tr. Evelyn Heepe. *MoDA* pp 45-60. [*Et lille Kræ* and *Under åben Himmel*, reminiscences, 1935.]

Tangiers. Tr. Jacob Wittmer Hartmann. In *Essays of the Masters*. Ed. Charles Neider. New York: Rinehart & Co., 1956. pp 268-287. [From the 1929 translation *(Days in the Sun)* of *Soldage*, travel description, 1903.]

Previous Translations: *111*

The Golden Watch.
Birds of Passage.
Days in the Sun.
Jacob's Wonderful Cruise.
In God's Land.
Under the Open Sky. My Early Years.
Greeting, Comrade, Give Me Your Hand.

Works about Martin Andersen Nexø

Koefoed, H. A. **Martin Andersen Nexø - Some Viewpoints.** *Scandinavica* vol. 4, no. 1 (May 1965) pp 27-37.

Lindsay, Jack. **Martin Andersen Nexø.** In Jack Lindsay, *Decay and Renewal: Critical Essays on Twentieth Century Writing*. Bombay: Kutub Popular, 1965. Sydney: Wild and Woolley; London: Lawrence and Wishart, 1976. pp 173-180.

Martin Andersen Nexø: A Symposium. *Scandinavica* vol. 8, no. 2 (Nov. 1969) pp 121-135.

Slochower, Harry. **The Marxist Homage to Creative Labour. »Pelle the Conqueror«.** In his *Mythopoesis: Myth Patterns in the Literary Classics*. Detroit: Wayne State Univ. Press, 1970. pp 284-289.

Thompson, Lawrence S. **Martin Andersen Nexø, 1869-1954.** *Books Abroad* (Norman, Oklahoma) vol. 28, no. 4 (1954) pp 423-424.

ANTON NIELSEN (1827-1897)

Sunset and Dawn. Tr. S. D. Rodholm. *HoS* p 39. [*Ved Solbjergslag*, poem published in *Den nye Almanak for 1871*, 1870.]

EDLE NIELSEN (b. 1926)

To An Adolescent Cub From a Pastor's Home. Tr. Martin S. Allwood. *TCScP* pp 103-104. [*Til en Pubertetshvalp i et Præstehjem*, poem from the collection *Sange til Karlsvognen*, 1946.]

EMANUEL NIELSEN

The Eagle and the Man. Boston: Bruce Humphries, 1962. p 63. [Collection of poems by Danish-born author.]

112 **The Heart Has Many Doors.** Cedar Rapids, Iowa: Torch Press, 1958. p 67. [Collection of poems by Danish-born author.]

HANS-JØRGEN NIELSEN (b. 1941)

The Body, A Burning Singing-machine. Tr. Tania Ørum. *CDPo* pp 275-277. [*Kroppen, den brændende Sangmaskine*, poem from the collection *Verdens/Billeder, Udvalgte Stykker*, 1972.

A Few Lines and a Dog. Tr. Tania Ørum. *CDPo* p 277. [*Nogle Linier og en Hund*, poem from the collection *Verdens/Billeder, Udvalgte Stykker*, 1972.]

From: **Figures Moved in Their Images. Not only Her.** Tr. Tania Ørum. *CDPo* pp 277-278. [Excerpts from *Figurerne bevæget i deres Billeder. Ikke blot hende*, poem from the collection *Verdens/ Billeder, Udvalgte Stykker 1972.*]

Mobiles. Variations on the Snow, 1, 2, 5. Tr. Tania Ørum. *CDPo* pp 273-275. [*Mobiler. Varitioner over Sneen, 1, 2, 5*, poems from the collection *Verdens/Billeder, Udvalgte Stykker*, 1972.]

On the Verge of Poetry. Tr. Tania Ørum. *CDPo* p 281. [*Digt*, poem from the collection *Verdens/Billeder, Udvalgte Stykker*, 1972.]

A Picture Somewhere in Language. Tr. Tania Ørum. *CDPo* pp 278-280. [*Et Billede et Sted i Sproget*, poem from the collection *Verdens/ Billeder, Udvalgte Stykker*, 1972.]

JØRGEN NIELSEN (1902-1945)

A Catastrophe. Tr. W. Glyn Jones. *CDPr* pp 263-269. [*En Katastrofe*, short story from the collection *Figurer i et Landskab*, 1944.]

Works about Jørgen Nielsen

Madsen, Børge Gedsø. **»Lavt Land« and Its Debt to »Himmerlandshistorier«.** *SS* vol. 31, no. 3 (August 1959) pp 121-128.

L. C. NIELSEN (1871-1931)

From Dover. Tr. Charles Wharton Stork. *SeBDV* pp 137-138. [*Tre Digte fra Dover, (II)*, poem from the collection *Broget Høst*, 1913.]

Sea Enfolding Denmark. Tr. R. P. Keigwin. *IDIWB* pp 97-99. [*Havet omkring Danmark*, poem from the play *Willemoes* 1908, published in the collection *Udvalgte Digte*, 1918.]

LEAN NIELSEN (b. 1935)

Brothers Meet. Tr. Kurt Hansen. *CDPo* pp 321-322. [*Brødre mødes*, poem from the collection *Egne Digte*, 1973.]

Kurt's Story. Tr. Kurt Hansen. *CDPo* pp 320-321. [*Beretningen om Kurt*, poem from the collection *Egne Digte*, 1973.]

MORTEN NIELSEN (1922-1944)

The Account. Tr. Helge Westermann and Martin S. Allwood. *MoDP* pp 22-23. Also *TCScP* p 97. [*Redegørelse*, poem from the collection *Krigere uden Vaaben*, 1943.]

Announcement of a Defeat. Tr. Poul Borum. *CDPo* pp 111-112. [*Meddelelse om et Nederlag*, poem from the collection *Krigere uden Vaaben*, 1943.]

I See in the Night . . . Tr. Phillip Marshall. *LitR-Dk* p 18. [*Jeg ser nu i Nat*, poem from the collection *Efterladte Digte*, 1945.]

I See Tonight. Tr. Poul Borum. *CDPo* p 112. [*Jeg ser nu i Nat*, poem from the collection *Efterladte Digte*, 1945.]

Meeting. Tr. Martin S. Allwood. *TCScP* p 98. [*Møde*, poem from the collection *Krigere uden Vaaben*, 1943.]

They Are Playing Ball on the Road. Tr. Poul Borum. *CDPo* p 114. [*De spiller Bold på Vejen*, poem from the collection *Efterladte Digte*, 1945.]

We Couldn't Stay Away from Each Other. Tr. Poul Borum. *CDPo* p 113. [*Vi kunne ikke blive fra hinanden*, poem from the collection *Efterladte Digte*, 1945.]

We're Sending Dance Music at Night. Tr. Poul Borum. *CDPo* pp 110-111. [*Vi sender Dansemusik om Natten*, poem from the collection *Krigere uden Vaaben*, 1943.]

Previous Translations:

A Horseman Is Riding. (Motif in a Carpet).

RASMUS NIELSEN

Spring. Tr. S. D. Rodholm. *HoS* p 142. Also *HinS* song nr. 94. [*Vaaren er i Luften*, poem published in *Højskolebladet*, 1. april 1892.]

TORBEN NIELSEN (b. 1918)

A Gallowsbird's Song. London: Collins, 1976. p 189. [*Galgesangen*, novel, 1973.]
See also *An Unsuccessful Man*.

Nineteen Red Roses. London: Collins [for] the Crime Club, 1978. p 196. [*Nitten røde Roser*, novel, 1973.]

An Unsuccessful Man. Tr. Marianne Helweg. New York: Harper & Row, 1976. p 147. [*Galgesangen*, novel, 1973.]

MOGENS JERMIIN NISSEN (1906-1972)

Confidentially. Tr. Martin S. Allwood. *TCScP* pp 81-82. [*Fortroligt*, poem from the collection *Ved Kløfterne*, 1946.]

The Titanic. Tr. Martin S. Allwood. *MoDP* p 18. [*Titanic*, poem from the collection *Ved Kløfterne*, 1946.]

HENRIK NORDBRANDT (b. 1945)

Aegean Sea. Tr. Henrik Nordbrandt, Alexander Taylor and Nadia Christensen. *SP-HN* p 14. [*Agæiske Hav*, poem from the collection *Opbrud og Ankomster*, 1974.]

Aegina. Tr. Henrik Nordbrandt, Alexander Taylor and Nadia Christensen. *SP-HN* p 32. [*Ægina*, poem from the collection *Glas*, 1976.]

Agoraphilia. Tr. Henrik Nordbrandt and Alexander Taylor. *Modern Poetry in Translation* no. 33 (Spring 1978) p 7. Also *SP-HN* p 57. [*Agoraphilia*, poem from the collection *Ode til Blæksprutten*, 1975.]

Alaren. Tr. Robert Salter. *Modern Poetry in Translation* no. 33 (Spring 1978) p 3. [*Alarahan*, poem from the collection *Glas*, 1976.]

Anaesthesia. Tr. Nadia Christensen. *CDPo* p 291. [*Narkose*, poem from the collection *Omgivelser*, 1972.]

As Though under a Lid. Tr. Nadia Christensen. *LR* p 40. [*Ligesom under et Laag*, poem from the collection *Miniaturer*, 1967.]

Ascent toward Akseki. Tr. Henrik Nordbrandt and Alexander Taylor. *SP-HN* p 53. [*Opstigning mod Akseki*, poem from the collection *Glas*, 1976.]

Ascent toward Akseki. Tr. Robert Salter. *Modern Poetry in Translation* no. 33 (Spring 1978) p 2. [*Opstigning mod Akseki*, poem from the collection *Glas*, 1976.]

Athens. Tr. Henrik Nordbrandt, Alexander Taylor and Nadia Christensen. *SP-HN* p 23. [*Athen*, poem from the collection *Omgivelser*, 1972.]

Autumn Mountainsides. Tr. Henrik Nordbrandt and Alexander Taylor. *SP-HN* p 46. [*Efterårsbjærgsider*, poem from the collection *Glas*, 1976.]

Baghlama. Tr. Henrik Nordbrandt and Alexander Taylor. *SP-HN* p 21. [*Baghlama*, poem from the collection *Glas*, 1976.]

Baklava. Tr. Nadia Christensen. *CDPo* p 292. Also in *The Minnesota Review* (Milwaukee, WI) no. 4 (Spring 1975) p 58. [*Baklava*, poem from the collection *Opbrud og Ankomster*, 1974.]

Baklava. Tr. Henrik Nordbrandt, Alexander Taylor and Nadia Christensen. *SP-HN* p 36. [*Baklava*, poem from the collection *Opbrud og Ankomster*, 1974.]

Because It Is October. Tr. Nadia Christensen. *New York Quarterly* 15 (Summer 1973) p 101. Also *LR* pp 44-45. [*Fordi det er Oktober*, poem from the collection *Digte*, 1966.]

Bodrum. Tr. Henrik Nordbrandt and Alexander Taylor. *SP-HN* p 60. [*Bodrum*, poem from the collection *Ode til Blæksprutten*, 1975.]

Byzantium. Tr. Nadia Christensen. *CDPo* pp 292-293. [*Byzantium*, poem from the collection *Opbrud og Ankomster*, 1974.]

Byzantium. Tr. Henrik Nordbrandt, Alexander Taylor and Nadia Christensen. *Modern Poetry in Translation* no. 33 (Spring 1978) p 6. Also *SP-HN* p 37 and in *The Pennypaper* (Willimantic, CT) vol. 1, no. 1 (Summer 1978). [*Byzantium*, poem from the collection *Opbrud og Ankomster*, 1974.]

Chase. Tr. Henrik Nordbrandt, Alexander Taylor and Nadia Christensen. *SP-HN* p 15. [*Jagt*, poem from the collection *Opbrud og Ankomster*, 1974.]

China Observed through Greek Rain in Turkish Coffee. Tr. Henrik Nordbrandt and Alexander Taylor. *SP-HN* pp 12-13. [*Kina betragtet gennem græsk Regnvejr i Cafe Turque*, poem from the collection *Syvsoverne*, 1969.]

Chora. Tr. Henrik Nordbrandt and Alexander Taylor. *SP-HN* p 44. [*Chora*, poem from the collection *Glas*, 1976.]

114

Chora. Tr. Robert Salter. *Modern Poetry in Translation* no. 33 (Spring 1978) p 2. [*Chora*, poem from the collection *Glas*, 1976.]

Civil War. Tr. Nadia Christensen. *CDPo* p 295. Also *Books* p 3 (no trans. given) [*Borgerkrig*, poem from the collection *Opbrud og Ankomster*, 1974.]

Civil War. Tr. Henrik Nordbrandt, Alexander Taylor and Nadia Christensen. *SP-HN* p 51. [*Borgerkrig*, poem from the collection *Opbrud og Ankomster*, 1974.]

Constellation. Tr. Henrik Nordbrandt, Alexander Taylor and Nadia Christensen. *SP-HN* p 61. [*Constellation*, poem published in *Necropolis*, 1977.]

Days Late in March. Tr. Henrik Nordbrandt and Alexander Taylor. *SP-HN* p 72. [*Dage sent i Marts*, poem from the anthology *Ode til Blæksprutten*, 1975.]

Decadence of Houses. Tr. Nadia Christensen. *LR* p 42. [*Villadekadence*, poem from the collection *Digte*, 1966.]

December Sun. Tr. Nadia Christensen. *International Poetry Review* (Greensboro, N. C.) vol. VI, no. 1 (Spring 1980) p 29. [*Decembersol*, poem from the collection *Istid*, 1977.] [Danish text included.]

Disconnection. Tr. Nadia Christensen and Alexander Taylor. *LR* pp 46-47. Also *CDPo* pp 288-289. [*Afbrydelse*, poem from the collection, *Digte*, 1966.]

Dissertation. Tr. Henrik Nordbrandt and Alexander Taylor. *SP-HN* pp 80-83. [*Om Islam og den danske Kunst*, poem published in *Gyldendals Lyrikmagasin*, 1977.]

The Door. Tr. Nadia Christensen. *International Poetry Review* (Greensboro, N. C.) vol. VI, no. 1 (Spring 1980) p 31. [*Døren*, poem from the collection *Istid*, 1977.] [Danish text included.]

Edward Munch's Lakes. Tr. Robert Salter. *Modern Poetry in Translation* no. 33 (Spring 1978) p 3. [*Munchs Søer*, poem from the collection *Istid*, 1977.]

Fragment. Tr. Nadia Christensen. *LR* p 47. [*Fragment*, poem from the collection *Digte*, 1966.]

A Funeral Portrait. Tr. Alexander Taylor. *CDPo* p 294. [*Et Gravportræt*, poem from the collection *Opbrud og Ankomster*, 1974.]

Funeral Portrait. Tr. Henrik Nordbrandt and Alexander Taylor. *SP-HN* p 42. Also *Poets On* vol. 2, no. 2 (Summer 1978) p 45. [*Et Gravportræt*, poem from the collection *Opbrud og Ankomster*, 1974.]

German Soldiers' Graves. Tr. Henrik Nordbrandt, Alexander Taylor and Nadia Christensen. *SP-HN* p 50. [*Tyske Soldatergrave*, poem from the collection *Miniaturer*, 1967.]

German Soldiers' Graves. Tr. Nadia Christensen. *LR* p 41. Also *CDPo* p 290 and *Prism International* (Vancouver, B. C.) vol. 12, no. 2 (1972) p 32. [*Tyske Soldatergrave*, poem from the collection *Miniaturer*, 1968.]

Gesture. Tr. Alexander Taylor. *Poetry Now* (Eureka, Ca.) vol. 4, no. 6 (1979) p 37. [*Gestus*, poem from the collection *Ode til Blæksprutten*, 1975.]

Gobi. Tr. Henrik Nordbrandt and Alexander Taylor. *Modern Poetry in Translation* no. 33 (Spring 1978) p 6. Also *SP-HN* p 59. [*Gobi*, poem from the collection *Ode til Blæksprutten*, 1975.]

God's House. Tr. Henrik Nordbrandt and Alexander Taylor. Copenhagen: Augustinus Forlag: Willimantic, CT: Curbstone Press, 1979. p 39. [*Guds Hus*, book-length poem, 1977.]

Going Ashore. Tr. Henrik Nordbrandt and Alexander Taylor. *Poets On* vol. 2, no. 1 (Winter 1978) p 45. Also *SP-HN* p 22. [*Landgang*, poem from the collection *Opbrud og Ankomster*, 1974.]

Guerilla Death Certificate. Tr. Henrik Nordbrandt and Alexander Taylor. *Modern Poetry in Translation* no. 33 (Spring 1978) pp 6-7. Also *SP-HN* p 52. [*Partisanens Dødsattest*, poem from the collection *Opbrud og Ankomster*, 1974.]

Head of Clay. Tr. Henrik Nordbrandt and Alexander Taylor. *Modern Poetry in Translation* no. 33 (Spring 1978) p 5. Also *SP-HN* p 68. [*Et Lerhoved*, poem from the collection *Syvsoverne*, 1969.]

Headlong Fall. Tr. Henrik Nordbrandt, Alexander Taylor and Nadia Christensen. *SP-HN* p 35. [*Styrt*, poem from the collection *Omgivelser*, 1972.]

Homage to Hans Christian. Tr. Nadia Christensen. *The Bridge* (Junction City, Oregon) no. 3 (1979) p 46. Also *SR* vol. 68, no. 1 (March 1980) p 49. [*Homage to Hans Christian*, poem from the collection *Istid*, 1977.]

The Homecoming. Tr. Nadia Christensen. *Mundus Artium* (Athens, Ohio) vol. 8, no. 2 (1975) p 141. [*Hjemkomsten*, poem from the collection *Opbrud og Ankomster*, 1974.] [Danish text included.]

The Homecoming. Tr. Henrik Nordbrandt, Alexander Taylor and Nadia Christensen. *SP-HN* p 25. [*Hjemkomsten*, poem from the collection *Opbrud og Ankomster*, 1974.]

Hooks. Tr. Alexander Taylor. *Portland.* p 87. [*Kroge*, poem from the collection *Spøgelseslege*, 1979.] [Danish text included.]

Howl for a Friend. Tr. Nadia Christensen. *International Poetry Review* (Greensboro, N. C.) vol. VI, no. 1 (Spring 1980) p 31. [*Hyl* *over en veninde*, poem from the collection *Istid*, 1977.] [Danish text included.]

I Have Squandered My Money on Roses. Tr. Henrik Nordbrandt and Alexander Taylor. *Modern Poetry in Translation* no. 33 (Spring 1978) p 5. Also *SP-HN* p 58. [*Jeg har købt mig fattig i Roser*, poem from the collection *Ode til Blæksprutten*, 1975.]

Idyl. Tr. Alexander Taylor. *Portland* p 89. [*Idyl*, poem from the collection *Spøgelseslege*, 1979.] [Danish text included.]

In an Asian Village. Tr. Linda Tagliaferro. *CDPo* p 293. [*I en asiatisk Landsby*, poem from the collection *Omgivelser*, 1972.]

It Is Winter Here. Tr. Henrik Nordbrandt, Alexander Taylor and Nadia Christensen. *SP-HN* p 64. [*Det er Vinter her*, poem from the collection *Necropolis*, 1977.]

It Was. Tr. Nadia Christensen. *LR* pp 43-44. [*Det var*, poem from the collection *Digte*, 1966.]

Kastelorizon. Tr. Henrik Nordbrandt and Alexander Taylor. *SP-HN* p 62. [*Kastelorizon*, poem from the collection *Ode til Blæksprutten*, 1975.]

Late Summers. Tr. Henrik Nordbrandt, Alexander Taylor and Nadia Christensen. *SP-HN* p 30 [*Eftersomre*, poem from the collection *Glas*, 1976.]

Late Summers. Tr. Robert Salter. *Modern Poetry in Translation* (New York) no. 33 (Spring 1978) p 1. [*Eftersomre*, poem from the collection *Glas*, 1976.]

A Life. Tr. Henrik Nordbrandt and Alexander Taylor. *SP-HN* p 65. [*Et Liv*, poem from the collection *Istid*, 1977.]

Little Essay on Language. Tr. Alexander Taylor. *Portland* p 88. [*Lille Essay om Sproget*, poem from the collection *Spøgelselege*, 1979.] [Danish text included.]

Little Morning Prayer. Tr. Henrik Nordbrandt and Alexander Taylor. *SP-HN* p 79. [*Lille Morgenbøn*, poem from the collection *Ode til Blæksprutten*, 1975.]

Meditating Camel. Tr. Henrik Nordbrandt and Alexander Taylor. *SP-HN* p 54. [*Mediterende Kamel*, poem from the collection *Glas*, 1976.]

Memory of Denizli. Tr. Henrik Nordbrandt and Alexander Taylor. *SP-HN* p 63. [*Erindring om Denizli*, poem from the collection *Ode til Blæksprutten*, 1975.]

Molyvos. Tr. Robert Salter. *Modern Poetry in Translation* no. 33 (Spring 1978) p 2. [*Molyvos*, poem from the collection *Glas*, 1976.]

Naxos, Sappho, Knossos. Tr. Henrik Nordbrandt and Alexander Taylor. *SP-HN* pp 17-20. [*Naxos, Sappho, Knossos*, poem from the collection *Glas*, 1976.]

No Matter Where We Go. Tr. Henrik Nordbrandt, Alexander Taylor and Nadia Christensen. *SP-HN* p 24. [*Hvor vi end rejser hen*, poem from the collection *Opbrud og Ankomster*, 1974.]

No Matter Where We Travel. Tr. Nadia Christensen. *Mundus Artium* (Athens, Ohio) vol. 8, no. 2 (1975) p 147. [*Hvor vi end rejser hen*, poem from the collection *Opbrud og Ankomster*, 1974.] [Danish text included.]

Now I Can No Longer Use You. Tr. Henrik Nordbrandt and Alexander Taylor. *Modern Poetry in Translation* no. 33 (Spring 1978) p 6. Also *SP-HN* p 77. [*Nu kan jeg ikke bruge dig længere*, poem from the collection *Ode til Blæksprutten*, 1975.]

October 20, 1971. Tr. Henrik Nordbrandt and Alexander Taylor. *SP-HN* p 47. [*Den 20. Oktober 1971*, poem from the collection *Omgivelser*, 1972.]

On the Plain. Tr. Henrik Nordbrandt and Alexander Taylor. *Modern Poetry in Translation* no. 33 (Spring 1978) p 6. Also *SP-HN* p 45. [*På Højsletten*, poem from the collection *Omgivelser*, 1972.]

On the Way to Ithaca. Tr. Henrik Nordbrandt, Alexander Taylor and Nadia Christensen. *SP-HN* p 31. [*På Vej mod Ithaka*, poem from the collection *Glas*, 1976.]

Ostrachon. Tr. Henrik Nordbrandt and Alexander Taylor. *SP-HN* p 28. [*Ostrachon*, poem published in *Gyldendals Lyrikmagasin*, 1976.]

Our Love Is like Byzantium. Tr. Henrik Nordbrandt and Alexander Taylor. *SP-HN* pp 40-41. [*Vores Kærlighed er som Byzantium*, poem from the collection *Ode til Blæksprutten*, 1975.]

The Poem That Wished a Flower. Tr. Nadia Christensen. *Mundus Artium* (Athens, Ohio) vol. 8, no. 2 (1975) p 145. [*Digtet som ville en Blomst*, poem from the collection *Digte*, 1966.] [Danish text included.]

Postcard with Angels. Tr. Henrik Nordbrandt, Alexander Taylor and Nadia Christensen. *SP-HN* p 38. [*Postkort med Engle*, poem from the collection *Istid*, 1977.]

Prayer. Tr. Henrik Nordbrandt and Alexander Taylor. *Modern Poetry in Translation* (New York) no. 33 (Spring 1978) p 5. Also *SP-HN* pp 26-27. [*Bøn*, poem from the collection *Opbrud og Ankomster*, 1974.]

Roads. Tr. Alexander Taylor. *Poetry Now* (Eureka, Ca.) vol. 4, no. 6 (1979) p 37. [*Veje*, poem from the collection *Istid*, 1977.]

The Rose from Lesbos. Tr. Henrik Nordbrandt and Alexander Taylor. *SP-HN* p 73. [*Rosen fra Lesbos*, poem from the anthology *Ode til Blæksprutten*, 1975.]

116 **Sailing.** Tr. Henrik Nordbrandt and Alexander Taylor. *SP-HN* p 78. [*Sejlads*, poem from the collection *Ode til Blæksprutten*, 1975.]

Selected Poems. Tr. Alexander Taylor and Henrik Nordbrandt. Willimantic, CT: Curbstone Press, 1978. p 83. Individual poems listed separately under *SP-HN*. [Some poems, translated by Nadia Christensen and Alexander Taylor, appeared earlier in *Modern Poetry in Translation* and *Poets On*.]

Shadow Race. Tr. Nadia Christensen. *International Poetry Review* (Greensboro, N. C.) vol. VI, no. 1 (Spring 1980) p 27. [*Skyggeløb*, poem from the collection *Istid*, 1977.] [Danish text included.]

Shadows. Tr. Henrik Nordbrandt and Alexander Taylor. *SP-HN* p 75. [*Skygger*, poem from the collection *Ode til Blæksprutten*, 1975.]

Simi. Tr. Richard McKane. *Modern Poetry in Translation* no. 33 (Spring 1978) pp 3-4. [*Simi*, poem from the collection *Opbrud og Ankomster*, 1974.]

Simple Psychoanalysis. Tr. Nadia Christensen. *The Bridge* (Junction City, Oregon) no. 3 (1979) p 47. [*Lille Psychoanalyse*, poem from the collection *Istid*, 1977.]

Smile. Tr. Henrik Nordbrandt and Alexander Taylor. *SP-HN* p 74. [*Smil*, poem from the collection *Ode til Blæksprutten*, 1975.]

Stairsong. Tr. Nadia Christensen. *LR* p 45. Also *CDPo* p 289. [*Trappesang*, poem from the collection *Digte*, 1966.]

Station. Tr. Nadia Christensen. *Mundus Artium* (Athens, Ohio) vol. 8, no. 2 (1975) p 143. [*Station*, poem from the collection *Digte*, 1966.] [Danish text included.]

Streets. Tr. Henrik Nordbrandt, Alexander Taylor and Nadia Christensen. *SP-HN* p 69. [*Gader*, poem from the anthology *Omgivelser*, 1972.]

Sultana. Tr. Robert Salter. *Modern Poetry in Translation* no. 33 (Spring 1978) p 2. [*Sultana*, poem from the collection *Glas*, 1976.]

Taurus. Tr. Henrik Nordbrandt and Alexander Taylor. *SP-HN* p 56. [*Taurus*, poem from the collection *Ode til Blæksprutten*, 1975.]

Tibetan Dream. Tr. Henrik Nordbrandt and Alexander Taylor. *SP-HN* p 71. Also *Poets On* (Chaplin, Connecticut) vol. 2, no. 2 (Summer 1978) p 44. [Poem.]

To a Death Mask. Tr. Henrik Nordbrandt, Alexander Taylor and Nadia Christensen. *SP-HN* p 49. [*Til en Dødsmaske*, poem from the collection *Syvsoverne*, 1969.]

To a Death Mask. Tr. Nadia Christensen. *LR* p 41. Also *CDPo* p 290 and *Prism International* (Vancouver, B. C.) vol. 12, no. 2 (1972) p 33.

[*Til en Dødsmaske*, poem from the collection *Syvsoverne*, 1969.]

To Capture Byzantium. Tr. Henrik Nordbrandt, Alexander Taylor and Nadia Christensen, *SP-HN* p 39. [*At indtage Byzantium*, poem from the collection *Glas*, 1976.]

To Sleep in Your Arms. Tr. Henrik Nordbrandt and Alexander Taylor. *SP-HN* p 76. [*At sove i dine Arme*, poem published as *Charlotte* in *Gyldendals Lyrikmagasin*, 1975.]

Tonight. Tr. Nadia Christensen. *Mundus Artium* (Athens, Ohio) vol. 8, no. 2 (1975) p 141. [*I Nat*, poem from the collection *Opbrud og Ankomster*, 1974.] [Danish text included.]

Tonight. Tr. Henrik Nordbrandt, Alexander Taylor and Nadia Christensen. *SP-HN* p 16. [*I Nat*, poem from the collection *Opbrud og Ankomster*, 1974.]

Troy. Tr. Henrik Nordbrandt, Alexander Taylor and Nadia Christensen. *SP-HN* p 34. [*Troja*, poem from the collection *Glas*, 1976.]

Troy. Tr. Robert Salter. *Modern Poetry in Translation* no. 33 (Spring 1978) p 3. [*Troja*, poem from the collection *Glas*, 1976.]

Une décadence immense. Tr. Nadia Christensen. *LR* p 43. [*Une décadence immense*, poem from the collection *Digte*, 1966.]

Variation. Tr. Nadia Christensen. *International Poetry Review* (Greensboro, N. C.) vol. VI, no. 1 (Spring 1980) p 27. [*Variation*, poem from the collection *Istid*, 1977.] [Danish text included.]

Voyage. Tr. Anne Born. *Outposts* (Thames, Surrey) no. 115 (Winter 1977) p 19. [*Sejlads*, poem from the collection *Ode til Blæksprutten*, 1975.]

Watch. Tr. Henrik Nordbrandt, Alexander Taylor and Nadia Christensen. *SP-HN* p 33. [*Vagt*, poem from the collection *Glas*, 1976.]

We Separate the Days. Tr. Nadia Christensen. *International Poetry Review* (Greensboro, N. C.) vol. VI, no. 1 (Spring 1980) p 25. [*Vi adskiller Dagene*, poem from the collection *Istid*, 1977.] [Danish text included.]

When a Person Dies. Tr. Nadia Christensen, *CDPo* p 291. Also in *Mundus Artium* (Athens, Ohio) vol. 8, no. 2 (1975) p 147. [*Når et Menneske dør*, poem from the collection *Omgivelser*, 1972.] [*Mundus Artium* also includes Danish text.]

When a Person Dies. Tr. Henrik Nordbrandt, Alexander Taylor and Nadia Christensen. *SP-HN* p 48. [*Når et Menneske dør*, poem from the collection *Omgivelser*, 1972.]

When We Leave Each Other. Tr. Henrik Nordbrandt and Alexander Taylor. *SP-HN* p 70. [*Når vi forlader hinanden*, poem from the anthology *Omgivelser*, 1972.]

You Resting in Me. *LR* p 48. [*Du som hviler i mig*, poem from the collection *Miniaturer*, 1967.]

Your Definitive Face. Tr. Nadia Christensen. *LR* p 46. [*Dit definitive Ansigt*, poem from the collection *Digte*, 1966.]

LISE NØRGAARD (b. 1917)

Mother at the Wheel. Tr. Carl Blechingberg. New York: Taplinger, 1963. p 288. [*Med Mor bag Rattet*, novel, 1959.]

HEINRICH VON NUTZHORN (1833-1925)

The Twinkling Stars Are Bright. Tr. S. D. Rodholm. *HoS* p 54. Also *HinS* hymn nr. 13. [*Nu Mørket bryder paa*, poem published in *Sange for den kristelige Folkeskole*, 1881.]

ADAM OEHLENSCHLÄGER (1779-1850)

Aladdin at his Mother's Grave. Tr. R. S. Hillyer. *IDIWB* pp 27-29. [*Aladdin paa sin Moders Grav*, poem from Act IV of the play *Aladdin eller Den forunderlige Lampe*, 1805.]

Aladdin, or the Wonderful Lamp. A Play. Tr. Henry Meyer. Intro. F. J. Billeskov Jansen. Copenhagen: Gyldendal, 1968. p 298. [*Aladdin eller Den forunderlige Lampe*, play, 1805.]

Aladdin's Lullaby. Tr. Robert Silliman Hillyer. *BoDV* pp 37-38. [*Aladdins Vuggesang*, from *Aladdin eller Den forunderlige Lampe*, play, 1805.]

Christ's Manhood. (From **The Gospel of the Year**). Tr. R. S. Hillyer. *IDIWB* p 33. [*Christi Manddom*, poem from *Jesu Kristi gientagne Liv i den aarlige Natur (Aarets Evangelium)*, from the collection *Poetiske Skrifter*, 1805.]

The Drive. Tr. Robert Silliman Hillyer. *BoDV* pp 26-27. [*De Kjørende*, poem from *Sanct Hansaften-Spil*, play, 1803.]

Fair Maiden! Tr. Charles Wharton Stork. *SeBDV* p 17. [*Skøn Jomfrue! Luk dit Vindue op*, (first line), song from the play *Sovedrikken*, 1808.]

Freya's Spinning Wheel. Tr. Charles Wharton Stork. *SeBDV* p 16. Also *A Little Treasury* pp 508-509. [*Freyas Rok*, poem first published in Simon Poulsen's *Nytaarsgave*, 1804, and then in *Poetiske Skrifter*, 1805.]

The Golden Horns. Tr. Robert Silliman Hillyer. *BoDV* pp 14-21. Also *AScL* pp 47-53. [*Guldhornene*, poem from the collection *Digte*, 1803.]

Hakon Jarl. Tr. Henry Meyer. *ADL* pp 147-153. [*Hakon Jarl hin Rige*, dramatic poem from the collection *Nordiske Digte*, 1807.]

Hakon Jarl's Death. Tr. Robert Silliman Hillyer. *BoDV* pp 21-26. [*Hakon Jarls Død*, poem from the collection *Digte*, 1803.]

Korsør. Tr. Charles Wharton Stork. *SeBDV* pp 18-19. [*Corsøer*, poem from the collection *Poetiske Skrifter*, 1805.]

The Life of Jesus Christ Symbolized in Nature. Christ's Birth. Christ's Manhood. The Holy Eucharist. Tr. Robert Silliman Hillyer. *BoDV* pp 32-37. [*Jesu Christi gientagne Liv i den aarlige Natur, (Aarets Evangelium)*, poem from the collection *Poetiske Skrifter*, 1805.

Morning Walk. Tr. Robert Silliman Hillyer. *BoDV* pp 27-29. [*Morgenvandring*, poem from the collection *Poetiske Skrifter*, 1805.]

Once More It Is the Springtime. Tr. Charles Wharton Stork. *SeBDV* pp 14-16. [*Vaarsang*, poem from the collection *Poetiske Skrifter*, 1805.]

The Rose of Roses. Tr. Charles Wharton Stork. *SeBDV* pp 17-18. Also *AScL* p 53. [*Saa dugbesprængte staae de Roser her*, (first line), poem from the song cycle *Freyas Alter* in the collection *Poetiske Skrifter*, 1805.]

Song. Tr. Robert Silliman Hillyer. *AScL* pp 52-53. [Poem.]

Song: Behind Black Woods. Tr. Robert Silliman Hillyer. *BoDV* p 39. [*Sang*, from *Aladdin eller Den forunderlige Lampe*, 1805.]

Summer Holiday. Tr. Robert Silliman Hillyer. *BoDV* pp 30-32. [*Freidigt Sommerliv*, poem from the collection *Poetiske Skrifter*, 1805.]

There Is a Charming Land. Tr. Robert Silliman Hillyer. *BoDV* p 13. [*Der er et yndigt Land*, (first line), or *Fædrelandssang*, poem from the collection *Samlede Digte*, II, 1823.]

There Is a Lovely Land. Tr. R. P. Keigwin. *IDIWB* p 31. [*Der er et yndigt Land*, (first line), or *Fædrelandssang*, poem from the collection *Samlede Digte*, II, 1823.]

There Is a Lovely Land. Tr. S. D. Rodholm. *HoS* p 134. Also *HinS* song nr. 91. [*Der er et yndigt Land*, (first line), or *Fædrelandssang*, poem from the collection *Samlede Digte*, II, 1823.]

118 Previous Translations:

The Bard.
The Adventurers.
The Little Shepherd-Boy.
Hakon Jarl, a Tragedy in Five Acts.
Thou Never Wilt Love?
Vahl.
Hiemvee.
Wiedewelt.
Sivald and Thora.
Sessrumnir.
Axel and Valborg, a Tragedy.
Thor's Fishing.
The Dwarfs.
Lines on Leaving Italy.
The Gods of the North.
Correggio. A Tragedy.
Vaulundurs Saga. A Legend of Wayland Smith.
Ewald.
Extracts from »Livserindringer«.
Extracts from »The Fisherman's Daughter«.
Palnatoke. A Tragedy in Five Parts.
Socrates (a 20-line Extract).
Death and His Victims.
The Children in the Moon.
Agnes.
The Treasure Seeker.
Aspiration.
The Gift of Aegir.
Judas the Apostate.
The Ice-Guard. A Christmas Ballad.
Lines, Supposed to Be Written by Christopher
    Columbus a Short Time before His Death.
The Requiem.
The Mystic Tree.
Time's Perspective.
The Death Raven.
Fridleif and Helga.
Elvir-Shades.
Cantata.
The Old Oak.
Nature's Temperaments.
The Violet-Gatherer.
The Broken Harp.
Hymn.

Works about Adam Oehlenschläger

Christiani, Dounia Bunis. **Oehlenschläger's**
»Aladdin« and Ibsen's »Peer Gynt«. A Com-
parison in Theme and Treatment. M. A.
thesis, Columbia University, 1956.

Hanson, Kathryn St. **Adam Oehlenschläger and**
Ludwig Tieck: A Study in Danish and Ger-
man Romanticism. Ph. D. diss., Princeton
University, 1978. (p 245.) [Diss. Abstr. 39,
2236-A.]
Ingwersen, Niels. **The Tragic Moment in Oeh-**
lenschläger's »Hakon Jarl Hin Rige«. *Scandi-*
navica vol. 9, no. 1 (May 1970) pp 34-44.

POUL ØRUM (b. 1923)

A Call from Jo-An. Tr. H. Raphael. *LitR-Dk*
pp 104-114. [*Hilsen fra Joan,* short story
published in *Perspektiv,* Summer 1963.]
Nothing but the Truth. Tr. Kenneth Barclay.
London: Gollancz; New York: Pantheon
Books, 1976. p 254. [*Kun Sandheden,* murder
mystery, 1974.]
The Rat. Tr. Paula Hostrup-Jessen. *DI* pp
145-149. [*Rotten,* short story from the collec-
tion *I Vandenes Dyb,* 1961.]
Scapegoat. Tr. Kenneth Barclay. New York:
Pantheon, 1975. p 255. [*Syndebuk,* murder
mystery, 1972.]
See also *The Whipping-boy.*
The Whipping-boy. London: Gollancz, 1975. p
255. [*Syndebuk,* murder mystery, 1972.]
See also *Scapegoat.*

KRISTIAN ØSTERGAARD (1855-1931)

The Gates of the Morning. Tr. S. D. Rodholm.
HoS p 35. Also *HinS* hymn nr. 6. [*Alt Morge-*
nens Porte, poem published in *Højskolebla-*
det, 1890, and in the collection *En Udvan-*
drers Digte, (mimiographed), 1956.]
Gracious and Mighty God. Tr. S. D. Rodholm.
HoS p 75. Also *HinS* hymn nr. 85. [*Gud, du*
er god og stærk, poem from the collection
Sange fra Prærien, 1912.]
In Far Distant Northland. Tr. Johannes Knudsen. *HinS* song nr. 93.
Lord I Wish to Be Thy Servant. Tr. J. C.
Aaberg. *HinS* hymn nr. 72. [*Herre, jeg vil*
gerne tjene, poem published in *Højskolebla-*
det, 12. feb. 1892, and in *Sange fra Prærien,*
1912.]
Lord, to Thee I Humbly Tender. Tr. S. D. Rodholm. *HoS* p 74. [*Herre, jeg vil gerne tjene,*
poem published in *Højskolebladet,* 12. feb.
1892, and in *Sange fra Prærien,* 1912.]

That Cause Can Never Be Lost or Stayed. Tr. J. C. Aaberg. *HinS* hymn nr. 81. [*Den Sag er aldrig i Verden tabt*, poem from the collection *Sange fra Prærien*, 1912.]

We are Stewards. Tr. S. D. Rodholm. *HoS* p 118. Also *HinS* hymn nr. 80. [*Vi er Fæstere*, poem from the collection *Sange fra Prærien*, 1912.]

JACOB PALUDAN (1896-1975)

All in a Writer's Day. Tr. Maureen Neiiendam. Copenhagen: Hasselbalch, 1957. p 32. [*Skribent at være*, 1957.] [Danish-English text.]

Aphorisms. *LitR-Dk* pp 46, 141. [*Små Apropos'er*, from collections of essays, 1929-1954.]

Artists of Style. Tr. David Stoner. *ADL* pp 408-423. [*Stilens Kunstnere*, essay from *Som om Intet var hændt*, 1938.]

Birds around the Light. Tr. Evelyn Heepe. *MoDA* pp 175-194. [Four extracts from *Fugle omkring Fyret*, novel, 1925.]

Chickens. Tr. Lydia Cranfield. *Nor* vol. 15, no. 1 (Jan.-Feb. 1957) 64-68. [*Høne og Hane*, essay from the collection *Landluft*, 1944.]

Conversation and Company. Tr. Lydia Cranfield. *Nor* vol. 9, no. 1 (Jan.-Feb. 1951) pp 45-51. [*Samtale og Samvær*, essay from the collection *Som om Intet var hændt*, 1938.]

Jørgen Stein. Tr. Carl Malmberg. Intro. P. M. Mitchell. Madison: The University of Wisconsin Press, 1966. p 724. [The Nordic Translation Series.] [*Jørgen Stein*, novel, 1937.]

On the Square. Tr. F. A. Rush. *CDPr* pp 213-225. [*Her paa Torvet*, short story from the collection *Facetter*, 1947.]

Works about Jacob Paludan

Heltberg, Niels. **Jacob Paludan.** *ASR* vol. 40, no. 2 (June 1952) pp 142-145.

FREDERIK PALUDAN-MÜLLER (1809-1876)

The Day of Judgment. Tr. Mark Baker. *IDIWB* pp 65-67. [*Basunen*, poem from the *Ahasverus* cycle, originally published in the collection *Tre Digte*, 1854.]

Oft in a Castle. Tr. R. P. Keigwin. *ASR* vol. 43, no. 1 (March 1955) p 69. [Poem.]

The Pearl. Tr. Robert Silliman Hillyer. *BoDV* pp 113-114. [*Perlen*, poem published in *Kjøbenhavns Morgenblad*, 1838, and later in *Ungdomsskrifter*, II, 1870.]

To the Star (from **The Dancer).** Tr. Robert Silliman Hillyer. *BoDV* pp 110-112. [Last stanzas from the first song of *Dandserinden*, 1832.]

The Trumpets of Doom. Tr. Robert Silliman Hillyer. *BoDV* pp 116-117. [*Basunen*, poem from the *Ahasverus* cycle, originally published in the collection *Tre Digte*, 1854.]

Two Sonnets. Tr. Robert Silliman Hillyer. *BoDV* pp 114-115. [From the *Alma Sonetter* in *Adam Homo*, 1842 and 1848.]

Previous Translations:

What Is, to Be?
The Fountain of Youth.
An Extract from »Adam Homo«.

LEIF PANDURO (1923-1977)

Kick Me in the Traditions. Tr. Carl Malmberg. New York: Eriksson-Taplinger Publishing Co., 1961. p 217. [*Rend mig i Traditionerne*, novel, 1959.]

One of our Millionaires Is Missing. Tr. Carl Malmberg. New York: Grove Press, Inc., 1967. p 174. [Evergreen Black Cat Book series.] [*Vejen til Jylland*, novel, 1966.]

Röslein auf der Heide. Tr. Paula Hostrup-Jessen. *DI* pp 223-235. [*Röslein auf der Heide*, short story published in *Vindrosen*, 1960.]

Tivoli. *DFOJ* Special Copenhagen Issue (1967) pp 32-33.

Works about Leif Panduro

Hugus, Frank. **The King's New Clothes: The Irreverent Portrayal of Royalty in the Works of Leif Panduro and Finn Søeborg.** *SS* vol. 51, no. 2 (Spring 1979) pp 162-176.

Kampmann, Christian. **A Popular Social Critic.** *DJ* no. 72 (1972) pp 46-49. Ill.

120 SVERRI PATURSSON (1871-1960)
Faroese author

Eliesar and the Basking Shark. Tr. from the Faroese by Hedin Brønner. *FSS* pp 35-45. [*Brugdan*, short story from the collection *Fuglar og Fólk*, 1935.]

The Winning of the Bounty. Tr. from the Faroese by Hedin Brønner. *FSS* pp 46-53. [*Ravnahjúnini*, short story from the collection *Fuglar og Fólk*, 1935.]

JACOB PEDER MYNSTER PAULI (1844-1915)

Your Home Must Be founded upon the Rock That Stands. Tr. P. C. Paulsen. *HinS* hymn nr. 87. [*Jert Hus skal I bygge paa Ordets Klippegrund*, wedding hymn printed in 1878, included in the collection *Skygger og Lys*, 1902.]

SIGFRED PEDERSEN (1903-1967)

Anthem to an Inn. Tr. Martin S. Allwood. *TCScP* pp 80-81. [*Hymne til et Værtshus*, poem from the collection *Nye og sørgelige Viser*, 1938.]

Little Poet Joker. Tr. Martin S. Allwood. *TCScP* p 80. [*Lille Digter Skrøne er saa fattig*, poem from the collection *Nye og sørgelige Viser*, 1933.]

LEIF PETERSEN (b. 1934)

Johnny's Dream. Tr. David Hohnen. In *Radio Plays from Denmark, Finland, Norway, Sweden*. Stockholm: Sveriges Radios förlag, 1971. [*Filejsens Drøm*, radio play, 1967.]

A Woman Is a Nuisance. (Resume with quotations of reviews in English and French). *World Theatre* (Paris) vol. 14, no. 6 (1965) p 638 (Technical Data: Denmark). [*En Kvinde er en Straf*, play, 1965.]

NIS PETERSEN (1897-1943)

The Cat without a Tail. Tr. Helge Westermann and Martin S. Allwood. *TCScP* pp 66-67. [*Den haleløse Kat*, poem from the collection *Til en Dronning*, 1935.]

Do You Love Man. Tr. Helge Westermann and Martin S. Allwood. *MoDP* pp 8-11. Also *TCScP* pp 68-69. [*Elsker du Mennesket*, poem from the collection *Nattens Pibere*, 1926.]

Elegy. Tr. R. P. Keigwin. *TCScP* p 73. [*Elegi*, poem from the collection *Stykgods*, 1940.]

Elegy 1940. Tr. Poul Borum. *CDPo* p 51. [*Elegi 1940*, poem from the collection *Stykgods*, 1940.]

Europe Aflame. Tr. Helge Westermann and Martin S. Allwood. *TCScP* pp 69-73. [*Brændende Europa*, poem from the collection *En Drift Vers*, 1933.]

The Evening Prayer. Tr. Eileen MacLeod. *CDPr* pp 229-237. [*Aftenbønnen*, short story from the collection *Muleposen*, 1942.]

Gipsy Privilege. Tr. R. P. Keigwin. *IDIWB* pp 103-105 and *TCScP* pp 67-68. [*Romaniernes Ret*, poem from the collection *Til en Dronning*, 1935.]

Hazard. Tr. R. P. Keigwin. *TCScP* pp 73-74. Also *A Little Treasury* p 511. [*Spillet*, poem from the collection *En Drift Vers*, 1933.] [Note: In *A Little Treasury* incorrectly listed as Nils Petersen.]

Kain. Tr. Erik Henning Jensen. *Nor* vol. 9, no. 5 (Sept.-Oct. 1951) pp 321-322. [*Kain*, poem from the collection *Nattens Pibere*, 1926.]

Lovest Thou Man? Tr. Henry Meyer. *ADL* pp 584-587. [*Elsker du Mennesket?* poem from the collection *Nattens Pibere*, 1926.]

Lovest Thou Man? Tr. Erik Henning Jensen. *Nor* vol. 10, no. 5 (Sept.-Oct. 1952) p 333. [*Elsker du Mennesket?* poem from the collection *Nattens Pibere*, 1926.]

Spring at Mariager Fjord. Tr. Lee Marshall. *ADL* pp 582-583. Also *CDPo* pp 49-50. [*Forår ved Mariager Fjord*, poem from the collection *Nattens Pibere*, 1926.]

Spring at Mariager Fjord. Tr. Martin S. Allwood and Knud Mogensen. *MoDP* pp 6-7. Also *TCScP* pp 65-66. [*Foraar ved Mariager Fjord*, poem from the collection *Nattens Pibere*, 1926.]

Tragedy. Tr. Dennis Lee. *Versuch* vol. 17 (1978) p 12. [*Tragedie*, poem from the collection *En Drift Vers*, 1933.]

Two Little Old Widows Playing Duet. Tr. Poul Borum. *CDPo* p 50. [*To små gamle Damer spiller firhændigt*, poem from the collection *Stykgods*, 1940.]

What an Old Peddlar Told Me about Girls. Tr. Mark J. Christensen. *Versuch* vol. 16 (1977) p 25. [*Hvad en gammel Bissekræmmer fortalte*, poem from the collection *Stykgods*, 1940.]

Previous Translations:

The Street of the Sandalmakers.
Spilt Milk. A Story of Ireland.
Hazard, or Game of Chance. (Spillet).
Beside Prayers.

ROBERT STORM PETERSEN (STORM P.) (1882-1949)

Ye Venerable Vikings and Noble Normans. By Storm P. Preface and tr. Poul Sørensen. Copenhagen: Carit Andersen, 1957. p 64. Ill. [*De gæve Vikinger og ædle Normanner*, Danish-English text, 1957.]

Works about Robert Storm Petersen

Chafetz, Henry. **Robert Storm Petersen.** *ASR* vol. 40, no. 3 (September 1952) pp 213-219.

CARL PARMO PLOUG (1813-1894)

Little Karen. Tr. R. P. Keigwin. *IDIWB* p 69. [*Husker du i Høst*, or *Folke-vise*, poem written in 1853, printed in *Samlede Digte*, 1862.]
The Unity of the North. Tr. Charles Wharton Stork. *SeBDV* p 58. [Abbreviated version of *Norden*, poem written in 1842, published in *Samlede Digte*, 1862.]

Previous Translations:

Sleep, Weary Child.
The Battle of Slesvig.

HENRIK PONTOPPIDAN (1857-1943)

Eagle's Flight. Tr. Lida Siboni Hanson. *AScL* pp 70-74. [*Ørneflugt*, short story, 1894.]
A Fisher Nest. Tr. Juliane Sarauw. *Nobel Prize Reader* pp 121-138. [Translation originally published in 1927.] [*En Fiskerrede*, short story from the collection *Landsbybilleder*, 1883.]
Gallows Hill at Ilum. Tr. David Stoner. *ADL* pp 333-359. [*Ilum Galgebakke*, short story, 1890.]

The Royal Guest. Tr. P. M. Mitchell and Kenneth H. Ober. *RG* pp 133-193. [*Den kongelige Gæst*, short novel, 1908.]

Previous Translations:

The Apothecary's Daughter.
Emanuel, or, Children of the Soil.
The Promised Land.
Extracts from the Poem »4 Februar« (The Realm He Created, Where Is It?).

Works about Henrik Pontoppidan

Ekman Ernst. **Henrik Pontoppidan as a Critic of Modern Danish Society.** *SS* vol. 29, no. 4 (November 1957) pp 170-183.
Gray. Charlotte Schiander. **Henri Pontoppidan's »Kingdom of the Dead«. Literary Production in Its Social Context.** Ph. D. diss., Univ. of California, Berkeley, 1976. (p 248).
Jones, W. Glyn. **»Det forjættede Land« and »Fremskridt« as Social Novels. A Comparison.** *SS* vol. 37, no. 1 (February 1965) pp 77-90.
Jones, W. Glyn. **Henrik Pontoppidan, the Church and Christianity after 1900.** *SS* vol. 30, no. 4 (November 1958) pp 191-197.
Madsen, Børge Gedsø. **Henrik Pontoppidan's Emanuel Hansted and Per Sidenius.** In *Scandinavian Studies: Essays Presented to Dr. Henry Goddard Leach*. Seattle: University of Washington Press for the American-Scandinavian Foundation, 1965. pp 227-235.
Mitchell, P. M. **Henrik Pontoppidan.** Boston: Twayne, 1979. p 158.
Ober, Kenneth H. **The Incomplete Self in Pontoppidan's »De Dødes Rige«.** *SS* vol. 50 (1978) pp 396-402.

VALDEMAR POULSEN (b. 1909)
Faroese author

The Huntsman. Tr. from the Faroese by Hedin Brønner. *FSS* pp 241-244. [*Veiðimaðurin*, short story from the collection *Meðan Havaldan Dúrar*, 1960.]

HANS POVLSEN (1886-1973)

You Aren't Big Enough. Tr. John Poole. *CDPr* pp 167-185. [*Du er for bitte*, extract from the novel *Himlens Fugle har Reder*, 1936.]

122 ORLA BUNDGÅRD POVLSEN (b. 1918)

The Blue Coffee Pot. Tr. Poul Borum. *CDPo* p 134. [*Den blå Kaffekande*, poem from the collection *Flammekrebsen*, 1971.]
The Dark House. Tr. Phillip Marshall. *LitR-Dk* p 42. [*Den mørke Hus*, poem from the collection *Vartegn*, 1959.]
Lizard. Tr. Poul Borum. *CDPo* p 133. [*Firben*, poem from the collection *Spor*, 1964.]
Love Poem. Tr. Poul Borum. *CDPo* p 133. [*Kærlighedsdigt*, poem from the collection *Spor*, 1964.]
Month of August Poem. Tr. Poul Borum. *CDPo* pp 131-132. [*Augustmånedsdigt*, poem from the collection *Mur og Rum*, 1962.]
My Black Windows Shining Miles Away in the Night. Tr. Poul Borum. *CDPo* p 134. [*Mine sorte Vinduer lyser milevidt i Natten*, poem from the collection *Flammekrebsen*, 1971.]
Patience among Trees. Tr. Poul Borum. *CDPo* p 135. [*Tålmod mellem Træer*, poem from the collection *Flammekrebsen*, 1971.]
A Superannuated Romantic. Tr. Nadia Christensen and Poul Borum. *CDPo* p 136. [*En afdanket Romantiker*, poem from the collection *Dag/lig/dag*, 1974.]

KNUD LYNE RAHBEK (1760-1830)

Drinking Song. Tr. Charles Wharton Stork. *SeBDV* pp 22-23. [Poem.]

Previous Translations:

The Women of Denmark.
Augustus Ehrman.
Peter Colbiornsen.
To My 'Bakkehuus'.
The Great Fire of Copenhagen in 1795.

HIERONYMUS JUSTESEN RANCH (1539-1609)

Nithing the Niggard. Tr. Frederick Marker. *ADL* pp 19-49. [*Karrig Niding*, dramatic comedy, c. 1598.]

GERHARD RASMUSSEN (1905-1968)

No Leave for the Captain. Tr. Mervyn Savill. New York: Crowell Company, 1958. p 154. [*Kaptajnen behøver ingen Orlov*, novel, 1955.]

HALFDAN RASMUSSEN (b. 1915)

Far Away. Tr. Martin S. Allwood. *TCScP* pp 99-100. [*Langt borte*, poem from the collection *Paa Knæ for Livet*, 1948.]
Halfdane's Nonsense and Nursery Rhymes. Tr. and recreated by Kurt Hansen. Ill. Ernst Clausen, Ib Spang Olsen and Arne Ungermann. Copenhagen: Schønberg, 1973. p 52. [Cover title: *Halfdanes Sense and Nonsense Verse.*]
Hocus Pocus. Nonsense Rhymes. Adapted by Peter Wesley-Smith. Ill. Ib Spang Olsen. London: Angus and Robertson, 1973. p 30. Ill. [*Hokus pokus og andre Børnerim*, children's rhymes, 1969.]
The Monument. Tr. Elizabeth Byrd. *MoDP* pp 28-29. [*Monument*, poem from the collection *Aftenland*, 1950.]
Old Johnson the Letterbox-painter. Tr. Kurt Hansen. *CDPo* p 108. [*Noget om relative Glæder*, poem from the collection *Tosserier*, 1956.]
Sardine. Tr. Kurt Hansen. *CDPo* pp 104-105. [*Sardin*, poem from the collection *Med Solen i Ryggen*, 1963.]
Snowman Frost and Lady Thaw. Tr. Kurt Hansen. *CDPo* p 109. [*Snemand Frost og Frøken Tø*, poem from the collection *Kaspar Himmelspjæt*, 1955.]
Something about Heroes. Tr. Kurt Hansen. *CDPo* pp 105-107. [*Noget om Helte*, poem from the collection *Tosserier*, 1955.]

CONRAD RAUN

The Sorting Machine. Tr. Robert Fred Bell. *LitR-Dk* pp 132-141. [*Sorteremaskinen*, short story published in *Vindrosen*, September 1963.]

ADOLPH RECKE (1820-1867)

Lord of Creation. Tr. S. D. Rodholm. *HoS* p 139. [*Bøn for Danmark*, published 1848, and in the collection *Viser*, 1868.]

CHRISTIAN RICHARDT
(1831-1892)

Evening Star Up Yonder. Tr. S. D. Rodholm. *HoS* pp 44-45. Also *HinS* hymn nr. 11. [*Lær mig!*, poem from the collection *Smaadigte*, 1861.]

Fearless Ever. Tr. R. P. Keigwin. *IDIWB* p 73. [*Altid frejdig, naar du gaar*, poem from the cycle *Tornerose*, in the collection *Texter og Toner*, 1868.]

The Forest Wedding. Tr. Charles Wharton Stork. *SeBDV* p 54. [*I Skoven*, poem from the collection *Smaadigte*, 1861.]

In the Verdant Hills Abiding. Tr. Johannes Knudsen. *HinS* hymn nr. 36. [*I Nazareth*, poem from the collection *Nyere Digte*, 1864.]

It Was a Cross. Tr. S. D. Rodholm. *HoS* p 86. Also *HinS* hymn nr. 38. [*Korsets Vei*, poem from the collection *Smaadigte*, 1861.]

Ninetta's Tom-Cat. Tr. Charles Wharton Stork. *SeBDV* pp 54-55. [*Pigen med Katten*, poem from the collection *Samlede Digte* II, 1895.]

On Your Way! Be Brave and True! Tr. S. D. Rodholm. *HinS* hymn nr. 84. [*Altid frejdig*, poem from the collection *Texter og Toner*, 1868.]

Onward. Tr. S. D. Rodholm. *HoS* p 117. [*Altid frejdig*, poem from the collection *Texter og Toner*, 1868.]

The Skylark. Tr. S. D. Rodholm. *HoS* pp 160-161. [*Ved Lærkens komme*, poem from the collection *Texter og Toner*, 1868.]

Teach Me! Tr. Charles Wharton Stork. *SeBDV* pp 53-54. [*Lær mig!* poem from the collection *Smaadigte*, 1861.]

Previous Translations:

Cradle Song.
In the Covert.

KLAUS RIFBJERG (b. 1931)

Afternoon. Tr. Alexander Taylor. *CDPo* p 233. [*Eftermiddag*, poem from the collection *25 desperate Digte*, 1974.]

Afternoon. Tr. Nadia Christensen and Alexander Taylor. *SP-KR* p 18. [*Eftermiddag*, poem from the collection *25 desperate Digte*, 1974.]

Assens. Tr. Nadia Christensen and Alexander Taylor. *SP-KR* p 27. [*Assens*, poem from the collection *Fædrelandssange*, 1967.]

Before the Mount of Venus. Tr. Nadia Christensen and Alexander Taylor. *SP-KR* pp 30-31. [*Foran Venusbjerget*, poem from the collection *Scener fra det daglige Liv*, 1973.]

Birth. Tr. Nadia Christensen and Alexander Taylor. *Scottish International* (Edinburgh) September 1973 p 34. Also *SP-KR* pp 6-7 and *CDPo* pp 224-226. [*Fødsel*, poem from the collection *Under Vejr med mig selv*, 1956.]

Board and Lodging. (Resume with quotations of reviews in English and French). *World Theatre* (Paris) vol. 14, no. 1 (1965) p 97 (Technical Data: Denmark). [*Diskret Ophold*, play by Jesper Jensen and Klaus Rifbjerg, 1965.]

The Burial of the Canary. Tr. Anne Born. *Orbis* p 51. [*Kanariefuglens Begravelse*, poem from the collection *Amagerdigte*, 1965.]

Byron and Company. Tr. Alexander Taylor. *CDPo* pp 229-231. [*Byron & Co.*, poem from the collection *Mytologi*, 1970.]

Byron & Co. Tr. Nadia Christensen and Alexander Taylor. *The Malahat Review*, (Victoria, B.C.). April 1975. Also *SP-KR* pp 28-29. [*Byron & Co.*, poem from the collection *Mytologi*, 1970.]

The Canary's Burial. Tr. Nadia Christensen and Alexander Taylor. *Modern Poetry in Translation* (London) no. 15 (1973) p 15. Also *SP-KR* p 12. [*Kanariefuglens Begravelse*, poem from the collection *Amagerdigte*, 1965.]

Chronic Innocence. *DFOJ* 59 (1967) pp 38-39. [Excerpt from the novel *Den kroniske Uskyld*, 1958.]

Conception. Tr. Jens Nyholm. *LitR-Dk* p 98. Also *DFOJ* vol. 59 (1967) pp 38-39. [*Undfangelse*, poem from the collection *Under Vejr med mig selv*, 1956.]

The Day Passes. Tr. Nadia Christensen and Alexander Taylor. *SP-KR* p 36. [*Dagen går*, poem from the collection *25 desperate Digte*, 1974.]

Developments. Tr. Pat Shaw. *MoNPl* pp 264-346. [*Udviklinger*, play, 1965.]

Donkey. Tr. Nadia Christensen and Alexander Taylor. *SP-KR* p 17. [*Æsel*, poem from the collection *Efterkrig*, 1964.]

Fetus. Tr. Jens Nyholm. *Tri-Quarterly* (Evanston, Ill.] vol. 5 (1968) p 103. [*Foster*, poem from the collection *Under Vejr med mig selv*, 1956.]

Grandparents. Tr. Jens Nyholm. *LitR-Dk* p 96. [*Bedsteforældre*, poem from the collection *Under Vejr med mig selv*, 1956.]

Grandparents. Tr. Nadia Christensen and Alexander Taylor. *Modern Poetry in Translation* (London) no. 15 (1973) p 15. Also *SP-KR* p 8. [*Bedsteforældre*, poem from the collection *Under Vejr med mig selv*, 1956.]

123

124 **Hung Over.** Tr. Nadia Christensen and Alexander Taylor. *SP-KR* pp 14-15. [*Tømmermænd*, poem from the collection *Under Vejr med mig selv*, 1956.]

Hvad en Mand har Brug for. (Resume with quotations of reviews in English and French). *World Theatre* (Paris) vol. 15, no. 5 (1966) p 449 (Technical Data: Danmark). [*Hvad en Mand har Brug for*, play, 1966.]

Kindergarten. Tr. Jens Nyholm. *Tri-Quarterly* (Evanston, Ill.) vol. 5 (1968) p 102. [*Børnehave*, poem from the collection *Under Vejr med mig selv*, 1956.]

A Kiss. Tr. John C. Pearce. *LitR-Dk* pp 99-103. [*Et Kys*, short story from the collection *Og andre Historier*, 1964.]

Marat. Tr. Nadia Christensen and Alexander Taylor. *Modern Poetry in Translation* (London) no. 15 (1973) p 14. Also *SP-KR* p 25. [*Marat*, poem from the collection *Mytologi*, 1970.]

Matter of Factness. Tr. Nadia Christensen and Alexander Taylor. *Modern Poetry in Translation* (London) no. 15 (1973) pp 15-16. Also *SP-KR* pp 9-11. [*Saglighed*, poem from the collection *Amagerdigte*, 1965.]

Medieval Morning. Tr. Tove Neville. *CDPo* pp 226-228. [*Middelaldermorgen*, poem from the collection *Konfrontation*, 1960.]

Midsummer. Tr. Nadia Christensen and Alexander Taylor. *SP-KR* pp 34-35. [*Midsommer*, poem from the collection *Konfrontation*, 1960.]

The New Star. Tr. Nadia Christensen and Alexander Taylor. *ASR* vol. 61, no. 4 (Winter, 1972) p 402. Also *SP-KR* p 5. [*Den nye Stjerne*, poem from the collection *Efterkrig*, 1964.]

Newly Married. Tr. Jens Nyholm. *LitR-Dk* pp 97-98. [*Nygift*, poem from the collection *Under Vejr med mig selv*, 1956.]

Newlyweds. Tr. Nadia Christensen and Alexander Taylor. *Modern Poetry in Translation* (London) no. 15 (1973) pp 13-14. [*Nygift*, poem from the collection *Under Vejr med mig selv*, 1956.]

Old Man Jensen. Tr. Paula Hostrup-Jessen. *DI* pp 32-41. [*Frække Jensen*, short story from the collection *Og andre Historier*, 1964.]

Portrait no. 31. Tr. Nadia Christensen and Alexander Taylor. *Scottish International* (Edinburgh) (September 1973) p 35. Also *The Wormwood Review* (Stockton, California) vol. 14, no. 30 (issue no. 55) (1974) pp 117-118. [The thirty-first poem in the collection *Portræt*, 1963.]

The Scorpion in Spodsbjerg. Tr. Nadia Christensen and Alexander Taylor. *SP-KR* pp 22-23. [*Ulken i Spodsbjerg*, poem from the collection *Fædrelandssange*, 1967.]

Selected Poems. Tr. Nadia Christensen and Alexander Taylor. Willimantic, CT: Curbstone Press, 1976. p 36. pb. Individual poems listed separately under *SP-KR*.

Slow Waltz. Tr. Alexander Taylor. *Portland* p 91. [*Langsom Vals*, poem from the collection *Scener fra det daglige Liv*, 1973.] [Danish text included.]

Spring. Tr. Alexander Taylor. *CDPo* pp 231-232. Also *Books* p 9. [*Forår*, poem from the collection *Scener fra det daglige Liv*, 1973.]

Spring. Tr. Nadia Christensen and Alexander Taylor. *The Malahat Review* (Victoria, B. C.) April 1975. Also *SP-KR* pp 32-33. [*Foraar*, poem from the collection *Scener fra det daglige Liv*, 1973.]

Terminology. Tr. Nadia Christensen and Alexander Taylor. *SP-KR* p 21. [*Terminologi*, poem from the collection *Konfrontation*, 1960.]

To Love. Tr. Nadia Christensen and Alexander Taylor. *The Wormwood Review* (Stockton, California) vol. 14, no. 30 (1974) (issue no. 55) pp 117-118. Also *Scottish International* (Edinburgh) (September 1973) p 35 and *SP-KR* p 13. [*At elske*, poem from the collection *Under Vejr med mig selv*, 1956.]

We Have Been Called Upon. Tr. Jens Nyholm. *ADL* pp 594-599. [*Det er blevet os pålagt*, poem from the collection *Konfrontation*, 1960.]

When We Conquered the Moon. Tr. Reginald Spink. *Adam International Review* (Bucharest and London) vol. 35, nos. 334-336 (1969) p 39. [Prose.]

The Willow in Longelse. Tr. Nadia Christensen and Alexander Taylor. *SP-KR* p 24. [*Piletræet i Longelse*, poem from the collection *Fædrelandssange*, 1967.]

Winter. Tr. Alexander Taylor and Nadia Christensen. *Contemporary Literature in Translation* (Vancouver, B. C.) no. 7 (Spring 1970) p 27. Also *SP-KR* p 16. [*Vinter*, poem from the collection *Efterkrig*, 1964.]

X-Ray. Tr. Anne Born. *Orbis* p 52. [*Røntgen*, poem from the collection *Konfrontation*, 1960.]

Zero Hour. Tr. Nadia Christensen and Alexander Taylor. *Modern Poetry in Translation* (London) no. 15 (1973) p 14. Also *SP-KR* pp 19-20. [*Nultime*, poem from the collection *Konfrontation*, 1960.]

Zeus in That Mood. Tr. Nadia Christensen and Alexander Taylor. *SP-KR* p 26. Also *CDPo* pp 228-229. [*Zeus i det Humør*, poem from the collection *Mytologi*, 1970.]

Works about Klaus Rifbjerg

Gray, Charlotte Schiander. **Klaus Rifbjerg: A Contemporary Danish Writer.** *Books Abroad* (Norman, Okla.) vol. 49 (1975) pp 25-28. Ill.

Kistrup, Jens. **Klaus Rifbjerg, Danish Author. The Latest Phase.** *DFOJ* no. 59 (1967) pp 8-11. Ill.

ERIK RIIS-CARSTENSEN

Northlight. New York: Philosophical Library, 1962. p 356. [Novel published in English.]

AGNES RINGBORG

Sunshine beyond Shadows. Blair, Nebraska: Lutheran Publishing House, 1959. [*Gaa væk, Skygge, lad Solen skinne*, novel by Danish-American writer published in Danish in Blair, Nebraska, 1956.]

HENRIK V. RINGSTED (b. 1907)

From a Garden in London. London: Jonathan Cape, 1952. p 279. [*En Have i London*, essays, rewritten in English by the author.]

EDITH RODE (1879-1956)

The Eternal Adorer. Tr. Evelyn Heepe. *MoDA* pp 205-209. [*Den evige Tilbeder*, short story from the collection *Af Kundskabens Træ*, 1912.

The Eternal Adorer. No trans. given. *Nor* vol. 8 no. 5 (September-October 1950) pp 344-346. [*Den evige Tilbeder*, short story from the collection *Af Kundskabens Træ*, 1912.]

Illusion. Tr. Ann and Peter Thornton. *CDPr* pp 120-121. [*Illusion*, short story from the collection *Afrodite smiler*, 1929.]

The Three Little Girls. Tr. Evelyn Heepe. *MoDA* pp 198-204. [Extracts from *De tre smaa Piger*, novel, 1943.]

HELGE RODE (1870-1937)

Clover. Tr. Charles Wharton Stork. *SeBDV* p 79. [*Kløver*, poem from the collection *Ariel*, 1914.]

Dream Kiss. Tr. S. Foster Damon. *BoDV* p 153. [*Drømmekysset*, poem from the collection *Digte, gamle og nye*, 1907.]

Early Spring. Tr. Charles Wharton Stork. *SeBDV* pp 78-79. Also *TCScP* p 41. [*Første Foraar*, poem from the collection *Ariel*, 1914.]

Morning. Tr. S. Foster Damon. *BoDV* pp 151-152. [*Morgen*, poem from the collection *Hvide Blomster*, 1892.]

Purple. Tr. S. Foster Damon. *BoDV* p 152. [*Purpur*, poem from the collection *Digte*, 1896.]

Snow. Tr. R. P. Keigwin. *IDIWB* p 99. [*Sne*, poem from the collection *Digte*, 1896.]

SØREN DAMSGAARD RODHOLM (1877-1951)

Creation. *HoS* p 183. [Song.]

David the Shephard Poet. *HoS* p 188. [Song.]

A Harvest of Song. Translations and original lyrics by S. D. Rodholm. With a biographical sketch by Enok Mortensen. Des Moines: American Lutheran Church, 1953. p 193. [Includes translations of Danish hymns.] Individual translations listed under the author with abbreviation *HoS*.

The Lord's Mercy and Loving Kindness. *HoS* p 186. [Song.]

The Pilgrim Song. *HoS* p 187. [Song.]

A Prayer of Moses, the Man of God. *HoS* p 185. [Song.]

With the Word All Things Began. Adapted from N. F. S. Grundtvig. *HinS* hymn nr. 31.

You Foolish Child. *HoS* p 184. [Song.]

Works about S. D. Rodholm

Mortensen, Enok. **A Note on S. D. Rodholm's Translations.** *HoS* pp 24-31.

Mortensen, Enok. **S. D. Rodholm, a Biographical Sketch.** *HoS* pp 9-22.

PETER RONILD (b. 1928)

Boxing for One. Tr. Pat Shaw. *MoNPl* pp 350-449. [*Boxning for én Person*, television drama, 1964.]

The Man in the Cannon. Tr. Paula Hostrup-Jessen. *DI* pp 94-107. [*Manden i Kanonen*, short story from the collection *I Morgen kommer Paddehatteskyen*, 1959.]

126 VALDEMAR RØRDAM
(1872-1946)

Winternight. Tr. Charles Wharton Stork. *TCScP* pp 48-49. [*Vinternat*, poem from the collection *Sol og Sky*, 1895.]

JØRGEN RYTTER (b. 1923)

Autumn Crocus; a Novel. Tr. Maurice Michael. London: Chatto and Windus, 1963. p 154. Ill. [*Høst tidløs*, novel, 1960.]

ULLA RYUM (b. 1937)

Relief. (Two Averted Faces). Tr. Mary Catherine Phinney. *LitR* p 83. [Poem.]

The Siamese Cat. Tr. Paula Hostrup-Jessen. *DI* pp 108-120. [*Kattedrabet*, short story published in the journal *Resonans* no. 1, 1963, and included in the collection *Noter om idag og igår*, 1971.]

OLE SARVIG (1921-1981)

Afternoon. Tr. Ole Sarvig and Alexander Taylor. *LD* p 38. [*Eftermiddag*, poem from the collection *Jeghuset*, 1944.]

Christ in the Grain Fields. Tr. Ole Sarvig and Alexander Taylor. *LD* p 39. Also *CDPo* p 121. [*Kristus i Kornet*, poem from the collection *Jeghuset*, 1944.]

Chrysalises. Tr. Ole Sarvig and Alexander Taylor. *Portland:* p 97. [*Pupper*, from the collection *Jeghuset*, 1944.] [Danish text included.]

Early Morning. Tr. Ole Sarvig and Alexander Taylor. *LD* p 32. [*Tidlig Morgen*, poem from the collection *Forstadsdigte*, 1974.]

From: Epilogue. Tr. Ole Sarvig and Alexander Taylor. *LD* p 43. [From *Epilog*, 1952.]

Fate Song. Tr. Ole Sarvig and Alexander Taylor. *LD* p 22. [*Skæbnesang*, poem from the collection *Jeghuset*, 1944.]

Fragment. Tr. Ole Sarvig and Alexander Taylor. *LD* p 41. [*Fragment*, poem from the collection *Menneske*, 1948.]

In the Suburbs. Tr. Ole Sarvig and Alexander Taylor. *LD* pp 16-17. [*I Forstaden*, poem from the collection *Menneske*, 1948.]

It Is Late. Tr. Ole Sarvig and Alexander Taylor. *LD* p 25. [*Det er sent*, poem from the collection *Forstadsdigte*, 1974.]

Lances. Tr. Ole Sarvig and Alexander Taylor. *LD* p 10. Also *Poetry Now* (Eureka, Ca.) vol. 4, no. 6 (1979) p 35. [*Lanser*, poem from the collection *Forstadsdigte*, 1974.]

Late Day. Tr. Ole Sarvig and Alexander Taylor. Ill. with graphics by Palle Nielsen. Willimantic, CT: Curbstone Press, 1976. p 43 pb. [Some trans. published previously in *Maine Edition.*] Individual poems listed separately under *LD*.

From: Legend. Tr. Ole Sarvig and Alexander Taylor. *LD* pp 33-37. [From *Legende*, 1946.]

The Lost Earth. Tr. Ole Sarvig and Alexander Taylor. *LD* pp 28-29. [*Den mistede Jord*, poem from the collection *Forstadsdigte*, 1974.]

The Moon's Day. Tr. Ole Sarvig and Alexander Taylor. *LD* p 13. Also *CDPo* p 120. [*Månens Dag*, poem from the collection *Jeghuset*, 1944.]

My Mind. Tr. Ole Sarvig and Alexander Taylor. *LD* p 8. [*Mit Sind*, poem from the collection *Jeghuset*, 1944.]

My Sorrow. Tr. Martin S. Allwood, Helge Westermann, and Knud Mogensen. *TCScP* p 95. [*Min Sorg*, poem from the collection *Jeghuset*, 1944.]

My Sorrow. Tr. Ole Sarvig and Alexander Taylor. *LD* pp 11-12. Also *CDPo* pp 115-116. [*Min Sorg*, poem from the collection *Jeghuset*, 1944.]

Overlooking the Cemetery. Tr. Ole Sarvig and Alexander Taylor. *LD* p 23. Also *CDPo* p 122. [*Over for Kirkegården*, poem from the collection *Forstadsdigte*, 1974.]

Pale Morning. Tr. Ole Sarvig and Alexander Taylor. *LD* p 14. Also *CDPo* p 116. [*Bleg Morgen*, poem from the collection *Jeghuset*, 1944.]

R^4. Tr. Ole Sarvig and Alexander Taylor. *LD* p 21. Also *CDPo* p 123. [*R^4*, poem from the collection *Forstadsdigte*, 1974.]

Ripe. Tr. Ole Sarvig and Alexander Taylor. *LD* p 24. [*Modne*, poem from the collection *Jeghuset*, 1944.]

SATURN. Tr. Ole Sarvig and Alexander Taylor. *LD* p 19. [*SATURN*, poem from the collection *Forstadsdigte*, 1974.]

The Sea. Tr. Ole Sarvig and Alexander Taylor. *LD* p 7. Also *Poetry Now* (Eureka, Ca.) vol. 4, no. 6 (1979) p 35. [*Havet*, poem from the collection *Forstadsdigte*, 1974.]

Skylights. Tr. Carl Nesjar, Martin S. Allwood, and Knud Mogensen. *TCScP* pp 96-97. [*Tagruder*, poem from the collection *Jeghuset*, 1944.]

Skylights. Tr. Ole Sarvig and Alexander Taylor. *LD* p 9. Also *CDPo* p 118. [*Tagruder*, poem from the collection *Jeghuset*, 1944.]

The Stone of Christ. Tr. Ole Sarvig and Alexander Taylor. *LD* p 42. [*Kristusstenen*, poem from the collection *Jeghuset*, 1944.]

Thistles. Tr. Ole Sarvig and Alexander Taylor. *LD* p 20. Also *CDPo* p 121. [*Tidsler*, poem from the collection *Forstadsdigte*, 1974.]

Thought Stillness. Tr. Carl Nesjar, Martin S. Allwood and Knud Mogensen. *MoDP* p 40. Also *TCScP* p 96. [*Tankestille*, poem from the collection *Jeghuset*, 1944.]

Thought Stillness. Tr. Ole Sarvig and Alexander Taylor. *LD* p 18. Also *CDPo* p 119. [*Tankestille*, poem from the collection *Jeghuset*, 1944.]

VOCABULARY. Tr. Ole Sarvig and Alexander Taylor. *LD* pp 26-27. [Written for Amnesty International on The Day of the Political Prisoner, Copenhagen, Oct. 21, 1975.]

Walk. Tr. Ole Sarvig and Alexander Taylor. *LD* p 15. Also *CDPo* p 117. [*Vandring*, poem from the collection *Jeghuset*, 1944.]

Wild Fear. Tr. Ole Sarvig and Alexander Taylor. *LD* p 40. Also *Poetry Now* (Eureka, Ca.) vol. 4, no. 6 (1979) p 35. [*Vild Angst*, poem from the collection *Jeghuset*, 1944.]

Yesterday, Today and Tomorrow. Tr. Ole Sarvig and Alexander Taylor. *LD* pp 30-31. [*Igår og idag og imorgen*, poem from the collection *Forstadsdigte*, 1974.]

Works about Ole Sarvig

Rossel, Sven. **Crisis and Redemption: An Introduction to Danish Writer Ole Sarvig.** *World Literature Today* (Norman, Oklahoma) vol. 53, no. 4 (Fall 1979) pp 606-609.

SAXO GRAMMATICUS (c. 1200)

Amleth's Revenge. Tr. Reginald Spink. Woodcuts by Povl Christensen. Copenhagen: Danish Ministry of Foreign Affairs, 1961. p 33. Ill. [From the Danish translation by Jørgen Olrik of *Gesta Danorum*.]

The History of Amleth, Prince of Denmark. Tr. into English from the editio princeps of the Latin text of *Historia Danica* by Oliver Elton. Preface by Henrik de Kauffmann. Intro. Israel Gollancz. Woodcuts by Sigurd Vasegaard. New York: Limited Editions Club, 1954. p 112. Ill. [Printed in Copenhagen by C. B. Nordlunde.]

Saxo Grammaticus. The History of the Danes. Tr. Peter Fisher. Ed. Hilda Ellis Davidson. Two volumes. I: Text, II: Commentary. Totowa, N.J.: Rowman & Littlefield, 1980. Cambridge: Brewer, 1979-80.

The Story of Amleth. Tr. Oliver Elton. *AScL* p 7-16. [Slightly abridged version of the tale in *Gesta Danorum*.]

Previous Translations:

Fragment of Biarkamal.
Song of Regner Lodbrock.
Lamentation of Starkader.
The Death-Song of Hagbard the Dane.
The First Nine Books of the Danish History of Saxo Grammaticus.
The Swords of the Vikings.

Works about Saxo Grammaticus

Bergsøe, Paul. **The Real Hamlet. Shakespeare and Elsinore.** Copenhagen: Turistforeningen, 1950. p 32. Ill.

Boberg, Inger Margrethe. **Saxo's Hamlet.** *ASR*, vol. 44, no. 1 (March 1956) pp 50-56.

Dollerup, Cay. **Denmark, Hamlet and Shakespeare. A Study of Englishmen's Knowledge of Denmark towards the End of the Sixteenth Century with Special Reference to Hamlet.** Vol. 1-2. Salzburg: Institut für eng. Sprache und Literatur, Universität Salzburg, 1975. p 338.

Hansen, George P. **Legend of »Hamlet, Prince of Denmark« as Found in the Works of Saxo Grammaticus and Other Writers of the 12th Century.** Ed. Charles B. Simons. 1887; rpt. New York: A M S Press, 1972. p 57.

Hansen, Richard Wagner. **Shakespeare and the Danish Hamlet.** *DFOJ* no. 48 (1964) pp 9-16. Ill.

Klem, Knud. **Kronborg - Hamlet's Castle.** *DFOJ* no. 46 (1963) pp 17-19.

Linneballe, Poul. **Hamlet and Kronborg.** *DFOJ* no. 8 (1953) pp 19-22.

HANS EGEDE SCHACK
(1820-1859)

Works about Hans Egede Schack

Jørgensen, Aage. **On »Phantasterne«, the Novel by Hans Egede Schack.** *Scandinavica*, vol. 5, no. 1 (May 1966) pp 50-53.

128 Madsen, Børge Gedsø. **Hans Egede Schack's »Phantasterne«.** *SS* vol. 35, no. 1 (February 1963) pp 51-58.

A. W. SCHACK VON STAFFELDT (1769-1826)

At the Rendezvous. Tr. Charles Wharton Stork. *SeBDV* pp 20-21. [*Paa et aftalt Samlingssted*, poem published in *Poulsens Nytaarsgave*, 1803.]

JENS AUGUST SCHADE (1903-1978)

At the Movies. Tr. Poul Borum. *CDPo* p 58. Also *Books* p 21 (no trans. given.) [*I Biografen*, poem from the collection *Helvede opløser sig*, 1953.]

The Bureau. Tr. Poul Borum. *CDPo* p 57. [*Chatollet*, poem from the collection *Jordens største Lykke*, 1949.]

Changed Eyes. Tr. Poul Borum. *CDPo* p 53. [*Forandrede Øjne*, poem from the collection *Den levende Violin*, 1926.]

Equinox. Tr. Poul Borum. *CDPo* p 54. [*Solhverv*, poem from the collection *Den levende Violin*, 1926.]

The Heavenly Sun. Tr. Poul Borum. *CDPo* p 52. [*Den himmelske Sol*, poem from the collection *Den levende Violin*, 1926.]

I Love You. Tr. Martin S. Allwood. *TCScP* p 79. [*Jeg elsker dig*, poem from the collection *Kællingedigte*, 1944.]

I Love You. Tr. Poul Borum. *CDPo* p 57. [*Jeg elsker dig*, poem from the collection *Kællingedigte*, 1944.]

Introduction. Tr. Martin S. Allwood. *TCScP* p 79. [*Indledning*, poem from the collection *Den levende Violin*, 1926.]

Life in Copenhagen. Tr. Dennis Preston. *Versuch* vol. 17 (1978) p 13. [*Københavnerliv*, poem from the collection *Det evige Liv*, 1948.]

Me. Tr. Martin S. Allwood. *TCScP* pp 78-79. [*Mig*, poem from the collection *Hjertebogen*, 1930.]

My Young Love. Tr. Poul Borum. *CDPo* p 54. [*Min unge Elskede*, poem from the collection *Den levende Violin*, 1926.]

Nattens Frelse (Resume with quotations of reviews in French and English). *World Theatre* (Paris) vol. 14, no. 6 (1965) p 639 (Technical Data: Denmark). [*Nattens Frelse*, scenic poem, 1965.]

Nocturnal Ride. Tr. Poul Borum. *CDPo* p 55. [*Natlig Køretur*, poem from the collection *Kærlighed og Kildevand*, 1936.]

People Meet and Sweet Music Fills the Heart. Tr. Carl Malmberg. New York: Dell, 1969. p 188. [A Seymour Lawrence book.] [*Mennesker mødes, og sød Musik opstår i Hjertet*, novel, 1944.]

Snow. Tr. Poul Borum. *CDPo* p 56. [*Sne*, poem from the collection *Kællingedigte*, 1944.]

Spring Storm. Tr. Elizabeth Byrd. *MoDP* pp 18-19. [*Foraarsstorm*, poem from the collection *Jordens største Lykke*, 1949.]

A Strawberry. Tr. Poul Borum. *CDPo* p 59. [*Et Jordbær*, poem from the collection *Schades Højsang*, 1958.]

Woman. Tr. Poul Borum. *CDPo* p 53. [*Kvinde*, poem from the collection *Den levende Violin*, 1926.]

The Wonderful Vase. Tr. Poul Borum. *CDPo* p 55. [*Den vidunderlige Vase*, poem from the collection *Hjertebogen*, 1930.]

HANS SCHERFIG (1905-1979)

Paris. Tr. Eileen MacLeod. *CDPr* pp 297-299. [From a chapter in the novel *Den døde Mand*, 1937.]

Works about Hans Scherfig

Møller Kristensen, Sven. **How to Castigate Your Public - and Write Best Sellers.** *DJ* no. 76 (1973) pp 26-29.

KARL SCHLÜTER (1883-1960)

Off the Rails. Tr. Anne R. Born. *CDPl* pp 251-326. [*Afsporet*, play, 1932.]

ASGER SCHNACK (b. 1949)

Language for Lost Places. Tr. Asger Schnack and Alexander Taylor. *Portland* p 92. [*Sproget for de tabte Steder*, poem from the collection *Jeg forsvinder og virker således*, 1978.] [Danish text included.]

PETER SEEBERG (b. 1925)

The Dent. Tr. Børge Gedsø Madsen. *LitR-Dk* pp 47-53. [*Bulen*, short story from the collection *Eftersøgningen*, 1962.]
The Dent. Tr. Paula Hostrup-Jessen. *DI* pp 150-157. [*Bulen*, short story from the collection *Eftersøgningen*, 1962.]
The Patient. A Story. Tr. Alexander Taylor and Nadia Christensen. *Boundary, A Journal of Post-modern Literature*, vol. 1, no. 3 (Spring 1973) pp 697-699. [*Patienten*, short story from the collection *Eftersøgningen*, 1962.]

HANS HARTVIG SEEDORFF PEDERSEN (b. 1892)

All's Well with the Compass. Tr. R. P. Keigwin. *ScSoB* pp 11-12. [*Rosvald*, poem from the collection *Fra Danmark til Dvina*, 1918.]
Autumn. Tr. Charles Wharton Stork. *SeBDV* pp 133-134. [*Høsten*, poem from the collection *Udvalgte Digte*, 1952.]
Introduction. In Werner, Sigvart: *Denmark, Land of Beauty.* Tr. R. P. Keigwin. Ill. Sigvart Werner. London: George Allen & Unwin, 1950. p 166. Ill. [Printed in Denmark.]
Knave of Hearts and the Four Queens. Tr. R. P. Keigwin. *TCScP* pp 58-59. [*Hjerterknægt og de fire Damer*, poem from the collection *Vinløv og Vedbend*, 1916.]
Sailor's Drinking Song. Tr. R. P. Keigwin. *TCScP* pp 59-60. [*Rosvald*, poem from the collection *Fra Danmark til Dvina*, 1918.]
The Swans from the North. Tr. Charles Wharton Stork. *SeBDV* pp 131-132. [*Svanerne fra Norden*, poem first published on Nordens Dag, October 27, 1936.]
The Swans of the North. Tr. Evelyn Heepe. *Nor* vol. 9, no. 4 (July-August 1951) pp 276-277. Also *SotN* pp 9-12. [*Svanerne fra Norden*, poem first published on Nordens Dag, October 27, 1936.]
Thoughts on Resurrection. Tr. Martin S. Allwood. *ScSoB* pp 46-47. [*Tanker om Genopstandelse*, poem from the collection *Hyben*, 1917.]
To a Silhouette. Tr. Charles Wharton Stork. *SeBDV* pp 135-136. [Poem.]
Two Silver Birds. Tr. Evelyn Heepe. *Nor* vol. 13, no. 1 (Jan.-Feb. 1955) pp 33-34. [Poem written on the occasion of the opening of the New Polar Air Route from the West Coast of the U.S.A. to Scandinavia.]

Previous Translations: *129*

Extracts from »1940, Christian X of Denmark« (Men asked me how does he dare).

ANNEMARIE SELINKO (b. 1914)
Danish-Austrian author who writes in German

Désirée. Tr. from the German by Arnold Bender and E. W. Dickes. London: Heinemann, 1953. p 674. London: Reprint Society, 1954. p 510. [*Désirée*, historic novel, 1952.]
Désirée. Tr. from the German. New York: Morrow, 1953. p 594. [*Désirée*, historic novel, 1952.]
Désirée. Queen of Sweden. London: Longman, 1975. p 106. Ill. [*Désirée*, historic novel, 1952.]
Désirée. Queen of Sweden. Abridged and simplified by A. G. Eyre. London: Longman, 1975. p 106. [Longman structural readers: fiction: stage 5.]
Désirée, Wife of Marshal Bernadotte. Tr. from the German by Arnold Bender and E. W. Dickes. Simplified and abridged by A. G. Eyre. London: Longman, 1975. p 100. Ill. [Longman structural readers: fiction: stage 4.]

JOHAN SKJOLDBORG (1861-1936)

Cotter's Song. Tr. Charles Wharton Stork. *SeBDV* p 106. [*Husmandssangen*, poem from the collection *Dynæs Digte*, 1915.]
Morning Song. Tr. Charles Wharton Stork. *SeBDV* p 107. [*Morgensang*, poem from the collection *Dynæs Digte*, 1915.]

Previous Translations:

Per Hywer's Summer Day.
The Lymfiord Huckster and the Furbo Maid.
In Life and Death.

TAGE SKOU-HANSEN (b. 1925)

The Naked Trees. Tr. Katherine John. London: Jonathan Cape, 1959. p 222. [*De nøgne Træer*, novel, 1957.]

130 FINN SØEBORG (b. 1916)

Four Cheers for Bureaucracy. Tr. Janet Gow. London: Sidgwick and Jackson, 1952. p 224. [*Sådan er der så meget*, novel, 1950.]

Works about Finn Søeborg

Hugus, Frank. **The King's New Clothes: The Irrevent Portrayal of Royalty in the Works of Leif Panduro and Finn Søeborg.** *SS* vol. 51, no. 2 (Spring 1979) pp 162-176.

HARRY SØIBERG (1880-1954)
Also spelled Søjberg

The School Teacher and His Family Take a Summer Holiday by the Sea. Tr. Anne R. Born. *CDPr* pp 122-134. [*Adjunktfamiliens Sommerferie ved Havet*, short story from the collection *Af Jordens Slægt*, 1910.]

Previous Translations:

The Old Boat.
The Sea King.

KNUD SØNDERBY (1909-1966)

The Blue Flashes. The Hawthorn. Danish Harbours. Tr. Reginald Spink. Ill. Hans Lollesgaard. Copenhagen: Udenrigsministeriets Pressebureau, 1966. p 39. Ill. [Presentation Books, 4.]
The Danish Harbours. Ill. Sven Havsteen Mikkelsen. *DFOJ* no. 56. (1966) pp 20-23. Ill. Also *ASR* vol. 54, no. 3 (1966) pp 254-259.
Inland Navigation. Tr. Evelyn Heepe. *SotN* pp 76-83. [*Indenskærs Sejlads*, essay from the collection *Hvidtjørnen*, 1950.]
An Inn in Jutland. Tr. Walter Foote. *LitR-Dk* pp 23-30. [*En Kro i Jylland*, essay from the collection *Gensyn med Havet*, 1957.]
Sonia. Tr. A. I. Roughton. *CDP* pp 326-330. [*Sonja*, essay from the collection *Grønlandsk Sommer*, 1941.]
Waiting. Tr. Lydia Cranfield. *Nor* vol. 11, no. 2 (March-April 1953) pp 130-134. [*Ventetiden*, essay from the collection *Forsvundne Somre*, 1947.]
A Woman Too Many. Tr. A. I. Roughton. *CDPl* pp 429-494. [*En Kvinde er overflødig*, play, 1942.]

JØRGEN SONNE (b. 1925)

Bird in Mountains. Tr. Nadia Christensen. *CDPo* p 210. [*Fugl i Bjerge*, poem from the collection *Italiensk Suite*, 1954.]
Chamber Cantata; Minor Mode. Tr. Jørgen Sonne and Alexander Taylor. *Portland* p 95. [*Kammerkantate i Moll*, poem included in the collection *År, sammenvalgte Digte 1950-1965*, 1965.] [Danish text included.]
The Fold-out Men. Tr. Tove Neville. *CDPo* pp 208-210. [*Foldemændene*, poem from the collection *Krese, Rhapsodi af Digte*, 1963.]
It Is You. Tr. Tove Neville. *CDPo* p 207. [*Det er dig*, poem from the collection *Krese, Rhapsodi af Digte*, 1963.]
A Man in Hvalsø. (A Critical Elegy in Memory of Paul La Cour). Tr. Richard B. Vowles. *LitR-Dk* p 40. [*En Mand i Hvalsø*, poem from the collection *Midtvejs*, 1960.]
Museum Music. Tr. Anne Born. *Orbis* p 54. [*Museumsmusik*, poem from the collection *Krese, Rhapsodi af Digte*, 1963.]
Northwester. Tr. Anne Born. *Orbis* pp 53-54. [*Nordvest*, poem from the collection *Midtvejs*, 1960.]
Shanty. Tr. Jørgen Sonne and Alexander Taylor. *Portland* p 93. [*Shanty*, poem from the collection *Delfiner i Skoven*, 1951.] [Danish text included.]
Shanty. Tr. Anne Born. *Orbis* p 53. [*Shanty*, poem from the collection *Delfiner i Skoven*, 1951.]
The Shepherds' Adoration. Tr. Tove Neville. *CDPo* pp 207-208. [*Hyrdernes Tilbedelse*, poem from the collection *Italiensk Suite*, 1954.]

LISE SØRENSEN (b. 1926)

Boy's Life. Tr. Nadia Christensen. *CDPo* p 150. [*Drengeliv*, poem from the collection *Tro dine Øjne*, 1973.]
Girl Who Is Waiting. Tr. Martin S. Allwood. *TCScP* p 102. [*Pige, der venter*, poem from the collection *Rødløs*, 1946.]
Hold My Hand. Tr. Nadia Christensen. *CDPo* pp 148-149. [*Hold mig i Hånden*, poem from the collection *Epistler*, 1966.]
In a White Kayak. Tr. Nadia Christensen. *CDPo* pp 153-154. [*I en hvid Kajak*, poem from the collection *Tro dine Øjne*, 1973.]
In the Dark. Tr. Nadia Christensen. *CDPo* p 149. [*I Mørket*, poem from the collection *Tro dine Øjne*, 1973.]

Longing. Tr. Mary Catherine Phinney. *LitR-Dk* p 76. [*Længsel,* poem from the collection *Blæsten udenfor,* 1956.]

Our Don John. Tr. Nadia Christensen. *CDPo* p 151. [*Vor Don Johan,* poem from the collection *Tro dine Øjne,* 1973.]

Previously Unpublished. Tr. Nadia Christensen. *CDPo* p 152. [*Hidtil utrykt,* poem from the collection *Tro dine Øjne,* 1973.]

POUL SØRENSEN (1906-1973)
Also known as »Poeten«

The Centaur. Tr. Charles Wharton Stork. *SeBDV* pp 144-145. Also *TCScP* pp 77-78. [*Kentaur,* poem from the collection *Europasange,* 1947.]

VILLY SØRENSEN (b. 1929)

Child's Play. Tr. Maureen Neiiendam. *Tiger* pp 79-88. [*Blot en Drengestreg,* short story from the collection *Sære Historier,* 1953.]

The Concert. 1. The Rumour. 2. The Journey There. 3. The Opening. Tr. Maureen Neiiendam. *Tiger* pp 35-78. [*Koncerten. I. Rygtet. II. På vej. III. Åbenbaringen,* short story from the collection *Sære Historier,* 1953.]

The Enemy. Tr. Lawrence S. Thompson. *LitR-Dk* pp 64-65. [*Fjenden,* short story from the collection *Ufarlige Historier,* 1955.]

In Strange Country. Tr. Paula Hostrup-Jessen. *DI* pp 52-67. [*I det fremmede,* short story from the collection *Formynderfortællinger,* 1964.]

The Murder Case. 1. The Police Station. 2. On the Trail. 3. The Hotel. 4. The Report. 5. The Messenger-boy. 6. The Murder is Solved. Tr. Maureen Neiiendam. *Tiger* pp 142-204. [*Mordsagen. En Kafka-Idyl. I. I Politigården. II. På Sporet. III. Hotellet. IV. Rapporten. V. Hoteldrengen. VI. Opklaringen,* short story from the collection *Sære Historier,* 1953.]

The Soldier's Christmas Eve. Tr. Alexander Taylor and Nadia Christensen. Ill. Victoria Schaaf, Willimantic, CT: Curbstone Press, 1973. p 24. [Ltd. ed. of 500, handnumbered.] [*Soldatens Juleaften,* short story from the collection *Ufarlige Historier,* 1955.]

The Soldier's Christmas Eve. Tr. Børge Gedsø Madsen. *ASR* vol. 52, no. 4 (December 1964) pp 435-440. [*Soldatens Juleaften,* short story from the collection *Ufarlige Historier,* 1955.]

Strange Stories. Tr. Maureen Neiiendam. Intro. Angus Wilson. London: Secker & Warburg, 1956. p 204. [*Sære Historier,* short story collection, 1953.] American ed. *Tiger in the Kitchen.* Individual stories listed separately under *Tiger.*

The Strange Tree. Tr. Maureen Neiiendam. *Tiger* pp 105-115. [*Det ukendte Træ,* short story from the collection *Sære Historier,* 1953.]

Tiger in the Kitchen and Other Strange Stories. Tr. Maureen Neiiendam. Intro. Angus Wilson. New York: Abelard-Schuman; Toronto: Nelson, Foster & Scott, 1957. Freeport, New York: Books for Libraries Press, 1969. p 204. [*Sære Historier,* short story collection, 1953.] British ed. *Strange Stories.* Individual stories listed separately under *Tiger.*

The Tigers. Tr. Maureen Neiiendam. *Tiger* pp 1-34. [*Tigrene,* short story from the collection *Sære Historier,* 1953.]

Two Legends. 1. Silvanus of Nazareth. 2. Theodora and Theodorus. Tr. Maureen Neiiendam. *Tiger* pp 116-141. [*To Legender. Silvanus af Nazareth. Theodora og Theodorus,* short stories from the collection *Sære Historier,* 1953.]

The Two Twins. Tr. Maureen Neiiendam. *Tiger* pp 89-104. [*De to Tvillinger,* short story from the collection *Sære Historier,* 1953.]

Youth in Revolt. *DJ* vol. 65 (1969) pp 2-7. [*Den oprørte Ungdom,* article originally published in *Berlingske Tidende,* 22. sept. 1968, and in the collection *Mellem Fortid og Nutid,* 1969.

CARL ERIK SOYA (b. 1896)

Bedroom Mazurka: Seven Erotic Stories. London: Sphere, 1971. p 156. [*Tilegnet Boccaccio,* short story collection, 1959.]

Farmor's House. A Portrait of an Epoch. Tr. Agnes Camilla Hansen. Revised and ed. Alan Moray Williams. Copenhagen: Borgens Publishing House, 1964. p 293. [*Min Farmors Hus,* memoirs in novel form, 1943.]

Grandmother's House. Tr. Agnes Camilla Hansen. Trans. rev. Alan Moray Williams. New York: Taplinger, 1966. p 293. [*Min Farmors Hus,* memoirs in novel form, 1943.]

Lion with Corset. Tr. Barbara Knudsen. In *Five Modern Scandinavian Plays.* Intro. Henry W. Wells. New York: American-Scandinavian Foundation and Twayne Publishers, 1971. pp 19-99. (Library of Scandinavian Literature, vol. 11). [*Løve med Korset,* play, 1950.]

An Order. *Story - The Magazine of the Short Story* (New York) vol. 35, issue 8, no. 137

132   (1962) pp 9-22. Also *ASR* vol. 51, no. 3
(September 1963) pp 288-298. [*En Ordre,*
short story in the collection *Fra mit Spejlka-*
binet, 1956.]

The Rites of Spring. New York: Pyramid, 1962.
p 205. pb. [Abridged version of *Seventeen.*]
[*Sytten: Erindringer og Refleksioner,* novel,
1953-1954.]

Seventeen: A Novel of Puberty. Tr. Carl Malmberg. New York: Paul S. Eriksson, 1961. p
369; rpt. London: Sphere, 1969, 1974. [*Syt-*
ten: Erindringer og Refleksioner, novel, 1953-
54.] [See also abridged version, *The Rites of*
Spring.]

Two Threads Tr. anonymously, revised by P. N.
Furbank and Elias Bredsdorff. *CDPl* pp 173-
250. [*To Traade,* play, 1943.]

The Unmentionable Part. An Ethnographic Re-
cord from Natahoa. Tr. Maureen Neiiendam.
Nor vol. 12, no. 2 (March-April 1954) pp
126-132. [*Den usømmelige Legemsdel. En et-*
nografisk Beretning fra Natahoa, short story
from the collection *Hvis Tilværelsen keder*
Dem, 1952.]

World Fame. Tr. R. H. Bathgate. *CDPr* pp 225-
228. [*Verdensberømmelse,* short story from
the collection *Hvis Tilværelsen keder Dem,*
1952.]

HENRIK STANGERUP (b. 1937)

Works about Henrik Stangerup

Monty, Ib. **An Unsentimental Dane. Portrait of**
Danish Author and Film Director Henrik
Stangerup. *DJ* no. 72 (1972) pp 15-19.

VAGN STEEN (b. 1928)

$a$capitalistic$society$. Tr. Vagn Steen. *CDPo*
p 272. [*Et%kapitalistisk%samfund%,* poem
from the collection *Teknisk er det muligt,*
1967.]

Concretism? *Scandinavica.* Special issue devoted to contemporary poetry, 1973 pp 23-39.
[Essay.]

I Am No Shower. *CDPo* p 267. [Poem written
in English.]

Mirror Mirror on the Wall. Tr. Vagn Steen.
CDPo p 272. [*Lille Spejl,* poem from the
collection *Digte?,* 1964.]

Technically It Is Possible. *CDPo* pp 268-271.
[Poem written in English.]

THORSTEINN STEFÁNSSON (b. 1912)
Icelandic author who writes in Danish

The Golden Future. Ill. Victor G. Ambrus.
London: Oxford University Press, 1974. p
165. Ill. [*Den gyldne Fremtid,* novel, 1958.]

NICOLAUS STENO (1638-1686)
Also known as Niels Stensen

The Earliest Geological Treatise (1667). Tr.
from the Latin *Canis Carchariae dissectum*
caput, with intro. and notes by Axel Garboe.
London: Macmillan; New York: St. Martin's
Press, 1958. p 51.

A Lecture on the Anatomy of the Brain. Intro.
Gustav Scherz. Copenhagen: Nyt Nordisk
Forlag - Arnold Busck, 1965. p 208. Ill. [Text
in French, English and German.]

Steno's Letter on the Grotto above Gresta. In
Hilsen til J. Christian Bay. Copenhagen: Rosenkilde & Bagger, 1951. pp 27-31. Ill.

Steno's Letter on the Grotto of Moncodeno. In
Hilsen til J. Christian Bay. Copenhagen: Rosenkilde & Bagger, 1951. pp 32-38. Ill.

Works about Nicolaus Steno

Billeskov Jansen, F. J. **Niels Stensen.** Tr. David
Stoner. *ADL,* 1972. [*Niels Stensen,* lecture,
1958.]

Cioni, Raffaelo. **Niels Steensen, Scientist Bi-**
shop. Tr. from the Italian by Dr. Genevieve
M. Camera. New York: J. J. Kenedy & Sons,
1962. p 192.

Garboe, Axel. **Niels Stensen's Grotto Letters**
(1671). An Episode in the Life of the Young
Niels Stensen (Steno). In *Hilsen til J. Chri-*
stian Bay. Copenhagen: Rosenkilde & Bagger, 1951. pp 13-26.

HANS CHRISTENSEN STHEN (1544-1610)

Lord Jesus Christ. Tr. J. C. Aaberg. *HinS* hymn
nr. 37. [*Du Herre Christ (En Christelig*
Supplicatz til Guds Søn), hymn from the
collection *En liden Vandring,* ca. 1589.]

O Lord, O Lord, a Heart So True. Tr. Henry
Meyer. *DB&FS* pp 256-257. [*Et trofast*
Hjerte, o Herre min, hymn, about 1609.]

Previous Translations:

The Grace of God (My God, My God, for Thee I Pine.

BINE STRANGE PETERSEN

Anything Goes. Tr. Hallberg Hallmundsson. New York: Grove, 1967. p 127. [*Alt er tilladt*, novel, 1965.]

AMBROSIUS STUB (1705-1758)

Aria. Tr. R. P. Keigwin. *IDIWB* pp 17-19. [*Aria*, (first line *Skal Dalens Lillie af Foragt)* from the collection *Arier og Sange*, I, 1773.]
Spring. Tr. S. D. Rodholm. *HoS* pp 143-145. [*Den kiedsom Vinter*, poem from the collection *Arier og andre Stykker*, published posthumously by T. S. Heiberg, 1771.]

Previous Translations:

O Beauteous Rosebud.
To Be Well Born Is Good.

VIGGO STUCKENBERG (1863-1905)

Confession. Tr. S. Foster Damon. *BoDV* pp 139-140. [*Bekendelse*, poem published in *Tilskueren*, 1896 and in the collection *Sne*, 1901.]
Early October. Tr. S. Foster Damon. *BoDV* pp 140-141. [*Først i Oktober*, poem from the collection *Sne*, 1901.]
Holiday. Tr. R. P. Keigwin. *IDIWB* pp 83-85. [*Første Maj*, poem from the collection *Sidste Digte*, 1906.]
Morning. Tr. Charles Wharton Stork. *SeBDV* p 74. [*Morgen*, poem from the collection *Sne*, 1901.]
My Mother. Tr. Charles Wharton Stork. *SeBDV* pp 74-75. [Part I of *Min Moder*, poem from the collection *Sne*, 1901.]
Snow. Tr. S. Foster Damon. *BoDV* p 142. [*Sne*, poem from a collection by that name, 1901.]

Previous Translations: *133*

Sadness.
Bliss.
By the Wayside; Little Tales and Legends.
Asa's Mound.
Now Burgeon in All the Fissures.
One Morning Was Your Tomb.
We Must Make Amends.

DIDERIK PETER SVENDSEN (1824-1884)

Jesus, Draw Thou near to Me. Tr. S. D. Rodholm. *HoS* p 64. [*Jesus, kom dog nær*, hymn published in *Dansk Kirke-Tidende*, 18. marts, 1860.]

VALDEMAR THISTED (1815-1887)

When Day Is Done. Tr. S. D. Rodholm. *HoS* p 5. Also *HinS* hymn nr. 10. [*Naar Solen ganger til Hvile*, stanzas from the poem *Min elskede Plet*, from the collection *Digte*, 1862.]

GRETHE RISBJERG THOMSEN (b. 1925)

Apple Blossoms. Tr. R. P. Keigwin. *ASR* vol. 39, no. 1 (March 1951) p 37. [*Æbleblomster*, poem from the collection *Digte*, 1945.]
The Drop. Tr. Elizabeth Falksen. *Versuch* vol. 18 (1979) p 13. [*Dråben*, poem from the collection *Havet og Stjernen*, 1959.]
The Law of Equilibrium. Tr. Martin S. Allwood. *TCScP* p 97. [*Ligevægtens Lov*, poem from the collection *De aabne Døre*, 1946.]
The Tree in the City. Tr. Elizabeth Falksen. *Versuch* vol. 18 (1979) p 34. [*Træerne i Byen*, poem from the collection *Træerne i Byen*, 1950.]

RICHARD BØRGE THOMSEN
(1888-1974) Faroese author

The Tyrants. Tr. Naomi Walford. New York: G. P. Putnam's Sons; London: Bodley Head, 1955. p 245. London: World Distributors, 1960. p 223. [*De stærke Viljer*, novel, 1952.]

134 KIRSTEN THORUP (b. 1942)

Baby. Tr. Nadia Christensen. Baton Rouge, Louisiana: Louisiana State University Press, 1980. p 208. [*Baby*, novel, 1973.]
Love from Trieste. Tr. Alexander Taylor and Nadia Christensen. Copenhagen: Augustinus Forlag; Willimantic, CT: Curbstone Press, 1980. p 59. [*Love from Trieste*, poetry collection, 1969.]

HERMANN ANDREAS TIMM (1800-1866)

Under His Wings. Tr. S. D. Rodholm. *HoS* pp 78-79. [*Under dine Vingers Skygge*, hymn from the collection *Christlige Sange*, 1852.]

HENRIK TJELE

Two and Two. Tr. Peter K. Nepperson. New York: Grove Press, 1970. [*To og to*, novel, 1965. Part Two of *Min Seng er mit Slot*, erotica.]

DAN TURÈLL (b. 1946)

Canto XLVI. *CDPo* pp 300-301. [Poem, written in English, from the collection *Another Draft of Space Cantos*, 1974.]
Canto XXXVII. *CDPo* p 299. [Poem, written in English, from the collection *Another Draft of Space Cantos*, 1974.]
From: **Karma Cowboy Theme Song.** *CDPo* pp 296-297. [Poem, written in English, from the collection *Karma Cowboy*, 1974.]
Nr. 5: Coda. Tr. Mark Hansen. *Versuch* vol. 18 (1979) p 10. [Poem.]
Parking Lot Rag. Tr. Mark Hansen. *Versuch* vol. 18 (1979) p 20. [*Parking Lot Rag* part of the poem *New York Suite* from the collection *Tre-D Digte*, 1977.]
From: **Song for Blake.** *CDPo* p 298. [Poem, written in English, from the collection *Karma Cowboy*, 1974.]

JØRGEN VIBE (1896-1968)

A Song of Sprats. Tr. Charles Wharton Stork. *SeBDV* pp 139-140. [*En Sang om Silden*, poem from the collection *Konkylier*, 1919.]

ERNST VON DER RECKE (1848-1933)

An Angel Touched Your Forehead. Tr. Charles Wharton Stork. *SeBDV* pp 89-90. [*En Engel har rørt ved din Pande*, poem from the collection *Smaadigte*, 1883.]
Methought. Tr. Charles Wharton Stork. *SeBDV* pp 90-91, [*Mig tyktes, du stod ved mit Leie*, poem from the collection *Smaadigte*, 1883.]
Oh, Is It Wrought —. Tr. Charles Wharton Stork. *SeBDV* p 89. [*Blev det mon spundet af Solens Skin*, poem from the collection *Smaadigte*, 1916.]
You Never Have Cared. Tr. Charles Wharton Stork. *SeBDV* pp 91-92. [*Jeg veed, jeg vorder dig aldrig kjær*, poem from the collection *Smaadigte*, 1916.]

WILHELM ANDREAS WEXELS (1797-1866)

Some Day I Know. Tr. S. D. Rodholm. *HoS* pp 92-93. [*Tænk naar en gang*, poem from the collection *Religiøse Digte*, 1845.]

DORRIT WILLUMSEN (b. 1940)

Complication. Tr. Paula Hostrup-Jessen. *DI* p 187-191. [*Komplikation*, short story from the collection *Knagen*, 1965.]

CHRISTIAN WINTHER (1796-1876)

At the Manor House. Tr. Charles Wharton Stork. *SeBDV* pp 33-34. [Poem.]
Darkness Is Falling. Tr. Harald Schiøtz. *HinS* hymn nr. 12. [Poem.]
Fly, Bird, Fly. Tr. Robert Silliman Hillyer. *BoDV* pp 80-82. Also *IDIWB* pp 55-57. [*Flyv, Fugl, flyv*, poem from the collection *Digte*, 1828.]
Going to Sleep. Tr. S. D. Rodholm. *HoS* p 47. [*Aftenbøn*, published in *A.B.C.* by Chr. Winther and Constatin Hansen, 1863.]
Had I Some Magic Power. Tr. Charles Wharton Stork. *SeBDV* pp 31-32. [*Kunde jeg Roser male* (first line), poem nr. 10 of the cycle *Til Een*, in *Digtninge*, 1843.]
Longing. Tr. Charles Wharton Stork. *SeBDV* pp 30-31. [*Længsel*, poem from the collection *Sang og Sagn*, 1840.]

My Home. Tr. Charles Wharton Stork. *SeBDV* p 32. [*Mit Hjem*, poem from the collection *Brogede Blade*, 1865.]

The Night Was Kindly and Vast. Tr. Robert Silliman Hillyer. *BoDV* pp 82-83. [*Natten var mild og kjær*, (first line) poem from the collection *Nye Digte*, 1851.]

Over the Ocean's Barren Meadow. Tr. Robert Silliman Hillyer. *BoDV* pp 83-84. [Poem.]

The Stork Goes South. Tr. R. P. Keigwin. *IDIWB* pp 57-61. [*Til Storken*, poem from the collection *Nye Digtninge*, 1853.]

A Summer Night. Tr. Robert Silliman Hillyer. *BoDV* pp 79-80. [*En Sommernat*, poem from the collection *Nogle Digte*, 1835.]

Previous Translations:

Henrik and Else.
The Confessional.
Knight Kalv (Calf).
Murad.

M. A. WINTHER
Faroese author

The Battle of Klandurskot. Tr. from the Faroese by Hedin Brønner. *FSS* pp 13-21. [*Orrustan i Klandurskoti*, short story from the collection *Úrvalsrit*, 1970.]

Hunger. Tr. from the Faroese by Hedin Brønner. *FSS* pp 28-31. [*Hungur*, short story from the collection *Úrvalsrit*, 1970.]

To Catch a Thief. Tr. from the Faroese by Hedin Brønner. *FSS* pp 22-27. [*Eitt heppið bragd*, short story from the collection *Úrvalsrit*, 1970.]

OLE WIVEL (b. 1921)

The Cologne Cathedral. Tr. Nadia Christensen. *CDPo* pp 137-138. [*Domkirken i Køln*, poem from the collection *Nike*, 1958.]

The Fish. Tr. Martin S. Allwood. *MoDP* p 42. Also *TCScP* p 101. [*Fisken*, poem from the collection *Jævndøgn*, 1956.]

Holy Andrew's Barrow. Tr. Alexander Taylor. *CDPo* p 138. [*Hellig Anders Høj*, poem from the collection *Gravskrifter*, 1970.]

Pax Americana. Tr. Chip Pedersen. *Versuch* vol. 16 (1977) p 17. [*Pax Americana*, poem from the collection *Gravskrifter*, 1970.]

The Repentant Magdalene of the Roadside. Tr. Alexander Taylor. *CDPo* p 139. [*Landevejens bodfærdige Magdalene*, poem from the collection *Gravskrifter*, 1970.]

Stenild Cemetery. Tr. Alexander Taylor. *CDPo* pp 139-140. [*Stenild Kirkegaard*, poem from the collection *Gravskrifter*, 1970.]

Thus. Tr. Alexander Taylor and Nadia Christensen. *Occum Ridge Review* (South Willington, Connecticut) (Spring-Summer 1973) p 35. [Poem.]

To Poul Winther. Tr. Alexander Taylor. *CDPo* p 140. [*Til Poul Winther*, poem from the collection *Gravskrifter*, 1970.]

Weep for Balder. Tr. Martin S. Allwood. *TCScP* pp 100-101. [*Græd for Balder*, poem from the collection *I Fiskens Tegn*, 1948.]

Winter Night. Tr. Norman C. Bansen. In *Christmas Chimes.* An Annual Christmas Publication. Vol. 38. Ed. Edward C. Eskildsen. Blair, Nebraska: Lutheran Publishing House, 1958. p 64. [Poem.]

JOHANNES WULFF (b. 1902)

Ecstasy of the Flesh. Tr. Kurt Hansen. *CDPo* pp 65-69. [*I Kødets Ekstase*, poem from the collection *Jeg tror minsandten at jeg lever*, 1970.]

The Friend Is Dead. Tr. Kurt Hansen. *CDPo* pp 62-65. [*Vennen er død*, poem from the collection *Jeg tror minsandten at jeg lever*, 1970.]

DANISH LITERATURE IN ENGLISH TRANSLATION 1950-1980

B. Individual Genres

Ballads

Aage and Else. Tr. E. M. Smith-Dampier. *BoDB* pp 86-90. Also *The World in Literature*. Ed. Robert Warnock and George K. Anderson. Chicago: Scott, Foresman and Co., 1950. Rev. ed. 1967. pp 250-251. [*Aage og Else.*]

Aage and Else. Tr. Alexander Gray. *FaF* pp 83-85. [*Aage og Else.*]

Agnes and the Merman. Tr. E. M. Smith-Dampier.*BoDB* pp 113-116. [*Agnete og Havmanden.*]

Agnete and the Merman. Tr. Alexander Gray. *FaF* pp 3-6. [*Agnete og Havmanden.*]

Alf of Odderskerry. Tr. E. M. Smith-Dampier. *BoDB* pp 83-86. [*Alf i Odderskær.*]

Angelfyr and Helmer Kamp. Tr. Henry Meyer. *DB&FS* pp 92-95. [*Angelfyr og Helmer Kamp.*]

The Avenging Daughters. Tr. Alexander Gray. *FaF* pp 38-39. [*Døtre hævner Fader.*]

The Avenging Daughters. Tr. E. M. Smith-Dampier. *BoDB* pp 202-204. Also *A Little Treasury* pp 507-508. [*Døtre hævner Fader.*]

The Avenging Sword. Tr. E. M. Smith-Dampier. *BoDB* pp 127-130. [*Hævnersværdet.*]

The Bald-pated Monk. Tr. Alexander Gray. *FaF* pp 140-144. [*Den skaldede Munk.*]

The Ballad of the Eagle. Tr. E. M. Smith-Dampier. *BoDB* pp 185-187. [*Ørnevisen.*]

The Banishment. Tr. Henry Meyer. *BD&FS* pp 68-70. [*Landsforvisningen.*]

The Battle of Lena. (King Sverker the Younger.). Tr. Alexander Gray. *HBD* pp 44-46. [*Kong Sverker hin Unge.*]

The Battle of Lena. Tr. E. M. Smith-Dampier. *BoDB* pp 142-144. [*Slaget ved Lena.*]

The Bear of Dalby. Tr. E. M. Smith-Dampier. *BoDB* pp 273-274. [*Dalby Bjørn.*]

Bedeblak. Tr. Alexander Gray. *FaF* pp 102-104. [*Bedeblak.*]

Birth in the Grove. Tr. Henry Meyer. *DB&FS* pp 130-133. [*Fødsel i Lunden*, or *Redselille og Medelvold.*]

The Bridal of Queen Dagmar. Tr. E. M. Smith-Dampier. *BoDB* pp 144-146. [*Dronning Dagmars Bryllup.*]

The Bride of Ribe. Tr. E. M. Smith-Dampier. *BoDB* pp 243-244. Also *The World in Literature*. Ed. Robert Warnock and George K. Anderson. Chicago: Scott, Foresman and Co., 1950. Rev. ed. 1967. pp 256-257. [*Bruden i Ribe.*]

The Buried Mother. Tr. Henry Meyer. *DB&FS* pp 43-46. [*Moderen under Mulde.*]

Carol Algotson. Tr. Henry Meyer. *DB&FS* pp 124-127. [*Karl Algotsøn.*]

The Corbie. Tr. Alexander Gray. *FaF* pp 131-133. [*Der Bauer und die Krähe*, ballad of supposedly Danish origin.]

The Corbie as Rune-bearer. Tr. Alexander Gray. *FaF* pp 118-119. [*Ravn fører Runer.*]

The Dagmar and Bengerd Cycle: Queen Dagmar and Sir Strange. The Marriage of Queen Dagmar. Death of Queen Dagmar. Queen Bengerd. Tr. Alexander Gray. *HBD* pp 47-76. [*Dronning Dagmar og Junker Strange.*]

Dame Gundelil's Harping. Tr. E. M. Smith-Dampier. *BoDB* pp 316-318. [*Fru Gundelils Harpeslæt.*]

The Dear Robe. Tr. Henry Meyer. *DB&FS* pp 139-141. [*Den dyre Kaabe.*]

The Death of Knight Stig. Tr. E. M. Smith-Dampier. *BoDB* pp 138-140. [*Ridder Stigs Død.*]

The Death of Queen Dagmar. Tr. E. M. Smith-Dampier. *BoDB* pp 147-150. [*Dronning Dagmars Død.*]

The Death of Sir Stig. Tr. Alexander Gray. *HBD* pp 25-27. [*Ridder Stigs Død.*]

The Dice Game. Tr. Henry Meyer. *DB&FS* pp 137-138. [*Terningspillet.*]

The Dragon. Tr. E. M. Smith-Dampier. *BoDB* pp 278-280. [*Lindormen.*]

The Dying Lover. Tr. Alexander Gray. *FaF* pp 73-76. [*Fæstemanden dør.*]

The Eagle Song. (Christian II). Tr. Henry Meyer. *DB&FS* pp 84-86. [*Ørnevisen.*]

Ebbe Skammelson. Tr. E. M. Smith-Dampier. *BoDB* pp 224-229. [*Ebbe Skammelsøn.*]

Ebbe Skammelsen. Tr. Henry Meyer. *DB&FS* pp 113-120. [*Ebbe Skammelsøn.*] [Different version of Meyer's translation than in *DB & FS.*]

Ebbe Skammelsen. Tr. Henry Meyer. *ADL* pp 20-29. [*Ebbe Skammelsøn.*]

Ebbe Skammelson. Tr. Alexander Gray. *FaF* pp 57-62. [*Ebbe Skammelsøn.*]

The Elf Hill. Tr. Henry Meyer. *DB&FS* pp 35-37. [*Elverhøj.*]

The Elfin Shaft. Tr. E. M. Smith-Dampier. *BoDB* pp 103-106. [*Elverskud.*]

Elfin Sorcery. Tr. Henry Meyer. *ADL* pp 14-19. [*Elverskud.*]

The Elf-Shot. Tr. Henry Meyer. *DB&FS* pp 33-35. [*Elverskud.*]

Ellen, Daughter of Ove. Tr. Alexander Gray. *FaF* pp 145-148. [*Ellen Ovesdatter.*]

Esbern Snare. Tr. E. M. Smith-Dampier. *BoDB* pp 141-142. [*Esbern Snare.*]

The False Kelpie. Tr. Alexander Gray. *FaF* pp 12-14. [*Nøkkens Svig.*]

Might of the Harp. *European Folk Ballads.* Ed. Erich Seemann, Dag Strömbäck and Bengt Jonsson. European Folklore Series, vol. 2. Copenhagen: Rosenkilde and Bagger for Council for Cultural Co-operation of the Council of Europe, 1967. pp 23-26. [*Harpens Kraft.*] [Danish text included.]

The Mighty Harp. Tr. E. M. Smith-Dampier. *BoDB* pp 106-108. [*Harpens Kraft.*]

Mimering. Tr. Alexander Gray. *FaF* pp 77-79. [*Mimering.*]

Morning Dreams. Tr. Alexander Gray. *FaF* pp 157-160. [*Møens Morgendrømme.*]

The Mother under the Mould. Tr. E. M. Smith-Dampier. *BoDB* pp 263-267. [*Moder under Mulde.*]

The Murder of Tord Iverson. Tr. Alexander Gray. *FaF* pp 31-34. [*Aage fælder Tord Iversøn.*]

Niels Ebbesen. Tr. Henry Meyer. *DB&FS* pp 71-84. [*Niels Ebbesøn.*]

Niels Ebbeson. Tr. E. M. Smith-Dampier. *BoDB* pp 174-185. Also *The World in Literature.* Ed. Robert Warnock and George K. Anderson. Chicago: Scott, Foresman and Co., 1950. Rev. ed. 1967. pp 252-255. [*Niels Ebbesøn.*]

Niels Ebbesøn. Tr. Alexander Gray. *HBD* pp 143-151. [*Niels Ebbesøn.*]

Niels Strangesen's Stone Tower. Tr. E. M. Smith-Dampier. *BoDB* pp 298-300. [*Nilus Strangesøns Stenstue.*]

Nilus and Hillelil. Tr. Henry Meyer. *DB&FS* pp 109-113. [*Nilus og Hillelil.*]

Nilus and Hillelille. Tr. E. M. Smith-Dampier. *BoDB* pp 191-195. Also *The World in Literature.* Ed. Robert Warnock and George K. Anderson. Chicago: Scott, Foresman and Co., 1950. Rev. ed. 1967. pp 255-259. [*Nilus og Hillelille.*]

Nilus and Hillelille. Tr. Alexander Gray. *FaF* pp 25-30. [*Nilus og Hillelille.*]

Nilus Strangesøn's Stone-House. Tr. Alexander Gray. *HBD* pp 156-158. [*Nilus Strangesøns Stenstue.*]

Oh, Seventy-seven. Tr. E. M. Smith-Dampier. *BoDB* pp 90-96. [*De vare syv og syvsindstyve.*]

The Outlaw. Tr. Alexander Gray. *FaF* pp 67-69. [*Jon rømmer af Land.*]

The Outlaws. Tr. Henry Meyer. *DB&FS* pp 70-71. [*De Fredløse.*]

The Power of Music. Tr. Henry Meyer. *THB* pp 10-11. Also *DB&FS* pp 31-32. [*Harpens Kraft.*]

The Power of the Harp. Tr. Alexander Gray. *FaF* pp 7-11. [*Harpens Kraft.*]

The Pridefu' Lass. Tr. Alexander Gray. *FaF* pp 127-130. [*Kong Erik og den spotske Jomfru.*]

Prood Signild and Queen Sophia. Tr. Alexander Gray. *FaF* pp 63-66. [*Stolt Signild og Dronning Sophia.*]

Proud Ellensborg. Tr. E. M. Smith-Dampier. *BoDB* pp 318-322. [*Stalt Ellensborg.*]

Queen Bengerd. Tr. E. M. Smith-Dampier. *BoDB* pp 150-152. [*Dronning Bengerd.*]

Queen Dagmar's Death. Tr. Henry Meyer. *THB* pp 22-25. [*Dronning Dagmars Død.*]

Queen Dagmar's Death. Tr. Henry Meyer. *DB&FS* pp 60-64, [*Dronning Dagmars Død.*] [Different version of Meyer's translation than in *THB.*]

The Raid of the King of Norway. Tr. Alexander Gray. *FaF* pp 179-182. [*Venderkongens Jomfrurov.*]

Ranil's Wedding. Tr. Alexander Gray. *FaF* pp 70-72. [*Rane Jonsøns Giftermaal.*]

Ribold and Goldborg. Tr. E. M. Smith-Dampier. *BoDB* pp 247-249. [*Ribold og Guldborg.*]

Ribold and Guldborg. Tr. Alexander Gray. *FaF* pp 49-52. [*Ribold og Guldborg.*]

St. Olaf and the Trolls. Tr. E. M. Smith-Dampier. *BODB* pp 109-112. [*Hellig Oluf og Troldene.*]

St. Olav's Race. Tr. Henry Meyer. *DB&FS* pp 49-52. [*Hellig Olavs Væddefart.*]

The Serpent Bride. Tr. E. M. Smith-Dampier. *BoDB* pp 271-272. [*Jomfru i Ormeham.*]

Sigurd and Hamling. Tr. Maud Karpeles. *Folk Songs of Europe.* Ed. Maud Karpeles. London: Novello & Co., Ltd., 1956. New York: Oak Publications, 1964. pp 2-3. [*Kong Diderik og hans Kæmper.*] [Danish text and guitar music included.]

Sir Bosmer in Elfland. Tr. E. M. Smith-Dampier. *BoDB* pp 257-260. [*Hr. Bøsmer i Elverhjem.*]

Sir Bosmer in Elfland. Tr. Alexander Gray. *FaF* pp 18-21. [*Hr. Bøsmer i Elverhjem.*]

Sir Cauline and Sir Guy. Tr. Alexander Gray. *FaF* pp 137-139. [*Esbern Snare.*]

Sir David and His Stepsons. Tr. E. M. Smith-Dampier. *BoDB* pp 331-334. [*Hr. David og hans Stesønner.*]

Sir Helmer. Tr. Alexander Gray. *FaF* pp 35-37. [*Hr. Hjelm.*]

Sir Hjelm. Tr. E. M. Smith-Dampier. *BoDB* pp 303-306. [*Hr. Hjælm.*]

Sir John the Outlaw. Tr. E. M. Smith-Dampier. *BoDB* pp 206-208. [*Jon rømmer af Land.*]

Sir Karel on His Bier. Tr. Alexander Gray. *FaF* pp 164-166. [*Hr. Karl paa Ligbaare.*]

Sir Karel's Lykewake. Tr. E. M. Smith-Dampier. *BoDB* pp 335-337. [*Hr. Karl paa Ligbaare.*]

Sir Laurens Steals a Bride. Tr. E. M. Smith-Dampier. *BoDB* pp 288-292. [*Laurens bortfører Bente Sunesdatter.*]

142 **Sir Luno and the Mermaid.** Tr. E. M. Smith-Dampier. *BoDB* pp 250-252. Also *The World in Literature.* Ed. Robert Warnock and George K. Anderson. Chicago: Scott, Foresman and Co., 1950. Rev. ed. 1967. pp 261-262. [*Hr. Luno og Havfruen.*]

Sir Malcolm in Prison. Tr. Alexander Gray. *FaF* pp 134-136. [*Hr. Verner i Fangetaarn.*]

Sir Morten of Fogelsang. Tr. Alexander Gray. *FaF* pp 86-88. [*Hr. Morten af Fuglsang.*]

Sir Oluf and His Gilded Horn. Tr. E. M. Smith-Dampier. *BoDB* pp 268-271. [*Hr. Oluf og hans forgyldte Ljud.*]

Sir Oluf and His Magic Lute. Tr. Alexander Gray. *FaF* pp 120-124. [*Hr. Oluf og hans forgyldte Ljud.*]

Sir Palle's Bridal. Tr. E. M. Smith-Dampier. *BoDB* pp 326-329. [*Rige Hr. Palles Bryllup.*]

Sir Peter & Sir Oluf. *European Folk Ballads.* Ed. Erich Seemann, Dag Strömbäck and Bengt Jonsson. European Folklore Series, vol. 2. Copenhagen: Rosenkilde and Bagger for Council for Cultural Co-operation of the Council of Europe, 1967. pp 59-65. [*Ridderens Runeslag.*] [Danish text included.]

Sir Peter's Harp. Tr. E. M. Smith-Dampier. *BoDB* pp 223-224. [*Hr. Peders Harpe.*]

Sir Peter's Leman. Tr. E. M. Smith-Dampier. *BoDB* pp 229-231. [*Hr. Peders Slegfred.*]

Sir Stig and His Runes. Tr. E. M. Smith-Dampier. *BoDB* pp 280-285. [*Ridder Stigs Runer.*]

Sir Stig's Runes. Tr. Alexander Gray. *FaF* pp 113-117. [*Ridder Stigs Runer.*]

Sir Verner's Escape. Tr. E. M. Smith-Dampier. *BoDB* pp 233-234. [*Hr. Verner i Fangetaarn.*]

Sir Walter's Daughter. Tr. Alexander Gray. *FaF* pp 40-42. [*Torbens Datter.*]

Sister Woos Brother. Tr. Henry Meyer. *DB&FS* pp 141-143. [*Søster beder Broder.*]

Siuord and Brynild. *European Folk Ballads.* Ed. Erich Seeman, Dag Strömbäck and Bengt Jonsson. European Folklore Series, vol. 2. Copenhagen: Rosenkilde and Bagger for Council for Cultural Co-operation of the Council of Europe, 1967. pp 145-149. [*Siuord og Brynild.*] [Danish text included.]

The Slaying at Thord Iverson. Tr. E. M. Smith-Dampier. *BoBV* pp 310-313. [*Aage fælder Tord Iversøn.*]

Son, Come Tell to Me. Tr. Maud Karpeles. *Folk Songs of Europe.* Ed. Maud Karpeles. London: Novello & Co., 1956. New York: Oak Publications, 1964. p 4. [*Svend i Rosengaard,* ballad.] [Danish text and guitar music included.]

Song of the Falcon. Tr. E. M. Smith-Dampier. *AScL* pp 17-18. Also *BoDB* pp 237-240. [*Falken og Duen.*]

The Sorrows of Hillelille. Tr. Alexander Gray. *FaF* pp 53-56. [*Hillelilles Sorg.*]

The Soul of the Child. Tr. Henry Meyer. *DB&FS* pp 54-56. [*Barnesjælen.*]

Squire Lavers. Tr. Alexander Gray. *HBD* pp 80-84. [*Laurens bortfører Bente Sunesdatter.*]

The Stolen Bride. Tr. E. M. Smith-Dampier. *BoDB* pp 286-288. [*Venderkongens Jomfrurov.*]

Svend among Rosebeds So Near. Tr. Henry Meyer. *THB* pp 18-19. [*Svend i Rosengård.*]

Svend Felding. Tr. Henry Meyer. *DB&FS* pp 103-108. [*Svend Felding.*]

Svend in the Rose Garden. Tr. Henry Meyer. *DB&FS* pp 133-134. [*Svend i Rosengård.*]

Svend Normand. (Svend Vonved). Tr. Henry Meyer. *DB&FS* pp 89-92. [*Svend Normand.*]

Svend of Vollerslov. Tr. E. M. Smith-Dampier. *BoDB* pp 306-310. [*Svend af Vollersløv.*]

The Talking Harp. Tr. Henry Meyer. *DB&FS* pp 46-48. [*Den talende Strengeleg.*]

Tit for Tat. Tr. E. M. Smith-Dampier. *BoDB* pp 219-220. [*Svar som Tiltale.*]

Torben's Daughter. Tr. E. M. Smith-Dampier. *BoDB* pp 204-205. [*Torbens Datter.*]

Torben's Daughter and His Slayer. Tr. Henry Meyer. *THB* pp 16-17. Also *DB&FS* pp 120-121. [*Torbens Datter og hendes Faderbane.*]

Torben's Daughter and His Slayer. Tr. Henry Meyer. *ADL* pp 10-13. [*Torbens Datter og hendes Faderbane.*] [Different version of Meyer's translation than in *THB.*]

Two Brides and One Groom. Tr. E. M. Smith-Dampier. *BoDB* pp 329-331. [*To Brude om een Brudgom.*]

Ulver and Vaenilil. Tr. Alexander Gray. *FaF* pp 45-48. [*Ulver og Vænilil.*]

Valdemar and Tove. Version A and Version B. Tr. Alexander Gray. *HBD* pp 33-39. [*Valdemar og Tove.*]

Valdemar and Tove (A). Tr. E. M. Smith-Dampier. *BoDB* pp 133-135. [*Valdemar og Tove.*]

Valdemar and Tove (B). Tr. E. M. Smith-Dampier. *BoDB* pp 135-138. Also *A Pageant of Old Scandinavia.* Ed. Henry Goddard Leach. 1946; rpt. Freeport, N. Y.: Books for Libraries Press, 1968. pp 293-295. [*Valdemar og Tove (B).*]

Valdemar and Tovelil. Tr. Henry Meyer. *DB&FS* pp 57-60. [*Valdemar og Tove.*]

Valraven and the Danish King. Tr. E. M. Smith-Dampier. *BoDB* pp 231-233. [*Valraven og Danskekongen.*]

The Wedding of Rane Jonson. Tr. E. M. Smith-Dampier. *BoDB* pp 293-294. [*Rane Jonsøns Giftermaal.*]

The Woman-Murderer. Tr. Henry Meyer. *DB&FS* pp 127-130. [*Kvindemorderen.*]

The Wood-Raven. Tr. E. M. Smith-Dampier. *BoDB* pp 274-277. [*Valravnen.*]

The Wounded Maiden. Tr. E. M. Smith-Dampier. *BoDB* pp 221-222. [*Den saarede Jomfru.*]

The Wounded Maiden. Tr. Alexander Gray. *FaF* pp 161-163. [*Den saarede Jomfru.*]

Wulfstan and Venelil. Tr. E. M. Smith-Dampier. *BoDB* pp 253-255. [*Ulver og Vænelil.*]

Young Danneved and Swain Trust. Tr. E. M. Smith-Dampier. *BoDB* pp 301-303. [*Unge Danneved og Svend Trøst.*]

Young Engel. Tr. E. M. Smith-Dampier. *BoDB* pp 195-202. Also *The World in Literature*. Ed. Robert Warnock and George K. Anderson. Chicago: Scott, Foresman and Co., 1950. Rev. ed. 1967. pp 259-261. [*Liden Engel.*]

The Young Man's Dream. Tr. Henry Meyer. *DB&FS* pp 143-144. [*Ungersvends Drøm.*]

Young Squire Dyre. Tr. Alexander Gray. *FaF* pp 170-174. [*Unge Svend Dyre.*]

Young Svejdal. Tr. E. M. Smith-Dampier. *BoDB* pp 120-124. [*Ungen Svejdal.*]

Young Svend Dyre. Tr. E. M. Smith-Dampier. *BoDB* pp 322-326. [*Unge Svend Dyre.*]

Bødker, Laurits. **The Brave Tailor in Danish Tradition.** *Studies in Folklore in Honor of Distinguished Service Professor Stith Thompson.* Bloomington: Indiana Univ. Press, 1957. pp 1-23. [A Study of AT1640 as it appears in Denmark.]

Christophersen, Paul. **The Ballad of Sir Aldingar: Its Origin and Analogues.** Oxford: Clarendon Press, 1952. p 258.

Jones, W. Glyn. **Valdemar and Tove - from Danish Ballad to Schönberg's Gurrelieder.** *Mosaic* (Manitoba) vol. 4, no. 2 (1970) pp 29-45. [Issue on *Scandinavian Literature: Reality and Vision.*]

Jørgensen, Aage. **Some Recent Contributions to Danish Ballad Research.** *Folklore* (London) vol. 87 (1976) pp 186-191. Also *Annali. Sezione Germanica* (Napoli) vol. 16, no. 3 (1973) pp 227-235.

Kabell, Aage. **DgF90 and the Danish Novel.** *Scandinavica* vol. 6, no. 2 (Nov. 1967) pp 85-94.

Piø, Iørn. **On Reading Orally-performed Ballads: The Medieval Ballads of Denmark.** *Oral Tradition, Literary Tradition; a Symposium.* Odense: Odense University Press, 1977. pp 69-82.

Richmond, W. Edson. **Some Norwegian Contributions to a Danish Ballad.** In *Studies in Folklore in Honor of Distinguished Service*

Professor Stith Thompson. Bloomington: Indiana Univ. Press, 1957. pp 177-186. [About *Frederik den Anden i Ditmarsken.*]

Rossel, Sven H. **The Medieval Ballad in Danish Literature until 1800.** *SS* vol. 49, no. 4 (Autumn 1977) pp 412-438.

Steenstrup, Johannes and Christopher Hagemann Reinhardt. **The Medieval Popular Ballad.** Tr. Edward Godfrey Cox. Seattle & London: University of Washington Press, 1968. New ed. includes foreword by David C. Fowler and bibliographic essay by Karl-Ivar Hildeman. p 269. [Rpt. of the 1914 trans. of the 1891 original.]

Syndergaard, Larry Edvard. **English-Scottish and Danish Popular Ballads. A Comparative Study.** Ph. D. diss., University of Wisconsin, 1970. (p 399). [Diss. Abstr. 31/10-A, 5377.]

Faroese Literature

1) Ballads

Ballad of William Curt-Nose. Tr. from the Faroese by E. M. Smith-Dampier. *ASR* vol. 40, no. 2 (June 1952) pp 134-135.

Sigurd and the Dragon. Tr. Maud Karpeles. *Folk Songs of Europe.* Ed. Maud Karpeles. London: Novello & Co., Ltd., 1956. New York: Oak Publications, 1964. pp 8-9. [*Sjurðar Kvæði.*] [Faroese text and guitar music included.]

Sigurd the Dragon-slayer. A Faroese Ballad-cycle. Tr. and intro. E. M. Smith-Dampier. New York: Kraus Reprint Co., 1969. Orig. pub. 1934. [*Sjurður Kvæði.*]

Song of Roland: Burden. The First Winding of the Horn. Karlmagnus Takes the Field. Conclusion. Tr. E. M. Smith-Dampier. With an introduction. *ASR* vol. 40, no. 1 (March 1952) pp 41-43.

Stephen He Looked Out. *European Folk Ballads.* Ed. Erich Seemann, Dag Strömbäck and Bengt Jonsson. European Folklore Series, vol. 2. Copenhagen: Rosenkilde and Bagger for Council for Cultural Co-operation of the Council of Europe, 1967. pp 187-191. [*Rúdisar visa.*] [Faroese text included.]

O'Neil. Wayne A. **The Oral-Formulaic Structure of the Faroese Kvaedi.** *Fróðskapparit Annales Societatis Scientiarum Faeroensis* (Tórshavn) vol. 18, 1970. pp 59-68.

144   2) **Folk Literature**

Agnus Dei. Tr. from the Faroese by E. M. Smith-Dampier. *ASR* vol. 38, no. 3 (September 1950) p 251. [Faroese folk song.]

Upsala-Paetur's Christmas, A Faroese Legend. Tr. Hedin Brønner. *ASR* vol. 57, no. 4 (December 1969) pp 397-399. [Legend entitled *Upsala-Pætur*, recorded by Jakob Jakobsen in the 1890s and published in his collection *Færøske Folkesagn og Eventyr*, 1898-1901.]

3) **Saga**

The Faroe Islanders' Saga. Tr. and ed. George Johnston. Drawings by William Heinesen. Ottawa: Oberon Press, 1975. p 144. [*Færeyinga saga.*]

The Faroese Saga Freely Translated with Maps and Genealogical Tables. By G. V. C. Young and Cynthis R. Clewer. Belfast: Century Services Ltd., 1973. p 60. Ill. [*Færeyinga saga.*]

Foote, Peter. **A Note on Some Personal Names in »Faereyinga saga«.** In *Otium et negotium. Studies in Onomatology and Library Science Presented to Olof von Feilitzen.* Ed. Folke Sandgren. Stockholm: Norstedt, 1973. pp 96-108. Also issued as *Acta Bibliotheca Regiae Stockholmiensis*, vol. XVI.

Foote, Peter. **On Legal Terms in Faereyinga Saga.** *Fróðskapparit Annales Societatis Scientiarum Faeroensis* (Tórshavn) vol. 18, 1970.

Foote, Peter. **On the Saga of the Faroe Islanders. An Inaugural Lecture Delivered at University College London, 12 November 1964.** London: H. K. Lewis & Co., 1965. p 24.

Folk Songs

The Banquet of the Bird. Tr. Henry Meyer. *DB&FS* pp 151-155. [*Fuglegildet*, jocular folk song.]

The Beautiful Tree. Tr. Henry Meyer. *DB&FS* pp 217-218. [*Det fagre Træ*, folk song.]

A Better Bargain. Tr. Henry Meyer. *DB&FS* pp 159-160. [*Her bliver vel bedre Køb*, jocular folk song.]

The Big Crow. Tr. Henry Meyer. *DB&FS* pp 164-165. [*Den store Krage*, jocular folk song.]

The Cassock. Tr. Henry Meyer. *DB&FS* pp 185-186. [*Munkekappen*, folk song.]

Cobbler and Nobleman. Tr. Henry Meyer. *DB&FS* pp 195-200. [*Skomager og Edelmand*, folk song.]

Danyser. (Tannhäuser). Tr. Henry Meyer. *DB&FS* pp 191-195. [*Danyser*, folk song.]

Disappointment Overcome. Tr. Henry Meyer. *DB&FS* pp 235-236. [*Overvunden Skuffelse*, folk song.]

Erik Lange to Sophie Brahe. Tr. Henry Meyer. *DB&FS* pp 222-224. [*E. L. til S. B.*, folk song. First line: *Lad fare, min Sjæl, din høje Attraa.*]

Faithlessness. Tr. Henry Meyer. *DB&FS* pp 255-256. [*Verdens Troløshed*, folk song.]

A Farmer Lived on a Danish Farm. Tr. Martin S. Allwood and Inga Wilhelmsen. *ScSoB* pp 9-10. [*Det var en god gammel Bondemand*, folk song.]

The German Band. Tr. S. D. Rodholm. *HoS* pp 177-178. [*Fra Tyskland uddrog*, children's song.]

Grandmother. Tr. S. D. Rodholm. *HoS* pp 174-175. [*Slig en Bedstemor som min*, children's song.]

Happiness in Love. Tr. Henry Meyer. *DB&FS* pp 221-222. [*Kærlighedslykke*, folk song.]

The Heart So True. Tr. Henry Meyer. *DB&FS* p 219. [*Et trofast Hjerte af al min Agt*, folk song.]

His Sweetheart's Death. Tr. Henry Meyer. *DB&FS* pp 212-213. [*Den Kærestes Død*, folk song.]

Jerusalem's Cobbler. Tr. Henry Meyer. *DB&FS* pp 171-175. [*Jerusalems Skomager*, folk song.]

The Jilted Maid. Tr. Henry Meyer. *DB&FS* pp 237-238. [*Den forskudte Pige*, folk song.]

Johny, Get Up! Tr. S. D. Rodholm. *HoS* p 176. [*Op, lille Hans*, children's song.]

The Lad Who Was Fooled. Tr. Henry Meyer. *DB&FS* pp 160-162. [*Den narrede Ungersvend*, jocular folk song.]

Lie and Truth. Tr. Henry Meyer. *DB&FS* pp 182-185. [*Løgn og Sandhed*, folk song.]

The Lost Falcon. Tr. Henry Meyer. *DB&FS* pp 201-202. [*Den bortfløjne Falk*, folk song.]

The Maid Who Trod on the Loaf. Tr. Henry Meyer. *DB&FS* pp 176-179. [*Pigen, der trådte på Brødet*, folk song.]

The Master's Counsel. Tr. Henry Meyer. *DB&FS* pp 155-158. [*Mesterens Råd*, jocular folk song.]

May Song. Tr. Henry Meyer. *DB&FS* pp 186-188. [*En Majvise*, folk song.]

The Nightingale Sent to the King. Tr. Henry Meyer. *DB&FS* pp 232-235. [*Nattergal sendes til Kongen*, folk song.]

On Saturday I Waited. Tr. Martin S. Allwood and Yvonne Parkes. *ScSoB* pp 35-36. [*Det var en Lørdag Aften*, folk song.]

Peasant's Wife Visits Courtier. Tr. Henry Meyer. *DB&FS* pp 162-164. [*Bondens Kone besøger Hovmand*, jocular folk song.]

Per Ræv Lille's Love Song. Tr. Henry Meyer. *DB&FS* pp 210-211. [*Per Ræv Lilles Kærlighedsvise*, folk song.]

The Princess and the Vagabond. Tr. S. D. Rodholm. *HoS* pp 152-154. [*Prinsessen sad i Højeloft*, folk song.]

The Re-union. Tr. Henry Meyer. *DB&FS* pp 207-209. [*Genkendelsen*, folk song.]

The Red Rosebud. Tr. Maud Karpeles. *Folk Songs of Europe.* Ed. Maud Karpeles. London: Novello & Co., Ltd., 1956. New York: Oak Publications, 1964. p 5. [*En yndig og frydefuld Sommer*, folk song.] [Danish text and guitar music included.]

The Rich Sister's Punishment. Tr. Henry Meyer. *DB&FS* pp 180-181. [*Rige Søsters Straf*, folk song.]

The Rose of Love. Tr. Henry Meyer. *DB&FS* pp 238-240. [*Kærlighedsrosen*, folk song.]

Rosina. Tr. Henry Meyer. *DB&FS* p 220. [*Rosina*, folk song.]

A Sad Complaint of Separation. Tr. Henry Meyer. *DB&FS* pp 213-217. [*Et bedrøveligt Klagemål over Skilsmisse*, folk song.]

Sophie Brahe to Erik Lange. Tr. Henry Meyer. *DB&FS* pp 225-232. [*S.B. til E.L.*, folk song. First line: *Nu vil jeg for Eder kvæde.*]

The Ten Maidens' Songs. Tr. Henry Meyer. *DB&FS* pp 169-170. [*De ti Jomfruers Vise*, folk song.]

The Three Noblemen. Tr. Henry Meyer. *DB&FS* pp 205-207. [*De tre Grever*, folk song.]

The Tree in the Forest. Tr. Maud Karpeles. *Folk Songs of Europe.* Ed. Maud Karpeles. London: Novello & Co., Ltd., 1956. New York: Oak Publications, 1964. pp 6-7. [*Langt udi Skoven*, folk song.] [Danish text and guitar music included.]

Twas on a Saturday Evening. Tr. Henry Meyer. *DB&FS* pp 236-237. [*Det var en Lørdag Aften*, folk song.]

The Two Royal Children. Tr. Henry Meyer. *DB&FS* pp 189-191. [*De to Kongebørn*, folk song.]

Unhappy Love. Tr. S. D. Rodholm. *HoS* pp 155-156. [*Det var en Lørdag Aften*, folk song.]

Upside Down Ditty. Tr. Henry Meyer. *DB&FS* pp 165-166. [*Bagvendt Vise*, jocular folk song.]

Watchman's Song. Tr. Henry Meyer. *DB&FS* pp 203-205. [*En Vægtervise*, folk song.]

The Wedding of the Fly. Tr. Henry Meyer. *DB&FS* pp 149-150. [*Fluens Bryllup*, jocular folk song.]

Folk Tales

Danish Fairy Tales. Retold by Inge Hack. New York: Follett, 1967. p 194.

Danish Fairy Tales. By Svend Grundtvig. Tr. J. Grant Cramer. Ill. Drew Van Heusen. 1919; rpt. New York: Dover Publications; London: Constable, 1972. p 124. Ill.

Fairy Tales of Denmark. Retold by Reginald Spink. Ill. Carl Hollander. London: Cassell; New York: Dutton, 1961. p 44. Ill. [Fairy Tales of Many Lands.]

Old Stories from Denmark. Ill. Axel Mathiesen. Ebeltoft: Kaj Elles boghandel, 1953. p 31. Ill. [*Molbohistorier.*]

Old Stories from Denmark. Ill. Poul Lundsgaard. Ebeltoft: Kaj Elles boghandel, 1967. p 31. [*Molbohistorier.*]

Old Stories from Mols. 20 funny stories about the humour-loving people of Mols. Ill. Axel Mathiesen. Ebeltoft: Kaj Elles boghandel, 1952. p 32. [*Molbohistorier.*]

Greenland Literature

Eskimo Poems from Canada and Greenland. Tr. Tom Lowenstein from material originally collected by Knud Rasmussen. London: Allison & Busby; Pittsburgh: University of Pittsburgh Press, 1973. p 149. [From *Snehyttens Sange*, 1930.]

Eskimo Songs: Songs about the Narwhales, Dead Man's Song, Dead Man's Song (2), Greeting to the Women of the Feastinghouse, Abduction, Sun and the Moon and the Fear of Loneliness, My Breath. Tr. from the Danish by Tom Lowenstein. *Chicago Review* vol. 24 no. 2 (1972) pp 126-133.

Eskimo Songs and Stories. Collected by Knud Rasmussen on the Fifth Thule Expedition. Selected and trans. Edward Field. Ill. Kiakshuk & Pudlo. New York: Delacorte Press / S. Lawrence, 1973. p 102. Ill. [From *Myter og Sagn*, vol. III, 1925.]

146 **The Great Hunter from Aluk, Whose Heart Broke When He Saw the Sin over His Settlement. A Legend.** *DFOJ* 58 (1967) pp 48-49. Ill.

Kågssagssuk. The Legend of the Orphan Boy. Tr. H. C. Huus. Ill. Jakob Danielsen. Preface Ph. Rosendahl. Lyngby: Lyngby Kunstforening, 1967. p 65. Ill. [*Sagnet om den Forældreløse*, Danish-English-Greenlandic text.]

Song of the Old Woman. Tr. from Greenl. into French by Paul-Emile Victor. Into English by Armand Schwerner. *The Other Voice. Twentieth-Century Women's Poetry in Translation.* New York: W. W. Norton, 1976. p 51. [Poem collected by Paul-Emile Victor at Angmagssalik, 1935, and published in *Poèmes esquimaux*, 1951.]

An Unusual Bearhunt. By Knud Rasmussen. Copenhagen: Inge og Carl Gustav Thorborg, 1956. p 42. [*Bjørnen i Vågen*, story from *I Bjørnejægernes og Aandemanernes Land.*] [Danish-English text.]

A Woman's Song about Men. Tr. from Greenl. into French by Paul-Emile Victor. Into English by Armand Schwerner. *The Other Voice. Twentieth-Century Women's Poetry in Translation.* New York: W. W. Norton, 1976. p 72. [Poem collected by Paul-Emile Victor at Angmagssalik, 1935, and published in *Poèmes esquimaux*, 1951.]

Rasmussen, Knud. **Tales from Greenland.** *J. L. News* (J. Lauritzen Lines, Copenhagen) no. 37. p 28.

van Dommelen, David B. **Folklore of the Greenland Eskimos.** *ASR* vol. 50, no. 1 (March 1962) pp 49-52.

DANISH LITERATURE
IN ENGLISH TRANSLATION
1950-1980

C. Anthologies

Anthology of Danish Literature. Ed. P. M. Mitchell and F. J. Billeskov-Jansen. Carbondale, Ill.: Southern Illinois University Press, 1972. p 606. hb.
Also as a two volume paperback, same year, same pagination. [Bilingual edition - Danish-English text.] [English version, with corrections and additions, of the Danish-French edition, 1964.]

An Anthology of Scandinavian Literature. From the Viking Period to the Twentieth Century. Ed. Hallberg Hallmundsson. New York: Collier-MacMillan Ltd., 1965. p 362.

A Book of Danish Ballads. Selected and intro. Axel Olrik. Tr. E. M. Smith-Dampier. 1939; rpt. New York: Books for Libraries Press, 1968. p 337. [Granger Index Reprint Series.]

Book of Danish Verse. Selected and annotated by Oluf Friis. Tr. in the original meters by S. Foster Damon and Robert Silliman Hillyer. 1922; rpt. New York: Kraus Reprint Co., 1976. p 176.

Contemporary Danish Plays. An Anthology. Intro. and supervision of trans. Elias Bredsdorff. Copenhagen: Gyldendal, 1955; rpt. Freeport, N. Y.: Books for Libraries Press, 1970. p 556.

Contemporary Danish Poetry. An Anthology. Ed. Line Jensen, Erik Vagn Jensen, Knud Mogensen and Alexander Taylor. Intro. Torben Brostrøm. Boston: Twayne Publishers, 1977. p 343. [Published under the auspices of the Danish Ministry of Cultural Affairs, with the cooperation of Gyldendal.] [The Library of Scandinavian Literature, vol. 31.]

Contemporary Danish Prose. An Anthology. Supervision of trans. and notes Elias Bredsdorff. Intro. F. J. Billeskov-Jansen. Copenhagen: Gyldendal, 1958; rpt. Westport. Connecticut: Greenwood Press, 1974. p 376.

Danish Ballads and Folk Songs. Selected and edited by Erik Dal. Tr. Henry Meyer. Woodcuts by Marcel Rasmussen. Copenhagen and New York: The American-Scandinavian Foundation and Rosenkilde and Bagger, 1967. p 303. [Revised and trans. ed. of *Danske Viser: Gamle Folkeviser. Skæmt. Efterklang*, 1962.]

The Devil's Instrument and Other Danish Stories. Ed. Sven Holm. Intro. Elias Bredsdorff. Tr. Paula Hostrup-Jessen. London: Peter Owen, 1971. p 266. [UNESCO Collection of Contemporary Works.]

Faroese Short Stories. Ed., tr. and intro. Hedin Brønner. New York: Twayne Publishers, 1972. p 267.

Five Modern Scandinavian Plays. Intro. by Henry H. Wells. New York: The American-Scandinavian Foundation and Twayne Publishers, 1971. p 424. [Library of Scandinavian Literature, vol. 11.]

Four and Forty. A Selection of Danish Ballads Presented in Scots. Tr., and with intro. and notes by Alexander Gray. Edinburgh: The University Press; Chicago: Albine Publishing Co., 1954. p 184. Ill.

The Genius of the Scandinavian Theater. Ed. and with intro. by Evert Sprinchorn. New York: New American Library of World Literature, 1964. p 637.

A Harvest of Song: Translations and Original Lyrics. By S. D. Rodholm. With a biographical sketch by Enok Mortensen. Des Moines: American Lutheran Church, 1953. p 193.

The Heart Book: The Tradition of the Danish Ballad. Idea, drawing and layout, Povl Abrahamsen. Text in collaboration with Erik Dal. Copenhagen: Royal Danish Ministry of Foreign Affairs, 1965. p 41. Ill. [Presentation Books, no. 3.]

Historical Ballads of Denmark. Tr. Alexander Gray. Ill. Edward Bawden and George Mackie. Edinburgh: The University Press, 1958. p 158. Ill.

A Heritage in Song. Ed. Johannes Knudsen. Ill. Philip Tascone. Askov, Minnesota: The American Publishing Company for the Danish Interest Conference of the Lutheran Church in America, 1978. Unp. Ill.

In Denmark I Was Born... A Little Book of Danish Verse. Selected and trans. (with contributions by other hands) by R. P. Keigwin. Copenhagen: Høst, 1950. p 112. [First ed. 1948.]

Modern Danish Authors. Evelyn Heepe and Niels Heltberg, eds. Tr. Evelyn Heepe. 1946; rpt. Folcroft, Pennsylvania: Folcroft Library Editions, 1974. p 222.

Modern Danish Poems. Ed. Knud K. Mogensen. Tr. Martin S. Allwood. 2nd ed. Copenhagen: Høst, 1951. [1st ed., 1949.] p 47. [Later included in *Twentieth Century Scandinavian Poetry.*]

Modern Nordic Plays: Denmark. Intro. Per Olsen. Tr. Pat Shaw. Oslo: Universitetsforlaget; New York: Twayne Publishers, 1974. p 449. [The Library of Scandinavian Literature, vol. 21.]

Modern Scandinavian Plays. By August Strindberg and others. New York: Liveright Corporation and The American-Scandinavian Foundation, 1954. p 366.

150 **The Royal Guest and Other Classical Danish Narrative.** Tr. and ed. P. M. Mitchell and Kenneth H. Ober. Chicago and London: The University of Chicago Press, 1977. p 235.

Scandinavian Plays of the Twentieth Century. Intro. A. Gustafson. 1944; rpt. New York: Kraus Reprint Co., 1972. 2 vols.

Scandinavian Songs and Ballads. Modern Swedish, Danish and Norwegian Songs. Ed. Martin S. Allwood. Music ed. Lindsay Lafford. Selected guitar accompaniments by Kurt Strid. Tr. Martin S. Allwood, Helen Asbury and Lars Forsell. Copenhagen: Arne Frost-Hansens Forlag; Mullsjö, Sweden: Anglo-American Center, 1953. p 56.

A Second Book of Danish Verse. Tr. and compiled by Charles Wharton Stork. Foreword by Johannes V. Jensen. 1947; rpt. Freeport, N. Y.: Books for Libraries Press, 1968. p 155.

Swans of the North and Short Stories by Modern Danish Authors. Tr. Evelyn Heepe. Copenhagen: Gad, 1953. p 84.

Twentieth Century Scandinavian Poetry. The Development of Poetry in Iceland, Denmark, Norway, Sweden and Finland, 1900-1950. Ed. Martin S. Allwood. Copenhagen: Gyldendal, 1950. p 397. Danish section ed. Knud K. Mogensen.

BOOKS ABOUT DENMARK
1950-1980

A Selection

Agriculture

Agricultural Policy in Denmark. Paris: OECD, 1974. p 63.

Agriculture in Denmark. Annotated Statistics. Copenhagen: The Agricultural Council of Denmark, 1974. p 24.

Cohen, Marshall H. **The Agricultural Economy and Trade of Denmark.** Washington, D. C.: Economic Research Service, U. S. Dept. of Agriculture, 1968. p 18. Ill.

Cohen, Marshall H. **Summary of: Projections of Supply and Demand for Agricultural Products in Denmark (1970-1980).** Washington, D. C.: U. S. Dept. of Agriculture, Economic Research Service, 1970. p 54. [ERS-foreign 303. Summary of a study conducted at the University of Århus.]

Danish Agriculture. Denmark as a Food Producer. Copenhagen & London: Danish Agricultural Organisations, 1954. p 96. Ill. 3rd ed. 1960. p 100. [Danish Agricultural Producers' Information Service.]

Ellert, Holger, ed. **The Dairy Industry of Denmark.** Århus: The Federation of Danish Dairy Associations, 1962. p 152. Ill.

Federation of Danish Dairy Associations. **Denmark Calling.** Århus: De danske Mejeriforeningers Fællesorganisationer, 1957. p 80. Ill.

Federation of Danish Dairy Associations. **Facts about the Danish Dairy Industry.** Århus: Federation of Danish Dairy Associations, 1962. p 66. Ill.

Heigham, N. **Agricultural Ideas and Practice and Social Conditions in Denmark, 1756-1786.** Ph. D. dissertation, Oxford University, 1964.

Institute of Farm Management and Agricultural Economics. **Technical and Economic Changes in Danish Farming. 40 Years of Farm Records 1917-1957.** Copenhagen: Landhusholdningsselskabet, 1959. p 75.

Jensen, Peter. **A Page from the History of the Cheese Trade in Denmark.** Copenhagen: Firmaet Peter Jensen, 1951. p 40. Ill.

Kampp, Aa. H. **An Agricultural Geography of Denmark.** Budapest: Akadémiai Kiadó, 1975. p 87. Ill.

Knudsen, P. H., ed. **Agriculture in Denmark.** London: Land Books, 1967. p 230. Ill.

Knudsen, P. H., ed. **Agriculture in Denmark.** Tr. F. A. Rush. Copenhagen: The Agricultural Council of Denmark, 1977. p 227. Ill. [*Landbruget i Danmark.*]

Landbrugsministeriet. **Livestock Products from Denmark. Quality Control.** Copenhagen: Landbrugsministeriet, 1961. p 36. Ill.

Landbrugsraadet. **Facts about Danish Agriculture. 1955-1959.** Copenhagen: Landbrugsraadet, 1955-1959. p 16.

Martin, Nancy (pseud.). **Young Farmers in Denmark.** By Nancy Martin, pseud. for Annie Elizabeth Salmon. Ill. Stuart Tresilian. London: Macmillan & Co.; New York: St. Martin's Press, 1954. p 176. Ill.

Mitchison, Naomi. **Karensgaard. The Story of a Danish Farm.** London: Collins, 1961. p 192. Ill.

Nash, E. F. **The Agricultural Policies of Britain and Denmark: a Study in Reciprocal Trade.** By E. F. Nash and E. A. Attwood. London: Land Books, 1961. p 94.

Petersen, Einar Ol. **Danish Dairying. Production, Manufacture, Organization and Marketing.** Tr. G. H. Wilster. Copenhagen: Technical Dairy Publishing House, 1956. 2nd ed. 1963. p 153. Ill.

Pritchard, Norris Taylor. **Food Marketing in Denmark: Developments, Prospects for 1980, Significance for U. S. Exports.** Washington, D. C.: U. S. Department of Agriculture, 1971. p 48. [Foreign Agricultural Economic Report no. 72.]

Rush, F. A. **Denmark Farms on . . . Danish Farm Products Today.** London: Danish Agricultural Producers, 1970. p 127. Ill.

Special Issue of the Danish Foreign Office Journal for the XVIth International Dairy Congress. Copenhagen: Ministry of Foreign Affairs, 1961. p 40. Ill. [Vol. 37.]

Spink, Reginald. **DBC, the Story of the Danish Bacon Company, 1902-1977.** Welwyn Garden City, Herts: DBC Ltd., 1977. p 96. Ill.

Steensberg, Axel. **Farms and Water Mills in Denmark during 2,000 Years.** With a contribution by Valdemar M. Mikkelsen. Copenhagen: Alfred G. Hassing, 1952. p 325. Ill. [The National Museum. 3rd Dept. Researches into Village Archaeology. Danish-English text.]

Webster, F. H. **Agricultural Co-operation in Denmark.** Oxford: The Plunkett Foundation for Co-operative Studies, 1973. p 152. Ill.

Agriculture - Periodicals

Danish Dairy Industry . . . Worldwide. Hjallese, Denmark: Danish Dairy Managers' Assoc. and the Danish Dairy Engineers' Assoc., 1976- .

154 Architecture, Planning, Housing

Bramsen, Henrik [et al.]. **Early Photographs of Architecture on View in Two Copenhagen Libraries.** By Henrik Bramsen, Marianne Brøns and Bjørn Ochsner. Copenhagen: Thaning & Appel, 1957. p 94. Ill.

Building. Copenhagen: Ministry of Foreign Affairs, 1974. p 31. Ill. [*Denmark Review*. Special ed.]

Dahlmann Olsen, Robert. **Art in Architecture and Townscape; Denmark.** Photographs by Jørn Freddie. Copenhagen: Ministry of Foreign Affairs, 1969. p 56. Ill.

Danish National Planning. Present State and Future Prospects. Copenhagen: The Secretariat of the National Planning Committee, 1972. p 97. Ill.

Dyssegaard, Søren, ed. **Arne Jacobsen - a Danish Architect.** Tr. Reginald Spink and Bodil Garner. Copenhagen: Ministry of Foreign Affairs, 1971, 1976. p 56. Ill. [A Presentation Book.]

Elling, Christian, ed. **Danish Architectural Drawings. 1660-1920.** Ed. Christian Elling and Kay Fisker. Tr. Ingeborg Nixon. Copenhagen: Gyldendal, 1961. p 402. Ill. [*Monumenta architecturae danicae. Danske Arkitekturtegninger.* Danish-English text.]

Faber, Tobias. **Arne Jacobsen.** Teufen: Arthur Niggli, 1964. Praeger, 1964. p 175. Ill. [German-English text.]

Faber, Tobias. **Danish Architecture.** Copenhagen: Det danske Selskab, 1978. p 316. Ill. [Denmark in Print and Pictures.] [Rev. ed. of *A History of Danish Architecture.*]

Faber, Tobias. **A History of Danish Architecture.** Tr. Frederic R. Stevenson. New York; Copenhagen: Det danske Selskab, with the cooperation of the American-Scandinavian Foundation, 1964. p 255. Ill. Rev. ed. 1978. p 316. Ill. [Denmark in Print and Pictures.]

Faber, Tobias. **New Danish Architecture.** Tr. E. Rockwell. London: Architectural Press; New York: Praeger Publishers; Teufen: Arthur Niggli, 1968. p 219. Ill. [English-German text.]

Federation of Danish Architects. **100 New Buildings in Copenhagen.** Publ. for the Federation of Danish Architects. Copenhagen: Arkitekten, 1956. p 24.

Finsen, Helge, ed. **Danish Architecture 1050-1850.** Ed. Helge Finsen and Esbjørn Hiort. Copenhagen: Arkitektens Forlag, 1975. p 16. Ill.

Hiort, Esbjørn. **Contemporary Danish Architecture 1958.** Ed. Finn Monies and Bent Røgind. Tr. Eve M. Wendt. Copenhagen: Arkitektens Forlag, 1958. p 87. Ill.

Hiort, Esbjørn, ed. **Danish Architecture of Today.** Exhibition at the Royal Institute of British Architects, London, 1950. Copenhagen and London, 1950. p 48. Ill.

Hiort, Esbjørn. **Housing in Denmark Since 1930.** Tr. Eve M. Wendt. Copenhagen: Gjellerup, 1952. p 112. Ill.

Ideal Danish Homes 1973. 14 Danish Architects. Copenhagen: Federation of Danish Architects, 1973. p 41. Ill.

Møller, C. F. **The Buildings of the Aarhus University 1933-1961.** The University Library. The Royal Dental College Århus. Illustrations, with an introduction in Danish and English. Århus: Architect C. F. Møller, 1961. p 36. Ill. [*Aarhus Universitets bygninger 1933-1961.*]

Nyboe Andersen, Svend Aage. **Building and the Environment.** Copenhagen: Ministry of Foreign Affairs, 1972. p 38. Ill.

Post-War Housing in Denmark. Tr. Reginald Spink. Copenhagen: Det danske Selskab, 1956. p 29. [Danish Reference Papers.]

Rasmussen, Steen Eiler. **Experiencing Architecture.** Tr. Eve Wendt. Cambridge, Mass.: M. I. T. Press; London: Chapman, 1959. p 251. Ill. 2nd ed., Cambridge, Mass.: M. I. T. Press, 1962. p 245. Ill. New rev. ed., London: Chapman & Hall, 1964. p 245. Ill.

Skovgaard, Joakim A. **A King's Architecture. Christian IV and his Buildings.** London: Hugh Evelyn, 1974. p 143. Ill.

Skriver, Poul Erik. **Danish Houses.** Copenhagen: Arkitektens Forlag, 1960. p 95. Ill. [*Danske huse. Særtryk af Arkitektur.*]

Skriver, Poul Erik, ed. **Guide to Modern Danish Architecture.** Ed. Poul Erik Skriver and Gunhild Starke. Tr. E. Rockwell. Copenhagen: Arkitekten, 1964. p 78. Ill. 3rd ed. Ed. and layout Poul Erik Skriver. Tr. David Hohnen. 1969. p 114. Ill. 4th ed. 1973. p 108. Ill.

Smith, Vincent. **The Sydney Opera House.** Sydney: Paul Hamlyn, 1974. p 160. Ill. [Designed by Danish architect Jørn Utzon.]

Steensberg, Axel. **Old Danish Farmhouses.** 2nd rev. ed., with David Yde-Andersen. Tr. Jean Olsen. Copenhagen: Haase, 1962. p 173. Ill. [*Gamle danske bøndergaarde.* Danish-English-German text.]

Town Planning Guide. Denmark. Copenhagen: Danish Town Planning Laboratory, 1973. p 85. Ill.

Town Planning in Denmark. Tr. Reginald Spink. Copenhagen: Det danske Selskab, 1956. p 34. [Danish Reference Papers.]

Architecture - Periodicals

Arkitektur. Copenhagen: Arkitektens Forlag. [Danish-English-German text.] Bi-monthly. 1957- . [Since vol. 16 (1972) called *Arkitektur DK.*]

Art - I.
General

Benzon, Gorm. **Art Treasures in Denmark.** Odense: Skandinavisk Bogtryk, 1966. p 182. Ill.

Grandjean, Bredo L. **Danish Art.** Foreword by Erik Zahle. Tr. Clive Bayliss and Jørgen Andersen. Copenhagen: Thaning & Appel, 1952. p 208. Ill. [*Dansk kunst. Arkitektur, skulptur, malerkunst og kunsthåndværk.* Danish-English text.]

Great Centres of Art: Copenhagen. New York: Barnes, 1969. p 251. Ill.

Lassen, Erik, ed. **The Arts of Denmark: Viking to Modern.** An exhibition organized by the Danish Society of Arts and Crafts and Industrial Design, 1960-1961, U.S.A. Copenhagen: Danish Society of Arts and Crafts and Industrial Design, 1960. p 160. Ill.

Poulsen, Vagn. **Illustrated Art Guide to Denmark.** Tr. Elaine Hagemann. Copenhagen: Gyldendal, 1959. p 85. Ill.

Art - II.
Painting and Sculpture

Bramsen, Henrik. **Danish Marine Painters.** Copenhagen: Burmeister & Wain, Nyt Nordisk Forlag, 1962. p 116.

A Catalogue of Wall-Paintings in the Churches of Medieval Denmark 1100-1600. Scania, Halland, Blekinge. Vols. 1-3. Copenhagen: Akademisk Forlag, 1976. Ill.

Pedersen, Poul. **Mankind, Granite Sculpture and Pictorial Blocks in Jutland.** Photography by Poul Pedersen. Århus: Marselis, 1973. p 71. Ill.

Poulsen, Vagn. **Danish Painters.** Tr. Elaine T. Hagemann. Copenhagen: Erichsen, 1961. p 88. Ill. [*Danske malere.* Danish-English-French-German text.] [Printed in Stuttgart.]

Poulsen, Vagn. **Danish Painting and Sculpture.** Tr. Sigurd Mammen. Copenhagen: Det danske Selskab, 1955. p 191. Ill. Rev. ed., with H. C. Nørregaard-Nielsen, 1976. p 234. Ill. [Denmark in Print and Pictures.]

Sloan, Thomas la Brie. **Neoclassical and Romantic Painting in Denmark 1754-1848.** Ph. D. diss., Evanston, Ill.: Northwestern University, 1972.

Art - III.
Individual Artists

[Bille]
Vad, Poul. **Ejler Bille.** Copenhagen: Munksgaard, 1961. p 44. Ill. [Contemporary Danish Artists Series, no. 1.] [Danish-English text.]

[Bo]
Lars Bo. Coloured Engravings. Illustrated Exhibition Catalogue. 19th August - 10th September 1977. Edinburgh: The Danish Institute, 1977. p 18. Ill.

[Bojesen]
Lübecker, Pierre. **Applied Art by Kay Bojesen.** Copenhagen: The National Association of Danish Handicrafts, 1955. p 35. Ill.

[Gauguin]
Severin, Mark F. **Pola Gauguin.** Tr. Louis Feinberg. Copenhagen: Areté, 1952. p 56. Ill. [Danish-English text.]

[Heerup]
Wilmann, Preben. **Henry Heerup.** Copenhagen: Munksgaard, 1962. p 104. Ill. [Contemporary Danish Artists Series, no. 3.] [Danish-English text.]

[Jacobsen]
Hovdenakk, Per. **Egill Jacobsen I: Paintings 1928-65.** Copenhagen: Borgen. 1980. p 223. Ill. [English-Norwegian text.]

[Jorn]
Andersen, Troels, ed. **Asger Jorn. 1914-1973. A Catalogue of Works in the Silkeborg Kunstmuseum.** Silkeborg: Silkeborg Kunstmuseum, 1974. p 176. Ill.

Atkins, Guy. **Asger Jorn in Scandinavia 1930-1953. A Study of Asger Jorn's Artistic Development from 1930 to 1953 and a Catalogue of His Oil Paintings from that Period.** With the help of Troels Andersen. Copenhagen: Borgen; London: Lund Humphries, 1968. p 418. Ill.

Atkins, Guy. **Asger Jorn. The Crucial Years: 1954-1964.** Copenhagen: Borgens Forlag; New York: Wittenborn Art Books, Inc., 1977. p 396. Ill. [A comprehensive catalogue.]

Atkins, Guy, ed. **Asger Jorn's Aarhus Mural.** Intro. Erik Nyholm. Photos by Dominique Darbois. Westerham, England: Printed by Westerham Press, 1964. p 16. Ill.

Schade, Virtus. **Asger Jorn.** Copenhagen: Stig Vendelkær, 1965. p 179. Ill.

[Mortensen]
Johansson, Ejner. **Richard Mortensen.** Copenhagen: Munksgaard, 1964. p 97. Ill. [Contemporary Danish Artists Series, no. 2.] [Danish-English and French-English editions.]

[Nielsen]
Larkin, David, ed. **Kay Nielsen.** Toronto and New York: Peacock Press/Bantam Books, 1975. p 7 text and p 40 plates. [Printed in Italy.]

Larkin, David, ed. **The Unknown Paintings of Kay Nielsen.** Toronto: Peacock Press, 1977. p 58. Ill.

[Skovgaard]
Skovgaard, Joakim. **Skovgaard's Pictures in Viborg Cathedral: 40 Reproductions.** Intro. Henning Høirup. Tr. Noëlle Davies. Viborg: Viborg Cathedral, 1962. p 52. Ill.

[Thommesen]
Vad, Poul. **Erik Thommesen.** Tr. Ann Born. Photos by Roald Pay. Copenhagen: Munksgaard, 1964. p 96. Ill. [Contemporary Danish Artists. Vol. V.]

[Thorvaldsen]
Thorvaldsen. Drawings and Bozzetti. Autumn Exhibition 30. October - 14. December 1973. London: Heim Gallery, 1973. p 61 text and p 79 plates.

[Wiinblad]
Wiinblad, Bjørn. **The Apparel Mart Tapestries in Dallas.** By Bjørn Wiinblad. Extracts from the Arabian Nights Tales in Translation. Woven by F. Silveiro of Portugal. Copenhagen: The Author, 1973. p 22.

Art - IV.
Crafts, Applied Art, Design

Bengtsson, Gerda. **Cross Stitch Embroidery.** Vol. 1-2. Copenhagen: Haandarbejdets Fremmes Forlag (Høst), 1963. p 51 & 52. Ill. [*Korsstingsarbejder.* Haandarbejdets Fremmes Haandbøger.]

Bengtsson, Gerda. **Gerda Bengtsson's Book of Danish Stitchery.** Tr. Paula Hostrup-Jessen. Published under the auspices of the Danish Handcraft Guild. New York: Van Nostrand Reinhold, 1972. p 136. Ill.

Bengtsson, Gerda. **Herbs and Medicinal Plants in Cross-stitch from the Danish Handcraft Guild.** New York: Van Nostrand Reinhold, 1979. p 64. Ill.

Bing, Jacob. **Bing & Grøndahl Copenhagen Porcelain.** Copenhagen: [The Factory], 1969. p 32. Ill.

Bjerregaard, Kirsten, ed. **Design from Denmark.** Tr. Harold Young. Copenhagen: World Pictures Corp., [no date.] p 127. Ill.

Broby-Johansen, R. **Body and Clothes.** Tr. Erik J. Friis and Karen Rush. Ill. Ebbe Sunesen. New York: Reinhold Book Corp., 1968, London: Faber & Faber, 1969. p 235. Ill. [Updated ed. of *Krop og klær*, 1953.]

Christmas Plates - juleplatter 1908-1972. The Royal Copenhagen Porcelain Manufactory. Copenhagen: Hall-Press, 1972. p 48. Ill.

The Danish Furnituremakers Control Association. **Danish Furniture.** Copenhagen: The Danish Furnituremakers Control Association, 1964. p 88. Ill. [English-French-German-Danish text.]

Danish Glass 1814-1914. The Peter F. Heering Collection. Exhibition in Victoria and Albert Museum. Arranged by Bent Wolstrup. London: Victoria and Albert Museum, 1974. p 72. Ill.

Danish Handcraft Guild. **Counted Cross-stitch Designs for Christmas.** New York: Charles Scribner's Sons, 1977. p 79. Ill.

Danish Handcraft Guild. **Danish Embroidery.** Foreword by Gertie Wandel. London: B. T. Batsford Ltd., 1959. p 210. Ill. [Danish-English text.]

Danish Handcraft Guild. **Danish Pulled Thread Embroidery.** By Haandarbejdets Fremme (The Danish Handcraft Guild); Esther Fangel, Ida Winckler, Agnete Wuldem Madsen. N. Y.: Dover Publications; London: Constable, 1977. p 100. Ill. [Dover Needlework Series.] [English-Danish text.] [Rpt. of parts 3 & 4 of *Danish Embroidery*, 1959.]

Danish Handcraft Guild. **Jul. Christmas.** Ed. Ida Winckler. Ill. Gerda Bengtsson, Else Thordur Hansen, Lisbeth Kjeldgaard Sørensen and Ida Winckler. Copenhagen: Haandarbejdets Fremme and Høst, 1967. p 44. Ill. [Danish-English text.]

The Danish Society of Arts and Crafts and Industrial Design. **Danish Ceramics. Exhibition Catalogue.** Copenhagen: Landsforeningen Dansk Kunsthaandværk, [no date.] Unp. Ill. [*Dansk keramik*, Danish-English text.]

Ditzel, Nanna, ed. **Danish Chairs.** Ed. Nanna Ditzel and Jørgen Ditzel. Photos by Erik Hansen and Keld Helmer-Petersen. Copenhagen: Høst, 1954. p 96. Ill. [*Danske stole*, Danish-English text, chiefly illustrations.]

Erlandsen, Ida-Merete. **Paris: a Book of Cross-stitch Designs.** Copenhagen: Høst, 1961. p 50. Ill. [*Paris i korssting.* Danish-English text.]

Erlandsen, Ida-Merete. **Tivoli in Cross-stitch.** Copenhagen: Høst, 1957. p 157. [Danish-English text.]

Georg Jensen Silversmithy. 77 Artists, 75 Years. Washington, D. C.: Smithsonian Institution Pr., 1980. p 127. Ill.

Grandjean, Bredo L. **The Flora Danica Service.** Copenhagen: Hassing, 1950. p 80. Ill. 2nd ed. Copenhagen: Forum, 1973. p 79. Ill. [*Flora Danica-Stellet.* Danish-English text.]

Hiort, Esbjørn. **A Century of Danish Design.** Tr. David Hohnen. Copenhagen: The Danish Society of Arts and Crafts and Industrial Design, 1968. p 75. Ill.
Guide to the exhibition of Danish furniture and crafts held at the Arts Gallery and Museum in Glasgow June 17 - July 14, 1968.

Hiort, Esbjørn, ed. **The Danish Poster. An Exhibit Sent out by Det danske Selskab.** Tr. Reginald Spink. Copenhagen: Det danske Selskab, 1951. p 39. Ill.

Hiort, Esbjørn. **Modern Danish Ceramics.** Tr. Eve M. Wendt. Photos by Aage Strüwing. Copenhagen: Gjellerup, 1955. p 132. Ill. [*Moderne dansk keramik.* English-Danish-French-German text.]

Hiort, Esbjørn. **Modern Danish Furniture.** Tr. Eve M. Wendt. Ill. Jonals Co. & Aage Strüwing. New York: Architectural Book Publishing Co.; Copenhagen: Gjellerup, 1956. p 135. Ill. [*Moderne danske møbler.* English-Danish-French-German text.]

Hiort, Esbjørn. **Modern Danish Silver.** Tr. Eve M. Wendt. Photos by Jonals Co. Copenhagen: Gjellerup; New York: Museum Books; London: A. Zwemmer Ltd., 1954. p 124. Ill. [*Moderne dansk sølv.* English-French-German-Danish text.] [Printed in Denmark.]

Jensen, Inge Lise. **Caucasian Rugs - a Private Danish Collection.** Photos by Poul Larsen. Copenhagen: Richard Levin, 1974. p 67. Ill.

Karlsen, Arne, ed. **Contemporary Danish Design.** Arne Karlsen, Bent Salicath and Mogens Utzon-Frank, eds. Tr. Birthe Andersen. Copenhagen: The Danish Society of Arts and Crafts and Industrial Design, 1960. p 117. Ill.

Karlsen, Arne. **Made in Denmark: a Picture-book about Modern Danish Arts and Crafts.** By Arne Karlsen and Anker Tiedemann. New York: Reinhold Publishing Co., 1960. p 175. Ill.

Kaufmann, Edgar, ed. **Fifty Years of Danish Silver in the Georg Jensen Tradition.** Photos by Keld Helmer-Petersen and Erik Hansen. Copenhagen: Schønberg, 1955. p 72. Ill.

Lassen, Erik. **Knives, Forks and Spoons.** Issued by Carl M. Cohr's Sølvvarefabriker A/S, Fredericia. Copenhagen: Høst, 1960. p 23, 80 pl. [*Ske, kniv og gaffel.* Danish-English text.]

Møller, Henrik Sten. **Danish Design.** Photographs by Steen Rønne. Copenhagen: Rhodos, 1975. p 262. Ill.

Møller, Henrik Sten. **Rud Thygesen. Johnny Sørensen. Industri & Design.** Copenhagen: Rhodos, 1976. p 52. Ill. [Danish-English text.]

Møller, Svend Erik, ed. **Danish Design.** Tr. Mogens Kay Larsen. Copenhagen: Det danske Selskab, 1974. p 163. Ill. [Denmark in Print and Pictures.]

Møller, Svend Erik. **Danish Design at Table.** Copenhagen: Høst, 1956. p 48. Ill. [*Brugskunst på bordet.* Danish-English-French-German text.]

Møller, Svend Erik. **Danish Design in the Living Room.** Copenhagen: Høst, 1956. p 48. Ill. [*Brugskunst i stuen.* Danish-English-French-German text.]

Møller, Svend Erik. **Georg Jensen 1866-1966.** Snekkersten: Mobilia, 1966. p 127. Ill.

Møller, Svend Erik. **Modern Danish Homes.** By Svend Erik Møller and Tyge Arnfred. Copenhagen: Høst, 1953. p 144. Ill. [*Moderne danske hjem.* Danish-English-German text.]

Nielsen, Agnete Bech. **Holbeinwork.** Copenhagen: Haandarbejdets Fremme and Høst & Søn, 1960. p 36. Ill. Pb. [*Mønstre til Holbeinsyning,* Danish-English text.]

Nyrop-Larsen, Johanne. **Lace-Making by Diagram.** Tr. Eve M. Wendt. Copenhagen: Jul. Gjellerups Forlag, 1955. p 48. Ill.

Olufsen, Birte, ed. **Danish Furniture: Questions and Answers.** Tr. Geoffrey Dodd, Hellerup, DK.: Danish Furniture Manufacturers' Association, [no date.] p 64. Ill.

183 Danish Craftsmen. Copenhagen: Danske Kunsthåndværkeres Landssammenslutning, 1980. p 110. Ill. [English-German text.]

One Hundred Great Danish Designs! Snekkersten: Mobilia, 1974. p 100. Ill. [Mobilia No. 230-233.]

Petersen, Grete. **Handbook of Stitches: 200 Embroidery Stitches, Old and New, with Descriptions, Diagrams and Samplers.** By Grete Petersen and Elsie Svennas. Foreword by Jacqueline Enthovan. Tr. from the Danish. New York: Van Nostrand Reinhold, 1970.

Petersen, Grete. **Hans Andersen's Fairy Tales, a Book of Cross-stitch Designs.** Copenhagen: Høst, 1961. p 48. Ill. [*H. C. Andersens eventyr i korssting.* Danish-English text.]

Rasmussen, Steen Eiler. **Danish Textiles.** Leigh-on-Sea: F. Lewis, 1956. p 24. Ill.

158 The Royal Copenhagen Porcelain Manufactory Plates. Copenhagen: Den Kongelige Porcelainsfabrik, 1970. p 115. Ill.

Salicath, Bent, ed. **Meals & Design.** Exhibition 1962 by the Danish Society of Arts and Crafts and Industrial Design. Tr. Birthe Andersen. Copenhagen: The Danish Society of Arts and Crafts and Industrial Design, 1962. p 78. Ill.

Salicath, Bent, ed. **Modern Danish Textiles.** Ed. Bent Salicath and Arne Karlsen. Tr. Birthe Andersen. Biblio. and layout Arne Karlsen. Copenhagen: The Danish Society of Arts and Crafts and Industrial Design in conjunction with The Federation of Danish Textile Industries and *Arkitekten*, 1959. p 72. Ill.

Starcke, Dagmar. **Hans Christian Andersen's Alphabet.** Copenhagen: Thaning & Appel, 1955. Unp. Ill. [Embroidery patterns, with captions in Danish and English.]

Art - V.
Periodicals

An Annual of New Art and Artists. Copenhagen: Lindhardt og Ringhof, 1973. [One issue only, 1973/1974.]

Danish Design. Copenhagen: Danish Design Council. 1980- . [English-Danish text.]

Danish Handcraft Guild. Copenhagen: Haandarbejdets Fremme, quarterly. 1934- . [Danish-English text.]

Hafnia. Copenhagen Papers in the History of Art. Copenhagen: University of Copenhagen, Institute of Art History, 1970- .

Ballet and Dance

Association for the Promotion of Folk Dances. **Old Danish Folk Dances.** Described by the Association for the Promotion of Folk Dances. Tr. Finn Dyhr. Copenhagen: Foreningen til Folkedansenes Fremme, 1960. p 39.

Bournonville, August. **My Theatre Life.** Tr. Patricia McAndrew. Middletown, Ct.: Wesleyan University Press, 1979. 3 vol. p 673. [Memoirs.]

Bruhn, Erik. **Bournonville and Ballet Technique: Studies and Comments on August Bournonville's »Etudes Choréographiques«.** By Erik Bruhn and Lillian Moore. New York: The Macmillan Co., 1961. p 70.

Dyssegaard, Søren, ed. **The Royal Danish Ballet.** Tr. Reginald Spink. Photos by Mogens von Haven and Jørgen Mydtskov. Copenhagen: Ministry of Foreign Affairs, 1969. p 50. Ill.

Fog, Dan. **The Royal Danish Ballet 1760-1958 and August Bournonville. A Chronological Catalogue of the Ballets and Ballet-divertisements Performed at the Royal Theatre of Copenhagen and a Catalogue of August Bournonville's Works. With a Musical Bibliography.** Copenhagen: Dan Fog Musikforlag, 1961. p 79.

Gruen, John. **Erik Bruhn. Danseur Noble.** New York: The Viking Press, 1979. p 252. Ill.

Kragh-Jacobsen, Svend. **The Royal Danish Ballet. An Old Tradition and a Living Present.** Preface by Arnold L. Haskell. Photos by Baron and Mydtskov. Copenhagen: Det danske Selskab, 1955. p 89. Ill.

Kragh-Jacobsen, Svend. **The Royal Danish Ballet To-day.** Photos by H. I. Mydtskov. Copenhagen: Thorkild Beck, 1951. p 20. [*Balletten i dag*. Danish-English text.]

Kragh-Jacobsen, Svend. **20 Solo Dancers of The Royal Danish Ballet.** Photos by Mogens von Haven. Tr. Esther Heilbuth. Copenhagen: Hans Reitzel, 1965. p 84. Ill. [*20 solodansere fra den kongelige Ballet*. Danish-English text.]

Lorenzen, Poul. **Dances of Denmark.** By Poul Lorenzen and Jeppe Jeppesen. Ill. Rowland A. Beard. New York: Chanticleer Press, 1950. p 40. Ill. The history of Danish folk dances with music and directions.

Ralov, Kirsten, ed. **The Bournonville School. The Daily Classes, Music, Benesh Notation, Labanotation.** New York: Audience Arts div. of Marcel Dekker, Inc., 1979. 4 vol. Ill.

Royal Danish Ministry of Foreign Affairs. **The Festival Arts.** Danish Drama, Ballet and Music. Tr. Reginald Spink. Copenhagen: Royal Danish Ministry of Foreign Affairs, 1958. p 52. Ill.

Royal Danish Ministry of Foreign Affairs. **The Royal Danish Ballet and Bournonville.** Special issue of *Danish Journal*. Ed. Anders Georg, Ebbe Mørk, Søren Dyssegaard. Tr. Henry Godfrey. Copenhagen: Ministry of Foreign Affairs, 1979. p 48. Ill. [In Honour of the Centenary of August Bournonville.]

Terry, Walter. **The King's Dancing Master. A Biography of Denmark's August Bournonville.** New York: Dodd, Mead & Co., 1979. p 173. Ill.

Von Haven, Mogens. **The Royal Danish Ballet.** Photographs by Mogens von Haven. Intro. John Martin. Tr. Maureen Neiiendam. 2nd rev. ed. Copenhagen: Gyldendal, 1964. p 120. Ill. [*Balletten danser ud*, 1961.]

Bibliography

Bredsdorff, Elias. **Danish Literature in English Translation.** Copenhagen: Ejnar Munksgaard, 1950. Rpt. Westport, Connecticut: Greenwood Press, 1973. p 178.

Danish Children's Books. Copenhagen: IBBY. 1971. p 40. Ill.

Hansen, Peter Allan. **A Bibliography of Danish Contributions to Classical Scholarship from the 16th Century to 1970.** Copenhagen: Rosenkilde and Bagger, 1977. p 335.

Jacobsen, Sven C., ed. **Denmark. A Bibliography. With a Special Section on Hans Christian Andersen.** Ed. Sven C. Jacobsen, Karsten Kromann and Jan William Rasmussen. Compiled by the Danish Department of the Royal Library. 2nd ed. Copenhagen: Royal Library, 1976. p 56.

Jansen, Henrik M. **A. Select Bibliography of Danish Works on the History of Towns Published 1960-1972.** By Henrik M. Jansen and Thomas Riis. Odense: Odense Universitet, 1973. p 46.

Jansen, Henrik M. **A Select Bibliography of Danish Works on the History of Towns Published 1960-1976.** With the assistance of Knud Hannestad and Thomas Riis. Odense: Odense Universitet, Institut for Historie og Samfundsvidenskab, 1977. p 85.

Jørgensen, Aage. **Contributions in Foreign Languages to Danish Literary History. 1961-1970.** Aarhus: Akademisk Boghandel, 1971. p 44.

Similar compilations and supplements in *Orbis Litt.* vols. 21 (1966), 24 (1969), 27 (1972) and 31 (1976).

List of Literature in English on Education in Denmark in the National Library of Education. Copenhagen: Danmarks Pædagogiske Bibliotek, 1975. p 18.

Mitchell, P. M. **A Bibliographical Guide to Danish Literature.** Copenhagen: Munksgaard, 1951. p 62.

Mitchell, P. M. **A Bibliography of 17th Century German Imprints in Denmark and the Duchies of Schleswig-Holstein.** Lawrence, Kansas: Univ. of Kansas, 1969. 2 vols. [University of Kansas Publications, Library Series no. 28.]

Mitchell, P. M. **English Imprints of Denmark through 1900.** Lawrence: The University of Kansas Libraries, 1960. p 85.

Munch-Petersen, Erland. **Bibliography of Translations into Danish 1800-1900 of Prose Fiction from Germanic and Romance Languages.** Copenhagen: Rosenkilde & Bagger, 1976. p 598. [Danish-English text.]

Munch-Petersen, Erland. **A Guide to Danish Bibliography.** By Erland Munch-Petersen assisted by Frederic J. Mosher. Copenhagen: The Royal School of Librarianship, 1965. p 140. pb.

Nielsen, Torben. **A Selection of Current Danish Periodicals.** Copenhagen: The Royal Library, 1965. p 45.

Ober, Kenneth H. **Contributions in Dutch, English, Faroese, German, Icelandic, Italian, and Slavic languages to Danish Literary History 1925-1970. A Provisional Bibliography.** Copenhagen: The Royal Library, 1976. p 32.

The Royal Danish Library. **Denmark: Literature, Language, History, Society, Arts. A Select Bibliography.** Copenhagen: The Royal Library, 1966. p 151. pb. [Cover title: *Denmark: Country, People, Culture.*]

Søndergaard, Jens. **Danish Legal Publications in English, French and German.** [1920-1962.] Göteborg: Almqvist & Wiksell, 1963. p 91.

Thorning, Ebba. **Danish Plays in English Translation.** By Ebba and Just Thorning. Copenhagen: The International Committee of Dansk Amatør Teater Samvirke, 1965. p 13.

University of Copenhagen Library, ed. **Danish Theses for the Doctorate 1927-1958. A Bibliography.** Copenhagen: University of Copenhagen Library, 1962. p 249. [Library Research Monographs no. 6.]

Bibliography - Periodicals

Dania Polyglotta. Literature on Denmark in languages other than Danish, and books of Danish interest published abroad. Compiled by the Danish Department of the Royal Library. Copenhagen: The Royal Library. Annual. New series 1970- .

160 Biography - I.
General

Pedersen, Poul Trier. **Danes of Today.** Vignettes by Paul Erlinger. Copenhagen: Statsministeriet, 1954. p 32. Ill.

Pedersen, Poul Trier. **Danes of Today.** Copenhagen: Committee for Danish Cultural Activities Abroad, 1961. p 32. Ill.

Biography - II.
Individual Biographies

Note: For additional biographies, see other subject headings, also »Literature in Translation« section for biographies of authors.

[Beck]
Beck, Vilhelm. **Memoirs.** Tr. C. A. Stub. Intro. Paul C. Nyholm. Philadelphia: Fortress Press, 1965. p 192.
The autobiography of a leader of religious renewal in Denmark.

[Bering]
Fischer, Raymond H. **Bering's Voyages. Wither and Why.** Seattle, University of Washington Press, 1977. p 217.

Lauridsen, Peter. **Vitus Bering: The Discoverer of Bering Strait.** Intro. Frederick Schwatka. Freeport, N. Y.: Books for Libraries Press, 1969. p 223.

Murphy, Robert. **The Haunted Journey.** Garden City, N. Y.: Doubleday, 1961. p 212. Juvenile ed.: New York: Farrar, Straus & Giroux, 1969. p 144. [An Ariel Book.]
About Vitus Bering.

[Bohr]
Moore, Ruth. **Niels Bohr, the Man, His Science and the World They Changed.** New York: Alfred A. Knopf, 1966. p 436.

Niels Bohr; His Life and Work as Seen by His Friends and Colleagues. New York: Wiley, 1967. p 355. Ill.

Pauli, W., ed. **Niels Bohr and the Development of Physics.** New York: McGraw-Hill Book Co., 1955. p 195. [Articles and essays presented on the occasion of Niels Bohr's 70th birthday.]

Robertson, Peter. **The Early Years. The Niels Bohr Institute 1921-1930.** Copenhagen: Akademisk Forlag, 1979. p 175. Ill.

Silverberg, Robert. **Niels Bohr: The Man Who Mapped the Atom.** Philadelphia: Macrae Smith Co., 1965. p 185. [A biography for teenagers.]

[Borge]
Borge, Victor. **Letter from a Father.** Ill. Arne Ungermann. *DFOJ* vol. 60 (1967), pp 13-15. [Memories and impressions of Copenhagen.]

[Brahe]
Dreyer, John Louis Emil. **Tycho Brahe. A Picture of Scientific Life and Work in the Sixteenth Century.** New York: Dover, 1964. p 205.

Gade, John Allyne. **The Life and Times of Tycho Brahe.** New York: Greenwood Press, 1969. p 209. Ill. [Rpt.]

[Egede]
Bobé, Louis. **Hans Egede, Colonizer and Missionary of Greenland.** Tr. Aslaug Mikkelsen. Intro. Harald Lindow. Copenhagen: Rosenkilde and Bagger, 1952. p 207. Ill.

Garnett, Eve. **To Greenland's Icy Mountains. The Story of Hans Egede, Explorer, Coloniser, Missionary, etc.** Foreword by Nils Egede Bloch-Hoell. Ill. with photos and drawings by the author. London: Heinemann; New York: Roy Publishers, 1968. p 189. Ill.

[Heiberg]
Fenger, Henning. **The Heibergs.** Tr. and intro. Frederick J. Marker. New York: Twayne Publishers, 1971. p 191. [Twayne's World Author Series, no. 105.]

[Jensen]
Eaton, Leonard K. **Landscape Artist in America. The Life and Work of Jens Jensen.** Chicago: University of Chicago Press, 1964. p 240.

[Jessen]
Jessen, Boy. **Living Under Three Flags. Biography of a Danish-American born in South Slesvig.** New York: Vintage Press, 1959. p 212. Ill.

[Juel]
Barfod, Jørgen H. **Niels Juel: a Danish Admiral of the 17th Century.** Copenhagen: Marinehistorisk Selskab, 1977. p 139. Ill.

[Kold]
Goodhope, Nana. **Christen Kold - The Little Schoolmaster Who Helped Revive a Nation.** Blair, Nebraska: Lutheran Publishing House, 1956. p 121. [Also spelled Kristen Kold.]

[Lassen]
Lassen, Suzanne. **Anders Lassen V. C. The Story of a Courageous Dane.** Tr. Inge Hack. London: Frederick Muller Ltd., 1965. New York: Sportshelf, 1966. p 244. Ill. [*Anders Lassen. Sømand og Soldat.*]

[Magnusson]
Bekker-Nielsen, Hans. **Arne Magnusson. The Manuscript Collector.** By Hans Bekker-Nielsen and Ole Widding. Tr. Robert W. Mattila.

Odense: Odense University Press, 1972. p 69.
Ill. [*Arne Magnusson: Den Store Håndskrift-samler*, 1963.]
[Malthe-Bruun]
Malthe-Bruun, Vibeke, ed. **Heroic Heart. The Diary and Letters of Kim Malthe-Bruun.** Tr. Gerry Bothmer. Postscript by C. Fitzsimmons Alleson. New York: Random House, 1955. Also New York: Seabury, 1966. p 177.
Two Letters. Tr. Evelyn Heepe. *MoDA* pp 215-222. [Letters written to mother and fiancé while prisoner during World War II.]
[Melchior]
Melchior, Marcus. **Darkness over Denmark.** London: New English Library, 1973. p 192. [Autobiography.]
[Munk]
Hansen, Thorkild. **The Way to Hudson Bay. The Life and Times of Jens Munk.** Tr. James McFarlane and John Lynch. New York: Harcourt, Brace and World, 1970. p 348. Ill. [Abridged tr. of *Jens Munk*, 1965.]
[Muus]
Muus, Flemming Braun. **The Spark and the Flame.** Tr. and ed. Varinka Muus and J. F. Burke. London: Museum Press. 1957. p 172. [*Ingen tænder et Lys*, memoirs from World War II, 1950.]
[Ørsted]
Hans Christian Ørsted, 1777-1977. Copenhagen: Ministry of Foreign Affairs, 1977. p 48. Ill.
[Pallandt]
Pallandt, Nina Van. **Nina.** New York: Walker, 1973. p 221. Ill. [Autobiography.]
[Rask]
Nykl, Dr. A. R. **Rasmus Rask's Grave.** Evanston, Ill.: privately printed, 1958.
[Riis]
Alland, Alexander. **Jacob A. Riis Photographer and Citizen.** Millerton, New York: Aperture, 1974. p 220. Ill.
Fried, Lewis. **Jacob A. Riis: A Reference Guide.** By Lewis Fried and John Fierst. Boston: Hall, 1977. p 168.
Lane, James B. **Jacob A. Riis and the American City.** Port Washington, N. Y.: Kennikat Press, 1974. p 267. Ill.
Patterson Meyer, Edith. **»Not Charity, but Justice«. The Story of Jacob A. Riis.** New York: Vanguard Press, 1974. p 172. Ill.
Riis, Jacob A. **The Making of an American.** New York: Macmillan, 1970. p 347. [Originally pub. in 1901; new ed. features epilogue by Dr. J. Riis Owre.]
[Rutzebeck]
Rutzebeck, Hjalmar. **Mad Sea. The Life and Loves of a Windjammer Sailor.** New York: Greenberg, 1956. p 284.

Rutzebeck, Hjalmar. **Sailor with a Gun.** New York: Pageant Press, 1957. p 182.
Rutzebeck, Hjalmar. **The Wind is Free.** London: Alvin Redman, 1957. p 288.
[Wichfeld]
Muus, Flemming Braun. **Monica Wichfeld. A very Gallant Woman.** By Flemming Braun Muus and Varinka Wichfeld Muus. Tr. Anthony Hinton. London: Arco Publishers, 1955. p 158. [*Monica Wichfeld*, biography, 1954.]

Biography - III. Royalty

[Alexandra]
Battiscombe, Georgina. **Queen Alexandra.** London: Constable; New York: Houghton Mifflin, 1969. p 336. Ill.
Biography of Danish princess, daughter of Christian IX, who became Queen of England as the wife of King Edward VII.
Fisher, Graham. **Bertie and Alix. Anatomy of a Royal Marriage.** By Graham Fisher and Heather Fisher. London: Robert Hale, 1975. p 192. Ill.
Maas, Jeremy. **The Prince of Wales's Wedding. The Story of a Picture.** London: Cameron and Tayleur, 1977. p 100. Ill.
Tisdall, E. E. P. **Unpredictable Queen. The Intimate Life of Queen Alexandra.** London: Stanley Paul, 1953. p 240. Ill.
[Anne]
Williams, Ethel Carleton. **Anne of Denmark. Wife of James VI of Scotland: James I of England.** London: Longman, 1970. p 236. Ill.
[Carolina Matilda]
Chapman, Hester W. **Carolina Matilda - Queen of Denmark.** London: Cape, 1971. New York: Coward, McCann & Geohegan, 1972. p 221. Ill.
A biography of the English princess, sister of George III, who married King Christian VII of Denmark.
[George]
George, prince of Greece and of Denmark. **The Cretan Drama. The Life and Memoirs of Prince George of Greece.** Ed. by A. A. Pallis. New York: R. Speller, 1959. p 432. Ill.
Part I: The Memoirs. Tr. from the Danish by Reginald Spink. Part II: Life of Prince George of Greece, High Commissioner on Crete, 1898-1906. (Selections). By A. S. Skandamis. Abridged and tr. from the Greek by A. A. Pallis.

162 [Royal family]

Abrahamsen, Povl. **Royal Wedding. Setting and Background.** Tr. Reginald Spink. Copenhagen: Royal Danish Ministry of Foreign Affairs, 1967. p 48. Ill. [Presentation Book no. 5.]

Aronson, Theo. **A Family of Kings: The Descendants of Christian IX of Denmark.** London: Cassell, 1976. p 252. Ill.

Hansen, Ernst F., ed. **Three Princesses through the Seasons.** Tr. Clive Bayliss. Copenhagen: Thorkild Beck (Nyt Nordisk Forlag) 1954-1962, annually. p 32. [*Med prinsesserne året rundt. Prinsesse Margrethe, prinsesse Benedikte, prinsesse Anne-Marie.* Danish-English text.]

Moe, Allan. **Princesses in Snow and Summer Sun.** By Allan Moe and Ernst Mentze. Tr. Ivy Dilling. Copenhagen: Naver, 1954. p 32. Ill. [*Prinsesser i sne, sol og sommer.* Danish-English text.]

Palsbo, Susanne. **The Daily Life of the King of Denmark. A Pictorial Account of Frederik IX in the Service of the Community.** Susanne Palsbo and Ernst Mentze, eds. Copenhagen: Press Dept. of the Ministry of Foreign Affairs, 1957. p 56. Ill. [*Kongens hverdag.*]

Palsbo, Susanne. **How the King Lives.** Tr. Ivy Dilling. Copenhagen: Rasmus Navers Forlag, 1953. p 56. [*Saadan bor kongen.* Danish-English text.]

Watson, Thomas J. Jr. **The Visit of King Frederik and Queen Ingrid to the United States of America.** By Thomas J. Watson Jr. and A. K. Watson. Copenhagen: International Business Machines, 1961. p 46. Ill.

Cooking

Bang, Asta. **Open Sandwiches and Cold Lunches.** By Asta Bang in collaboration with Edith Rode. Tr. Kris Winther. Copenhagen: Gjellerup, 1951, 1955. New York: Pitman Publishing Corp., 1957. p 112. Ill.

Berg, Karen, ed. **Danish Home Baking. Traditional Danish Recipes.** Compiled by Kaj Viktor Hansen and Kirsten Hansen. Ed. Karen Berg. Copenhagen: Høst & Søn, 1957. London: W. H. Allen, in assoc. with Høst & Søn, 1961. p 83. Ill. New York: Dover Publications, 1972. p 87. Ill. 6th ed. Copenhagen: Høst, 1973. 7th ed. Copenhagen: Høst, 1980. p 85. Ill.

Christiansen, Grethe. **Traditional Danish Food. My Grandmother's Recipes.** Tr. Ian C. Curran. Ill. Thor Moving. Malling: Forlaget Tommeliden, 1972. p 48. Ill.

The Danish Center Ltd. **The Danwich Guide to Danish Party Foods.** London: The Danish Center Ltd., 1970. p 55. Ill.

De danske Husholdningsorganisationer. **Danske nationale retter. 46 opskrifter.** Copenhagen: De danske Husholdningsorganisationer, 1950. p 44. [Danish-English text.]

Dedichen, Hetna. **88 Danish Dishes.** Ill. Preben Zahle. 9th revised ed. Copenhagen: Høst & Søn, 1962. p 62. Ill. 10th ed. 1969. p 52. Ill.

Fenneberg, Emo. **Favorite Danish Dishes.** Ill. Sys Gauguin. Copenhagen: Berlingske, 1953. p 64. Ill.

Grumme, Grete. **Danish Food.** Tr. David Hohnen. Photos by Kirsten Kyhl. Copenhagen: Chr. Erichsen; London: Allen, 1964. p 94. Ill.

Hazelton, Nika Standen. **The Art of Danish Cooking.** Garden City, N. Y.: Doubleday, 1964. p 240. Ill.

Hazelton, Nika Standen. **Danish Cooking.** Harmondsworth: Penguin, 1974. p 237. New ed. 1978. [Revised ed. of *The Art of Danish Cooking.*]

Herborg, Mette. **Danish Open Sandwiches.** Tr. Kathleen and Erik Brøndal. Copenhagen: Høst, 1980. p 76. Ill.

Jensen, Bodil. **Take a Silver Dish . . .** Tr. David Hohnen. Copenhagen: Høst & Søn, 1962. p 152. Ill.

Jensen, Ingeborg Dahl. **Wonderful, Wonderful Danish Cooking. 500 Danish Specialties That Americans Love to Eat.** Intr. Victor Borge. Ill. Edward Kasper. N. Y.: Simon and Schuster, 1965. p 335. Ill.

Kirkeby, Henning. **Danish Akvavit. How to Savour and How to Flavour it.** Tr. Reginald Spink. Copenhagen: Høst & Søn, 1975. p 64. Ill.

La Cour, Tage. **The Book of Open Sandwiches.** Photographs by Jes Buusmann. Copenhagen: Lademann, 1973. 4 vols. Ill.

Lind, Mogens. **A Gastronomical Journey Through Denmark. A Guide to the Best Restaurants in Copenhagen and the Danish Provinces.** Ill. Paul Høyrup. Tr. David Hohnen. Copenhagen: Høst, 1962. p 152. [Danish-English-French text.]

Lind, Mogens. **Say Cheese.** Tr. Mary Fulford. Ill. Ib Ohlsson. Copenhagen: Rasmus Hansen Ltd., 1957. p 26. Ill.

Meal Ideas with Danish Bacon. London: Wolfe, 1973. p 128. Ill.

Møller, Carl [et al.]. **Danish Cakes.** By Carl Møller, Leo Madsen and Helmut Rosenthal. London: Maclaren & Sons, 1959. p 236. Ill.

Møller, Carl [et al.]. **Danish Pastries.** By Carl Møller, Leo Madsen and Helmut Rosenthal. London: Maclaren & Sons, 1959. p 277. Ill.

Palsbo, Susanne. **Danish Cookery.** By Susanne [pseud.]. Photos by Vagn Gulbrandsen. 1st ed. Copenhagen: Høst & Søn, 1950. New York: Bonniers, 1951. 2nd rev. ed. Copenhagen: Høst & Søn, 1953. p 77. Ill. 9th ed. 1972, Høst.

Palsbo, Susanne. **Droll, Danish and Delicious. 77 Festive Danish Recipes.** By Susanne [pseud.]. Tr. Virginia Allen Jensen and Mandy Behrendt. Copenhagen: Høst & Søn, 1966. p 92.

Slebsager, Astrid. **Cooking with the Danes.** Copenhagen: Høst & Søn, 1978. p 73. Ill.

»Tommy«. **Victuals for Vikings.** A Danish cookery book by »Tommy« with recipes by »Kate«. Copenhagen: Samleren, 1955. p 32. Ill.

Van Wagnen, F. I. **Danish Menus Translated.** Jackson, Michigan: E. H. Van Wagnen, 1972. p 46.

White, James. **Good Fare from Denmark and Norway.** By James White and Elizabeth White. London: F. Müller, 1955. p 223. Ill. 4th ed. 1965. [International Cookery Series.]

White, James R. **The Oskar Davidsen Book of Open Sandwiches.** 3rd rev. ed. Copenhagen: Høst & Søn, 1962. p 114. Ill.

A Word about Entertaining in the Danish Manner. Copenhagen: Peter F. Heering, 1962. p 28.

Description - I. General

Aistrup, Inga. **Danmark. The Four Seasons.** Tr. David Hohnen. Intro. and captions Ib Permin. Photos by I. Aistrup. 3rd rev. ed. Copenhagen: Høst & Søn, 1963. p 91. Ill. hb. and pb. New ed. 1980. Text by Kirsten Skaarup. p 74. Ill. [*Danmark. De fire aarstider.* Danish-English-French-Spanish-German text.]

Aistrup, Inga. **Dejlige Danmark. Denmark.** Tr. David Hohnen. Photos by I. Aistrup. Captions Ib Permin. 6th ed. Copenhagen: Høst & Søn, 1964. p 48. Ill. Unp. 1973, 8th rev. ed. [French-English-German-Danish text.]

Anderson, Robert Thomas. **Denmark: Success of a Developing Nation.** Cambridge, Mass.: Schenkman Publishing Co., 1975. p 178. Ill.

Appleton, Ted. **Denmark.** Drawings by Barbara Crocker. London and Glasgow: Collins; Chicago and New York: Rand McNally, 1968, 1974. p 96. [American ed., Rand McNally Europe Pocket Guide Series.]

Bailhache, Jean. **Denmark.** Tr. from the French by Patricia Champness. London: Vista Books; New York: Viking Press, 1961. p 191.

Bernild, Bror. **It's Danish.** Photos Bror Bernild and Jesper Høm. Text Henning Nystad. Tr. Maureen Neiiendam. Copenhagen: Gyldendal, 1961. p 42. Ill.

Bjørnsen, Mette Koefoed, ed. **Facts about Denmark.** Mette Koefoed Bjørnsen and Erik Hansen, eds. Tr. Erik Langkjær. 19th ed. Copenhagen: Politikens Forlag, 1976. p 104. Ill.

Boisen, Ingolf. **Iran and Denmark through the Ages.** Tr. David Hohnen. Copenhagen: Kampsax, 1965. p 124. Ill.

Bryans, Robin. **Danish Episode.** By Robin Bryans. (Pseud. for Robert Harbinson-Bryans). London: Faber & Faber, 1961. p 219. Ill.

Christiansen, Tage. **The Village. Pictures from Denmark's Countryside.** Tr. Reginald Spink. Copenhagen: Det danske Selskab, 1954. p 124. Ill. [Denmark in Print and Pictures.]

Clissold, Stephen. **Denmark, the Land of Hans Andersen.** London: Hutchinson, 1955. p 202. Ill.

The Danes. Opinions, Attitudes, Habits. Copenhagen: Observa, 1977. p 806.

Denmark: A National Profile. New York: Ernst & Ernst, Inc., 1971. p 34.

Denmark in Britain 68. Copenhagen: Ministry of Foreign Affairs, 1969. p 84. Ill. A selection of cuttings from the British press.

Drost, Kurt. **Denmark.** Tr. G. A. Colville. Intro. Erich Lüth. Garden City, New York: Doubleday, 1965. p 61.

Hansen, Aage Sikker. **Danish Summer.** Copenhagen: Politiken, 1950. p 32. Ill.

Hansen, J. Grønborg, ed. **Denmark, Places and People.** Photographs by Jonals Co., selected and arranged by J. Grønborg Hansen. Foreword and text by Monica Redlich. Copenhagen: Schønberg, 1950. p 176. Ill.

Harvey, William James. **Denmark and the Danes. A Survey of Danish Life, Institutions and Culture.** By William James Harvey and Christian Reppien. London and Port Washington, New York: Kennikat Press, 1970. p 346. Ill. [Reprint of the 1915 ed.]

Hohnen, David. **A Portrait of Denmark.** Copenhagen: Høst & Søn, 1966. p 148. Ill. [From the author's earlier work, *The Scandinavians.*]

Hohnen, David. **With Kind Regards.** Four minibooks. Vol. I. Hans Christian Andersen's *The Tinder-Box.* Vol. II. Christmas in Denmark. Vol. III. Denmark in the Summertime. Vol. IV. Seven Danish Dinners. Copenhagen: Høst, 1957. Each vol. p 38.

164 Huhle, Robert. **Introduction to Denmark.** Sønderborg, 1959. p 16.

Jones, W. Glyn. **Denmark.** London: Ernest Benn; New York: Praeger Publishers, 1970. p 256. Ill. [Nations of the Modern World Series.]

Kaaris, Viggo Emil. **Do You Know Denmark? Denmark in Pictures with Descriptive Text in English and Danish.** 9th ed. Aarhus: Copyright the Author, 1962. 10th ed. 1964. 12th ed. 1968. 15th rev. ed. 1974. p 164. Ill. [*Kender De Danmark?*]

Knudsen, Mogens. **Hans Andersen's Denmark Described in Pictures and Text.** Pictures selected by Chr. Bang. Copenhagen: Illustrationsforlaget, 1950. p 88. Ill.

Kraks Legat. **Kraks Maps of 50 Danish Provincial Towns.** 2nd ed. Copenhagen: Kraks Legat, 1964. p 130. Ill. [*Kraks kort over 50 provinsbyer.*]

Larsen, Helge, ed. **Facts about Denmark.** International Who-What-Where. Helge Larsen and Torben J. Meyer, eds. English text reviewed by Reginald Spink. 12th ed. Copenhagen: Politiken, 1962. p 64. Ill. [Politikens Håndbøger no. 23.]

Lembourn, Hans Jørgen. **The Denmark Book.** By Hans Jørgen Lembourn, Palle Lauring, Hans R. van Bülow, Esbjørn Hiort, Mogens Brandt and Svend Kragh-Jacobsen. Copenhagen: Grønlund, 1962. p 64. Ill.

Lind, Mogens. **Denmark. Where the Tuborg Comes from.** Ill. Hakon Mielche. Copenhagen: The Tuborg Breweries, 1958. p 32. Ill.

Lind, Mogens. **We Danes - and You.** Ill. Herluf Jensenius. Copenhagen: The National Travel Association of Denmark, 1956. 3rd ed. 1959. p 32. Ill.

MacHaffie, Ingeborg S. **Of Danish Ways.** By Ingeborg S. MacHaffie and Margaret A. Nielsen. Ill. Henning Jensen. Minneapolis, Mn.: Dillon Press, 1976. p 250. Ill.

Madsen, Herman. **Denmark.** Tr. C. J. Frejlev. Ill. Thormod Kidde. Odense: Munksgaard & Skandinavisk Bogforlag, 1960. p 478. Ill.

Miles, Beryl. **Candles in Denmark.** Levittown, New York: Transatlantic Arts, Inc.; London: John Murray, 1958. p 235. Ill.
Observations of daily life in Denmark.

Møller, Svend Erik. **This is Denmark.** Photos by Jørgen Schytte. Copenhagen: Ministry of Foreign Affairs, 1974. p 30. Ill.

Nystad, Henning. **It's Danish.** Tr. Maureen Neiiendam. Photographs Bror Bernild and Jesper Høm. Copenhagen: Gyldendal, 1961. p 80. Ill. [*Sådan er Danmark, sådan da . . .*]

Nystad, Henning. **Meet the Danes.** Photos by Jesper Høm. Copenhagen: Rhodos, 1965. p 128. Ill.

Oestermann, Richard. **God's Own Country - and Mine; America and Denmark.** By Richard Oestermann and Donald E. Nuechterlein. Copenhagen: Nyt Nordisk Forlag/Arnold Busck, 1951. p 244.

Olsen, Erling. **Like to Know Something about Denmark?** Language revision Jean Olsen. Ill. Peder Nyman. Copenhagen: The Author, 1977. p 47. Ill.

Riismøller, Peter. **Rebild. The Fourth of July Celebration in Denmark.** Issued in connection with the 40th anniversary of the first Rebild festival. Tr. Karen Randolf. Copenhagen: Hassing, 1952. p 146. Ill.

Royal Danish Ministry of Foreign Affairs, ed. **About Denmark.** 2nd ed. Copenhagen: Royal Ministry of Foreign Affairs, 1958. p 64. Ill.

Royal Danish Ministry of Foreign Affairs. **Denmark: An Official Handbook.** Press and Information Dept., Royal Danish Ministry of Foreign Affairs. Copenhagen: Ministry of Foreign Affairs, 1956. p 356. 1970. p 806. Ill. 15th ed. 1974. p 902. Ill.
A thorough introduction to many different aspects of Denmark, presented in the form of articles by different authors, with illustrations throughout. Also included are bibliography and complete index.

Royal Danish Ministry of Foreign Affairs. **Denmark Today. The World of the Danes.** Ed. Anders Georg, Søren Dyssegaard and Helge Knudsen. Copenhagen: Ministry of Foreign Affairs of Denmark, 1979. p 120. Ill.

Royal Danish Ministry of Foreign Affairs, ed. **Life in Denmark.** 2nd ed. Sep. British and American editions. Copenhagen: Ministry of Foreign Affairs, 1957. p 48. Ill.

Rying, Bent, ed. **Denmark. An Official Handbook.** Ed. Bent Rying and Mikal Rode. Tr. Reginald Spink. 13th ed. Copenhagen: Royal Danish Ministry of Foreign Affairs and Krak, 1964. p 889. Ill.

Sitwell, Sacheverell. **Denmark.** London: B. T. Batsford, 1956. p 168. Ill. [Batsford's The Countries of Europe Series.]

Sneum, Gunnar. **Denmark, Now and Then.** Copenhagen: Erichsen, 1974. p 120. Ill.

Spears, Heather. **The Danish Portraits.** Toronto: Ryerson Press, 1967. p 26.
Poems with Danish settings.

Spink, Reginald. **The Land and People of Denmark.** New York: Macmillan; London: Adam & Charles Black, 1957. p 87. Ill. [Lands and People Series.]

Strode, Hudson. **Denmark is a Lovely Land.** New York: Harcourt Brace & Co., 1951. p 304. Ill.

A literary diary describing the author's impressions of Danish civilization.

Weimar, Stig. **Denmark is Like This.** London: Kaye & Ward, 1977. p 30. Ill.

Welcome to Denmark. Vedbæk: Chief of Defence Denmark, 1976. p 30. Ill.

Description - II.
Tourist and Travel

Aistrup, Inga. **Castles and Manors.** Photos by Inga Aistrup. Copenhagen: Høst & Søn, 1962. p 96. Ill. [*Slotte og herregårde.* Danish-English text.]

Aistrup, Inga. **Denmark Town and Country.** Photos by Inga Aistrup. 4th rev. ed. Copenhagen: Høst & Søn, 1964. p 96. Ill. hb. and pb. Also 1974. p 72. Ill. [Danish-English-French-German text.]

Bendix, Hans. **Wonderful, Wonderful Denmark.** Tr. Gerda M. Andersen. Copenhagen: Martins Forlag, 1953. p 122. Ill. [*Saadan ligger landet.*]
Drawings of Denmark with English text.

Boesgaard, Eric. **Denmark in Pictures.** Tr. H. B. Ward. Copenhagen: Grønlund, 1956. p 72. Ill. [*Danmarkbogen.* See also later ed. by Ernst Mentze.]

Bornemann, Ove von, ed. **Esso Guide. Danish Harbours and Waters.** Copenhagen: Dansk Esso A/S, 1963. p 214. Ill. [*Danske havne og farvande.*]

Burke, J. F. **The Happy Invaders: Springtime in Denmark.** By J. F. Burke and William Luscombe. London: Robert Hale, 1956. p 192. Ill.

Christensen, Karsten [et al.]. **Zealand, Lolland, Falster and Møn.** By Karsten Christensen, Barbara Marcus-Møller and Jokum Smith. Copenhagen: Forum, 1975. p 96. Ill.

Christiansen, Tage. **Denmark.** 4th ed. Geneva: Nagel, 1968. p 120. [Nagel's Encyclopedia-guide.]

Colam, Lance (pseud.). **Denmark of £ 25.** By Lance Colam. (pseud. for Charles Gordon Towers Cooper). London: Frederick Muller, 1957. p 88. Ill.

Cooper, C. Gordon T. **A Fortnight in Denmark.** London: Percival Marshall, 1955. p 92. Ill. [Fortnight Holiday Series.]

Dark, Irene. **Come to Denmark.** Ill. John Berry. Loughborough: Wills & Hepworth, 1971. p 50. Ill.

Denmark. Greenland. 3rd rev. ed. Geneva: Nagel, 1975. p 522.

Denmark in Colorphoto. Copenhagen: Grønlund, 1963. p 48. Ill. [English-French-Italian-Russian-Spanish-German text.]

Dennis-Jones, Harold. **Letts Go to Denmark.** London: Letts, 1975. p 96. Ill.

Dennis-Jones, Harold. **Your Guide to Denmark.** London: Alvin Redman, 1963. New York: International Publications Service, 1965. p 312. Ill.

Det danske Lejrpladsudvalg. **Officiel fortegnelse over godkendte campingpladser i Danmark (1964).** Copenhagen: Det danske Lejrpladsudvalg, 1960-64. p 231. Ill. [Danish-English text.]

Ewerlöf, Paul H. [et al.]. **Gateway Guide to Denmark.** By Paul H. Ewerlöf, Paul Baker and Hjalmar Petersen. Ill. P. Hagen Jørgensen and Ib Withen. London: Methuen, 1967. p 63. Ill.

Grimble, Ian. **Denmark.** Ill. John Moore. London: Routledge & Kegan Paul, 1966. p 82. Ill.

Hotels, Pensions, Inns, Motels 1975. Copenhagen: The Danish Tourist Board, 1975. p 63.

Jacobsen, Niels Kingo, ed. **Guidebook Denmark; Contributions to Problems Discussed in Symposia and Excursions.** Copenhagen: Københavns Universitets Geografiske Institut, 1960. p 272. Ill.

Kringelbach, George. **Where to Eat in Denmark.** Copenhagen: Erichsen, 1975. p 96. Ill.

Lind, Mogens. **A Gastronomical Journey through Denmark.** Tr. David Hohnen. Ill. Paul Høyrup. Copenhagen: Høst, 1962. p 152. Ill. [Danish-English-French text.]

Marcus-Møller, Barbara. **Funen and the Neighboring Islands.** Copenhagen: Forum, 1974. p 48. Ill.

Martin-Meyer, Povl, ed. **Denmark in Pictures.** Copenhagen: Alfr. Th. Øberg, 1961. p 84. Ill. [Danish-English-French-German text.]

Mathiassen, Therkel. **Castle and Manor.** Tr. Ingelise Holst. Ill. Sigvart Werner. 2nd rev. ed. Copenhagen: Berlingske 1954. p 96. Ill. [*Borg og slot.* Danish-English text.]

Mentze, Ernst. **Denmark in Pictures.** Tr. H. B. Ward. Copenhagen: Grønlund, 1959. p 72. Ill. [*Danmarkbogen.* See also earlier ed. by Eric Boesgaard.]

Meyer, Torben J., ed. **Tourist in Copenhagen and Northern Zealand.** Ed. Torben J. Meyer and Hjalmar Petersen. Tr. Reginald Spink and R. L. Taylor. Ill. Ib Withen. Copenhagen: Politiken, in collaboration with The Tourist Association of Copenhagen, 1961. p 64. Ill. [Politikens Håndbøger no. 27.]

Morris, Elizabeth. **Passport to Denmark.** Ill. Michael Clante. Copenhagen: Høst & Søn, 1956. p 63. Ill.

166 Muirhead, Litellus Russell. **Denmark.** London: Benn, 1955. p 231. Ill.

Nelson, Nina. **Denmark.** Copenhagen: Høst & Søn; New York: Hastings House; London: Batsford Books, 1973. p 200. Ill. [Countries of Europe Series.]

Nielsen, Grete Gunnar. **Danish Inns.** Ill. Hans Lollesgaard. Copenhagen: Forum, 1973. p 67. Ill.

Nielsen, Kay. **Denmark as Seen from Above.** Photographs by Torkild Balslev. Tr. Georg Rona. Copenhagen: Lademann, 1968, 1972. p 208. Ill. [English-German-French-Spanish text.]

Oppenhejm, Inger. **Denmark . . . a Lovely Land.** Ill. Laus Lauesen. Copenhagen: Alfred Th. Øberg, 1960. p 34. Ill.

Permin, Ib. **Along the West Coast of Jutland.** Photographs by Inga Aistrup. Copenhagen: Høst, 1973. p 71. Ill. 2nd ed. 1977. p 60. Ill. [*Langs Jyllands Vestkyst.* Text in major languages.]

Permin, Ib. **Danmark. Between Sound and Sea.** Photos by Inga Aistrup. 3rd ed. Copenhagen: Høst, 1974. p 74. Ill. [Danish-English-French-German- Spanish text.]

Petersen, Hjalmar, ed. **Tourist in Denmark. Travel Guide.** Tr. Flemming Christensen and Erik Liebst. Ill. P. Haagen Jørgensen and Ib Withen. 5th rev. ed. Copenhagen: Politiken, in co-operation with the National Tourist Association of Denmark, 1963. p 224. Ill. [Politikens Håndbøger no. 26.] [Based on *Danmark Rundt.*]

Pilkington, Roger Windle. **Small Boat to Elsinore.** Ill. David Knight. London: Macmillan; New York: St. Martin's Press, Inc., 1969. p 230. Ill.

Pilkington, Roger Windle. **Small Boat to Skagerrak.** David Knight. London: Macmillan & Co., 1960. p 232. Ill.

Reiss, Toby A. **Denmark in Pictures.** Prepared by Toby A. Reiss. New York: Sterling Pub. & Co., London: The Oak Tree Press, 1961, 1966, 1969. p 64. Ill. [Visual Geography Series.]

Rossiter, Stuart, ed. **Denmark.** With an atlas and 19 other maps and plans. 2nd ed. London: Benn, 1965. p 237 & 16 maps.

Royal Danish Ministry of Foreign Affairs. **A Guide to Denmark.** Copenhagen: Press Department, Royal Danish Ministry of Foreign Affairs, 1951. p 60.

Rutland, Jonathan. **Looking at Denmark.** London: Black; Philadelphia: Lippincott, 1968. p 64. Ill. [Looking at Other Countries Series.]

Schlanbusch, Anna Grete, ed. **Tourist in Denmark; Travel Guide.** Ed. Anna Grete Schlan-busch and Erik Liebst. Tr. Flemming Christiansen and Erik Liebst. Copenhagen: Politikens Forlag, 1951. p 224. Ill.

Schultz, Hans Joakim. **The Traveller's Guide to Denmark - Land of the Welcoming Heart!** Copenhagen: Danish Tourist Board, 1975. p 96. Ill. 2nd ed. 1977. p 96. Ill. 3rd ed. 1979. p 96. Ill.

Toksvig, Harald. **Copenhagen. North Sealand.** English text by Harald Toksvig. 3rd enl. ed. Copenhagen: Grønlund, 1957. p 48. Ill. [English-French text.]

Toksvig, Harald, ed. **Denmark in Colour.** Text by Harald Toksvig. 3rd rev. ed. Copenhagen: Grønlund, 1955. p 72. Ill. 4th ed., 1957. p 84. Ill. [*Danmark i farver. 64 billeder gengivet direkte fra farvefoto.*]

Toksvig, Harald. **From Sea to Shining Sea.** Copenhagen: Burmeister & Wain, with Høst, 1956. p 100. Ill.

Tourist Associations of Jutland. **A Guide to Jutland. (Through Jutland, Denmark.)** Ringkøbing: The Combined Tourist Associations of Jutland with the assistance of The Official Tourist Association of Denmark, 1950. p 64.

Trampe, Poul-Henrik. **Møn.** Photographs by Lars Hansen. Stege: Møns Turistforening, 1975. p 64. Ill.

A Visit to Jylland. Ebeltoft: Elles Offset, 1970. p 51. Ill.

Werner, Sigvart. **Denmark: Land of Beauty.** Photographs by Sigvart Werner. Intro. Hans Hartvig Seedorff Pedersen. Tr. R. P. Keigwin. London: George Allen & Unwin, 1950. p 166. Ill. Printed in Denmark.

White, James. **A Short Guide to Denmark.** Copenhagen: Høst, 1950. p 116. Ill.

Wolfram, Richard. **Denmark.** Photographs by Toni Schneiders, Inga Aistrup, et al. New York: Hill & Wang, 1962. p 88. Ill. [Terra Magica Series.]

Description - III. Copenhagen

Aistrup, Inga. **København - Gader og Stræder. Streets and Alleyways.** Photos by Inga Aistrup. 2nd ed. Copenhagen: Høst & Søn, 1964. p 96. Ill. [English-Danish-French-German text.]

Aistrup, Inga. **Kongens København.** 6th ed. Danish text, Niels Høst, 1960. 7th rev. ed. Danish text, Ib Permin. Tr. David Hohnen. Copenhagen: Høst & Søn, 1964. p 48. Ill. [Danish-English-French-German text.]

Bing, Hanne, ed. **Tourist in Copenhagen and Environs.** Ed. Hanne Bing and Jens Friis Hansen. Copenhagen: Politiken, 1973. p 64. Ill.

Bjerregaard, Jørgen. **Historical Copenhagen.** Tr. David Hohnen. Copenhagen: Høst & Søn, 1959. 2nd ed. 1967. p 48. Ill. [*Det idylliske København.* Danish-English text, French-German resume.]

Black, William. **Copenhagen. A Sketchbook.** 2nd ed. Copenhagen: Hirschsprung, 1959. p 46. Ill. [English-Danish-French-German text.]

Broby-Johansen, R., ed. **Hans Andersen's Copenhagen.** Photos and commentary by R. Broby-Johansen. Drawings by Eiler Krag. Texts by Hans Christian Andersen. Tr. Niels Haislund and Helen Fogh. Copenhagen: Gyldendal, 1963. p 48. Ill.

Brochmann, Odd. **Copenhagen. A History of the City Told through Its Buildings.** Copenhagen: Arkitektens Forlag, 1970. p 96. Ill.

Buchwald, Gunnar. **Sunny Copenhagen Seaside.** By Gunnar Buchwald and Ebbe Fog. Copenhagen: Branner og Korch, 1950. p 96. Ill. [*Sol over sommerlandet.*]

Christensen, Karsten. **Copenhagen and Environs.** Copenhagen: Forum, 1974. p 96. Ill.

Copenhagen. Ill. Michael Buselle. Intro. William Sansom. London: Spring Books, 1966. p 160. Ill.

Copenhagen. Photos by Erling Mandelmann. Lausanne: Berlitz, 1979. p 128. Ill.

Det danske Selskab. **Capital of a Democracy. An Introduction to Copenhagen.** Tr. Reginald Spink. Copenhagen: Det danske Selskab, 1951. 3rd ed. Tr. Maureen Neiiendam, 1964. p 164. Ill. [Denmark in Print and Pictures.]

Eider, Preben. **Copenhagen.** Photos by Preben Eider. Copenhagen: Berlingske, 1972. p 64. Ill.

Eider, Preben. **Tivoli.** Photos by Preben Eider. Copenhagen: Eider, 1973. p 48. Ill.

Eilstrup, Per. **Tivoli. The Story of the Fairytale Garden.** Kastrup: Skandinavisk Idé-Tryk, 1975. p 64. Ill.

Elling, Christian. **Copenhagen Confidentially.** Photos by the Author. Copenhagen: Berlingske, 1961. p 60. Ill. [*København i fortrolighed.* Danish-English text.]

Fenneberg, Paul. **Copenhagen and Environs.** 4th ed. Copenhagen: Gad, 1957. p 50. Ill.

Fog, Ebbe. **Our Copenhagen Sketchbook.** Ebbe Fog and Carl Stuhr. Copenhagen: J. C. Hempels Skibsfarve-Fabrik A/S, 1952. p 48. Ill. [*Vor københavnske skitsebog.* Danish-English text.]

Fuchs, Horst. **Copenhagen: Get to Know It; Get to Like It.** Tr. from the German by Karl Westenberger. Drawings by Howard Williams. New York: Drake Publishers, Inc.; London: Interauto Book Co., Ltd., 1973. p 112. Ill. pb.

Hansen, Christen. **Wonderful Copenhagen.** English text by Christen Hansen. 5th ed. Copenhagen: Grønlund, 1964. p 64. Ill. [*Herrliches Kopenhagen.* English-German text.]

Hellssen, Henry. **Copenhagen.** Photos by Inga Aistrup. New ed. Copenhagen: Høst, 1950. p 100. Ill. [*København.* Danish-English text.]

Hjort, Angelo. **Copenhagen.** Intro. Temple Fielding. Tr. H. B. Ward. Copenhagen: Grønlund, 1959. p 84. Ill. [*København.* English-German-French text.]

København. A Short Description of the Origin of Copenhagen, the City's Physical Structure and Planning. Copenhagen: City Engineers' Department, 1973. p 47. Ill.

Kraks Legat. **Map of Copenhagen and Environs.** Copenhagen: Kraks Legat, 1964. p 64. Ill. [*Kraks kort. København og omegnen.*]

Living and Shopping in Copenhagen. 3rd rev. ed. Copenhagen: Mostrup, 1975. p 63. Ill.

Moltke, Erik. **The Churches of Copenhagen County.** By Erik Moltke and Elna Møller. Summary by Olaf Olsen. Copenhagen: The Danish National Museum and Gad, 1956. p 88. Ill. [Danish Churches Series.]

Pallis, Kis. **The Complete Guide to Wonderful Copenhagen.** Copenhagen: Carit Andersen, 1974. p 105. Ill.

Runnquist, Åke. **Copenhagen - Day and Night. What to See, Where to Eat, Where to have Fun, Where to Shop and Where to Sleep.** Tr. Carl Blechingberg. Ill. Ulla Kampmann. Copenhagen: Spektrum, 1974. p 96. Ill.

Sadolin, Ebbe. **Hans Christian Andersen's Copenhagen. 1805-1875. A Walk in the Footsteps of the Fairy-tale Writer.** With Ebbe Sadolin, who has also done the illustrations. Copenhagen: The Tourist Association of Copenhagen, 1964. Unp. Ill.

Sadolin, Ebbe. **Wanderings in Copenhagen.** Foreword by Francis Hackett. Tr. Mary Fulford. Copenhagen: Carit Andersen, 1953. p 168. Ill.

Shinkfield, Michael. **A Student's Guide to Copenhagen.** 2nd ed. Copenhagen: DIS, 1961. p 64.

Simon, Mike, ed. **Copenhagen, Malmö and the Øresund Area.** 13th ed. Copenhagen: SAS, 1972. p 67. Ill.

Stadsingeniørens Direktorat. **The Parks of Copenhagen.** Copenhagen: Stadsingeniørens Direktorat, 1954. p 20.

168

Strandberg, Julius. **A Necessary Warning to Everyone Who Visits Copenhagen from a Man Who Knows the Town: Time and Money-saving.** With an epilogue on 19th century life in the Danish capital by Poul Strømstad. Ed. Poul Strømstad and Hans Jørgen Strandberg. Tr. Fradley Hamilton Garner and English ed. edited by Christopher Follet. Copenhagen: Strandberg, 1978. p 75. Ill.

Tivoli. Copenhagen: 1973. p 26. Ill.

Tivoli and Georg Carstensen. Copenhagen: Tivoli, 1962. p 31. Ill. [*Tivoli og Georg Carstensen.* Udsendt af Tivoli i anledning af 150-årsdagen for Georg Carstensens fødsel. Danish-English text.]

Williams, Alan Moray. **Autumn in Copenhagen.** Selected poems by »Robert the Rhymer«. Ill. Poul Høyrup. Copenhagen: Scandinavian Features Service, 1963. p 96. Ill.

Williams, Alan Moray, ed. **Copenhagen - Praise and Protest.** Copenhagen: Høst, 1965. p 94. Ill.

Wright, Clifford. **Poetic Copenhagen.** Danish and English text by Clifford Wright. Photographs by Lilian Bolwinkel. Copenhagen: Spectator, 1965. p 92. Ill.

Description - III. Copenhagen - Periodicals

Coming Events in Copenhagen. This Week. Copenhagen: Dansk Bladforlag for The Tourist Association of Copenhagen, 1973- . [Supersedes *This Week.*]

Guide to Copenhagen. Copenhagen: Forlaget Folia, 1973- .

This Week. Guide to Wonderful Copenhagen. Copenhagen: Dansk Bladforlag for The Tourist Association of Copenhagen, 1947-1973. [Replaced by *Coming Events in Copenhagen. This Week.*]

Description - IV. Other Towns and Places.

[Aalborg]
Schultz, Hans Joakim. **Aalborg.** Photographs by J. Brems. Aalborg: Brems Foto, 1973. p 54. Ill.

Simon, Mike, ed. **Aalborg, Aarhus.** 2nd ed. Copenhagen: SAS, 1973. p 31. Ill.

[Aarhus]
Århus in Pictures. Århus: Forlaget Aros, 1956. Unp. ill. [*Århus i billeder. 100 fotos fra den jydske hovedstad.* Danish-English-German text.]

Det danske Selskab. **Aarhus. Meeting-Place of Tradition and Progress. An Account Written by a Group of Its Citizens.** Tr. Reginald Spink. Copenhagen: Det danske Selskab, 1956. 2nd ed. 1962. p 112. Ill. [Denmark in Print and Pictures.]

Ellert, Holger. **Aarhus.** Planned and published by Kjeld Woersaa. Photos: Camera foto, Aarhus. Aarhus: Kjeld Woersaa, 1954. p 32. Ill.

Sejr, Emmanuel. **Århus. A Picture Book of Photographs.** Århus: Århus Byråd, 1967. p 219. Ill.

[Ærø]
Ege, Ole. **Ærø.** Marstal: Oliver Press, 1974. p 80. Ill. 2nd ed. Marstal: Marstal Turistforening, 1980. p 80. Ill. [English-German text.]

[Als]
Lenz, Siegfried. **Als. The Wind Has Free Access.** Photos by Bram van Leeuwen. Sønderborg: Dy-Po, 1976. p 43. Ill. [English-German text.]

[Fanø]
Meesenburg, H. [et al.]. **The Island of Fanö - Its Dwellings and Its Countryside.** Esbjerg: Bygd, 1978. p 75. Ill.

[Fyn]
Det danske Selskab. **Funen, the Heart of Denmark. An Account Written by a Group af Its Inhabitants.** Tr. Graham D. Caie, Ann Caie. Copenhagen: Det danske Selskab, 1980. p 160. Ill. [Denmark in Print and Pictures.]

[Gladsaxe]
Mortensen, Tage, ed. **Gladsaxe Today.** Copenhagen: Forlaget Idag, 1960. p 196. Ill. [*Gladsaxe i dag.* Danish-English-German text.]

[Helsingør]
Egevang, Robert. **Old Elsinore.** Ed. Henning Dehn-Nielsen. Tr. Niels-Holger Larsen. Copenhagen: Nationalmuseet, 1977. p 88. Ill.

Klem, Knud. **Helsingør. Elsinore.** Helsingør: Ernst Hansen, 1950. p 32. Ill.

Leth, André. **Kronborg. The Castle and the Royal Apartments.** Helsingør: Kronborg Slot, 1960 (1st ed.), 1964 (2nd ed.), 1972 (4th ed.). p 66. Ill. [*Slottet og de kongelige sale.* Danish-English-French-German text.]

Magnussen, Arne. **The Atmosphere of Elsinore.** Photos by Arne Magnussen. Helsingør: Arne Magnussen, 1961. [62] unp. Ill. [*Helsingør stemninger.* Danish-English-German text.]

Manniche, Peter. **Elsinore in the Setting of Danish Social and Cultural Condition.** Elsinore: The Author, 1952. p 24. Ill.

Mikkelsen, Birger. **Kronborg.** Ill. and ed. Elisabeth Bjørn-Petersen. Helsingør: Nordisk Forlag for Videnskab og Teknik, 1978. p 107. Ill.

Old Houses in Elsinore 1973. Copenhagen: The National Museum, 1975. p 28. Ill.

Ring, H. **Elsinore. A Brief History of the Town and Its Historic Monuments.** Helsingør: H. Ring, 1950. p 32. Ill.

[Limfjorden]
Det danske Selskab. **The Limfjord. Its Towns and People.** Tr. Elsa Gress Wright and Percy Wait. Copenhagen: Det danske Selskab, 1964. p 220. Ill. [Denmark in Print and Pictures.]

[Odense]
Dreslov, Aksel. **A River - a Town - a Poet. A Walk together with Hans Christian Andersen.** Ill. William Hansen. Odense: Scandinavisk Bogforlag; Chester Springs, Pennsylvania: Dufour Editions, 1961. p 149. Ill.

[Præstø amt]
Jensen, Chr. Axel. **The Churches of Præstø County.** Summary by Hans Stiesdal. Copenhagen: The Danish National Museum and Gad, 1956. p 86. Ill. [Danish Churches Series.]

[Ribe]
Bencard, Mogens. **Ribe through 1,000 Years.** Photos by Svend Tougaard. Esbjerg: Bygd, 1978. p 71. Ill.

[Ringsted]
Hansen, Niels-Jørgen. **St. Bendt's Church in Ringsted.** Ringsted: Flensborg, 1979. p 24. Ill.

[Roskilde]
The Cathedral of Roskilde. Roskilde: Flensborg, 1974. p 32. Ill.

Moltke, Erik. **Roskilde Cathedral.** By Erik Moltke and Elna Møller. Copenhagen: The Danish National Museum and Gad, 1956. p 104. Ill. [Danish Churches Series.] [Condensed version of Danish ed.]

[Skagen]
Hardervig, Bent. **Dejlige Skagen.** Skagen: Skagen Turistforening, 1976. p 68. Ill. [English-French-German-Swedish text.]

Dictionaries

Bailey, I. E. **Dansk-Engelsk handels- og fagordbog.** Copenhagen: Det Schønbergske Forlag, 1972. p 521.

Bolbjerg, Alfred. **Dansk-Engelsk ordbog.** 4th ed. Copenhagen: Berlingske, 1975. p 558. [Berlingske Ordbøger.]

Bredsdorff, Ruth. **Bygge-ordbog. Dansk-Engelsk, Engelsk-Dansk.** Copenhagen: Nyt Nordisk Forlag, 1960. p 240.

Haislund, Niels. **Engelsk-Dansk ordbog.** By Niels Haislund and Aage Salling. 2nd ed. Copenhagen: Berlingske, 1950. 3rd exp. ed. 1964. p 564. [Berlingske Ordbøger.]

Hansen, Helge. **Engelsk-Dansk teknisk ordbog.** By Helge Hansen and Hans Hinrichsen. Copenhagen: Det Schønbergske Forlag, 1968. p 381.

Høegh, Nielsen, E. **Engelsk-Dansk ordbog.** Ill. L. Taaning. Copenhagen: Gyldendal, 1963. p 247. Ill. 2nd ed. 1976. p 251. Ill. [Gyldendals blå Ordbøger.]

Hohnen, David. **Høst's Engelsk-Dansk, Dansk-Engelsk lommeordbog. Høst's English-Danish and Danish-English Pocket Dictionary.** 3rd ed., expanded and rev. by David Hohnen. Copenhagen: Høst, 1966. p 512.

Kjærulff Nielsen, B. **Engelsk-Dansk ordbog.** Co-edited by Jens Axelsen. C. A. Bodelsen, consultant. Copenhagen: Gyldendal, 1964. p 1294. 1977. p 1471.

Løye, C. V. **Høst's Engelsk-Dansk, Dansk-Engelsk lommeordbog.** Høst Pocket Size Dictionary. Copenhagen: Høst, 1955. p 349. 2nd ed. For 3rd ed., see Hohnen, David. [Høsts Lommeordbøger.]

Munck, Evald. **Dansk-Engelsk ordbog.** Ill. L. Taaning. Copenhagen: Gyldendal, 1963. p 300. Ill. [Gyldendals blå Ordbøger.]

Schibsbye, Knud. **English-Danish Dictionary.** By Knud Schibsbye and H. Kossmann, with the assistance of Rees Taylor et al. Copenhagen: Politikens Håndbøger, 1957. p 556. [Politikens blå Ordbøger.]

Vinterberg, Hermann. **Dansk-Engelsk ordbog.** By Hermann Vinterberg and C. A. Bodelsen, with the assistance of H. J. Uldall and B. Kjærulff Nielsen. Copenhagen: Gyldendal, 1954 and 1956. Two vols., p 952 and p 906. 2nd ed., with Jens Axelsen, B. Kjærulff Nielsen and Edith Frey, 1966. p 918 and p 880.

Vinterberg, Hermann. **Dansk-Engelsk ordbog.** By Hermann Vinterberg, Johannes Magnussen and Otto Madsen. Copenhagen: Gyldendal, 1960. 6th rev. ed. 1964. p 447. 7th rev. ed. by Hermann Vinterberg and Jens Axelsen, 1969. p 464. 8th rev. ed. also by Hermann Vinterberg and Jens Axelsen, 1978. p 538. [Gyldendals røde Ordbøger.]

Vinterberg, Hermann. **Engelsk-Dansk ordbog.** By Hermann Vinterberg and Jens Axelsen. 7th ed. Copenhagen: Gyldendal, 1959. p 480.

170   8th ed. 1964. p 496. 9th ed. 1975. p 521. [Gyldendals røde Ordbøger.]

Vinterberg, Hermann [et al.]. **McKay's Modern Danish-English and English-Danish Dictionary.** By Hermann Vinterberg, Johs. Magnussen and Otto Madsen. New York: David McKay Co., 1954. p 882.

Vinterberg, Hermann. **McKay's Modern Danish-English and English-Danish Dictionary.** By H. Vinterberg and J. Axelsen. Rev. ed. New York: David McKay Co., 1965. [Modern Dictionaries Series.] p 447, 496.

Warrern, Allan. **Danish-English, English-Danish Technical Dictionary. Dansk-Engelsk, Engelsk-Dansk teknisk ordbog.** 2nd ed. Copenhagen: J. Fr. Clausen, 1957. 2 vols., p 333 and p 317. 3rd ed. 1964. 4th ed. 1970. 5th ed. 1976. New York: William S. Heinman, 1957-1960. 2 vols.

Economy - I.
General

Association of Savings Banks in Denmark. **Some Facts about Savings Banks' Activities in Denmark.** Copenhagen: The Association of Savings Banks in Denmark, 1950. p 20.

Blegvad, Britt-Mari. **The Consumer in Denmark: Law and Dispute Treatment.** Copenhagen: New Social Science Monographs, 1979. p 43.

The Co-operative Movement in Denmark. 2nd ed. Copenhagen: Andelsudvalget (The Central Cooperative Committee) and Det kooperative Fællesforbund (The Urban Cooperative Union), 1954. 3rd rev. ed. 1956. p 31. Ill. New ed. 1970. p 47. Ill.

Co-Ownership - Co-Determination: Danish Government Bills on Economic and Industrial Democracy. Copenhagen: Danish Federation of Trade Unions, 1974. p 26.

The Danish Banking System. Copenhagen: Danish Bankers Association, 1979. p 42.

The Danish Economy in 1975. Copenhagen: Royal Danish Ministry of Foreign Affairs, 1975. p 60.

Denmark in Europe 1990. Copenhagen: Børsen, 1977. p 377.

Denmark in the World. A Survey. London: Economist Newspaper, 1978. p 30. Ill.

Ølgaard, Anders. **The Danish Economy.** Luxembourg: Office for Official Publications of the European Communities, 1980. p 255.

Organization for Economic Cooperation and Development. **The Capital Market, International Capital Movements, Restrictions on Capital Operations in Denmark.** Washington, D.C.: O.E.C.D. Committee for Invisible Transactions, 1970. p 64.

Organization for Economic Cooperation and Development. **OECD Economic Surveys: Denmark.** Washington, D.C.: O.E.C.D., 1969. p 54. 1977. p 68.

Pedersen, Clemens, ed. **The Danish Cooperative Movement.** Rev. 2nd ed. Tr. Patricia Steen Hansen. Copenhagen: Det danske Selskab 1977. p 153. Ill. [Danish Information Handbooks.]

Ravnholt, Henning. **The Danish Cooperative Movement.** Copenhagen: Det danske Selskab, 1950. p 97. Ill. [Danish Information Handbooks.]

Royal Danish Ministry of Foreign Affairs. **Economic Survey of Denmark 1968.** Copenhagen: Ministry of Foreign Affairs, 1968. p 97.

Royal Danish Ministry of Foreign Affairs. **Investment of Foreign Capital in Denmark.** Copenhagen: Royal Danish Ministry of Foreign Affairs, 1957. p 40. Ill.

Special Edition of the Danish Foreign Office Journal for the Annual Meetings in Copenhagen of the International Monetary Fund and International Bank for Reconstruction and Development and its Institutions. Copenhagen: Ministry of Foreign Affairs, 1970. [Vol. 69.]

Stancke, Bent. **The Danish Stock Market 1750-1840.** Copenhagen: Københavns Universitets Fond til Tilvejebringelse af Læremidler (Gad), 1971. p 118. Ill.

Thorsteinsson, Th. **Mortgaging of Real Estate in Denmark.** 2nd rev. ed. Copenhagen: Østifternes Kreditforening, 1960. p 46.

Economy - II.
Business, Trade, Industry

British Import Union. **A Survey of Danish Imports from the United Kingdom.** Copenhagen: British Import Union, 1960. p 28. Ill.

Callesen, Gerd. **Social-Demokraten and Internationalism. The Copenhagen Social Democratic Newspaper's Coverage of International Labor Affairs, 1871-1958.** By Gerd Callesen and John Logue. Kent, Ohio: Kent Popular Press, 1979. p 73. Ill.

Carlsen, Peter. **The Danish Trade Union Movement.** Copenhagen: The Danish Federation of Trade Unions, 1977. p 28. Ill.

Castro Lopo, Joao C. De. **Denmark's Export Trade with Western Europe in the 1960's.** Copenhagen: Landsplanudvalgets Sekretariat (Secretariat of the National Planning Committee), 1966. p 62. Ill.

Danish Industry in Facts and Figures. Copenhagen: Federation of Danish Industries, 1970. p 49. Ill.

The Danish Labour Market. Copenhagen: Ministry of Labour, 1972. p 126.

Denmark. Hints to Businessmen. London: British Overseas Trade Board, 1977. p 52.

Doing Business in Denmark. Ill. Poul Holck. Copenhagen: Ministry of Foreign Affairs, 1972. p 39. Ill.

Engell, Preben, ed. **The 1,000 Largest Companies in Denmark.** 10th ed. Copenhagen: Teknisk Forlag, 1977. p 191. 11th ed. 1978. p 195.

Entering Denmark, Residence and Employment. Copenhagen: The Danish Employers' Confederation, 1973. p 16. Ill.

Establishing Business in Denmark. Copenhagen: Den Danske Landmandsbank, 1973. p 20. Ill.

Federation of Danish Industries. **The Case for Industry. An Open-ended Discussion on the Future of Industry in Denmark.** Copenhagen: Federation of Danish Industries, 1978. p 95.

Federation of Danish Industries. **Danish Industry in Facts and Figures.** Copenhagen: Federation of Danish Industries, 1963. p 25. Ill.

Federation of Danish Industries. **Industrial Denmark. Facts and Figures.** Copenhagen: Federation of Danish Industries, 1961. p 48.

Fog, Bjarke. **Industrial Pricing Policies; an Analysis of Pricing Policies of Danish Manufacturers.** Amsterdam: North-Holland Publishing Co., 1960. p 229. Ill. [Tr. of thesis, *Priskalkulation og prispolitik.* Univ. of Copenhagen.]

Galenson, Walter. **The Danish System of Labor Relations. A Study in Industrial Peace.** Cambridge, Mass.: Harvard University Press, 1952. New York: Russell & Russell, 1969. p 321.

Hastrup, Bjarne. **The Trades and Danish Economic Development since 1945.** Copenhagen: The Chamber of Danish Trade and Crafts, 1977. p 43.

Hirsch, Seev. **The Export Performance of Six Manufacturing Industries; A Comparative Study of Denmark, Holland and Israel.** New York: Praeger, 1971. p 196. [Praeger Special Studies in International Economics and Development.]

Jessen, Tage, ed. **How Why When.** Ed. Tage Jessen and Bent Jensen. Ill. Poul Andersen. 3rd printing. Copenhagen: Danish Employers' Confederation, 1972. p 58. Ill.

Kjær-Hansen, Max, ed. **Readings in Danish Theory of Marketing.** Copenhagen: Nyt Nordisk Forlag/Arnold Busck, 1966. p 325.

Korst, Mogens. **Industrial Life in Denmark. A Survey of Economic Development and Production.** Copenhagen: Det danske Selskab, 1976. p 172. Ill. [Denmark in Print and Pictures.]

Kraks legat. **Export Directory of Denmark.** Copenhagen: Kraks legat, 1927- . Irregular annual.

Krohn, Søren. **Investing in Denmark.** Copenhagen: Danish Employers' Confederation, 1980. p 36.

Kuhlmann, Stig. **Danish Labour Market Conditions, 1974.** Copenhagen: Ministry of Labour, Economic-Statistic Advisor, 1975. p 190.

Kuhlmann, Stig. **Industrial Relations.** Copenhagen: Ministry of Labour, 1977. p 48.

Manpower Policy in Denmark. Paris: OECD, 1974. p 59.

The Merchant's Guild. **Denmark, the Centre of Trade with Centuries of Traditions.** Copenhagen: The Merchant's Guild, 1953. p 34. Ill. 2nd ed. 1957. p 36.

Pan American Union. **Policies and Institutions for the Promotion of Exports of Manufactures; a Selected Case Study: Denmark.** Washington, D. C.: Pan American Union, Dept. of Economic Affairs, 1964. p 45. Ill.

Raffaele, Joseph A. **Labor Leadership in Italy and Denmark.** Madison, Wi.: University of Wisconsin Press, 1962. p 436.

Ravn, Bent, ed. **Setting up in Denmark. A Business Survey of Economical, Legal and Financial Aspects of Foreign Investment in Denmark.** Copenhagen: Copenhagen Handelsbank, 1976. p 43. Ill.

Riise, Allan [et al.]. **Employers and Workers. Development and Organization of the Danish Labour Market.** By Allan Riise, Peer Carlsen and Henning Lindegaard. Tr. Reginald Spink. Copenhagen: Det danske Selskab, 1956. 2nd rev. ed. 1962. p 52. 3rd ed., by Allan Riise, 1974. p 46. Ill. [Danish Reference Papers.]

Special Issue of the Danish Foreign Office Journal for the XVIIth Congress of the International Chamber of Commerce. Copenhagen: Ministry of Foreign Affairs, 1962. p 52. Ill. [Vol. 42.]

Thomsen, Birgit Nüchel. **Anglo-Danish Trade 1661-1963. A Historical Survey.** By Birgit

Nüchel Thomsen and Brinley Thomas. Århus: Universitetsforlag, 1966. p 438. [Danish-English text.]

The 2000 Largest Companies in Denmark. 13th ed. Copenhagen: Teknisk Forlag, 1980. p 193.

Zelenko, Morton. **A Businessman's Guide to Denmark. For Business Combined with Holiday, What to Do before Leaving and after Arriving.** Copenhagen: The Scandinavian Times, 1963. p 192. Ill.

Economy - III.
Specific Industries and Companies

Alkjær, Ejler. **The Market for Agriculture Machinery and Implements in Denmark.** Copenhagen: Børsen, 1953. p 44. [Market Handbooks. International Chamber of Commerce Collection.]

Alkjær, Ejler. **The Market for Photographic Articles in Denmark.** Copenhagen: Børsen, 1955. p 32. [Market Handbooks. International Chamber of Commerce Collection.]

Alkjær, Ejler. **The Market for Wine in Denmark.** Copenhagen: Børsen, 1952. p 34. [Market Handbooks. International Chamber of Commerce Collection.]

The Book of Carlsberg. Ill. Sikker Hansen. Vignettes by Poul Høyrup and Fritz Kraul. Copenhagen: Carlsberg, 1973. p 92. Ill.

The Book Trade in Denmark. A Short Guide on Its History, Organization and Functions. Copenhagen: The Danish Publishers' Association, 1953. p 32.

Brinck, Anker. **Tuborg. Tuborg Breweries Ltd.** Copenhagen: Tuborg, 1957. p 24.

Christiani & Nielsen. **Christiani & Nielsen. 60 Years of Civil Engineering 1904-1964.** Copenhagen: privately printed, 1965. p 146. Ill.

Danmarks skibsfart. Special Edition: Denmark-England. Copenhagen: The Association of Denmark's Shipmasters, 1973. p 34. Ill. [English trans. of title is *Denmark's Shipping.*]

Dansk Radio Industri. **Danish Radio and Television Industry.** Export ed. of the Danish publication, *Dansk radio industri.* Copenhagen: Dansk Radio Industri, 1961. p 94.

Estrup, Chr. **The Danish Chemical Industry: Structure and Development.** Lyngby: Polyteknisk Forlag, 1971. p 127. Ill.

Jacobsen, J. C. **The Book of Carlsberg.** By J. C. and Carl Jacobsen. Copenhagen: Carlsberg, 1967. p 94. Ill.

The foundation, manufacturing process, employee programs and cultural activities of the Carlsberg breweries.

Kirkeby, Henning. **Danish Akvavit.** Copenhagen: Høst, 1975. p 63. Ill.

Kjeldsen, Marius. **Industrialised Building in Denmark.** By Marius Kjeldsen and W. R. Simonsen. Published on the occasion of the Third CIB Congress 1965 in collaboration with »Byggeindustrien«. Copenhagen: Teknisk Forlag, 1965. p 128. Ill.

Det Østasiatiske Kompagni. **The East Asiatic Company, Ltd.** Rev. ed. Copenhagen: A/S Det Østasiatiske Kompagni, 1963. p 110. Ill.

Det Østasiatiske Kompagni. **Industrial Activities of the East Asiatic Company.** Copenhagen: The East Asiatic Company, 1969. p 143. Ill.

Pazic, Milan. **A Short Survey of the Danish Tourist Market and Travel Trade.** Copenhagen: Scandinavian Media, 1976. p 215. Ill.

The Royal Copenhagen Porcelain Manufactory 1775-1975. Copenhagen: Den Kongelige Porcelainsfabrik, 1975. p 134. Ill.

The Tuborg Story. Copenhagen: Tuborg, 1971. p 33. Ill.

Economy - IV.
Periodicals

Danish Economic Review. Copenhagen: Privatbanken, 1972-.

Danish Export News. Ballerup: Forlaget Fischer, 1977-.

Denmark. Paris: Organization for Economic Cooperation and Development, 1961-. Annual. (OECD Economic Surveys).

Denmark. Quarterly Review. Copenhagen: Copenhagen Handelsbank. 1938-.

Economic Survey of Denmark. Copenhagen: Royal Danish Ministry of Foreign Affairs, 1949-1972.

Monetary Review. Copenhagen: Danmarks Nationalbank. Vol. 1-, (1962-.).

Education

Advice Guide for Foreign Students. Copenhagen: The Student Council at the University of Copenhagen, 1973. p 22.

Belding, Robert E. **Worker Education in Denmark.** Iowa City: Center for Labor & Management, University of Iowa, 1968. p 20.

Branth, Ellen. **The University of Copenhagen. A Brief Survey of Its Organization and Activities.** Copenhagen: University of Copenhagen, 1965. p 25.

Brickman, William W. **Denmark's Educational System and Problems.** Washington, D. C.: U. S. Office of Education, 1968. p 46.

Christensen, Viktor A. **An Analysis of Critical Issues in Higher Education in Denmark.** Ph. D. diss., University of Southern California, 1969. p 173.

Committee for Health Education. **What the Teacher Sees.** Copenhagen: Committee for Health Education, 1969. p 47.

Council of Europe. **Educational Institutions - Terminology. Denmark.** By Ad Hoc Committee for Educational Documentation and Information. Working party on the Multilingual Eudised Thesaurus. Strasbourg: Council of Europe. Council for Cultural Cooperation, 1973. p 44.

Danish Unesco Schools Projects: Literature for Children and Young People as a Means of Promotion of International Understanding. Contributions made to the seminar at Skarrildhus September 1970. U. S., 1970. p 89. dupl.

Danmarks Internationale Studenterkomité. **The Foreign Student in Denmark.** Copenhagen: Danmarks Internationale Studenterkomité, 1967. p 78.

Danmarks Pædagogiske Bibliotek. **List of Literature in English on Education in Denmark in the National Library of Education.** Copenhagen: Danmarks Pædagogiske Bibliotek, 1975. p 18.

Det danske Selskab. **Methods of Teaching Retarded Readers in Denmark.** Copenhagen: Det danske Selskab, 1955. p 29. [Danish Reference Papers.]

Davis, David C. L. **Model for a Humanistic Education: The Danish Folk High School.** Columbus, Ohio: Merrill, 1971. p 132. [Studies of the Person.]

Dixon, C. Willis. **Education in Denmark.** Copenhagen: Centraltrykkeriet, 1959. p 233.

Gravesen, Ernst. **A Survey of the Administration of the Educational System in Denmark.** Copenhagen: Ministry of Education, 1978. p 43.

Hansen, Elin. **The Travelling Folk High School, the Necessary Teacher Training College, Tvind Continuation School: A Brief Introduction - Especially for Our Guest.** Ulfborg: Skipper Clement, 1978. p 83. Ill.

Hansen, Erik Jørgen. **Equality Through Education?** Copenhagen: The Danish National Institute of Social Research, Teknisk Forlag 1978. p 46. [Booklet no. 1.]

Hjernov, Børge. **Education in Denmark: A Background, 1971-1972.** Copenhagen: Danish International Student Committee, 1972. p 18.

The International People's College. 1921-1971. Elsinore: The International People's College, 1971. p 89. Ill.

Jansen, Mogens [et al.]. **The Teaching of Reading - without Really Any Method. An Analysis of Reading Instruction in Denmark.** By Mogens Jansen, Bo Jacobsen and Poul Erik Jensen. Copenhagen: Munksgaard; Atlantic Highlands, N. J.: Humanities Press, 1978. p 190. Ill.

Jensen, Jesper. **The Little Red Schoolbook.** By Jesper Jensen and Søren Hansen. With Wallace Roberts. Tr. Berit Thornberry. New York: Pocket Book Division of Simon and Schuster, 1971. London: Stage 1; New Zealand: Alister Taylor. p 255. [*Den lille røde bog for skoleelever*, 1969.]

Kiil, Per. **Adult Vocational Training.** Copenhagen: Ministries of Labor and Social Affairs, 1969. p 22.

Københavns Kommunale Skolevæsen. **The Municipal Schools of Copenhagen.** Copenhagen: Københavns Kommunale Skolevæsen, 1954, 1957. p 29.

Københavns Kommune. **The Child Welfare Institution Store Vigerslevgaard.** Copenhagen: Københavns Kommune, 1957. p 30.

Københavns Universitet, Studenterrådet. **Advice Guide for Foreign Students.** Copenhagen: Københavns Universitet, 1973. p 22. Ill.

Manniche, Peter, [et al.]. **Rural Development and the Changing Countries of the World: A Study of Danish Rural Conditions and the Folk High School with Its Relevance to the Developing Countries.** Prefaces by Jawaharlal Nehru and K. Helveg Petersen. Ed. James F. Porter. Oxford and New York: Pergamon Press, 1969. p 525. Ill. 2nd rev. and abbr. ed. by Jakob Kjær and the Author. Copenhagen: Borgen, 1978. p 288. [In part published earlier as *Denmark, a Social Laboratory*. See under »Social Affairs«.]

Ministry of Education, see Undervisningsministeriet.

Nellemann, Aksel [et al.]. **Schools and Education in Denmark.** Tr. John B. Powell. Copenhagen: Det danske Selskab, 1964. p 152. Ill. Rev. ed. 1972. Tr. Roy Duffel. p 160. Ill. New ed. 1981. [Danish Information Handbooks.]

Novrup, Johannes. **Adult Education in Denmark.** Copenhagen: Det danske Forlag, 1954. p 81. [Orig. pub. 1949.]

174 Pedersen, Mogens N. **State and University in Denmark: From Coexistence to Collision Course.** Odense: Odense Universitet, 1976. p 62. 1977. p 79.

Petersen, Jørgen Kjerulf. **How to Study in Denmark.** By Jørgen Kjerulf Petersen and Bjarne Nørretranders. Copenhagen: Danmarks Internationale Studenterkomité, 1950. p 89.

Rasmussen, Werner. **The Concept of Permanent Education and Its Application in Denmark.** Strasbourg, Austria: Council for Cultural Cooperation, 1968. p 39. [Studies on Permanent Education, no. 2.]

Rishøj, Tom. **Semester in Copenhagen. Motivation and Evaluation. A Research Project Based on the DIS Spring Semester 1973.** Copenhagen: DIS Study Division, 1973. p 61.

Rørdam, Thomas. **The Danish Folk High Schools.** Tr. Sigurd Mammen. Copenhagen: Det danske Selskab & Foreningen for Højskoler og Landbrugsskoler, 1965. p 200. Ill. 2nd rev. ed. 1980. Tr. Alison Borch-Johansen. p 198. Ill. [Danish Information Handbooks.]

The Royal Danish College of Education. **Further Training of Teachers in Denmark.** Copenhagen: The Royal Danish School of Educational Studies, 1973. p 21.

Skov Jørgensen, I. **Segregated versus Integrated Education. New Dimensions in Rehabilitation.** Copenhagen: Ministry of Education, 1976. p 28.

Skov Jørgensen, I. **Special Education for Handicapped Children in the Municipal Schools in Denmark.** 3rd ed. Copenhagen: Ministry of Education, 1969. p 89.

Skov Jørgensen, I., ed. **Special Education in Denmark.** Ed. I. Skov Jørgensen and Søren Dyssegaard. Copenhagen: Ministry of Education, Ministry of Foreign Affairs, 1973. p 52. Ill.

Skov Jørgensen, I., ed. **Special Education in Denmark: Handicapped Children in Danish Primary Schools.** Tr. Roy Duffel. Copenhagen: Det danske Selskab, 1970. p 132. Ill. Rev. ed. 1979. Tr. Ejvind Rosenberg. p 220. Ill. [Danish Information Handbooks.]

Skov Jørgensen, I. **Special Education in the Rehabilitation Programme.** Copenhagen: Undervisningsministeriet, 1968. p 40.

Skrubbeltrang, Fridlev. **The Danish Folk High Schools.** 2nd ed. rev. by Roar Skovmand. Copenhagen: Det danske Selskab, 1952. p 88. [First ed. 1947.] [Later edition see Rørdam.]

Stybe, Svend Erik. **Copenhagen University. 500 Years of Science and Scholarship.** Copenhagen: Ministry of Foreign Affairs, 1979. p 219. Ill.

Thomsen, Ole B. **Relationships between Government and Universities: A Danish View.** Lecture delivered at the University of Toronto on February 10th, 1965. n. d. p 30.

Thomsen, Ole B. **Some Aspects of Education in Denmark.** Toronto: University of Toronto Press, 1967. p 105. [Ontario: Institute for Studies in Education.]

Thrane, Eigil. **Education and Culture in Denmark. A Survey of the Educational, Scientific and Cultural Conditions.** Tr. Harold Young. Copenhagen: G. E. C. Gad, 1958. p 91.

Undervisningsministeriet. **Access to Higher Education in Denmark.** Copenhagen: Ministry of Education, 1972. p 16.

Undervisningsministeriet. **Commercial Education in Denmark.** Copenhagen: Ministry of Education, International Relations Division, 1969. p 16.

Undervisningsministeriet. **A Condensed Outline of the Danish Apprenticeship Act and a List of Recognized Trades. Industry, Handicraft and Commerce.** Copenhagen: Undervisningsministeriet, Direktoratet for Erhvervsuddannelserne, 1970. p 16.

Undervisningsministeriet. **Curriculum Regulations for the Gymnasium (Upper Secondary School).** Copenhagen: Danish Ministry of Education, International Relations Division, 1979. p 50. [Education in Denmark.]

Undervisningsministeriet. **Curriculum Regulations for the Upper Secondary School (gymnasium) in Denmark.** Ministry of Education notice of 16th June 1971 concerning the instruction in the upper secondary school, the examination requirements and the syllabus to be offered at the upper secondary school leaving examination (studentereksamen). Copenhagen: Undervisningsministeriet, Det internationale Kontor, 1972. p 75.

Undervisningsministeriet. **The Danish Gymnasium. The Official Regulations (1953).** Copenhagen: Undervisningsministeriet, 1959. p 66.

Undervisningsministeriet. **Developments Towards a Coherent System of Education for the Handicapped.** Copenhagen: Ministry of Education, International Relations Division, 1970. p 16.

Undervisningsministeriet. **Education in Visual Arts in Primary and Lower Secondary Schools in Denmark.** Copenhagen: Ministry of Education, International Relations Division, 1966. p 18.

Undervisningsministeriet. **The Education System.** Copenhagen: Danish Ministry of Education, 1980. p 96. [Education in Denmark.]

Undervisningsministeriet. **Educational Statistics.** Copenhagen: Ministry of Education, 1972. p 52.

Undervisningsministeriet. **Guidance on the Curriculum in the gymnasium.** Copenhagen: Undervisningsministeriet, 1964. p 67.

Undervisningsministeriet. **Higher Education in Denmark. A Short Survey of the Organization and Activities of the University and Other Institutions of Higher Education in Denmark.** Copenhagen: Danish Ministry of Education, 1954. p 55.

Undervisningsministeriet. **Primary and Lower Secondary Education in Denmark.** Copenhagen: Undervisningsministeriet, 1961. p 26.

Undervisningsministeriet. **Problems of Long-term Economic Planning in Denmark. 1970-85: Education.** Copenhagen: Undervisningsministeriet, Den Økonomisk-statistiske Konsulent, 1972. p 66.

Undervisningsministeriet. **Recent Development and Trends in the Educational System in Denmark.** Copenhagen: Ministry of Education, 1978. p 18.

Undervisningsministeriet. **Regulations Concerning the Curriculum in the gymnasium.** Copenhagen: Undervisningsministeriet, 1961. p 21.

Undervisningsministeriet. **The School, the Pupil and the Parents.** A guide to co-operation between the home and the school. (Extract from the Ministry of Education's Teaching Guide *Skole, elev og forældre*). Copenhagen: Ministry of Education, 1979. p 53.

Undervisningsministeriet. **School Systems - A Guide.** Copenhagen: Ministry of Education, International Relations Division, 1970. p 18.

Undervisningsministeriet. **Secondary Education in Denmark.** Copenhagen: Undervisningsministeriet, 1961. p 26.

Undervisningsministeriet. **Sex Education in Primary and Secondary Schools.** Copenhagen: Ministry of Education, International Relations Division, 1966. p 17.

Undervisningsministeriet. **Sexroles and Education.** Copenhagen: The Committee of Sex Roles and Education, Ministry of Education, 1979. p 106. Ill.

Undervisningsministeriet. **Survey of Danish Elementary, Secondary and Further (Non-vocational) Education.** 2nd ed. Copenhagen: Ministry of Education, 1951. p 36.

Undervisningsministeriet. **U 90 - Danish Educational Planning and Policy in a Social Context at the End of the 20th Century.** Copenhagen: Central Council of Education, Ministry of Education, 1978. p 365. Ill.

United States Educational Foundation in Denmark, ed. **The Fulbright Scholar in Denmark.** Copenhagen: United States Educational Foundation in Denmark, 1966. p 72.

Environment

Christensen, Wilfred. **The Water Supply of Copenhagen.** Copenhagen: Københavns Vandforsyning, 1961. p 34. Ill.

Danish Pollution Control Equipment and Know How. Copenhagen: Federation of Danish Industries, 1974. p 31.

Garner, Fradley. **Environment Denmark.** English text by Fradley Garner. Copenhagen: Ministry of Foreign Affairs, 1972. p 57. Ill.

Haagen Jensen, Claus. **The Law and Practice Relating to Pollution Control in Denmark.** London: Graham and Trotman, 1976. p 208. Updating Supplement: London: Graham and Trotman, for the Commission of the European Communities, 1978. p 30.

Kofoed-Hansen, O. **The Negotiators - The Challenge of the Atomic Age.** Copenhagen: Ejnar Munksgaard, 1964. p 157.

Olsen, Kirsten, ed. **Forestry in Denmark.** Ed. Kirsten Olsen and Poul Hauberg. Copenhagen: The Danish Forestry Society, 1971. p 27. Ill.

Faroe Islands

Do You Know Klaksvik. Photographs by Eiler Rasmussen. Klaksvik: Klaksvik Kommune, 1975. p 61. Ill.

Ebbesen, Sven, ed. **The Faroe Islands.** Ed. Sven Ebbesen and Søren Dyssegaard. Copenhagen: Ministry of Foreign Affairs, 1971. p 45. Ill.

Elkjær-Hansen, Niels, ed. **The Faroe Islands. Scenery, Culture and Economy.** Niels Elkjær-Hansen and Carl Hermansen, eds. Tr. Reginald Spink. Copenhagen: Royal Ministry of Foreign Affairs, 1959. p 33. Ill. Also 1965, with Jacobsen, Jørgen-Frantz. *The Farthest Shore.* p 40.

Exner, Bent. **Faeroese Church Silver-ware.** Ill. Bent Exner. Photographs by Svend Thomsen. Copenhagen: Rhodos, 1975. p 292. Ill.

Faroe Sea Food. 1948-1973. Tórshavn: Föroya Fiskasöla, 1973. p 90. Ill.

Faroes in Pictures. Tórshavn: Ásmundur Poulsen, 1978. p 60. Ill. [Faroese-English-German-Danish text.] [*Føroyar i myndum.*]

176 Franceschi, Gérard. **The Faroe Islands.** By Gérard Franceschi and William Heinesen. Copenhagen: Rhodos, 1971. p 183. Ill.

Islands and People. Tórshavn. Leikur, 1979. p 144. Ill.

Lockwood, W. B. **The Faroese Bird Names.** Copenhagen: Munksgaard, 1961. p viii & 100. [Faroensia, no. 5.]

Lockwood, W. B. **An Introduction to Modern Faroese.** Copenhagen: Munksgaard, 1955. p xii & 244. Also 1964. 3rd printing, Tórshavn: Føroya Skúlabókagrunnur, 1977. p 244.

Rasmussen, Jóannes. **Geology of the Faeroe Islands (Pre-Quarternary).** By Jóannes Rasmussen and Arne Noe-Nygaard. Copenhagen: Reitzel, 1970. p 141. Ill.

Rasmussen, Stig G., ed. **Tórshavn. The Capital of the Faroe Islands.** Ed. Stig G. Rasmussen and Susanne Barding. Tórshavn: Tórshavnar Býrad, 1976. p 175. Ill.

Special Edition of the Danish Foreign Office Journal: The Faroe Islands. Copenhagen: Ministry of Foreign Affairs, 1971. p 56.

Thomsen, Hans. **Faroes in Pictures.** Tórshavn: Ásmundur Poulsen, 1975. p 60. Ill.

West, John F., ed. **Faroe: The Emergence of a Nation.** London: C. Hurst; New York: Eriksson, 1971. p 220.

West, John F., ed. **The Journals of the Stanley Expedition to the Faroe Islands and Iceland in 1789.** Vol. I: Introduction and Diary of James Wright. London: C. Hurst, 1970. p 216. Vol. II: Tórshavn: Føroya Fróðskaparfelag, 1975. p 167. Ill.

Williamson, Kenneth. **The Atlantic Islands. A Study of the Faeroe Life and Scene.** With an additional chapter on the Faroes today by Einar Kallsberg. Ill. with pen-and-ink drawings and photographs by the author. London: Routledge & Kegan Paul; New York: Fernhill House, 1970. p 385. Ill. [Rpt. of first ed. with an additional chapter on the Faroes today by Einar Kallsberg.]

Young, G. V. C. **From the Vikings to the Reformation. A Chronicle of the Faroe Islands up to 1538.** Douglas: Shearwater Pr., 1979. p 184. Ill.

Faroe Islands - Periodicals

Faroe Isles Review. Tórshavn: Bokagardur, 1976- . Twice yearly.

Faroes in Figures. Tórshavn: Føroya Sparikassi, Færøernes Realkreditinstitut, Føroya Banki, etc. 1957-1970.

Føroyar, Welcome to the Faroes. Rungsted Kyst: Anders Nyborg A/S, 1974-1976. [English-Danish-German text.] [Supersedes *Welcome to the Faroes.* Replaced by *North Atlantic.*]

North Atlantic. Welcome to Greenland, Iceland, the Faroes. Hørsholm: Anders Nyborg, 1977. p 218. Ill. 1978. p 210. Ill. [English-Danish-German text.]

Welcome to the Faroes. Rungsted Kyst: Anders Nyborg A/S, 1967-1973. [English-Danish-German text.] [Replaced by *Føroyar. Welcome to the Faroes.*]

Film

Bay, Hugo, ed. **The Danish Film Institute, Museum, School.** Ed. Hugo Bay and Ib Monty. English text by David Hohnen. Copenhagen: The Danish Film Institute, 1974. p 18. Ill.

Bergsten, Bebe. **The Great Dane and the Great Northern Film Company.** Los Angeles, Ca.: Locare Research Group, 1973. p 116. Ill.

Bordwell, David. **Filmguide to La passion de Jeanne d'Arc. (By Carl Dreyer).** Bloomington, Indiana: Indiana University Press, 1973. p 83.

Danish Films 1978. Copenhagen: The Danish Film Institute, 1978. p 48. Ill. [English-French-German text.]

Danish Government Film Foundation. **The Cinema in Denmark.** Designed by Morten Peetz-Schou. Copenhagen: Danish Film Foundation, [no date.] p 35.
The history of the Danish film industry and the role of the Government Film Foundation.

Danish Government Film Foundation. **Danish Films 66.** Copenhagen: Danish Government Film Foundation, 1966.

Dreyer, Carl Th. **Dreyer in Double Reflection.** Ed. Donald Skoller. New York: Dutton, 1973. p 205. Ill. [*Om filmen,* 1959.]

Dreyer, Carl Th. **Four Screen Plays.** Tr. Oliver Stallybrass. Intro. Ole Storm. London: Thames & Hudson, 1970. p 312. Ill. [Contents: *La passion de Jeanne d'Arc, Vampyr, Vredens Dag,* and *Ordet.*]

Dreyer, Carl Th. **Jesus. A Great Filmmaker's Final Masterwork.** New York: Dial Press, 1972. Paperback ed., New York: Dell Publishing Co., Delta Book div., 1973. p 312. Ill. [Contains three essays, *My only Great Passion, Who Crucified Jesus?* and *The Roots of Anti-Semitism.* Written in English.]

Dyssegaard, Søren, ed. **Carl Th. Dreyer: Danish Film Director 1889-1968.** English text by Reginald Spink. Copenhagen: Royal Danish Ministry of Foreign Affairs, 1968. p 50. Ill. [A Presentation Book.]
Including an excerpt from the script for *Jesus*.

Mielke, Ulla, ed. **Danish Films. Denmark Presents.** Copenhagen: The Danish Film Institute, 1980. p 32. Ill. [English-French-German text.]

Milne, Tom. **The Cinema of Carl Dreyer.** New York: Barnes, 1971. p 191. Ill.

Nash, Mark. **Dreyer.** London: British Film Institute, 1977. p 81.

Neergaard, Ebbe. **Carl Dreyer. A Film Director's Work.** Tr. Marianne Helweg. London: British Film Institute, 1950. p 42. Ill. [New Index Series, no. 1.]

Neergaard, Ebbe. **Educational and Scientific Films from Denmark. A Catalogue with Synopses.** Copenhagen: Statens Filmcentral, 1950. p 56.

Neergaard, Ebbe. **The Story of Danish Film.** Tr. Elsa Gress. Preface by Carl Th. Dreyer. Appendix by Erik Ulrichsen. Copenhagen: Det danske Selskab, 1963. p 118. Ill.
Appendix: *Danish feature films 1956-1962.*

Statens Filmcentral. **46 New Danish Short Films.** A supplement to *117 Short Films from Denmark.* Copenhagen: Statens Filmcentral, 1963. p 32.

Statens Filmcentral. **117 Short Films from Denmark.** Copenhagen: Statens Filmcentral, 1960. p 59.

Stormgaard, Uffe, ed. **Danish Films.** Ed. Uffe Stormgaard and Søren Dyssegaard. Copenhagen: The Danish Film Institute, 1973. p 77. Ill.

Film - Periodicals

Danish Film. Copenhagen: Danish Film Foundation, 1966-. [Also known as *Danish Film News* and *Danish Films.*]

Folk Customs and Costumes

Andersen, Ellen. **Folk Costumes in Denmark. Pictures and Descriptions of Local Dresses in the National Museum.** Tr. Birthe Andersen. Copenhagen: Hassing, 1952. p 68. Ill.

Kyhl, Kirsten. **Julebogen. Christmas in Denmark.** By Kirsten Kyhl and Merete Zacho. Danish text by Marie Amble Hansen. Copenhagen: Erichsen, 1962. p 48. Ill.

Mentze, Ernst. **Life and Fun in Denmark.** Tr. H. B. Ward. Copenhagen: Grønlund, 1958. p 40. [*Fest og hverdag i Danmark.* Danish-English-German-French text.]

Nielsen, Richard G. **The Pig in Danish Culture and Custom.** Odense: Historisk Topografisk Information, 1978. p 47. Ill.

Petersen, Grete. **Dolls in Danish Dresses.** Ill. Grete Petersen. Tr. David Hohnen. Copenhagen: Høst, 1960. p 48. Ill. [*Dukker i nationaldragt.* Danish-English text.]

Geography

Aagesen, Aage. **Atlas of Denmark.** 2 vols. Vol. II: The Population. Copenhagen: Det Kongelige Danske Geografiske Selskab and C. A. Reitzel, 1961. p 124. [*Atlas over Danmark. 2. Befolkningen.* Danish-English text.]

Aalen, F. H. A. **A Geographical Survey of North West Zealand, Denmark. (A Sample of East Danish Landscape).** M. A. thesis, Trinity College, Dublin, 1963.

Andersen, Otto. **The Population of Denmark.** Copenhagen: C. I. C. R. E. D., 1977. p 149. Ill.

Bjerre, Arne G. **Geography of Agricultural Land Resource Use in Denmark.** M. A. thesis, Oregon State College, 1960.

Bunting, B. T. **Danish Agriculture: A Revaluation from the Standpoint of Cultural Geography.** M. A. thesis, Sheffield University, 1957.

Frydendahl, Knud. **The Climate of Denmark. 1. Wind. Standard-normals 1931-1960.** Charlottenlund: Danish Meteorological Institute, 1971. p 240.

Gade, Ole. **Land Reclamation and the Cultivation of Reclaimed Wastelands in Denmark.** M. A. thesis, Florida State University, 1964.

Iversen, Johs. **The Development of Denmark's Nature since the Last Glacial.** Copenhagen: Reitzel, 1973. p 125. Ill.

Jacobsen, Niels Kingo, ed. **Collected Papers: Denmark; Some Contributions Concerning the Geography of Denmark and Other Topics Discussed by Copenhagen Geographers.** Copenhagen: Københavns Universitets Geografiske Institut, 1964. p 153. Ill.

Matthiesen, Poul Chr. **Population of Denmark. Trend and Prospects.** Copenhagen: Ministry of Foreign Affairs, 1974. p 23.

178 Matthiesen, Poul Chr. **Some Aspects of the Demographic Transition in Denmark.** Copenhagen: Københavns Universitet, 1970. p 226. Ill. [Diss.]

Scott, D. **Changes in the Settlement Pattern of the Island of Amager in Copenhagen. 1850-1952.** M. A. thesis, Birmingham University, 1954.

Wheeler, P. T. **Viborg and Its Region.** Nottingham: Geographical Field Group, 1973. p 189. Ill.

Greenland

Aron fra Kangek. **The Norsemen and Skraelings.** With Eigil Knuth. Godthåb, Greenland: Det grønlandske Forlag, 1968. p 109. Ill.

Bailey, Bernadine. **Greenland in Pictures.** New York: Sterling, 1974. p 64. Ill.

Balle, Povl E., ed. **Greenland's Newspaper and Periodical Index 1950-1954.** Ed. Povl E. Balle and Åse Reymann. Ballerup: Bibliotekscentralen, 1976. p 124.

Balle, Povl E., ed. **Greenland's Newspaper and Periodical Index 1955-1959.** Ed. Povl E. Balle and Åse Reymann. Ballerup: Bibliotekscentralen, 1977. p 182.

Banks, Michael. **Greenland.** London: David and Charles, 1975. p 208. Ill.

Berry, Francis. **I Tell of Greenland. An Edited Translation of the Saudarkrokur Manuscripts.** London: Routledge & Kegan Paul, 1977. p 205.

Berthelsen, Chr. **Development of the Educational System in Greenland 1950-1970.** Godthåb: Director of Education in Greenland, 1974. p 40. Ill.

Böcher, Tyge W. [et al.]. **The Flora of Greenland.** By Tyge W. Böcher, Kjeld Holmen and Knud Jakobsen. Ill. Ingeborg Frederiksen. Copenhagen: Haase, 1968. p 312. Ill.

Bornemann, Claus: **Greenland.** Copenhagen: The Ministry for Greenland, 1976. p 38. Ill.

Bure, Kristjan, ed. **Greenland.** Copenhagen: Royal Danish Ministry of Foreign Affairs, 1953. p 167. Ill. Also 1954, Tr. Reginald Spink. 1956, Tr. Reginald Spink and A. Anslev. Also 1961, p 192.

De Laguna, Frederica. **Voyage to Greenland. A Personal Initiation into Anthropology.** New York: W. W. Norton, 1977. p 285. Ill.

Ebbesen, Sven, ed. **Greenland.** Ed. Sven Ebbesen and Søren Dyssegaard. Copenhagen: Ministry of Foreign Affairs, 1971. p 53. Ill.

Education in Greenland. Godthåb: Skoledirektøren for Grønland, 1977. p 44. Ill.

Egede, Hans. **A Description of Greenland.** New ed. Millwood, N. Y.: Kraus, 1973. p 118 & p 225. Ill.

Erngaard, Erik. **Greenland. Then and Now.** Copenhagen: Lademann, 1972. p 240. Ill.

Fristrup, Børge. **The Greenland Ice Cap.** Tr. David Stoner. Copenhagen: Rhodos; Seattle: Univ. of Wahington Press, 1967. p 312. Ill.

Gad, Finn. **The History of Greenland.** Tr. from the Danish by Ernst Dupont. In four volumes. Vol. I: Earliest Times to 1700. p 350. Vol. II: 1700-1782. [Vol. III: 1782-1910. Vol. IV: 1910 to present. In progress.] London: G. Hurst, 1970-1971. Montreal: McGill, Queen's University Press, 1971.

Giæver, John. **In the Land of the Musk-ox. Tales of Wild Life in North-East Greenland.** Tr. Munda Whittaker and Walter Oliver. London: Jarrolds, 1958. p 191. Ill.

Gilberg, Rolf. **The Polar Eskimo Population, Thule District, North Greenland.** Copenhagen: Nyt Nordisk Forlag, 1976. p 87.

Greenland. Arctic Denmark. Copenhagen: Ministry of Foreign Affairs, 1972. p 66. Ill.

The Greenland Criminal Code. South Hackensack, N. J.: Rothman, 1970. p 47. [The American Series of Foreign Penal Codes, no. 16.]

Henriksen, Edvard, ed. **Kalâtdlit-nunât. Greenland.** Ed. Edvard Henriksen and Sven Klitgaard. Copenhagen: Edvard Henriksen, 1971. p 93. Ill.

Herbert, Marie. **The Snow People.** London: Barrie & Jenkins; New York: Putnam, 1973. p 229. [About the Greenland Eskimos.]

Hertling, Knud [et al.], eds. **Greenland Past and Present.** Copenhagen: Edvard Henriksen, 1970. p 370. Ill.

Ingstad, Helge Marcus. **Land under the Pole Star. A Voyage to the Norse Settlement of Greenland and the Saga of the People that Vanished.** Tr. from the Norwegian by Naomi Walford. New York: St. Martin's Press; London: Jonathan Cape Ltd., 1966. p 381. Ill.

Jakobshavn. A Town in Greenland. Copenhagen: Ministry of Foreign Affairs, 1977. p 40. Ill.

Kent, Rockwell. **Greenland Journal. A Private Diary and Sketchbook.** New York: Ivan Obolensky, 1962. p 302. Ill.

Knuth, Eigil. **Aron of Kangeq 1822-1869. The Seal Hunter Who became Father of Greenland's Art of Painting.** Copenhagen: Danish National Museum. 1960. p 24. Ill.

Kornerup, Andreas. **Kornerups Grønland. Andreas Kornerup, Sketches from Greenland, 1876-1879.** Copenhagen: The Commission for Scientific Research in Greenland, 1978. p 136. Ill.

Krogh, Knud J. **Viking Greenland. With a Supplement of Saga Texts.** Copenhagen: The National Museum, 1967. p 187. Ill.

Leth Nielsen, Bjarne. **A Survey of the Economic Geology of Greenland (Exclusive Fossil Fuels).** Copenhagen: Geological Survey of Greenland, 1973. p 45. Ill.

Mackersey, Ian. **Rescue Below Zero.** New York: W. W. Norton & Co., 1954. p 155. Ill.

Malaurie, Jean. **The Last Kings of Thule; a Year among the Polar Eskimos of Greenland.** Tr. from the French by Gwendolen Freeman. Preface G. de Poncons. New York: Thomas Crowell, 1956. p 295. Ill.

Mattox, William G. **Fishing in West Greenland 1910-1966. The Development of a New Native Industry.** Copenhagen: Hans Reitzel, 1973. p 469. Ill. [*Meddelelser om Grønland*, vol. 197, nr. 1.]

Nielsen, Bent. **Med Kongefamilien på Grønland. A Royal Visit.** Photos Allan Moe. Text Bent Nielsen. Tr. Niels Haislund. Ed. Per Hjald Carlsen. Copenhagen: Illustrationsforlaget, 1960. p 15 and p 24 plates.

Nørlund, Poul. **Viking Settlers in Greenland and Their Descendants during Five Hundred Years.** Foreword by Ellis H. Minns. Tr. from the Danish by W. E. Calvert. New York: Kraus Reprint Co., 1971. p 160. Ill. [Rpt. of 1937 ed.]

Oldenow, Knud. **Printing in Greenland.** Copenhagen: Munksgaard, 1959. p 44. Ill.

Oldenow, Knud. **The Spread of Printing: Greenland.** Amsterdam: Van Gendt & Co., 1969.

Rasmussen, Knud. **The Bear in the Ice Hole. Greenland and Its People.** Ed. Bent Rying. Tr. Reginald Spink. Ill. Knud Berthelsen. *Greenland and Its People* by P. H. Lundsteen. Copenhagen: Royal Danish Ministry of Foreign Affairs, 1962. p 40. Ill.

Rasmussen, Knud J. V. **Greenland by the Polar Sea: The Story of the Thule Expedition from Melville Bay to Cape Morris Jesup.** Tr. Asta and Rowland Kenney. Preface Sir Lewis Beaumont. 1921; rpt. New York: AMS Press, 1976. p 326. Ill.

Rasmussen, Knud J. V. **Knud Rasmussen's Posthumous Notes on East Greenland Legends and Myths.** Ed. H. Ostermann. 1939; rpt. New York: AMS Press, 1976. p 182.

Rasmussen, Knud J. V. **Knud Rasmussen's Posthumous Notes on the Life and Doings of the East Greenlanders in Olden Times.** Ed. H. Ostermann. 1938; rpt. New York: AMS Press, 1976. p 214. Ill.

Rasmussen, Knud J. V. **The People of the Polar North, a Record.** Compiled from the Danish originals and ed. G. Herring. Ill. Count Harald Moltke. 1908; rpt. Detroit: Gale Research Co., 1975. p 358. Ill. New York: AMS Press, 1976. p 358. Ill. [First is a rpt. of London ed. of 1908, second a rpt. of the Philadelphia ed. of the same year.]

Regional Development Programme for Greenland 1977-1979. Brussels: Commission of the European Communities, 1977. p 49.

Rink, Hinrich (Henry) Johannes. **Danish Greenland, Its People and Products.** Tr. from Danish by the author. 1877; rpt. with a new intro. by Helge Larsen. Montreal: McGill-Queen's University Press; London: Hurst, 1974. p 468. Ill. [Ed. and expanded trans. of *Grønland, geografisk og statistisk beskrevet.*]

Rosendahl, Philip. **Jakob Danielsen - A Greenlandic Painter.** Tr. Douglas Holmes and David Stoner. Copenhagen: Rhodos, in collaboration with The Greenland Society and The Ministry for Greenland, 1967. p 355. Ill. [Danish-English-Greenlandic text.]

Secher, Alex. **Greenland Revisited.** Tr. David Hohnen. Copenhagen: Chr. Erichsens Forlag, 1958. p 92. Ill.

Simpson, C. J. W. **North Ice, the Story of the British North Greenland Expedition.** Drawings by Ann Simpson. London: Hodder & Stoughton, 1957. p 384. Ill.

Svarlien, Oscar. **The Eastern Greenland Case in Historical Perspective.** Gainesville: University of Florida Press, 1964. p 74. [Univ. of Florida Monographs, no. 21.]

Therkelsen, Kjeld Rask. **Grønland.** Copenhagen: Det Schønbergske Forlag, 1953. p 127. Ill. [Danish-English text.]

Udbye, Knud. **The Greenlandic Summer.** Text and photographs by Knud Udbye. Copenhagen: Rhodos, 1972. p 61. Ill.

Wager, Walter. **Camp Century: City Under the Ice.** Philadelphia: Chilton Co., 1962. p 144. Ill.

Williamson, Geoffrey. **Changing Greenland.** Intro. Ole Bjørn Kraft. London: Sidgwick & Jackson, 1953. New York: Library Publishers, 1954. p 288. Ill.

Wright, Theon. **The Knife.** Ill. Rus Anderson. Canada: Copp Clark Co., New York: Gilbert Press, 1955. p 300. Ill.

Greenland - Periodicals

Danish Arctic Research. (Greenland). Report from Arktisk Institut, 1960- .

180 **Grønland. Welcome to Greenland.** Rungsted Kyst: Anders Nyborg, 1974-1976. [English-Danish-German text.] [Supersedes *Welcome to Greenland.* Replaced by *North Atlantic.*]

North Atlantic. Welcome to Greenland, Iceland, the Faroes. Hørsholm: Anders Nyborg, 1977. p 218. Ill. 1978. p 210. Ill. [English-Danish-German text.]

Welcome to Greenland. Rungsted Kyst: Anders Nyborg in cooperation with Grønlands Landsråd, 1971-1973. [English-Danish text.] [Replaced by *Grønland. Welcome to Greenland.*]

Health and Medicine

Deaf in Denmark. Exhibition, City Hall of Copenhagen, August 1977. Copenhagen: The National Association of the Deaf, 1977. p 30. Ill.

Ejlers, Erik [et al.]. **The Danish National Service for the Mentally Retarded. The Years' Planning and Building 1959-1969.** By the architects Erik Ejlers, Henning Gravesen and Jens Malling Pedersen, Foreword by N. E. Bank-Mikkelsen. Copenhagen: Nyt Nordisk Forlag/Arnold Busck, 1969. p 126. Ill.

Engberg, Eugenie, ed. **Rehabilitation and Care of the Handicapped in Denmark.** Ed. Eugenie Engberg and Carl Lange. Copenhagen: Socialministeriets Afdeling for Internationalt Socialpolitisk Samarbejde, 1963. p 100. Ill.

Engberg, Eugenie. **Rehabilitation and Care of the Handicapped.** Copenhagen: Ministries of Labour and Social Affairs, 1967. p 84. [Social Conditions in Denmark, no. 6.]

Felbo, Mogens. **Old Age and Work. Relation between Condition of Limps and Capacity for Work in 65 and 70 Year Old Natives of the Danish Island Bornholm.** Tr. Anna la Cour. Copenhagen: Munksgaard, 1958. p 236. Ill. [diss.]

Flash on the Danish National Service for the Mentally Retarded. Copenhagen: The Personnel Training School, 1974. p 142. Ill. 2nd ed. 1976. p 183. Ill.

Hegeler, Inge. **Living Is Loving.** By Inge Hegeler and Sten Hegeler. Ill. Eiler Krag. New York: Stein & Day, 1972. p 189.

Hegeler, Inge and Sten Hegeler. **The X. Y. Z. of Love: Frank Answers to Every Important Question about Sex in Today's World.** Tr. David Hohnen. New York: Crown, 1970. p 216. [*Spørg Inge og Sten.*]

Høybye-Mortensen, Preben. **The Society and Home for the Disabled. 1872-1972.** Copenhagen: The Society and Home for the Disabled, 1972. p 39. Ill.

Jensen, V. Gaunø. **The History of Pharmacy in Denmark. A Survey.** By V. Gaunø Jensen and A. Schæffer. Copenhagen: Dansk Farmacihistorisk Selskab, 1960. p 42. Ill. [Theriaca. 6.]

Koch, J. H. [et al.]. **Health Services in Denmark.** By J. H. Koch, C. Toftemark and P. Andersen-Rosendal. Copenhagen: Amtsrådsforeningen i Danmark, 1976. p 36. Ill.

Møller, P. Flemming. **History and Development of Radiology in Denmark 1896-1950.** Copenhagen: Nyt Nordisk Forlag/Arnold Busck, 1968. p 528. Ill.

National Association for the Fight against Tuberculosis. **Fight Against Tuberculosis in Denmark.** Copenhagen: National Association for the Fight against Tuberculosis and Nyt Nordisk Forlag, 1950. p 134.

Samfundet og Hjemmet for Vanføre. **The Society and Home for Cripples in Denmark.** Copenhagen: Samfundet og Hjemmet for Vanføre, 1957. p 40. Ill.

Schwalbe-Hansen, P. **Care of the Mentally Defective in Denmark.** Copenhagen: Munksgaard, 1953. p 16. Ill.

The Society and Home for the Disabled. Copenhagen: The Society and Home for the Disabled, 1974. p 109. Ill.

Health and Medicine - Periodicals

Danish Medical Bulletin. Danish Medical Association. Annual. 1954- .

History - General

Birch, J. H. S. **Denmark in History.** Westport, Conn.: Greenwood Press, 1976. [Rpt. of 1938 ed.]

Georg, Anders, ed. **Denmark-USA, 200 Years of Close Relations.** Ed. Anders Georg and Ole Kjær Madsen. Copenhagen: Ministry of Foreign Affairs, 1976. p 48. Ill.

Hellsen, Henry. **Danske Malere fortæller Fædrelandshistorie.** English text by W. Glyn Jones. Copenhagen: Berlingske, 1953. p 96. Ill.

Kjersgaard, Erik. **A History of Denmark.** Tr. Reginald Spink. Copenhagen: Royal Danish Ministry of Foreign Affairs, 1974. p 102. Ill.

Kjølsen, Klaus. **The Foreign Service of Denmark 1770-1970.** Copenhagen: Ministry of Foreign Affairs, 1970. p 38. Ill.

Lauring, Palle. **A History of Denmark in Pictures.** Pictures from before 1937 selected by Otto Andrup. Tr. W. Glyn Jones. Copenhagen: Hasselbalch, 1963. p 299. Ill. [New ed. of *Dansk dåd*, vol. I.]

Lauring, Palle. **A History of the Kingdom of Denmark.** Tr. David Hohnen. Copenhagen: Høst & Søn, 1960. p 260. Ill. 2nd rev. ed. 1963. p 280. 4th ed. 1973. p 274. Ill.

Møller, Th. **Old Danish Military Weapons.** Tr. David Hohnen. Ill. by the author. Copenhagen: Høst & Søn, 1963. 2nd rev. ed. 1970. p. 93. Ill. [Danish-English text. Scale drawings.]

Oakley, Stewart. **A Short History of Denmark.** New York: Praeger, 1972. p 269. Ill.
See also British ed., *The Story of Denmark.*

Oakley, Stewart. **The Story of Denmark.** London: Faber & Faber, 1972. p 269. Ill.

Royal Danish Ministry of Foreign Affairs. **Short History of Denmark.** English text revised by Reginald Spink. Prepared by the Institute of History at the University of Århus. Copenhagen: Royal Danish Ministry of Foreign Affairs, 1957. p 64. Ill. [Reprinted from *Denmark.*]

Starcke, Viggo. **Denmark in World History. The External History of Denmark from the Stone Age to the Middle Ages, with Special Reference to Danish Influence on the English-speaking Nations.** Tr. Frank Noel Stagg, Ingeborg Nixon and Elmer Harp. Philadelphia: University of Pennsylvania Press; London: Oxford University Press, 1963. p 381. Ill.

History - I.
Prehistory and
Archaeology

Broholm, H. C. **Early Bronze Age.** Copenhagen: Gyldendal. 1952. p 65. [*Ældre Bronzealder.* Danish-English text.] [Danske Oldsager. Danish Antiquities. III.]

Broholm, H. C. **Late Bronze Age Culture in Denmark.** Copenhagen: Gyldendal, 1953. p 104. [*Yngre Bronzealder.* Danish-English text.] [Danske Oldsager. Danish Antiquities. IV.]

Bröste, Kurt. **Prehistoric Man in Denmark. A Study in Physical Anthropology.** In collaboration with J. Balslev Jørgensen. Archeological contributions by C. J. Becker and Johannes Brønsted. 2 vols. Copenhagen: Munksgaard, 1956. p 159 and p 439.

Davidsen, Karsten. **The Final TRB Culture in Denmark. A Settlement Study.** Tr. Lars Broholm Tharp. Copenhagen: Akademisk Forlag, 1978. p 206. Ill. [Arkæologiske studier, V.]

Dyer, James. **Discovering Archaeology in Denmark.** Aylesbury: Shire, 1973. p 88. Ill.

Glob, Peter Vilhelm. **The Bog People. Iron-Age Man Preserved.** Tr. Rupert Bruce-Mitford. London: Faber & Faber; Ithaca, New York: Cornell University Press, 1969. p 200. Ill. Paperback ed., London: Granada Publishing Ltd.; New York: Ballantine Books, 1971. p 144. Ill.

Glob, Peter Vilhelm. **Danish Prehistoric Monuments; Denmark from the Stone Age to the Vikings.** Tr. Joan Bulman. London: Faber & Faber, 1971. p 351. Ill. [*Danske oldtidsminder,* 1967.]
See also American ed. *Denmark. An Archaeological History.*

Glob, Peter Vilhelm. **Denmark; an Archaeological History from the Stone Age to the Vikings.** Tr. Joan Bulman. Ithaca, New York: Cornell University Press, 1971. p 351. [*Danske oldtidsminder,* 1967.]
See also British ed. *Danish Prehistoric Monuments.*

Glob, Peter Vilhelm. **The Mound People: Danish Bronze-age Man Preserved.** Tr. Joan Bulman. London: Faber & Faber, 1970 and 1974. Ithaca, New York: Cornell University Press, 1974. p 184. Ill. [*Højfolket.*]

Hald, Margrethe. **Ancient Danish Textiles from Bogs and Burials. A Comparative Study of Costume and Iron Age Textiles.** Tr. Jean Olsen. Copenhagen: The National Museum 1980. p 398. Ill. [*Olddanske Tekstiler,* 1950.] [Archaeological-Historical Series, 21.]

Hald, Margrethe. **Primitive Shoes. An Archaeological-Ethnological Study Based upon Shoefinds from the Jutland Peninsula.** Tr. Ingeborg Nixon. Copenhagen: The National Museum, 1972. p 216. Ill. [Archaeological-Historical Series, 13.]

Hansen, Hans-Ole. **I Built a Stone-Age House.** Tr. Maurice Michael. London: Phoenix House, 1962. New York: John Day Co., 1964 p 80. Ill. [*Lerhusene i Lejre.*]

Hatt, Gudmund. **Nørre Fjand. An Early Iron-age Village Site in West Jutland.** Wih a contribution by Holger Rasmussen. Copen-

182

hagen: Munksgaard, 1957. p 382. Ill. [Det kgl. danske Videnskabernes Selskab. Arkæologisk-kunsthistoriske Skrifter. Vol. 2, no. 2.]

Klindt-Jensen, Ole. **The Bronze Cauldron from Brå. Early Celtic Influences in Denmark.** Aarhus: Universitetsforlaget, 1953. p 98. [*Bronzekedelen fra Brå. Tidlige keltiske indflydelser i Danmark.* Danish-English text.] [Jysk arkæologisk Selskabs Skrifter. III.]

Klindt-Jensen, Ole. **Denmark before the Vikings.** Tr. Eva and David Wilson. London: Thames and Hudson, 1957. New York: Praeger, 1957, 1969. p 212. Ill.

Klindt-Jensen, Ole. **Foreign Influences in Denmark's Early Iron Age.** Tr. W. E. Calvert. Copenhagen: Munksgaard, 1950. p 248. Ill. [Diss.]

Lauring, Palle. **Land of the Tollund Man; the Prehistory and Archaeology of Denmark.** Tr. Reginald Spink. Photos Lennart Larsen. London: Lutterworth Press, 1957. New York: Macmillan, 1958. p 160. Ill. [*De byggede riget.*]

Levy, Janet Elizabeth. **Social and Religious Change in Bronze Age Denmark.** Ph.D. diss., Washington University (St. Louis, Missouri), 1977. p 365. [Diss. Abstr. 38/07-A, 4236.]

Liversage, David. **Material and Interpretation - the Archaeology of Sjælland in the Early Roman Iron Age.** Copenhagen: The National Museum, 1980. p 204. Ill. [Archaeological-Historical Series, 20.]

Munksgaard, Elisabeth. **Denmark: An Archaeological Guide.** London: Faber & Faber; New York: Praeger, 1970. p 144. Ill. [Archaeological Guide Series.]

Ramskou, Thorkild. **Prehistoric Denmark.** Vignettes by Inge Thomasen. Photography by Lennart Larsen. Copenhagen: The National Museum, 1970. p 87. Ill.

Rasmussen, Holger. **Prehistoric Danes.** By Holger Rasmussen and Arne Andersen. Copenhagen: Telefon Fabrik Automatic, 1956. p 36. Ill.

Steensberg, Axel. **Draved. An Experiment in Stone Age Agriculture. Burning, Sowing and Harvesting.** Copenhagen: The National Museum, 1979. p 116. Ill.

History - II.
800-1500

Andrup, Otto. **Bonds of Kinship between the Royal Houses of Great Britain and Denmark.** Tr. John R. B. Gosney. 2nd ed. Copenhagen: Royal Danish Ministry of Foreign Affairs and Gyldendal, 1957. p 32. Ill. [Orig. pub. 1948.]

Cohen, Sidney L. **Viking Fortresses of the Trelleborg Type.** Copenhagen: Rosenkilde and Bagger, 1965. p 104. Ill.

Garmonsway, G. N. **Canute and his Empire.** London: H. K. Lewis & Co., 1964. p 28. [The Dorothea Coke Memorial Lecture in Northern Studies, delivered at University College, London, 28 October 1963.]

Jacobsen, Grethe. **Guilds in Medieval Denmark: The Social and Economic Role of Merchants and Artisans.** Ph.D. diss. University of Wisconsin, 1980. (p 334.)

Larson, Laurence Marcellus. **Canute the Great, 995-1035, and the Rise of Danish Imperialism during the Viking Age.** New York: AMS Press, 1970. p 375. Ill. [Rpt. of 1912 ed. Heroes of the Nations Series.]

Madsen, Hans Jørgen. **Århus of the Vikings.** Drawings by Flemming Bau. Photographs by Preben Delholm. Aarhus: Moesgård, 1975. p 16. Ill.

McGuire, Brian Patrick. **Conflict and Continuity at Øm Abbey: A Cistercian Experience in Medieval Denmark.** Copenhagen: Museum Tusculanum, 1976. p 151. Ill. [Opuscula Graecolatina, 8.]

Møller-Christensen, Vilhelm. **Ten Lepers from Næstved in Denmark. A Study of Skeletons from a Medieval Danish Leper Hospital.** Preface by Erik Waaler. Tr. Hans Andersen. Copenhagen: Danish Science Press, 1953. p 164. [Medical Monographs, 2.]

Olsen, Olaf. **Five Viking Ships from Roskilde Fjord.** Olaf Olsen and Ole Grumlin-Pedersen. Tr. Barbara Bluestone. Copenhagen: The National Museum, 1978. p 136. Ill.

Olsen, Olaf. **Fyrkat. The Viking Camp near Hobro.** 2nd rev. ed. Copenhagen: The National Museum, 1975. p 16. Ill.

Pratt, Fletcher. **The Third King.** Maps by Rafael Palacios. New York: Sloane, 1950. p 313. Ill. About Valdemar IV (1320-1375).

Randsborg, Klavs. **The Viking Age in Denmark: the Formation of a State.** London, Duckworth, 1980. p 206. Ill.

Rebane, P. Peter. **Denmark and the Baltic Crusade.** Ph.D. diss. Michigan State University, 1969. (p 235.)

Thorvildsen, Knud. **The Viking Ship of Ladby.** 2nd ed. Copenhagen: The National Museum, 1975. p 42. Ill.

The Vikings in Denmark. Eds. Anders Georg, Søren Dyssegaard and Thorkild Borre. Tr. Reginald Spink. Copenhagen: Ministry of Foreign Affairs, 1980. p 31. Ill. [Special Issue of *Danish Journal.*]

History - III.
1500-1914

Andersen, A. Feldborg. **Denmark Delineated or Sketches of the Present State of That Country 1824.** Copenhagen: Rosenkilde & Bagger, 1976. p 400. Ill.

Baack, Lawrence J. **Agrarian Reform in Eighteenth-Century Denmark.** Lincoln, Nebr., University of Nebraska Press, 1977. p 44. [University of Nebraska Studies, New Series, 56.]

Bamberger, Ib Nathan. **A Cultural History of the Jews of Denmark 1622-1900.** D. H. L. diss., Yeshiva University, 1974. (p 238). [Diss. Abstr. 36/03-A, p 1712.]

Carr, William. **Schleswig-Holstein, 1815-1864: A Study in National Conflict.** Manchester: Manchester University Press; New York: Barnes and Noble, 1963. p 341.

Danaher, Kevin, ed. **The Danish Force in Ireland 1690-1691.** Ed. K. Danaher and J. G. Simms. Dublin: Irish Manuscripts Commission, 1962. p 169. Ill.

Feldbæk, Ole. **Denmark and the Armed Neutrality 1800-1801. Small Power Policy in a World War.** Copenhagen: Akademisk Forlag, 1980. p 308. [Københavns Universitet, Institut for Økonomisk Historie, publikation 16.]

Feldbæk, Ole. **India Trade under the Danish Flag 1772-1808. European Enterprise and Anglo-Indian Remittance and Trade.** Lund: Studentlitteratur, 1969. p 359. [Scandinavian Institute of Asian Studies. Monograph Series, no. 2.]

Friis, Astrid. **A History of Prices and Wages in Denmark 1660-1800.** By Astrid Friis and Kristof Glamann. London: Longmans, Green and Co. for the Institute of Economics and History, Copenhagen, 1958. p 352.

Gold, Carol. **The Danish Reform Era 1784-1900.** Ph. D. diss., University of Wisconsin, 1975. (p 327). [Diss. Abstr. 36/12-A, p 8244.]

Halicz, Emanuel. **Danish Neutrality during the Crimean War (1853-1856). Denmark between the Hammer and the Anvil.** Tr. from the Polish. Odense: Odense University Press, 1977. p 247.

Hansen, Svend Aage. **Early Industrialisation in Denmark.** Copenhagen: Københavns Universitets Fond til Tilvejebringelse af Læremidler and Gad, 1970. p 77.

Hassø, Arthur G. **Danish Department of Foreign Affairs until 1770.** By Arthur G. Hassø and Erik Kroman. Copenhagen: Rigsarkivet, 1973. p 196. [Vejledende arkivregistraturer, 16.]

Hjelholt, Holger. **British Mediation in the Danish-German Conflict 1848-1850.** 2 vols. Part I: From the March Revolution to the November Government. Part II: From the November Cabinet until the Peace with Prussia and the London Protocol (the 2nd of July and the 2nd of August 1850). Copenhagen: Det Kongelige Danske Videnskabernes Selskab and Munksgaard, 1965-1966. [Historiske-Filosofiske Meddelelser 41:1 and 42:1.]

Hjelholt, Holger. **Great Britain, the Danish-German Conflict and the Danish Succession 1850-1852. From the London Protocol to the Treaty of London (the 2nd of August 1850 to the 8th of May 1852).** Copenhagen: Munksgaard, 1971. p 323. Ill.

Kjærgaard, Thorkild. **Denmark Gets the News of '76.** Copenhagen: Danish Bicentennial Committee. 1975. p 43. Ill.

Loftin, Joseph Evans, Jr. **The Abolition of the Danish Atlantic Slave Trade.** Ph. D. diss. The Louisiana State University and Agricultural and Mechanical College, 1977. (p 327). [Diss. Abstr. 38/06-A, p 3651.]

Molesworth, Robert. **An Account of Denmark as It Was in the Year 1692.** Copenhagen: Rosenkilde & Bagger, 1976. p 271. [Rpt. of 1693 original.]

Munck, Thomas. **The Peasantry and the Early Absolute Monarchy in Denmark 1660-1708.** Norwich: University of East Anglia, 1977. p 229. Ill.

Petersen, Charles William. **English and Danish Naval Strategy in the Seventeenth Century.** Ph. D. diss., University of Maine. 1975. (p 362). [Diss. Abstr. 36/10-A, p 6868.]

Petersen, Erling Ladewig. **The Crisis of the Danish Nobility 1580-1660.** Odense: Odense Universitetsforlag, 1967. p 35.

Pope, Dudley. **The Great Gamble. Nelson at Copenhagen.** London: Weidenfeld & Nicolson, 1972. p 579. Ill.

Von Schmidt-Phiseldek, C. F. **Europe and America.** Tr. Joseph Owen. Postscript by Thorkild Kjærgaard. Copenhagen: Danish Bicentennial Committee with the Danish Ministry of Foreign Affairs and Rhodos, 1976. p 307. Ill. [Rpt. of 1820 trans., with new postscript and ill.]

History - IV.
1914-1980

Agerbak, H. **Light out of Darkness.** London: University College, 1972. p 19. [A lecture delivered 28 November 1972.]

184

About British co- operation with the Danish Resistance Movement.

Bennett, Jeremy. **British Broadcasting and the Danish Resistance Movement, 1940-1945; a Study of the Wartime Broadcasts of the B.B.C. Danish Service.** Cambridge, England: Cambridge University Press, 1966. p 266. Ill.

Bertelsen, Aage. **October '43. An Account of the Rescue of 6,000 Jews from Occupied Denmark in October 1943.** Foreword by Sholem Asch. Tr. Molly Lidholm and Willy Agtby. New York: G. P. Putnam's Sons, 1953. p 246. London: Museum Press, 1955. p 160. Ill. London: John Spencer & Co., 1956. p 189. [Spencer ed., True War Series, no. 3.]

Flender, Harold. **Rescue in Denmark.** New York: Simon and Schuster, 1963. p 281. Ill. About the rescue of the Jews during World War II.

Hæstrup, Jørgen. **From Occupied to Ally: Denmark's Fight for Freedom 1940-1945.** Tr. Reginald Spink. Copenhagen: Danish Ministry of Foreign Affairs, 1963. p 40. Ill. [Panorama Denmark no. 1.]

Hæstrup, Jørgen. **Secret Alliance: a Study of the Danish Resistance Movement, 1940-45.** Tr. Alison Borch-Johansen. Odense: Odense University Press, 1976-1977. 3 vols. [*Hemmelig alliance.*]

Hanssen, Hans Peter. **Diary of a Dying Empire.** Tr. Oscar O. Winther. Indiana: Indiana University Press, 1955. p 409. [*Fra Krigstiden.*] Personal narratives about World War I, 1924.

Holm-Christensen, Marianne. **The Fight for Freedom and Its Significance for Denmark's Future.** Tr. J. D. Ambler. Copenhagen: Hirschsprung, 1960. p 23. [*Frihedskampen og dens betydning for Danmarks fremtid.* Danish-English text.]

Kaarsted, Tage. **Great Britain and Denmark 1914-1920.** Tr. Alison Borch Johansen. Odense: Odense University Press, 1979. p 244. Ill.

Karup Pedersen, Ole. **The Great Powers and the Nordic Countries 1939-40. Denmark's Policy 1939-1940.** Copenhagen: University of Copenhagen, 1976. p 22.

Kristiansen, Erling. **Denmark, 1918-1968: a Lecture Delivered 11 November 1968.** London: University College London (Scandinavian Dept.), 1970. p 20. [Scandinavian Studies jubilee lectures.]

Kruse, Fr. Vinding. **The Fate of Southern Slesvig.** Copenhagen: The South Slesvig Committee of 5th May 1945, 1954. p 46.

Lampe, David. **The Savage Canary. The Story of Resistance in Denmark.** Foreword by Air Chief Marshal Sir Basil Embry, G. C. B. London: Cassell & Co., 1957. p 236. Ill.

Lund, Erik. **A Girdle of Truth. The Underground News Service Information 1943-1945.** Copenhagen: Ministry of Foreign Affairs, 1970. p 25. Ill.

Merrill, James Arthur. **The Effect of the European Economic Community on Trade with Denmark.** Ph. D. diss., Columbia University (New York), 1976. [Diss. Abstr. 4504-A, 1977.]

Nytrup, Per. **An Outline of the German Occupation of Denmark 1940-1945.** Copenhagen: The National Museum, 1968. p 46. Ill.

Petrow, Richard. **The Bitter Years; the Invasion and Occupation of Denmark and Norway, April 1940-May 1945.** New York: William Morrow & Co., 1974. p 403. Ill.

Reilly, Robin. **The Sixth Floor.** London: Frewin, 1969. p 223. About World War II, underground, etc.

Thomas, John Oram. **The Giant-killers: The Story of the Danish Resistance Movement, 1940-45.** London: Michael Joseph, 1975. p 320. Ill.

Udenrigsministeriet. **Denmark and the Marshall Plan (1948-1952). Final Survey by the Danish Government of Operations and Progress under the European Recovery Programme.** Copenhagen: Udenrigsministeriet, 1952. p 52.

Voorhis, Jerry Livingston. **A Study of Official Relations between the German and Danish Governments in the Period between 1940-1943.** Ph. D. diss., Northwestern University, 1968. (p 306). [Diss. Abstr. 29/08-A, p 2661.]

Werstein, Irving. **That Denmark Might Live. The Saga of the Danish Resistance in World War II.** Philadelphia, Pa.: Macrae Smith, 1967. p 143. Ill.

Yahil, Leni. **The Rescue of Danish Jewry. Test of a Democracy.** Tr. from the Hebrew by Morris Gradel. Philadelphia, Pa.: The Jewish Publication Society of America, 1969. p 536.

History - V. Immigration

Alland, Alexander. **From Aalborg to America with Heinrich Tönnies.** A photographic walk through history guided by Alexander Alland. Preface by Bjørn Ochsner. New York: Camera/Graphic Press Ltd., 1975. p 128. Ill. [Danish-English text.] [Written for an exhibit in Aalborg in 1975.]

Andersen, A. L. **Norsewood. The Centennial Story. A History of the District of Norsewood.** Ngamoko: The Author, 1972. p 182. Ill.

Andersen, Arlow W. **The Salt of the Earth. A History of Norwegian-Danish Methodism in America.** Nashville, Tennessee: Norwegian-Danish Methodist Historical Association and Parthenon Press, 1962. p 338. Ill.

Bille, John H. **A History of the Danes in America.** San Francisco, Ca.: Rand E. Research Associates, 1971. p 48. [Rpt. of the 1896 ed., which was vol. 11 of the Transactions of the Wisconsin Academy of Sciences, Arts and Letters.]

Chrisman, Noel J. **Ethnic Influence on Urban Groups: The Danish-Americans.** Ph. D. diss., University of California, Berkeley, 1966.

Christensen, Thomas Peter. **A History of the Danes in Iowa.** Solvang, California: Dansk Folkesamfund, 1952. p 282. Ill.

Christensen, William. **Saga of the Tower.** Blair, Nebraska: Lutheran Publishing House, 1959. p 242.
Story of Dana College and Trinity Seminary.

Dickerson, Inga Hansen. **Trina.** New York: Comet Press Books, 1956. p 204.
Semi-biographical story about the author's mother, a Danish pioneer woman in South Dakota.

Dugan, James. **American Viking. The Saga of Hans Isbrandtsen and His Shipping Empire.** New York: Harper & Row, 1963. p 305.

Faralla, Dana. **Circle of Trees.** New York: Lippincott, 1955. p 221.
A story of Danish emigrants during their second year in Minnesota.

Friedman, Philip Scott. **The Danish Community of Chicago, 1860-1920.** Evanston, Ill.: Northwestern University, 1976. p 106. Rev. ed. 1977, p 128.

Hansen, Thorvald, ed. **Reflections. The Story of Luther Memorial, Des Moines, Iowa.** Askov, Minnesota: American Publishing Co., 1974. p 112. Ill.

Hansen, Thorvald. **School in the Woods. The Story of an Immigrant Seminary.** Askov, Minnesota: American Publishing Co., 1977. p 150. Ill.

Hansen, Thorvald. **We Laid Foundation Here... the Early History of Grand View College.** Des Moines, Iowa: Grand View College, 1972. p 144. Ill.

History of the West Denmark Lutheran Church 1873-1973. West Denmark, Wisconsin: The Church, 1973. p 68.

Hvidt, Kristian. **Danes Go West: a Book about the Emigration to America.** Tr. and ed. Ole

Duus. Maps and diagrams by Thor Drejer and Arne Gaarn Bak. Skørping: Rebild National Park Society, 1976. p 302. Ill. [*Danske veje vestpå*, 1976.]

Hvidt, Kristian. **Flight to America; the Social Background of 300,000 Danish Emigrants.** Tr. Anne Zeeberg and Virginia Laursen. New York: Academic Press, 1975. p 214. Ill. [Studies in Social Discontinuity.]

Jacob Riis Revisited. Poverty and the Slum in Another Era. Ed. with an introduction by Francesco Cordasco. Clifton, N. J.: Augustus M. Kelly, 1973. p 22, 418. Ill.

Jensen, John M. **The United Evangelical Lutheran Church. An Interpretation.** Minneapolis, Mn.: Augsburg, 1964. p 311.

Knudsen, Johannes. **The Danish-American Immigrant, Phases of His Religion and Culture.** By Johannes Knudsen and Enok Mortensen. Des Moines, Iowa: Grand View College, 1950. p 43.

Knudsen, Johannes. **Roots.** Askov, Minn.: American Publishing Co., 1973. p 94.
Autobiography of a Danish-American educator and clergyman.

McDonald, Julie. **Amalie's Story.** New York: Simon & Schuster, 1970. p 249.
The story of a young girl growing up in 19th-century Denmark and her subsequent emigration to America.

Marzolf, Marion T. **The Danish-Language Press in America.** Ph. D. diss., Ann Arbor, Michigan, 1972. New York: Arno Press, 1979. (p 276). [Scandinavians in America.]

Mortensen, Enok. **The Danish Lutheran Church in America: the History and Heritage of the American Evangelical Lutheran Church.** Philadelphia, Pennsylvania: Board of Publication, Lutheran Church in America, 1967. p 320. Ill.

Mortensen, Enok. **Seventy-Five Years at Danebod.** Tyler, Minnesota: Danebod Lutheran Church, 1961. p 103. Ill.

Mortensen, Enok. **Stories from our Church; a Popular History of the Danish Evangelical Lutheran Church of America.** Des Moines: Committee on Publications of the Danish Evangelical Lutheran Church of America, 1952. p 180.

Mose, H. Einar. **Dania Society of Chicago - The Centennial History, 1862-1962.** Chicago: Dania Society, 1962. p 84. Ill.

Nielsen, Alfred C. **Life in an American Denmark.** Des Moines, Iowa: Grand View College, 1962. p 142.

Nielsen, Eivind H. **Daneville Colony and Church Through Fifty Years.** Blair, Nebraska: Lutheran Publishing House, 1956. p 179.

186 Nyholm, Paul C. **A Study in Immigration: The Americanization of the Danish Lutheran Churches in America.** Copenhagen: Institute for Danish Church History, University of Copenhagen, 1963. p 480. [Ph. D. diss.]

Paulsen, Frank M. **Danish-American Folk Traditions: A Study in Fading Survivals.** Ph. D. diss., Indiana University, 1967.

Paulsen, Frank M. **Danish Settlements on the Canadian Prairies: Folk Traditions, Immigrant Experiences, and Local History.** Ottawa: National Museum of Canada, 1974. p 114. [Canadian Centre for Folk Culture Studies, no. 11.]

Price, Willadene. **Gutzon Borglum - The Man Who Carved a Mountain.** McLean, Virginia: E P M Publications, 1974. p 224.

Reid, Agnes Just. **Letters of Long Ago.** Salt Lake City, Utah: University of Utah Library, 1973. p 93. Ill.

Simonsen, Anker. **Builders with a Purpose.** Askov: American Publishing Company, 1963. p 144. Ill.

Smith, Frank. **Genealogical Guidebook and Atlas of Denmark.** By Frank Smith and Finn A. Thomsen. Salt Lake City, Utah: Bookcraft, 1969. p 164. Ill.

Smith, George T. **A Young Dane Finds His Promised Land.** New York: Vantage Press, 1970. p 118.

Wheelwright, Valborg Rasmussen. **Valborg. An Autobiography.** As told to her son Lorin F. Wheelwright. Salt Lake City, Utah: Pioneer Music Press, 1978. p 224. Ill.

Winther, Sophus Keith. **Take All to Nebraska.** Lincoln and London: University of Nebraska Press, 1976. p 306. [Rpt. of 1936 ed., First volume of a trilogy on Danish immigrant life.]

History - VI.
Colonies

Anderson, John L. **Night of the Silent Drums. A Narrative of Slave Rebellion in the Virgin Islands.** New York: Charles Scribner's Sons, 1975. p 406.

Bredsdorff, Peter [et al.]. **Three Towns. Conservation and Renewal of Charlotte Amalia, Christiansted and Frederiksted of the U. S. Virgin Islands.** Copenhagen: Danish West Indian Society, 1980. p 122. Ill.

Christensen, Carlo. **Peter von Scholten: A Chapter of the History of the Virgin Islands.** Lemvig: Gadgaard Nielsen, 1955. p 31. Ill.

Danish West Indian Festival 1975. Copenhagen: Danish West Indian Society, 1975. p 47. Ill. **Festival 1977.** 1977. p 63. Ill.

Danish West Indian Society. Copenhagen: Danish West Indian Society, annual. Ill.

The Danish West Indies in Old Pictures. Copenhagen: The Danish West Indian Society, 1967. p 102. Ill.

Gosner, Pamela W. **Plantation and Town. Historic Architecture of the United States Virgin Islands.** Durham, N. C.: Moore Publishing Co., 1971. p 110. Ill.

Heckert, Eleanor. **Muscavado.** Garden City, New York: Doubleday, 1968. p 348.
A novel set in the Virgin Islands at the end of the 17th century, based on actual people and events.

Hørlyk, Lucie. **In Danish Times: Stories about Life in St. Croix and St. Thomas in the Last Century.** Tr. Betty Nilsson. Stockholm: Tiden-Barnängen tryckerier, 1969. p 83. Ill. [Three stories originally published in the collection *Under Tropesol*, 1913.]

Lawaetz, Eva. **The Danish Heritage of the U. S. Virgin Islands.** St. Croix: The St. Croix Friends of Denmark Society, 1977. p 48. Ill.

Lawaetz, Eva. **Free Coloured in St. Croix, 1744-1816.** Comp., ed. and tr. Eva Lawaetz. Christiansted: The Author, 1979. p 51.

Lewisohn, Florence. **Divers Information on the Romantic History of St. Croix.** 4th printing. Christiansted: St. Croix Landmarks Society, 1964. p 71. Ill.

Lewisohn, Florence. **St. Croix under Seven Flags.** Hollywood, Fla.: The Dukane Press, 1970. p 432. Ill.

Lewisohn, Florence. **»What so proudly we hail«. The Danish West Indies and the American Revolution.** St. Croix: Prestige Press, 1975. p 51. Ill.

Morton, Henry. **St. Croix, St. Thomas, St. John. Danish West Indian Sketchbook and Diary. 1843-44.** Copenhagen: The Danish West Indian Society, 1975. p 183. Ill.

Nørregaard, Georg. **Danish Settlements in West Africa 1658-1850.** Tr. Sigurd Mammen. Brookline, Mass.: Boston University Press, 1966. p 287. Ill.

Paquin, Lyonel. **Historical Sketch of the American Virgin Islands.** St. Thomas: Lyonel Paquin, 1970. p 20.

Tansill, Charles Callan. **The Purchase of the Danish West Indies.** London & Westport, Connecticut: Greenwood Press, 1968. p 548. [Rpt. of 1932 ed.]

Taylor, Charles Edwin. **Leaflets from the Danish West Indies.** Westport, Conn.: Negro University Press, 1970. p 208. Ill.

Willis, Jean Louise. **The Trade between North America and the Danish West Indies, 1756-1807, with Special Reference to St. Croix.** Ph. D. diss., Columbia University, 1963. (p 364). [Diss. Abstr. 24/09, p 3724.]

History - VII.
Fiction

Andrews, Lynda M. **The Danish Queen.** London: Hale, 1978. p 157.
A novel based on the life of Anne of Holstein.
Arnold, Elliot. **Night of Watching.** New York: Charles Scribner's Sons, 1967. p 441.
About the rescue of Danish Jews during World War II. For young adults.
Halck, Jørgen. **Strictly Confidential.** Tr. Estrid Bannister. London: Jonathan Cape, 1961. p 176. [*I streng fortrolighed.*]
Lofts, Norah. **The Lost Queen. The Tragedy of a Royal Marriage.** Garden City, N. Y.: Doubleday and Co., p 302.
Novel based on the life of Queen Carolina-Matilda.
Sørensen, Virginia (Eggersten). **Kingdom Come.** New York: Harcourt, Brace & Co., 1960. p 497.
Set in Denmark in the 1850's, this novel deals with the impact of the first Mormon missionaries from America on the state church and on the lives of the people.

Language

Andersen, Gerda M. **Say It in Danish.** New York: Dover, 1957. p 165. pb. [Say It Series.]
A guide to 1,000 simple phrases needed for travel and everyday life.
Austin, John S. **Topics in Danish Phonology.** Ph. D. diss., Cornell University, 1971. [Diss. Abstr. 33:294-A.]
Bender, Eric L. **English Language Programs in Denmark and Aspects of Danish Phonology and Syntax.** New York: City University of New York, 1973. p 59.
Bredsdorff, Elias. **Danish: an Elementary Grammar and Reader.** 1st ed. London: Cambridge University Press, 1956. 2nd rev. ed. 1958. Rpt. pb. and hb. 1965, 1970, 1973, 1977, 1979. p 301.
Danish. 28 page booklet and five records. New York and Cleveland: World Publishing Co.;

Canada: Nelson, Foster & Scott, Ltd., 1961. [World Foreign Language Record series.]
Danish in Three Months. Revised by C. Crowley from *Danish Simplified.* London: Hugo's Language Books Ltd.; New York: David McKay Co., 1969. p 160.
Designed to form a self-instructing text in practical, everyday Danish.
Dearden, Jeannette. **Spoken Danish. Colloquial Everyday Speech.** By Jeannette Dearden and Karin Stiig-Nielsen. Ithaca, N. Y.: Spoken Language Services, Inc. 2 books, an album of 6 long playing records and a key to the recorded units.
Diderichsen, Paul. **Danish Pronunciation.** Key to gramophone record written for the Danish Graduate School for Foreign Students. 2nd rev. ed. Copenhagen: Munksgaard, 1953. p 20. [1st ed. 1949.]
Diderichsen, Paul. **Essentials of Danish Grammar.** Copenhagen: Akademisk Forlag, 1964, 1972. p 78. [See also *Danish Pronunciation*, Record and Key to Record.]
Fenneberg, Paul. **Speak Danish. A Practical Guide to Colloquial Danish.** 5th ed. New York: Oxford University Press, 1953. Copenhagen: Gad, 6th ed. 1956. p 138.
Henriksen, Caroline Coble. **A Study in Early Eighteenth-century Danish Grammar.** Ph. D. diss., Harvard University, 1973.
Hjemslev, Louis. **Language. An Introduction.** Tr. Francis J. Whitfield. Madison, Wi.: University of Wisconsin Press, 1970. p 145. [*Sproget.*]
Kjelds, Niels Tonnisen. **Suffixal Word Derivation in New Danish.** Ph. D. diss., University of Pennsylvania, 1954. (p 186). [Diss. Abstr. 14/05, p 835.]
Koefoed, H. A., ed. **Modern Danish Prose.** A selection of Danish texts for foreign students, annotated and with a glossary for each text. Copenhagen: Høst & Søn, 1955. p 160. pb.
Koefoed, H. A. **Poetry and Prose.** Copenhagen: Danmarks Internationale Studenterkomité, 1961. p 124. [Scandinavian Literature Texts, no. 1.]
Koefoed, H. A. **Teach Yourself Danish.** London: English Universities Press, 1958. New York: David McKay Co., 1959. p 232. Printed in English. [Teach Yourself Series.]
Mogensen, Knud K. **Basic Danish Word List. English Equivalents; Frequency Grading; A Statistical Analysis.** Copenhagen: Frost-Hansen; Hollywood, Ca.: Knud K. Mogensen; Franklin Park, New Jersey: The Scandinavian Book Club, 1951. Printed in Denmark. p 72.
Norlev, Erling. **The Way to Danish. A Textbook in the Danish Language Written for**

188

Americans. By Erling Norlev and H. A. Koefoed. 1st ed. Copenhagen: Munksgaard, and International Booksellers and Publishers, Ltd., 1959. 2nd ed. 1964. 3rd ed. 1968. p 300.

Novakovich, A. S. The Danish Language. Moscow: Institute of International Relations (IMO), 1962. p 63.

Over, Paul Douglas. Some Regularities in the Syntax of Negation and Related Areas in Modern Danish. Ph. D. diss., University of Texas at Austin, 1977. (p 119). [Diss. Abstr. 38/05-A. p 2748.]

Stemann, Ingeborg. Danish - A Practical Reader. In collaboration with Angus Macdonald and Niels Haislund. Copenhagen: Hagerup, 1938. 2nd ed. 1953. p 296. Ill. 3rd rev. ed. 1962. p 288. Ill. 5th ed. 1969.

Vasil'eva, I. G. The Danish Language: Phonetics and Morphology. A Short Outline. Moscow: Moscow University, 1962. p 104.

White, James R. Danish Made Easy. Phrases and Useful Information for Your Stay in Denmark. Compiled and edited by James R. White. 4th rev. ed. Copenhagen: Høst & Søn, 1961. 11th ed. 1978. p 64. [Høsts lommeparlører.]

Law

Danish Committee on Comparative Law. Danish and Norwegian Law. A general survey ed. by the Danish Committee on Comparative Law. Copenhagen: Gad, 1963. p 251.

Danish Committee on Comparative Law. The Danish Criminal Code. Intro. Knud Waaben. Copenhagen: Danish Committee on Comparative Law, and Gad, 1958. p 118.

The Penal System of Denmark. Copenhagen: Ministry of Justice, 1971. p 52. Ill.

Philip, Allan. American-Danish International Law. Published under the auspices of the Parker School of Foreign and Cooperative Law, Columbia University. New York: Oceana Publications, 1957. p 80. [Bilateral Studies in Private International Law.]

Riismandel, V. J. Divorce by Administrative Decree. Denmark. Washington, D. C.: Library of Congress Law Library, 1957. p 18.

Libraries

Drehn-Knudsen, Erik [et al.]. Public Libraries in Denmark. Text by Erik Drehn-Knudsen. Ed. Ib Koch-Olsen. Tr. Reginald Spink. Photos by Ole Woldbye. Copenhagen: State Inspectorate of Public Libraries (Bibliotekstilsynet) 1967. p 118. Ill.

Gimbel, Henning, ed. Work Simplification in Danish Public Libraries. Tr. Rudolph C. Ellsworth. Chicago: American Library Association, Library Technology Program, 1969. p 256. Ill. [Library Technological Program Publication no. 15.] [Rationalisering i danske folkebiblioteker.]

Jensen, Povl Johns. Catalogue and Scholarship. D. G. Moldenhawer's Catalogue in The Royal Library of Copenhagen. Copenhagen: The Royal Library, 1973. p 38. Ill.

Kirkegaard, Preben. Public Libraries in Denmark. Tr. Harriet Oppenhejm. Adapted by Carl Thomsen. Copenhagen: Det danske Selskab, 1950. p 104. Ill. [Danish Information Handbooks.]

Det Kongelige Bibliotek. The Royal Library, Copenhagen. A Brief Introduction. Copenhagen: Det Kongelige Bibliotek, 1951. p 32. Ill.

The New Danish Archives. Copenhagen: Rigsarkivet, 1970. p 47. Ill.

Plovgaard, Sven, ed. Public Library Buildings. Standards and Type Plans for Library Premises in Areas with Populations of between 5,000 and 25,000. Tr. Oliver Stallybrass. London: The Library Association, 1971. p 135. Ill. [Folkebiblioteksbygningen.]

School Libraries in Denmark. Kirke Hyllinge: The Danish Association of School Libraries, 1975. p 36. Ill.

Statens Bibliotekstilsyn. The Danish Public Libraries Act 1964. Copenhagen: Statens Bibliotekstilsyn, 1965. p 19.

Thorsen, Leif. Public Libraries in Denmark. Tr. Mogens Kay-Larsen. Copenhagen: Det danske Selskab, 1972. p 174. Ill. With Supplement, 1975. [Danish Information Handbooks.]

Literary Criticism and the Press

Barfoed, Niels E. Danish Literature 1962. Copenhagen: Committee for Danish Cultural Activities Abroad, 1963. p 31.

Barfoed, Niels E. Danish Literature 1963. Copenhagen: Committee for Danish Cultural Activities Abroad, 1964. p 28.

Barfoed, Stig Krabbe. Danish Literature 1966. Copenhagen: Committee for Danish Cultural Activities Abroad, 1967. p 27.

Borum, Poul. **Danish Literature. A Short Critical Survey.** Copenhagen: Det danske Selskab, 1979. p 140. Ill. [Danes of the Present and Past.]

Brask, Peter. **Danish Literature 1967.** Copenhagen: Committee for Danish Cultural Activities Abroad, 1968. p 37.

Brask, Peter. **Danish Literature 1968.** Tr. David Stoner. Copenhagen: Committee for Danish Cultural Activities Abroad, 1969. p 31.

Brask, Peter. **Danish Literature 1969.** Tr. David Stoner. Copenhagen: Committee for Danish Cultural Activities Abroad, 1970. p 31.

Bredsdorff, Elias. **An Introduction to Scandinavian Literature from the Earliest Time to Our Day.** By Elias Bredsdorff, Brita Mortensen and Ronald Popperwell. 1951; repr. Westport, Conn.: Greenwood Press, 1970. p 245.

Christensen, Nadia Margaret. **A Comparative Study of the Anti-Hero in Danish and American Fiction.** Seattle, Washington: University of Washington Press, 1972. p 222.

Claudi, Jørgen. **Contemporary Danish Authors. With a Brief Outline of Danish Literature.** Tr. Jørgen Andersen and Aubrey Rush. Copenhagen: Det danske Selskab, 1952. Los Angeles, Ca.: Knud K. Mogensen, 1953. p 164. Ill.

Danske Reklamebureauers Brancheforening. **Who Reads the Danish Weeklies?** Copenhagen: Danske Reklamebureauers Brancheforening, 1959. p 48. [*Hvem læser ugebladene? Observa læserindex.* Danish-English text.]

Ditlevsen, Knud, H., ed. **The World of Papers and Books in Denmark.** 5th ed. Copenhagen: Politiken, 1961. p 224. [Danish-English-French-German text. Politikens Håndbøger no. 12.]

Frederiksen, Emil. **Danish Literature 1960-61.** Tr. David S. Thatcher. Copenhagen: Committee for Danish Cultural Activities Abroad, 1962. p 41.

Frederiksen, Emil. **Danish Literature 1964.** Tr. David Stoner. Copenhagen: Committee for Danish Cultural Activities Abroad, 1965. p 23.

Frederiksen, Emil. **Danish Literature 1965.** Tr. David Stoner. Copenhagen: Committee for Danish Cultural Activities Abroad, 1966. p 31.

Jensen, Rudolf Jay. **Danish Novels of the 1920's: a Study of Structure and Theme.** Ph. D. diss., University of Wisconsin, 1978. (p 284). [Diss. Abstr. 39: p 2948-A.]

Kristensen, Sven Møller. **Contemporary Danish Literature.** Tr. Sigurd Mammen. Copenhagen: Det danske Selskab, 1956. p 32. [Danish Reference Papers.]

Mitchell, Phillip M. **A History of Danish Literature.** Intro. Mogens Haugsted. 1st ed. Copenhagen: Gyldendal, 1957. New York: American-Scandinavian Foundation, 1958. p 322. Ill. Rev. 2nd ed. New York: Kraus-Thomsen, 1971. p 339.

Olrik, Axel. **The Heroic Legends of Denmark.** Tr. from the Danish and rev. in collaboration with the author by Lee M. Hollander. New York: Kraus Reprint Co., 1971. p 530. [Rpt. of the 1919 ed.] [Scandinavian Monographs, vol. iv.]

Roger-Henrichsen, Gudmund. **A Decade of Danish Literature, 1960-1970.** Photographs by Gregers Nielsen, Klaus Lindewald, Poul Olsen. Copenhagen: Ministry of Foreign Affairs, 1972. p 48. Ill.

Siegmund, William Ian. **A Comparative Study of »Earl Brand« (Child 7) and its Danish and Icelandic Analogues.** Ph. D. diss., Ohio State University, 1973.

Stangerup, Hakon. **Danish Literature in 1955.** Tr. Ronald Harry Bathgate. Copenhagen: Committee for Danish Cultural Activities Abroad, 1957. p 30.

Stangerup, Hakon. **Danish Literature in 1956.** Copenhagen: Committee for Danish Cultural Activities Abroad, 1957. p 34.

Stangerup, Hakon. **Danish Literature in 1957.** Tr. W. Glyn Jones. Copenhagen: Committee for Danish Cultural Activities Abroad, 1958. p 31.

Stangerup, Hakon. **Danish Literature in 1958.** Tr. Ingeborg Nixon. Copenhagen: Committee for Danish Cultural Activities Abroad, 1959. p 33.

Stangerup, Hakon. **Danish Literature in 1959.** Tr. Ingeborg Nixon. Copenhagen: Committee for Danish Cultural Activities Abroad, 1960. p 28.

Thorsen, Svend. **Newspapers in Denmark.** Tr. Sigurd Mammen. Copenhagen: Det danske Selskab, 1953. p 168. Ill. [Danish Information Handbooks.]

Museums

Association of Museums of Arms etc. **Repertory of Museums of Arms and Military History.** Ed. by Tøjhusmuseet. Issued by the Association of Museums of Arms and Military History. Copenhagen: Tøjhusmuseet, 1960. p 159.

Boesen, Gudmund. **Danish Museums.** Ed. and arranged by Kristjan Bure. English text by Reginald Spink. Copenhagen: Committee for Danish Cultural Activities Abroad, 1966. p 246. Ill.

190 Bramsen, Bo. **The History of the Old Town Museum in Aarhus.** Tr. David Hohnen. Designed by Palle Christoffersen. Aarhus: Aarhus Oliefabrik A/S, 1971. p 221. Ill. [Published to mark the centenary of the company's foundation. 1,000 copies published in English, not sold commercially.]

Bramsen, Henrik, ed. **Treasures from Danish Museums.** Copenhagen: Udenrigsministeriet, Pressebureauet, 1954. 2nd ed. 1956. p 48. Ill.

The Cannon Hall. Copenhagen: The Tøjhusmuseum, 1971. p 91. Ill.

Danish Prehistory at Moesgaard: Guide to the Collections. Højbjerg: Forhistorisk Museum, 1973. p 32. Ill.

Eller, Poul. **Det Nationalhistoriske Museum paa Frederiksborg: Frederiksborg Museum, Illustrated Guide.** Tr. David Hohnen. Hillerød: The Museum of National History at Frederiksborg Castle, 1978. p 143. Ill.

Erichsen, John [et al.]. **Danish Museums 1648-1848:** Exhibition in the Thorvaldsen Museum 30 May - 30 September 1974. Selection and text John Erichsen, Bjarne Jørnæs, and Marianne Saabye. Tr. Jean Olsen. Copenhagen: Thorvaldsens Museum, 1974. p 36. Ill.

The Funen Village. Farm and Country Buildings Museum. Guide. Odense, 1980. p 23. Ill.

Den gamle By. **The Open Air Museum »Den gamle By«. A Guide through the Collections.** Århus: Den gamle By, 1962. 11th ed. p 32.

Hoff, Arne. **Royal Arms at Rosenborg.** By Arne Hoff, H. D. Schepelern and Gudmund Boesen. Vol I: Text. Vol. II: Plates. Copenhagen: The Chronological Collection of the Danish Kings at Rosenborg and Vaabenhistorisk Selskab, 1956. p 223 & 193. Ill.

Jensen, Jørgen [et al.]. **Nationalmuseet: Prehistoric Denmark. (The National Museum).** By Jørgen Jensen, Elisabeth Munksgaard and Thorkild Ramskou. Photos by Lennart Larsen et al. Copenhagen: Nationalmuseet and Gyldendal, 1978. p 80. Ill.

Københavns Bymuseum. **Københavns Bymuseum. Short Guide.** Copenhagen: Københavns Bymuseum, 1961. p 32.

Koefoed-Petersen, Otto. **Egyptian Sculpture in the Ny Carlsberg Glyptothek.** Tr. Eric Jacobsen. Copenhagen: Glyptoteket, 1951. p 92. Ill. 2nd rev. ed., tr. Eric Jacobsen and Bent Sunesen. 1962. p 42. Ill.

Langberg, Harald. **Kronborg Castle, Elsinore.** Copenhagen: Ministry of Housing, 1979. p 64. Ill.

Langberg, Harald. **Protection of Historic Buildings in Denmark.** Copenhagen: Foreningen til gamle Bygningers Bevarelse, 1952. p 20. Ill.

Louisiana. Humlebæk: Louisiana, 1978. p 96. Ill.

Michelsen, Peter. **Danish Peasant Culture. A Guide to the Danish Folkmuseum.** By Peter Michelsen and Holger Rasmussen. Copenhagen: Nationalmuseet, 1955. p 91. Ill.

Michelsen, Peter. **Frilandsmuseet. The Danish Museum Village at Sorgenfri.** Photographs by Lennart Larsen. Copenhagen: The National Museum of Denmark, 1973. p 236. Ill.

Mortensen, Otto. **Jens Olsen's Clock. A Technical Description.** Tr. A. Bildsøe, Helge Hansen and Hans H. Hinrichsen. Copenhagen: Teknologisk Instituts Forlag, 1957. p 159.

The Museum of National History at Frederiksborg Castle. Official Guide. 5th ed. Hillerød: Frederiksborg Castle, 1971. p 86. Ill.

The National Museum. General Guide. Copenhagen: National Museum, 1973. p 23. Ill.

Odense Bys Museer. **City of Odense Museums.** Ill. Svend Saabye. Photos by Wermund Bendtsen. Odense: Odense Bys Museer, 1960. p 52. Ill. [*Odense bys museer*. Danish-English text.]

The Old Town. Guide to the Collections. Aarhus, 1980. p 35. Ill.

Paulsen, Jørgen [et al.]. **Pictures from Frederiksborg.** Picture selection and text by Jørgen Paulsen, H. D. Schepelern and Povl Eller. Tr. Ingeborg Nixon. Hillerød: Det Nationalhistoriske Museum, 1961. p 172. Ill. [*Billeder fra Frederiksborg*. Danish-English text.]

Pedersen, Johannes. **The Carlsberg Foundation: The Carlsberg Laboratory. Scientific Grants. The Museum of National History at Frederiksborg Castle. The New Carlsberg Foundation.** Copenhagen: Carlsbergfondet, 1956. p 96. Ill.

Petersen, J. C. **The Danish Post and Telegraph Museum through 50 Years.** 1913 - 3rd November - 1963. Copenhagen: Generaldirektoratet for Post- og Telegrafvæsenet, 1963. p 57. Ill.

Poulsen, Vagn. **Ny Carlsberg Glyptothek. A Guide to the Collections.** 2nd ed. Copenhagen: Glyptoteket, 1955. p 104. Ill. 10th ed. 1965. 16th rev. ed. 1973. p 113. Ill.

Rosenborg Slot. **Rosenborg Castle. A Guide to the Chronological Collection of the Danish Kings.** Copenhagen: Rosenborg Slot, 1961, rev. ed. 1963. p 72.

Rosenborg Slot. **Treasures of Rosenborg.** Copenhagen: The Chronological Collection of the Danish Kings at Rosenborg, 1961. p 32. Ill.

Roussell, Aage. **The Museum of the Danish Resistance Movement 1940-1945.** 8th ed. Copenhagen: The National Museum, 1974. p 30.

Roussell, Aage, ed. **The National Museum of Denmark.** Copenhagen: Nationalmuseet, 1957. p 328. Ill.

Royal Museum of Fine Arts. **Catalogue of Old Foreign Paintings.** Copenhagen: Royal Museum of Fine Arts, (Statens Museum for Kunst), 1951. p 430. Ill.

Royal Museum of Fine Arts. **Modern Danish Paintings. Catalogue.** Copenhagen: Royal Museum of Fine Arts, 1970. p 345. Ill.

Royal Museum of Fine Arts. **Old Danish Paintings. Catalogue.** Copenhagen: Royal Museum of Fine Arts, 1970. p 329. Ill.

Royal Museum of Fine Arts. **A Short Guide to the Collections.** Copenhagen: The Royal Museum of Fine Arts, 1973, 1974. p 24. Ill.

Saabye, Marianne. **Thorvaldsen. Guide Book for Young People.** Copenhagen: Thorvaldsens Museum, 1972. p 37. Ill.

Steenberg, Jan. **The Round Tower.** Copenhagen: The National Museum, 1962. p 88. Ill. [*Rundetaarn.* Danish-English text.] [Published on the occasion of the 325th anniversary of the laying of the foundation stone.]

Thorvaldsens Museum. **Thorvaldsen's Museum. Official Guide.** Tr. Bengt Jürgensen. Copenhagen: Thorvaldsens Museum, 1953. p 158. Ill. 2nd ed. tr. Ingeborg Nixon, 1961. p 166. Ill. 1972. p 164. Ill.

Tøjhusmuseet. **The Royal Danish Arsenal Museum. Illustrated Guide to the Permanent Exhibition.** Copenhagen: Tøjhusmuseet, 1962. p 128. Ill. [*Tøjhusmuseet. Billedkatalog for den permanente udstilling.* Danish-English-French-German text.]

Tougaard, S. **The Aquarium, Esbjerg.** By S. Tougaard and H. Meesenburg. Photographs by S. Tougaard. Esbjerg: Fiskeri- og Søfartsmuseet, 1972. p 47. Ill.

Why Museums? Special Edition of the Danish Foreign Office Journal. Copenhagen: Ministry of Foreign Affairs, 1974. p 73. Ill. [Vol. 77.]

J. F. Willumsens Museum. **J. F. Willumsen's Museum. Catalogue.** Frederikssund: J. F. Willumsens Museum, 1962. p 37. Ill.

Music

Balzer, Jürgen, ed. **Carl Nielsen 1865-1965. Centenary Essays.** Copenhagen: Nyt Nordisk Forlag, 1965. London: Dennis Dobson; New York: Dover, 1966. p 130. Ill. [Eight essays by various authors on Carl Nielsen's life and works.]

Borge, Victor. **My Favourite Intervals.** By Victor Borge and Robert Sherman. Ill. Thomas Winding. London: Sphere, 1977. p 187. Ill.

Dickinson, Alis. **Keyboard Tablatures of the Mid-seventeenth Century in the Royal Library, Copenhagen: Edition and Commentary (Parts I & II).** Ph. D. diss., North Texas State University, 1973.

Fabricius, Johannes. **Carl Nielsen 1865-1931.** Copenhagen: Berlingske, 1965. p 72. Ill. [*Carl Nielsen 1865-1931 - en billedbiografi.* Danish-English text.]

Fabricius-Bjerre, Carl. **Carl Nielsen. A Discography.** Copenhagen: Nationaldiskoteket, 1965. 2nd ed. 1968. p 44.

Glahn, Henrik, ed. **The Clausholm Music Fragments.** Reconstructed and ed. Henrik Glahn and Søren Sørensen. Tr. John Bergsagel. Copenhagen: Wilhelm Hansen, 1974. p 210.

Hammerich, Angul. **Mediaeval Musical Relics of Denmark.** Tr. Margaret Williams Hamerik. (sic.). New York: AMS Press, 1976. p 124. Ill. [Rpt. of 1912 ed. publ. in Leipzig.]

Hansen, Hans. **Lauritz Melchior. A Discography.** 2nd rev. ed. Copenhagen: Nationaldiskoteket, 1972. p 40.

Hjorth, Arne. **Danish Violins and Their Makers.** Tr. Johanne Kastor Hansen. Copenhagen: Emil Hjorth & Sønner Violinbyggere, 1963. p 16. Ill.

Jones, William Isaac. **A Study of Tonality in the Symphonies of Carl Nielsen.** Ph. D. diss., Florida State University, 1973.

Kappel, Vagn. **Contemporary Danish Composers against the Background of Danish Musical Life and History.** Copenhagen: Det danske Selskab, 1950. p 116. 3rd rev. ed., 1967. p 84. Ill. [Danes of the Present and Past.]

Kappel, Vagn. **Danish Music from the Lur to the Vibraphone.** Notes to a series of records. Ed. Det danske Selskab. Tr. Reginald Spink. Copenhagen: Det danske Selskab, 1951. p 36.

Nielsen, Carl. **Living Music.** Tr. Reginald Spink. London: Hutchinson, 1953. p 80. Copenhagen: Edition Wilhelm Hansen, 1968. p 72. [*Levende musik*, music theory, 1925.]

Nielsen, Carl. **My Childhood.** Tr. Reginald Spink. London: Hutchinson, 1953. p 168. Copenhagen: Wilhelm Hansen, 1971, 1977. p 152. [*Min fynske Barndom*, memoirs, 1927.]

Petersen, Frede Schandorf. **Carl Nielsen, the Danish Composer.** Copenhagen: Press Department of the Ministry of Foreign Affairs, 1953. p 24.

Rapoport, Paul. **Vagn Holmboe: A Catalogue of his Music.** London: Triad Press, 1974. p 80.

192 Simpson, Robert W. L. **Carl Nielsen: Symphonist, 1865-1931.** Intro. H. E. Count Reventlow. Biographical appendix, Torben Meyer. London: J. M. Dent, 1952, 1965. Rev. ed. London: Kahn and Averill, 1979. p 236. Ill.

Simpson, Robert W. L. **Sibelius and Nielsen; a Centenary Essay.** London: British Broadcasting Corp. Publications, 1965. p 40.
Background information for the orchestral and choral concerts devoted to Sibelius and Nielsen in 1965.

The Society for Publishing Danish Music 1871-1971. Catalogue. Copenhagen: Dan Fog Musikforlag, 1972. p 114. Ill.

Music - Periodicals

Musical Denmark. Copenhagen: Det danske Selskab. Annual. 1952-.

Periodicals - General

American Dane Magazine. March 1972-. Omaha: Danish Brotherhood of America. [Supersedes *Danish Brotherhood* magazine.]

Anglo-Dania. Magazine for Anglo-Danish Relations. Copenhagen: The British Import Union. Irregular periodical 1928-.

The Bridge. Journal of the Danish American Heritage Society. (Junction City, Oregon). 1978-.

Contact with Denmark. Copenhagen: Det danske Selskab, 1970-. Annual.

Dane Review. Blair, Nebraska: Dana College.

Danish Brotherhood. [Replaced by *American Dane Magazine* in March of 1972.]

Danish Foreign Office Journal. Copenhagen: Danish Ministry of Foreign Affairs. 1920-1940, 1945-1968. Irregular. [Replaced by *Danish Journal.*]

Danish Journal. A magazine about Denmark. Copenhagen: Danish Ministry of Foreign Affairs. 1969-. Irregular. [Supersedes *Danish Foreign Office Journal.*]

Danish Outlook. Pub. and ed. Johs. Hansen. »Bakkerne«, Holte: Johs. Hansen, 1948-1958. Published six times a year.

Danish Press Summary. Prepared by Ritzaus Bureau. Copenhagen: Ministry of Foreign Affairs, 1973-.

Den Danske Pioneer. Elmwood Park. Ill. Bertelsen Publishing Co., 1872-.

Denmark. A Quarterly Review of Anglo-Danish Relations. London: The Anglo-Danish Society, 1946-1973.
1946 published with subtitle: *A Monthly Review of Anglo-Danish Relations.*

Denmark Cavalcade. Copenhagen: Danmarks Turistråd, 1950-1969.

Denmark Review. Copenhagen: Royal Danish Ministry of Foreign Affairs, 1961-. Irregular periodical.

Denmark Views. Travel news from the Danish Tourist Board. Copenhagen: Danish Tourist Board, 1978-. Ill.

News from Denmark. A socialist information bulletin. Irreg. periodical. 1971-1972.

North Atlantic. Hørsholm: Anders Nyborg A/S, 1977-1978. [Supersedes *Føroyar* and *Grønland.*]

The Rebild Newsletter. Skørping: Rebild National Park Society, 1970-.

Theses Accepted for the Doctorate and other Publications Issued by the University. Copenhagen: University of Copenhagen, 1970-1972. Replaced by *Theses and other Publications of the University of Copenhagen.*

Theses and other Publications of the University of Copenhagen. Copenhagen: University of Copenhagen, 1973-.

Tivoli Times. Copenhagen: Harlekin Publishing House, 1977-.

Who's Who in Corps Diplomatique in Denmark. Copenhagen: Børsen, 1975-.

Political Science and Government

Borre, Ole. **Party and Ideology in Denmark.** Aarhus: University of Aarhus, 1973. p 47.

Borre, Ole. **A Social Structure and Aggressive Voting: A Study of the Danish Election Survey 1971-1973.** Aarhus: University of Aarhus, 1978. p 20.

Buksti, Jacob A. **Variations in Organizational Participation in Government. The Case of Denmark.** By Jacob A. Buksti and Lars Nørby Johansen. Aarhus: University of Aarhus, 1978. p 33.

Consular Meeting in Denmark June 1970. Copenhagen: Press and Information Dept. of the Ministry of Foreign Affairs, 1970. p 62. Ill.

Damgaard, Erik. **External Participation in Danish Law-making: Corporatism or Pluralism?** By Erik Damgaard and Kjell A. Eliassen. Aarhus: University of Aarhus, 1978. p 34.

Damgaard, Erik. **Functions of Parliament in the Danish Political System.** Luxembourg: European Parliament, 1974. p 24.

Danish National Planning. Present State and Future Prospects. Copenhagen: The Secretariat of the National Planning Committee, 1972. p 100.

Det danske Selskab. **Major Danish Foundations for the Support of Science and Art.** Copenhagen: Det danske Selskab, 1955. p 31. [Danish Reference Papers.]

Denmark's Presidency of the European Communities, January-June 1978. Copenhagen: Ministry of Foreign Affairs, 1978. p 32. Ill.

Direct Taxation in Denmark. Copenhagen: The Inland Revenue Department, 1974. p 56.

Einhorn, Eric S. **National Security and Domestic Politics in Post-war Denmark: Some Principal Issues, 1945-1961.** Odense: Odense University Press, 1975. p 105.

Einhorn, Eric S. **Security Policy and International Politics in a Small State: the Case of Denmark, 1945-1960.** Ph. D. diss., Harvard University, 1972.

Elklit, Jørgen. **Election Laws and Electoral Behaviour in Denmark from the 1830's to 1920.** Aarhus: University of Aarhus, 1978. p 38.

Elklit, Jørgen. **The Formation of Mass Political Parties in the late 19th Century: The Three Models of the Danish Case.** Aarhus: University of Aarhus, 1978. p 37.

Esping-Andersen, Gösta. **The Social Democratic Party and the Welfare State: A Comparative Analysis of the Sources and Consequences of Party Decomposition in Advanced Capitalism.** Copenhagen: Institute of Organisation and Industrial Sociology, 1976. p 101.

Harder, Erik. **Local Government in Denmark.** Tr. Roy Duffel. Copenhagen: Det danske Selskab, 1973. p 186. [Danish Information Handbooks.]

Hurwitz, Stephan. **The Ombudsman. Denmark's Parliamentary Commissioner for Civil and Military Administration.** Tr. Elaine Hagemann. Copenhagen: Det danske Selskab, 1962. p 64. 1968. p 49. [Danish Reference Papers.]

Introduction to Danish Civil Defence. Copenhagen: Danish National Civil Defence Directorate, 1968. p 24.

Lerhard, Mogens, ed. **The Danish Ombudsman 1955-1969. Seventy-five Cases from the Ombudsman's Reports.** Selected and ed. Mogens Lerhard. Tr. Reginald Spink. Copenhagen: Schultz, 1972. p 116.

Miller, Kenneth E. **Government and Politics in Denmark.** Boston: Houghton Mifflin; London: George Allan and Unwin, 1968. p 308. Ill. [Contemporary Government Series.]

Ministry of Foreign Affairs. **Asiatisk Plads. The Danish Foreign Service's New Headquarters in Copenhagen.** Anders Georg, J. F. A. Holck Colding and Klaus Kjelsen, eds., tr. Reginald Spink. Copenhagen: Ministry of Foreign Affairs, 1980. p 96. Ill. [A Presentation Book.]

Mouritzen, Poul Erik. **Current Trends and Issues in Central Government Steering of Local Governments. The Danish Case.** Aarhus: University of Aarhus, 1979. p 30.

Murphy, Jeremiah Lawrence. **Coalition Politics in Denmark: Cooperation and Opposition in the Danish Parliament.** Ph. D. diss., Indiana University, 1968. p 199.

Nørby Johansen, Lars. **The Corporatist Elite in Denmark, 1946-1975.** Odense: Odense Universitet, 1980. p 24.

Nørby Johansen, Lars. **Corporatist Traits in Denmark, 1946-76.** By Lars Nørby Johansen and Ole P. Kristensen. Aarhus: University of Aarhus, 1978. p 33.

Petersen, Mogens N. **Political Development and Elite Transformation in Denmark.** London: Sage Publications, 1976. p 61. Ill.

Royal Danish Ministry of Foreign Affairs. **Denmark and the United Nation's Expanded Program of Technical Assistance.** Copenhagen: Ministry of Foreign Affairs and the Danish National Committee on Technical Assistance, 1956. p 24. Ill.

Royal Danish Ministry of Foreign Affairs. **Denmark's Participation in International Technical Assistance Activities.** Report of the Danish National Committee on Technical Assistance on Danish participation in international technical cooperation. Copenhagen: Ministry of Foreign Affairs and the Danish National Committee on Technical Assistance, 1961. p 84. Ill.

Sørensen, Max. **Denmark and the United Nations.** By Max Sørensen and Niels J. Haagerup. Prepared for the Carnegie Endowment for International Peace. New York: Manhattan Publishing Co., 1956. p 154.

Thomas, Alastair H. **Parliamentary Parties in Denmark 1945-1972.** Dissertation, Glasgow, University of Strathclyde, 1973. p 114.

194 # Religion

Hartling, Poul, ed. **The Danish Church.** Tr. Sigurd Mammen. Copenhagen: Det danske Selskab, 1965. p 161. Ill. [Denmark in Print and Pictures.]

Social Affairs

Anderson, Robert T. **The Vanishing Village. A Danish Maritime Community.** By Robert T. Anderson and Barbara Gallatin (Anderson). Seattle: University of Washington Press, 1964. p 160. [A Publication of the American Ethnological Society.]
An anthropological evaluation of Copenhagen's suburb Dragør, Amager.

Aude-Hansen, Carl, ed. **A Summary of the Report of the Danish Commission on Prison Labour.** Copenhagen: Direktoratet for Fængselsvæsenet, 1960. p 52.

Blum, Jacques. **Christiania - a Freetown. Slum, Alternative Culture or Social Experiment?** Copenhagen: The National Museum, 1977. p 66.

Children in Denmark. Special issue of *Contact with Denmark*. Copenhagen: Det danske Selskab, 1979. p 43. Ill.

Danish Youth Council. **Danish Youth.** Prefaces by Viggo Kampmann and Knud Enggaard. Copenhagen: The Danish Youth Council, 1962. p 48. Ill.

Det danske Selskab. **The Danish Mothers' Aid Centers. Review of Their History and Activities.** Tr. Elaine Hagemann. Copenhagen: Det danske Selskab, 1957. p 36.
Second edition see Skalts, Vera.

Fürstnow-Sørensen, Bent. **Migrant Worker in Denmark.** Tr. Else Giersing. English ed. rev. by counsellors concerning migrant workers. Copenhagen: Ministry of Social Affairs, 1974. p 66. Ill. [Danish ed. *Fremmedarbejder i Danmark.*]

Halck, Niels. **Social Welfare in Denmark.** Copenhagen: Danish Ministries of Labour and Social Affairs, 1961. p 72.

Hansen, Judith Friedman. **Danish Social Interaction: Cultural Assumptions and Patterns of Behavior.** Ph. D. diss., University of California, Berkeley, 1970.

Jensen, Orla. **Social Welfare in Denmark.** Tr. Else Giersing. Copenhagen: Det danske Selskab, 1961. p 136. Ill. 2nd rev. ed., 1966. 3rd rev. ed., edited by Jørgen Kock and Otto Wandall-Holm, 1972. p 157. Ill. [Danish Information Handbooks.]
Fourth edition see Marcussen, Ernst.

Kandel, Denise B. **Youth in two Worlds: United States and Denmark.** By Denise B. Kandel and Gerald S. Lesser. Foreword by James S. Coleman. San Francisco, Ca.: Jossey-Bass, 1972. p 237.

Koch-Nielsen, Inger. **The Future of Marriage in Denmark.** Tr. Charles Pendley. Graphics by Gitte Forsting. Copenhagen: The Danish National Institute of Social Research, 1978. p 45. Ill.

Kutschinsky, Berl. **Studies on Pornography and Sex Crimes in Denmark.** A Report to the U. S. Presidential Commission on Obscinity and Pornography. Copenhagen: New Social Science Monographs, 1970. p 197. [Monograph E:5.]

Kyst, Johannes. **What to Do with »Farmor«? Should »The Little Home« be the Answer.** Copenhagen: Pro Senectute, 1963. p 108. Ill.

Launspach, Jan. **Greetings from Christiania. A Foreigner's Experiences.** Copenhagen: Støt Christiania, 1978. p 33.

Lauret, Jean Claude. **The Danish Sex Fairs, Copenhagen-Odense, 1969/1970.** Foreword Fernando Henriques. Tr. from the French by Arlette Ryvers. London: Jasmine Press, 1970. p 179. Ill. [*La foire au sexe.*]
An account of the first trade fairs held for the pornography industry.

Levy, Janina. **Danish Youth Clubs: Focus on Copenhagen.** Copenhagen: University of Copenhagen, 1978. p 24.

Low, Anni Frandsen. **Growing up in Denmark: How Cultural Values Shape and Influence the Danish Personality.** Ph. D. diss., Claremont Graduate School, 1978. (p 180). [Diss. Abstr. 39. p 1466-A.]

Magnussen, Jan. **Urban Change and Urban Policy in Denmark.** Copenhagen: University of Copenhagen, 1979. p 33.

Manniche, Peter [et al.]. **Denmark, a Social Laboratory.** By Peter Manniche and an international group of writers. Oxford: Pergamon Press, 1969. p 264. Ill.
Earlier editions 1939, 1952. [The text forms Book I, part 1-2 of the author's *Rural Development... 1969.* See under EDUCATION.]

Manniche, Peter. **Living Democracy in Denmark. Independent Farmers, Farmers' Cooperation, the Folk High Schools, Cooperation in the Towns, Social and Cultural Activities, Social Legislation, a Danish Village.** Copenhagen: Gad, 1952. Westport, Ct.: Greenwood Press, 1952, 1970. p 240. Ill.
Revised edition of *Denmark, a Social Laboratory.*